D1607709

THE MIND OF

GERMANY

The Education of a Nation

HANS KOHN

CHARLES SCRIBNER'S SONS NEW YORK

$5.95

Hans Kohn

THE MIND
OF GERMANY

THE EDUCATION OF A NATION

The history of modern Germany is a study in national suicide. The enormous prestige won by the Germans, especially in scholarship and music, literature and philosophy, was deliberately destroyed by the Germans themselves. Now that Germany is once again bound to the western world, we cannot help asking why this suicide took place.

Hans Kohn, who has spent a lifetime studying the manifestations of nationalism, believes that the responsibility for the disaster must be borne by those Germans who rejected the humanitarian traditions of western Europe. Goethe was not one of these. As the author makes plain in the opening chapter, Goethe was a cosmopolitan who spurned the cult of the Middle Ages fostered by the romantics. This cult, as Goethe suspected, inspired an abnormal interest in the "Germanness" of the Germans. This was one reason why Heinrich Heine warned the French that a unified Germany, whether led by the Right or the Left, would terrorize Europe.

Later chapters deal with the heroic yearnings of Richard Wagner, the contempt of Friedrich Nietzsche for anything resembling "Germanity," and the surrender of liberal intellectuals to the might of Bismarck's empire. There were, of course, many Germans who

CONTINUED ON BACK FLAP

THE MIND OF GERMANY

The author acknowledges with thanks permission to quote from the following sources:

to ALFRED A. KNOPF, Inc.

The Life of Richard Wagner by Ernest Newman
The Decline of the West by Oswald Spengler
Hour of Decision by Oswald Spengler

to HENRY HOLT & Co , Inc

Jean-Christophe by Romain Rolland

To PROFESSOR *and* MRS. HANS BARTH-BRUNNER

My Zurich friends

Preface

GERMAN INTELLECTUAL and political history in modern times presents a fascinating spectacle. A great and numerous people living in the center of Europe has enriched the intellectual heritage of mankind with contributions equal, in several fields, to the greatest achievements in the history of civilization At the same time they have developed attitudes which separated them from the main trends characteristic of modern western civilization. A short book cannot do justice to the many facets of German history and cultural life. The present work wishes to provide a tentative reply to the one question on which much of the fascination of German history rests: how the alienation of Germany from the West came about.

A study in the history of ideas encounters that "most serious difficulty" which Jacob Burckhardt pointed out. "A great intellectual process," or rather a most complex interplay of several and often contradictory intellectual and social processes, "must be broken up into single, and often into what seems arbitrary (categories or divisions) in order to be in any way intelligible."

The writing of history is always selective. The accents and stresses are determined by the experiences of our generation and by our own value judgments. To re-think history is the task of every generation which has witnessed great historical changes. An effort to try to understand anew what has happened is the duty not only of the Germans but of all of us, not only with regard to German history but to all recent history. For the political and moral problems involved in modern German history are not only those of the Germans; to a varying degree they are those of all modern nations. Perhaps the Germans have presented the most outstanding example in our times of the moral catastrophe, into which the malady of a self-centered nationalism and the accompanying *trahison des clercs* can lead. But the malady is in no way confined to the Germans.

It is superfluous to mention that descent or "race" has nothing to do with man's political allegiance or moral attitudes. Such attitudes are influenced by historical traditions and circumstances, by environment and education, but again and again individuals have freed themselves from such influences, in Germany as much as elsewhere. Man's spirit does not depend on "blood." People of German descent living in Switzerland or in the United States have shown little inclination to model themselves on the Germany of recent times.

In the last decade an astonishing change of mind seems to have come over the Germans themselves. Perhaps this, too, is characteristic of other peoples than the Germans. An editorial "Power and Principle" in *The Times Literary Supplement* of July 17, 1959, in discussing the relationship of ethics and power politics in modern German history, concluded that at present "the tide beneath the waves . . . has set towards a Free Society again: a revised version of individualism, safeguarded from abuses but still reposing on the irreducible social unit of the individual conscience, and on self-realization of the citizen in the widest possible range of freedoms. That we have learned, is Society's best dynamic and its best cement. Society is not the State. . . . The younger generation might well find inspiration and social solidarity in a return to the principles of individual freedom." This is today the hope for Germany as well as for the whole fabric of modern civilization.

New York, Autumn 1959   H K.

Contents

THE MIND OF GERMANY

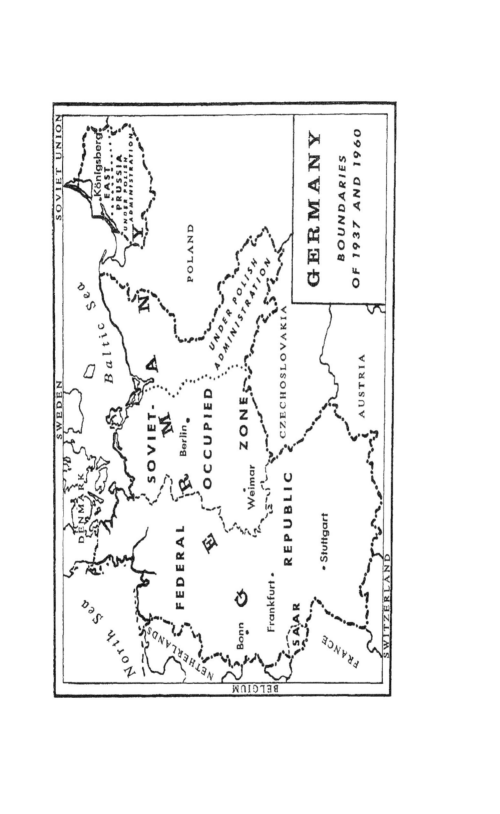

GERMANY

BOUNDARIES
OF 1937 AND 1960

SOVIET UNION

Königsberg

EAST
PRUSSIA
UNDER POLISH
ADMINISTRATION

POLAND

Baltic Sea

SWEDEN

UNDER POLISH
ADMINISTRATION

CZECHOSLOVAKIA

AUSTRIA

SOVIET-
OCCUPIED
ZONE

Berlin

Weimar

DENMARK

FEDERAL

REPUBLIC

Stuttgart

North Sea

Frankfurt

Bonn

SAAR

NETHERLANDS

FRANCE

SWITZERLAND

BELGIUM

Chapter One

THE COURSE OF

MODERN GERMAN HISTORY

The Legacy of the Middle Ages

ON OCTOBER 29, 1268, Konradin, the last of the Hohenstaufen, Germany's most ambitious medieval dynasty, mounted a scaffold in the market place of Naples and was put to death He was then in his seventeenth year. With him the splendor of German imperial grandeur that had dazzled Western Christendom and the Levant for a century ended in tragedy. The reign of the Hohenstaufen was followed by the great interregnum in Germany, the *schreckliche kaiserlose Zeit,* the terrible era without an emperor, as the Germans called it, during which the empire disintegrated, torn by centrifugal forces at a time when the other peoples of Western Christendom, with the exception of Italy, began to consolidate into modern territorial nations. This catastrophe came quite suddenly; only one hundred years before Konradin's birth his great-great-grandfather Frederick Barbarossa had raised German prestige to unprecedented heights.

The memory of Barbarossa's power fascinated the Germans for many centuries after he died leading a crusade in the Near East. A legend originally involving his grandson Frederick II was soon transferred to Barbarossa; it portrayed him asleep deep down inside a mountain—the Untersberg near Salzburg or the Kyffhäuser in Thuringia. But even asleep the hidden emperor remained the guardian of his nation's destiny. If Germany were ever in need of a savior he would be awakened by the ravens encircling his mountain top; he would then rise and lead Germany from defeat and despair to the glory of a new golden age. Compared with this certainty of salvation the actual events of German history and the realities of the world outside were pale indeed: deep down in their hearts the Germans felt that their true ruler, Germany's *heimliche Kaiser,* was ever ready to come to her rescue. Under the spell of such legends Germans were sometimes in danger of losing sight of political realities and of abandoning themselves to wistful dreams.

Barbarossa's gifted grandson Frederick II inherited his grand-father's imperial ambitions. He claimed superiority not only over all kingdoms of Christendom but even over the Pope. To the king-dom of Germany and the imperial dignity, to the crowns of Lom-bardy and Sicily, he added the kingdom of Jerusalem where he was crowned in the Church of the Holy Sepulcher in 1229. Twenty-one years later he died a broken man, exhausted by the unending strug-gles in which his overreaching ambition involved him. The claim of the Hohenstaufen prince that he had redeemed and unified the world in the light of ancient Biblical and Roman traditions col-lapsed in a catastrophe which spared no member of his family. The most handsome and beloved of his many bastard sons, Enzio, whom he had made king of Sardinia, was captured by the Bolognese in 1249, one year before his father's death, and though he lived on for twenty-two more years, he never left his prison. Enzio's half-brother Manfred was killed in battle in 1266 and his wife and sons were kept prisoners until their deaths. Frederick's only surviving legitimate son, Konrad IV, died four years after he succeeded his father. Then only twenty-five years old, he left an infant son, Kon-radin, who promised to equal his grandfather as a warrior and poet. His fate marked the end of the dynasty when, as a boy of fifteen, he crossed the Alps to restore the imperial splendor.

These overreaching ambitions of the thirteenth century left their mark upon German history: they prevented the consolidation of a rationally circumscribed German political order. When, in the Age of Nationalism, the attempt was made to create German national unity in a modern state the heritage of the Middle Ages was re-vived: nationalism fused with the consciousness of the imperial mis-sion and with a feeling of superiority of the imperial people, the *Reich.* Modern western science and technology penetrated the new Reich and rapidly transformed it into a nation with the most up-to-date equipment. Yet the social and intellectual substructure re-mained unchanged: its preservation was even regarded as a mark of true German strength. As a result the tragic story of the Middle

Ages repeated itself—great efforts and great achievements ended in an unexpected collapse.

The center of this new Reich was no longer Swabia, the south-western part of Germany, the home of the Hohenstaufen The center shifted from western and southern Germany, which from Roman times had been an integral part of the western world, to the lands beyond the Elbe, which in their social and political structure had not followed the development of modern Europe. There Prussia, a small, poor, and backward country on the eastern border of Germany, in many ways culturally and ethnically the least "German" part of the many Germanies of the period, was transformed through the exemplary will power and spartan devotion of Frederick the Great's subjects into a powerful militarized state. But in 1806, only twenty years after the death of its soldier-king, the military might of Prussia ignominiously collapsed. The intercession of the Russian Tsar with Napoleon, at that time, saved Prussia from complete extinction. In ten years, however, a highly intelligent and relentless concentration of all the nation's resources succeeded beyond all expectations in rebuilding Prussian power. Reforms were instituted affecting the political and legal structure of the nation.

Resented by most eighteenth century German intellectuals for its militarism, Prussia became, as a result of these reforms, a center for those who agitated for a strong German nation-state. The great historian Johann Gustav Droysen, then teaching at the University of Kiel, stressed, in a memorandum of April 26, 1848, Germany's need of a "powerful ruling house" He was convinced that only Prussia could fill the need by offering her *Machtorganisation,* her power concentration, especially her military and financial system, as a model for the whole of Germany "To the Hohenzollern," Droysen concluded, "belongs the place which has been empty since the days of the Hohenstaufen."

Droysen's wish came true. Bismarck, Prime Minister for twenty-eight years, made Prussia the brain and heart of modern Germany. It has often been said that in this process Prussia, which covered about three-fourths of the imperial territory, was only partly Germanized whereas the large parts of Germany which had fallen under Prussian leadership became Prussianized. Yet this Prussian-ization was hardly a blessing for Germany. Her temporary security was based upon Bismarck's moderation in foreign policy. Catastrophe quickly overtook Germany, and with her Europe, when Bismarck's successors, the victims of a psychological dynamism created by the great Chancellor himself, abandoned his moderation for aspirations as vague as those of any Hohenstaufen.

For the rapid deterioration of post-Bismarckian German states-manship Bismarck himself was responsible. In his foreign policy after 1871 he rarely used the crude and violent methods which characterized his actions before the moment when Prussia reached, in his opinion, the saturation point of her or his territorial aspira-tions; after that, however, he applied this aggressive manner even more openly in his domestic policy. His cynical contempt for par-liamentary liberalism and his insistence on authoritarian leadership kept the German middle class from active participation in govern-ment and precluded its growth to political maturity and responsible thinking. Nor did he inspire confidence in German intentions abroad.

The situation grew worse after the young Emperor William II dismissed Bismarck in 1890. The Emperor, who wished to be his own chancellor, exhibited Bismarck's ideological and temperamental shortcomings to a heightened degree without the old man's strength and judgment. Year by year, the world grew more and more con-cerned.

In 1912 Romain Rolland, a fervent European pacifist and a sharp critic of French nationalism who was wholly free of anti-German sentiment, conveyed in his novel *Jean-Christophe* the deep misgivings about Germany which by then were felt by even the most dispassionate observers of the European scene. His hero, a German musician who had lived most of his mature life in France and Italy, stressed Germany's responsibility for a Europe which Bismarck's victory over France at Sedan in 1870 had trans-formed into a military camp seething with mutual suspicions: "Although [Jean-Christophe] had spent a few months in Germany and returned there from time to time to conduct performances of his works, he did not settle there. He found too many things there which hurt him. They were not peculiar to Germany; he found them elsewhere too. But a man expects more of his own country than of any other, and he suffers more from its foibles. It was true too, that Germany was bearing the greatest burden of the sins of Europe. The victor incurs the responsibility of his victory, a debt toward the vanquished: tacitly the victor is pledged to march in front of them to show the way. The conquests of Louis XIV gave Europe the splendor of French reason. What light has the Ger-many of Sedan given to the world? The glitter of bayonets, thought without wings, action without generosity, brutal realism, which has not even the excuse of being the realism of healthy men;

force and interest; Mars turned traveling salesman. Forty years ago (1871) Europe was led astray into the night and the terrors of the night. The sun was hidden beneath the conqueror's helmet. If the vanquished can claim only pity mingled with contempt, what shall be given to the victor who has done this thing?"

At the beginning of the twentieth century Germany's neighbors feared her vague aspirations and her threatening gestures. As in the time of the Hohenstaufen, the German *Reich* in 1914 entered a gigantic struggle without a true estimate of its real strength and without understanding the changing realities of Europe and of the world. As a result, only twenty years after Bismarck's death, the mighty empire which he had established through war and which seemed so impregnable in its armed might, economic strength, and advanced scholarship foundered in defeat. The warning against the *hubris* of power which the defeat of 1918 should have carried remained unheeded by the Germans. On the contrary, in an effort surpassing all those of the past, and with all the deep earnestness of their dedicated discipline and feeling of superiority, the Germans rallied around a man who in his appeal to many of their folk myths and resentments appeared to them as the *heimliche Kaiser*, risen from the depth in Germany's hour of direst need to waken her and lead her to the glorious fulfillment of her mission. But this third attempt, which promised to last a thousand years, ended in an unprecedented catastrophe in which the last vestiges of the Bismarckian Reich and of Prussia itself disappeared.

The Tragic Character of German History

FROM THE HOHENSTAUFEN to the Hohenzollern, Germany has written some truly tragic pages in the history of Europe Perhaps for this reason Germans have claimed to feel the tragic character of history more strongly and to meditate more intensely about it than do others. This pessimistic attitude toward history divides the Germans from the English-speaking peoples and has made mutual understanding in the realm of political thought difficult indeed. The Germans easily succumb to the strange fascination which words such as *Schicksal* (fate) or *Verhangnis* (doom) exercise upon them. These are both words which are used as a matter of course in their scholarly writings and among the general public. They convey an untranslatable overtone of inevitability. They endow many Ger-

mans with the certainty of understanding the course of history in
a deeper way than the more superficial peoples of the West. In this
higher spirituality these Germans found a compensation for Germany's allegedly undeserved national misfortunes.

The question whether German history has formed the German
character or whether the character of the Germans has influenced
the course of their history has been widely discussed in recent years.
Many observers asked themselves whether National Socialism was
a natural outcome of German intellectual and political development, or whether Hitlerism—as some Germans maintained—was
alien to the German character and traditions and imposed upon
Germany by events and influences from without. Did National
Socialism represent the "organic" culmination of German history
or a monstrous deviation from it? Some German historians went
so far in their attempt to vindicate recent German history as to
argue that National Socialism was only the German manifestation
of a general European movement, characteristic of the age of the
rising masses, in which the true Germany, represented by the educated upper class, was swept away by the mounting tide of "democracy." Did not the essential elements of National Socialism
originate abroad, they asked· the totalitarian state in Russia, fascism
in Italy, the racial theory in France? Was not genuine German
"idealism" drowned in the onrush of industrial technology and
economic materialism which had come from the West and which
alone had rendered Hitler's mass-demagogy possible? Though these
attempts to burden the West and modern society with the responsibility for Germany's National Socialism contain, as does every
theory, an element of truth, they are fundamentally mistaken; worse,
however, they render a disservice to Germany, for they overlook the
specific German intellectual and political heritage which made the
Germans acclaim Hitler's rise to power. Germany did not succumb
to Hitler because she had become part of modern western society;
she succumbed because this modern society had been imposed on premodern social and intellectual foundations which were proudly
retained.

National Socialism and German History

NATIONAL SOCIALISM WAS as little the natural or logical outcome of
German history as Leninism was of Russian history. There is no

inevitability in history. Before 1914 there was good hope that the liberal and western trends in Germany and in Russia might slowly grow in strength and transform the social structure, political thought, and institutions of the two nations. Without the catastrophe of the First World War, without the ensuing economic chaos, and probably without the decisive personalities of Lenin and Hitler, neither Bolshevism nor National Socialism would have come to power. But the recognition of these historical circumstances does not imply that the success of the extremist movements was accidental or primarily due to external factors. Communism and National Socialism were made possible by the historical and political traditions of the two nations involved—not by what they had in common with the West but by what separated their intellectual and social development from that of the West.

Hitler's claim to represent the true interests of the German people could find credence because he appealed to sentiments deeply rooted both in the educated classes and in the people. His was not the only country in which such sentiments existed, but in Germany they were not held in check by the liberal-humanitarian considerations Western Europe inherited from the Enlightenment. Hitler was especially successful in appealing to what the Germans regarded as deep and idealistic in their past and their minds. He knew that the best way to lead Germans was by invoking a metaphysical system that would confer on their political actions and on their national desires the consecration of history and divine guidance. Thus National Socialism—in spite of its distortions—could pretend to lead a crusade to realize Germany's age-old longings and her sense of historical mission. Once National Socialism had assumed control its claims were supported by the German habit of trusting those in authority. This century-old disposition had been powerfully reinforced by Germany's unification through Bismarck's authoritarian methods and Prussia's military might. For Hitler was the heir—even if illegitimate—of German romantic myth and of Prussian militarist efficiency. His was a vulgarized form of the militarism which, to quote a contemporary German scholar, "made everything instrumental to the demands of dark, subconscious urges." National Socialism succeeded among many Germans in removing the rational and moral restraints imposed by "alien" Christianity and "alien" liberal western thought.

The Germans have been fascinated by the concepts of *Geist*, a term best translated as spiritual depth, and *Macht*, authoritarian power. In the eighteenth century German intellectuals and the

German people underrated the importance of power and overrated purity of spirit. They seemed to the western world an idyllic apolitical people of poets and thinkers. This attitude changed in the nineteeth century. From one extreme the Germans moved to another. They remained fundamentally apolitical, animated by haughty contempt for politics, but they became a dynamic nation whose will centered upon power and the power-state. From the life of the spirit, which characterized the period from 1740 to 1814, they turned to the pursuit of power. Having lived so long outside of active participation in political history, educated Germans tended to overstress the concepts of state and power. They rejected the rational and critical control of *Macht* by *Geist;* instead, under the pretext of a synthesis of spirit and power, they idealized the power-state and transformed it from an instrument of the spirit into its embodiment. Their leading thinkers of the early nineteenth century—Fichte, Hegel, and Marx—raised the nation, the state, and the economy to supreme concepts, regarded history with its conflicts as the unfolding of an ultimate and self-justifying reality, and distorted political processes to fit a semireligious utopianism. Under the influence of these and similar thinkers German thought after 1812 consciously deviated from the main lines of western development.

Throughout history, and especially in modern times, many people everywhere have succumbed to the demonic temptation of power and of the will-to-power which Nietzsche proclaimed the fundamental life-force. But beginning with their greatest nineteenth century philosopher, Hegel, and their greatest modern historian, Ranke, the Germans have often refused to recognize the demonic character of power; on the contrary, they have surrounded power with the halo of a philosophy which they extolled for its alleged understanding of history and human nature, an understanding, as they claimed, deeper than the superficial western moralism which to them only masked the power-drive. In the modern West, people distrusted power and feared its abuse; the modern Germans felt an almost religious reverence for power—Ranke regarded it as the manifestation of a spiritual essence—and for its embodiment in the authority of the state. State and power found in later nineteenth century Germany their most popular symbol in the army and the uniform—to partake of them gave even the humblest German a proud feeling of belonging, of belonging to a national whole whose armed power, whose loftiness of ideas, whose sense of discipline and service were without rivals.

Farewell to Liberalism

IN THE SIXTH DECADE of the nineteenth century, liberalism was in the ascendancy throughout Europe. The whole continent seemed destined to follow the example set by the English model of state and society. This prevailing trend toward liberalism was reversed—in Germany first and in much of the European continent thereafter—when Bismarck, with the enthusiastic acclaim of the German people, forged a new Reich in conscious opposition to liberal democracy. Richard Wagner, the greatest German artist of the period, in most ways quite unlike Bismarck, with equal incisiveness rejected the liberal West. On his grandiose stage he revived primitive native heroes and gods singing of fate and doom and rushing toward their own annihilation through a web of crime and deceit. Neither Bismarck in his statesmanship nor Wagner in his art, neither Germany groping for leadership before 1914, nor Germany overreaching itself for an even more ambitious goal in 1939, had any generous universal message to carry to other peoples. Other European nations, too, had tried to dominate the scene: all of them—from Catholic Spain under Philip II to Communist Russia under Lenin—thought of mankind as well as of their own nation. They brought a spiritual or social message which inspired millions in other lands In an exemplary way, seventeenth century England embodied the universal idea of liberty; eighteenth century France that of reason. Among all the great nations Germany alone, when its turn came, had nothing to offer but self-centered power and self-glorification.

Beginning with the early nineteenth century, many Germans dismissed the demand of the French classical mind for clarity and common sense, and the preference of the pragmatic English-speaking peoples for the reasonable and the useful. To the Germans such standards encouraged superficiality. There is no doubt that certain characteristics of the German romantics, when not overemphasized, were inextricably fused into superb achievements. These romantics left a great legacy as mystics, poets, philosophers, and musicians. These very characteristics, if overindulged, however, may foster attitudes harmful to political and social relationships. Few Germans recognized this danger as clearly as Goethe, who had to overcome in himself Titan-like tendencies. Faustus, with his overreaching will

was, after all, a German figure; a German, Oswald Spengler, characteristically, though wrongly, saw in Faust the embodiment of
western man as a whole; when, in 1947, Thomas Mann wrote about
the German madness which had involved Germany and Europe in
an unprecedented catastrophe, he again found the unifying symbol,
with much greater appropriateness, in *Doktor Faustus*.

Franz Grillparzer, the Austrian dramatist who struggled all his
life for balance and restraint, pointed in a truly Goethean spirit to
Mozart as a model for those who opposed the German lust for the
measureless in fears and hopes, in expectations and rejections. "You
call him great?" Grillparzer asked in a poem written in 1842. "He
was, but by accepting limits. What he did, and what he denied
himself, are of equal importance in judging his work. Because he
never determined to do more than human beings could, there is a
harmony in everything he created. In his art he preferred appearing
smaller than he was to growing beyond human measurement. The
world of art is a second world, but it is as real as the first world is,
and all reality is a matter of proportion." Grillparzer warned the
Germans against losing their sense of proportion and called on
them to appreciate the possible and the permissible. His call was in
vain. Their straining after the measureless went hand in hand with
their pride in meticulous organization and strict discipline; it was
this unique combination which made the Germans a European
problem.

In *The Dawn*, written in 1880, Nietzsche alluded to "the hostility
of the Germans to the Enlightenment" But he hoped that the
"obscurantist, enthusiastic and atavistic spirit" which caused the
German alienation from the West was passing. He was mistaken.
The alienation from the West grew deeper. The heritage of Bismarckism with its emotional rejection of western democracy and its
overrating of German strength prevented a realistic reappraisal of
the political and intellectual world situation. The influence of a
misunderstood Nietzsche strengthened the romantic devaluation of
common sense and of the rational-ethical forces in history. The
word *Mythus* (myth) began, at this time, to occupy a central position in German thought. Friedrich Gundolf, in his book on Stefan
George (1920), defined myth as "Wort und Schau von Volk und
Gott, von wirklichem (!) Geschehen," as word and vision telling of
folk and God, of what really (!) happens. Myth, it was believed,
not only opened the way to a deeper understanding of reality and
of its fundamental values—the concrete folk and a rather vague
God—myth was also acclaimed as a life-enhancing and life-renewing

force. This myth of folk and God gave to National Socialism whatever it had of intellectual content. In the preface to his *Der Mythus des 20. Jahrhunderts* (The Myth of the Twentieth Century, 1930) Alfred Rosenberg defined the task of our century as the creation of "a new type of man out of a new myth of life." As in a witches' caldron all the various antiwestern ingredients of modern German thought were thrown together in this confused book of the intellectual spokesman of National Socialism. The brew was not only intoxicating; it was poisonous.

The Longing for the "Hidden Savior"

RELIANCE ON POWER, a feeling of superiority, and a disregard for moral factors led Germany into the war of 1914 and, in spite of some very great military successes, into defeat. The fall of the Hohenzollern at the end of the war and the proclamation of the undesired Republic did not establish liberal democracy in Germany. The republican constitution preserved the essential features and even the name of the Reich. Most Germans regarded the Republic only as an interim state; in fact many refused to call it a state—a word which to Germans conveys pride, power, and majesty. Instead they contemptuously called the republic a mere system, a system of western corruption. The first President of the Reich (a significant title) to be elected by the people after the consolidation of economic stability and the reappearance of prosperity was the aged imperial Field Marshal Paul von Hindenburg, who had remained faithful to the antidemocratic convictions he inherited. The people were untrained in the practice and responsibility of self-government; democracy seemed an importation from the West unsuited to the German mind; German self-confidence was not shaken by the "undeserved" defeat but morbidly increased as a protest against the historical injustice of a lost war, the struggle against the peace treaty of Versailles was regarded as part of a war against the moral and social ideas of the West. Many German intellectuals saw in such a war the fulfillment of German history and the mission of the German people. A German Catholic essayist Eugen Gurster pointed out that the spokesmen of this generation— Oswald Spengler, Moeller van den Bruck, Ernst Junger—aimed at something more radical than revenge for Versailles or simply the resumption of the war they felt was merely interrupted in 1918. By a total and radical refusal to recognize any longer the eternal standards of a universal Christian or humanistic tradition, the Germans believed that they would be able to throw off, for good and all, those "ideological fig-leaves" with which humanity, craving for power, "has covered its shame for centuries." A totally new era in history had begun, Junger proclaimed, which promised big rewards for bold gamblers who dared to face reality. He saw the Germans marching "toward a magical zero point. Only those who tap invisible sources of strength can march beyond this point." The West had defeated Germany in the name of democracy; the West represented all the old values—Germany's great historical chance would now lie at the opposite pole.

A representative of this German generation came to the attention of the Swiss historian and diplomat Carl J. Burckhardt in 1925. Writing to the Austrian poet Hugo von Hofmannsthal, he reported a talk with a young man, apparently then in his middle thirties, whom he had known as a fellow-student at the University of Gottingen. What he had to say appeared to Burckhardt extremely "absurd" yet in no way ridiculous, for he recognized in the man the spokesman of a phalanx on the march. The man foretold the coming of the *heimliche Kaiser,* the hidden Emperor-Savior, the Hohenstaufen in the Kyffhauser who would remove the last trace of shallow western civilization and bring real health (Gesundung) to the German people. Burckhardt asked the grim fanatic what he really wanted—the answer was "Entfesselung mythischer Urkraft gegen civilisatorische Tucke," the unchaining of mythical primeval folk-strength against the perfidy of western civilization. Burckhardt knew that the young man was not intelligent, but he rightly saw in this deadly serious Ph.D. the German of the near future. Myths, Burckhardt wrote, are always intoxicating for the Germans. Far from being harmless allegories they are doomladen invitations to danger.

Burckhardt showed an acute understanding of the obsessions clouding the German mind in the first half of the twentieth century: a romantic interpretation of the past; a feeling of having been unjustly treated by history and of having suffered at the hands of inferior people; a conviction that Germany's great merits were not recognized by mankind; finally, the expectation of a future in which the myths of the past would turn into realities and thereby German history and destiny find their fulfillment. This point of view, so difficult for Anglo-Americans to understand, made many Germans jubilantly welcome the Third Reich. What was it but a fusion and consecration of the many myths that had defeated the Enlightenment in Germany? The Third Reich claimed to be the realization not only of German nationalism but also of *German* socialism, of a *German* revolution, and of a *German* theology bestowing its blessings upon the German historical mission, a true *imperium sacrum* or Holy Empire built upon the mystical and yet natural reality of the German race As Julius Petersen, for many years professor of German literature and editor of the works of Lessing, Goethe, and Schiller, put it in 1934 in *Die Sehnsucht nach dem Dritten Reich in deutscher Sage und Dichtung* (The Longing for the Third Reich in German Saga and Literature): "Now tomorrow has become today, the mood of the approaching end of the world (*Weltuntergangsstimmung*) has changed into the feeling of a new beginning (*Aufbruch*), the final goal has become visible. In the depth of the Volk all the forces of ancient longing are alive, and the dream pictures (*Traumbilder*) which inspired the past are entering the light of day." The final words of the book proclaimed the arrival of the transfigured German people and hero: "The new Reich has been firmly planted. The longed-for . . . leader has appeared."

In the early twentieth century the youth of Germany lived in a bewildering tension between a rapidly industrialized and outwardly westernized environment and an *Innenleben,* an inner life, dominated by neo-romanticism and myth. The growing strains created by the application of the most modern technology in a still partly patriarchal and feudal society deprived many young men of the sense of fulfillment and perplexed their minds, especially when a misunderstood Nietzscheanism and naturalism caused the progressive weakening of the moral restraints imposed by the Christian tradition. The forebodings of a great crisis, of a seminal catastrophe, propagated by a few intellectuals before the war of 1914, seemed confirmed by the consequences of the war and the defeat. To the German youth movement which started around 1900, the Germans appeared to lead the search for new foundations of life, which they believed all people had to find if they wished to overcome a deadly crisis of mind and society. The Germans quickly and eagerly assumed that western civilization was as rotten in the West as it appeared to be in Germany and Russia. The antiwestern traditions of the War of Liberation against Napoleon were revived. There was an end to reasonableness In its stead there was a fostering of the cult of the German people and its historical mission. After the war of 1914—which left upon many of the German front-generation a long-lasting impression very different from the average experience of the English-speaking soldiers—many young men, animated by a new fanatical faith, believed that they were living in a unique time of decision when almost anything could happen if willed with wholehearted determination. These young men accepted from Nietzsche not his ethical individualism, his sense of personal responsibility, his cold contempt for nationalism and the state; instead they accepted, and outdid, his rejection of western bourgeois civilization and his ecstatic expectation of a new man able to live reality in all its stark and tragic truth. These young men longed for a nebulous true community with a living center embodied in a trusted leader who by his magic power would carry his followers to some wonderland, far away from the prosaic mediocrity of the old middle class society. This was the generation that Max Kommerell deprecated as "youth without Goethe."

At the end of the nineteenth century German social science inclined to contrast two ideal types of social organization. One type, *Gemeinschaft* (community) presupposed that the individual could live a full and meaningful life only as a part of, and through his partnership in, the group. The cohesion of such a group was believed to be shaped by unconscious factors, by deep vital forces of instinct, growing organically as a part of nature and independent from man's free will. The other type, *Gesellschaft* (society), emphasized the individual who existed prior to the group, which owed its origin to the will of individuals and to their rational motives. Society in that sense was declared to be characteristic of western bourgeois civilization; it demanded as its foundation a respect for universal truth, a sense of reciprocity and of contractual fidelity which were not needed for the existence and cohesion of the more primeval and immediate vitality of Community. Some Germans regarded Community and its organic depth as peculiarly German (though the Russian Slavophils claimed it as specifically Russian), and extolled it above the "mechanic or purely legal superficiality" of Society.

This contrast was also often expressed as that between German spiritual *Kultur* and western technological civilization. The latter word soon acquired a pejorative meaning. Some even went so far as to doubt the value of any rational civilization, placing their faith instead in the elemental force of nature. They hailed the war of 1914 as the beginning of a new period of history in which *Kultur* or the German idea would replace civilization and the western ideas of 1789. In 1916 Professor Johann Plange, a political scientist at the University of Munster, published *1789 and 1914: Symbolic Years in the History of Political Ideas,* in which he proclaimed: "In us lives the twentieth century. However the war may end, we are the exemplary people. Our ideals will determine the goals of mankind. At present world history experiences the tremendous spectacle of the great new historical ideal breaking through to final victory among us, while in England the [old] world-historical principle is collapsing. . . . Impelled by the needs of war, the socialist idea has taken hold of German economic life; its organization has coalesced in a new spirit, and thus the defense of our nation has given birth to the new idea of 1914, an idea destined for the whole of mankind, the idea of German organization, the folk-community of national socialism." Opposing the individualism and egoism of the capitalistic West, especially of commercial England, the Germans in World War I spoke for a true socialism in which the individual became part of the community and regarded its growth and strength as his own. The planned economy introduced during the war years out of military necessity was interpreted as a higher form of social life in which the common weal took absolute precedence over individual rights and interests. When the great moral and material effort unexpectedly ended in defeat, Oswald Spengler's message of the inevitable decline and fall of western civilization comforted and inspired many Germans. The defeat was viewed as a temporary setback soon to be turned into an unprecedented triumph But in spite of all the enthusiasm engendered by National Socialism, the end was a greater catastrophe than that of 1918.

The Germany of Today and Tomorrow

IN 1945 GERMANY and Europe faced an entirely different situation. Prussia had ceased to exist. The rural nobility which formed its backbone was irretrievably uprooted. The lands to the east where its power was entrenched were resettled by Slavs. German life and civilization moved westward and the link with older German traditions, deflected and disfigured in the nineteenth century, was restored. The centralization and uniformity fostered by the cult of power and overrated in the name of efficiency were replaced by a federal structure and by the respect for diversity which had characterized German history in the past. With the total collapse of the Bismarckian Reich, the myth of the Reich lost its hold over the German mind. Sober and responsible thinking began to assert itself. Characteristically, the only effort to rekindle the spirit and enthusiasm of the antiwestern nationalist uprising, the *Volkserhebung* of 1813, was started by publicists and historians in the communist-occupied part of Germany, not in the German Federal Republic.

In the Federal Republic German scholars began in earnest to do what they should have done after 1918: to re-evaluate modern German history and to reassess its principal trends in the light of reality and of universal ethical principles. After 1918 most German intellectuals were obsessed with the vindication of Bismarck's Germany; their denunciations of the Treaty of Versailles did much to prepare the new generation for the joyous acceptance of the Third Reich In the campaign against Versailles German scholarship expressed its resentment of modern civilization. In *Luther, Gestalt und Symbol* (1928), Gerhard Ritter, one of the most prominent German historians of the period, declared: "There has been much discussion lately as to whether Luther belongs to the Middle Ages or to the modern world. Much more important seems to us the question whether we ourselves belong or wish to belong to the modern world, if by that is meant the spirit of Anglo-Saxon or Latin civilizations." Ten years later the disastrous consequences of this point of view once it spread beyond the narrow circle of scholars, were revealed in the triumph of a movement which had nothing in common with the spirit of the Anglo-Saxon or Latin civilizations

It has frequently been pointed out that there have been in history, and still are, several Germanies. First came western Germany, which formed part of the Roman *orbis*, where cities existed in ancient times and enjoyed all the amenities of the civilized life of antiquity This Germany was separated by the *Limes Germanicus* from the primitive barbaric lands which the victory of Arminius—celebrated later by German nationalists—saved from becoming part of the universal western civilization of the period. To the east of the *Limes* lay central Germany, incorporated into Christianity and civilization by Charlemagne around 800 A D , and an eastern Germany which German knights conquered from its Slav and Lithuanian inhabitants in the thirteenth century—a semicolonial land of barons and serfs where the few cities did not develop an independent life and where a thriving middle class developed only much later. It would be a mistake to overstress these historical differences as factors in twentieth century German civilization. Nevertheless it is not an

accident that the statesmen representing the new Germany after
1945 came from the west. Konrad Adenauer was by origin, background, and loyalties a Rhenish Catholic and Theodor Heuss a
Protestant from southwestern Germany with its liberal tradition.
Their policy was based upon the understanding that the new Germany could again become part and partner of the West only if it
succeeded, beyond and above military and economic considerations,
in re-establishing those moral and intellectual ties with the West
which in the course of the nineteenth century had become progressively loosened until they were completely cut in the National
Socialist era.

One of the most promising mid-twentieth century developments
is the fact that the alienation of German from Western thought is
coming to an end. This process of alienation had been going on for
a long time; first very slowly and against strong opposition from
1812 to 1870; then faster and against a rapidly diminishing opposition from 1871 to 1918; finally with dizzying acceleration and
against a crumbling opposition from 1919 to 1933. In 1924 Oswald
Spengler wrote in his *Politische Pflichten der deutschen Jugend*
(Political Duties of the German Youth) · "The fact that we as
Germans can finally hate, is one of the few developments in our
time which can assure our future." Twenty years later Spengler
was proved wrong in this as in most of his predictions. But many
of his German fellow intellectuals of the 1920's regarded it as supreme wisdom and as a sign of intellectual honesty and maturity to
insist upon the separation of the political from the moral sphere.
In 1937 a leading German philosopher, Heinrich Rickert, who was
no National Socialist, expressed this abdication of ethics before
life, of the intellectual before the man of action, in his *Grund-
probleme der Philosophie* (Fundamental Problems of Philosophy):
"What we Germans have to do today and tomorrow depends not on
philosophical but on entirely different considerations. If the philo-
sophical-ethical attitude of the German (*des Deutschen Weltanschauung*) does not agree with the demands of the day, he has to
accommodate his views to the historical situation. Otherwise he
must renounce every effective cultural activity, for in the long run
such an activity is only possible within his people." This personally
honest and well-meaning philosopher overlooked the fact that not
accommodation but a critical ethical opposition to the historical
situation and its official national spokesmen and interpreters will in
the long run contribute to the cultural growth of a nation.

Before 1914 some German philosophers viewed with deep apprehension the darkening of the German intellectual and moral scene through the gathering clouds of antiwestern neo-romanticism. They were neither radicals nor Westerners. They were part of the great stream of German European thought that included Leibnitz and Kant, Lessing and Goethe. One such philosopher was Wilhelm Dilthey, born in the Rhineland one year after Goethe's death, and in the closing years of the century professor of philosophy at the University of Berlin. Hajo Holborn, in his analysis of Dilthey's historical thought, has stressed its affinities with American pragmatism. Dilthey "praised the Enlightment for its confidence in the power of human reason and its secular interpretation of the world. He stated that it had been the dominant impulse of his own philosophical thinking 'in the spirit of the great Enlightment to cling to the world of experience as the *one* world of our knowledge.'" In the one book which during his lifetime reached a wide circle of readers, *Das Erlebnis und die Dichtung* (Experience and Poetry), Dilthey asked whether "we should not return to some of the ideas of the Enlightenment which we have abandoned." Even more prophetic were the words of Wilhelm Windelband, born in 1848 in Potsdam, who held the chair of philosophy at Heidelberg in the first decades of the twentieth century. To him, philosophy was the critical science of universal values. In his survey of the place of philosophy in the German intellectual life of the nineteenth century (*Die Philosophie im deutschen Geistesleben des 19. Jahrhunderts,* 1907), he stated that "we must resume the battle for the achievements of the Enlightenment . . . perhaps a more difficult struggle than that which the Enlightenment successfully waged."

If the war of 1914 had not inflamed the antiwestern, folk-centered, and militaristic passions in Germany, a rapprochement with the West and liberal democracy would have come about. But Germany's initial military successes aroused her national pride to feverish heat and the majority of her intellectuals and scholars were as irresponsible as her political and military spokesmen. Under these circumstances, the defeat in 1918 only stiffened resistance to parliamentary democracy and Western liberalism This situation changed twenty years later. The defeat of Germany in 1945 preserved liberty and civilization not only in the greater part of western and central Europe but also for much of Germany itself.

In the spring of 1941 the whole of Europe (with the exception of two minor enclaves) was under the domination of totalitarian and antiwestern doctrines; only in the small island of Britain, its original home, did parliamentary democracy survive, and Britain alone fought on, not only for its life but also for the survival of human values and individual liberty. Few men at that time dared to hope that within four years the empires of Mussolini and Hitler would crumble to dust and that great parts of Europe—even Italy and the larger part of Germany—would be restored to modern western civilization which fascism and communism had derided and despised. That not all of Europe could be liberated by the West from the blight of totalitarian tyranny was the result of German *hubris*. Drunk with victory and power, claiming to fulfill Germany's historical destiny, Hitler revived Germany's medieval *Drang nach Osten*, the urge to eastward expansion, in order to enslave the Slav and other inferior peoples to German *Kultur*. By the carefully planned annihilation of Poland Germany destroyed with Stalin's help the barrier which had protected Europe from the terror of Leninism. Two years later Hitler betrayed his ally Stalin; the German attack on Russia opened to Stalin's armies, which otherwise never would have got there, the access into central Europe and to the Elbe river. Characteristically, the plans drawn up for the invasion of Russia and the final establishment of the great Reich were called Operation Barbarossa. The tie with the Hohenstaufen myth was emphasized. But this time, too, Germany's attempt to incorporate the whole of central and eastern Europe into an antiwestern and antiliberal empire ended in failure. The equally antiwestern and antiliberal empire of communist Russia replaced German leadership in eastern Europe. To the greater part of Germany, however, the year 1945 brought freedom which had seemed lost to the Germans "for a thousand years." Since then Germany has been well on the road back not only to the cultural community of the West but also to her own great traditions.

Chapter Two

GOETHE AND HIS TIME

The Inheritance of the Enlightenment

GOETHE WAS THE LAST and the greatest of the eighteenth century literary figures who made German culture the equal of the older civilizations of the West. In his time German intellectual life was far in advance of the country's political and social development. Though the Holy Roman Empire of the German Nation, which preserved a loose and antiquated framework of German unity, was still in existence, and though two of its princes—Frederick II of Prussia and especially Joseph II of Austria—stood out among the enlightened monarchs of the period, Germany had no statesman to quicken the pace of its political life. After 1760 German intellectual and artistic culture had rapidly caught up with that of the more advanced West; politically and socially Germany remained a quiet backwater, unstirred by the political storms and the social changes sweeping the lands around the North Atlantic. In 1776 and again in 1789 some German intellectuals expressed profound sympathy with the American and French revolutions and wrote flaming protests against suppression of human and civic rights, but their protests were either couched in abstract terms or directed against situations under foreign skies. No attempt was made—nor could it be made under German conditions—to convert these sentiments, borrowed from the West and often passionately expressed, into concrete action at home. Neither an enterprising middle class nor a political tradition of self-government existed in Germany. The so-called free cities were dreamy relics of the past where a stagnant narrowness of view and the rule of a conceited oligarchy went hand in hand. Absolute princes dominated the life of many courts; some of those rulers cared for the welfare of their subjects; others cared only for their ruthless exploitation. In either case their subjects, whether commoners or intellectuals, never contested the ruler's prerogatives. The aristocracy was separated from the traditional middle class, the burghers, not only by legal privileges but also by an unbridgeable gulf, a gulf which some of the burghers began to resent but which practically all of them accepted without protest.

In the middle of the eighteenth century the spirit of Enlightenment spread from France and England to Germany, it awakened the dormant genius of the nation, but backward economic and political conditions confined its effects to the realm of thought. Thus the German philosopher, Immanuel Kant, the greatest philosophical genius of the Enlightenment, who launched one of the most daring revolutions of the mind, remained an obedient even subservient subject of the King of Prussia. The great German poets of the Enlightenment, Gotthold Ephraim Lessing and Friedrich Schiller, who created the German national theatre and were equally prominent as critics, were more concerned with freedom of speech and tolerance than with purely political rights. Yet in spite of its political weakness Germany, historically a borderland of western civilization, became for a brief time—roughly from 1770 to 1830—its intellectual center. Its influence penetrated more deeply throughout central and eastern Europe than did that of the French Revolution. Herder, Hegel, Schiller, Schlegel, and Schelling, these were men who also stirred the Slav mind.

This new German development drew its strength not only from modern England and France but also from a rediscovery of classical antiquity and a reassertion of its perennial value as a universal standard and guide. No one was more deeply inspired by classical antiquity than Goethe. With his almost Greek confidence in the all-encompassing security and unity of the cosmos, he was the last European "universal man"—poet, scientist, statesman, and critic,—for whom all the fields of human experience formed a harmonious whole. Nature was everywhere: in life and poetry, in science and artistic vision. From a brief period of youthful revolt and romantic self-assertion in the years of the "Storm and Stress"—he was then in his early twenties—Goethe finally reached, through many personal crises, a state of serenity far removed from the pessimism and national exclusiveness of many of his contemporaries. "Goethe illustrates," Walter Pater wrote in his essay on Winckelmann (1868), "that union of the Romantic spirit in its adventure, its variety, its profound subjectivity of soul, with Hellenism, in its transparency, its rationality, its desire of beauty—that marriage of Faust and Helena—of which the art of the nineteenth century is a child, the beautiful lad Euphorion, as Goethe conceives him, on the crags, in the splendor of battle and in harness as for victory, his brows bound with life. Goethe illustrates, too, the preponderance in this marriage of the Hellenic element."

The eighteenth century ended for Germany in 1806, when, under the impact of French victories, the Prussian army collapsed and the Holy Roman Empire was dissolved. From then until 1848 Germany passed through a transitional period in which the problems of modern Germany began to emerge and to assume the form in which they dominated the social and intellectual scene until 1945. From 1848 onward the character of Germany underwent a profound change. Economically and technologically Germany caught up with—and even occasionally surpassed—the more advanced countries of the West. At the same time she alienated herself more and more, intellectually and culturally, and grew ever more conscious and proud of this estrangement. Its origin can be traced to the spirit in which the war against Napoleon in 1813 was undertaken, or at least to the frame of mind of many German intellectuals at the time. It was understandable that many Germans welcomed the end of French occupation. The same sentiment of satisfaction in 1814 filled the hearts of the people in the Netherlands, which had become a province of the French Empire, and of Switzerland, whose political destiny was shaped by Napoleon. Yet neither in the Netherlands nor in Switzerland did there arise a deep and lasting hostility to French or western civilization. Such a hostility did, however, become characteristic of many German intellectual circles and, through their influence, of the people as a whole. The Dutch and the Swiss, though people of Germanic origin, continued gratefully to acknowledge French and western influence and to shape their political life after western models. On the other hand, the Germans, in the nineteenth century, began to feel themselves fundamentally different from and culturally and morally superior to France and the West.

Goethe remained, deep into the nineteenth century, a representative man of the eighteenth. He never succumbed to the growing Germanophilism. He retained to the end the humanism, optimism, and universalism of the eighteenth century. He was as aware as any twentieth century writer, of the dark abyss in the human heart and of the follies and tragedies of history. Yet this knowledge did not make him despair. He was born in the age of Voltaire, the age of confidence in reason. His youth was overshadowed by the passionate sentimentality of Rousseau and Werther, his manhood was lived amid the turmoil of the French Revolution and of the Napoleonic Wars, when the old order crumbled and man was at the mercy of elemental forces. He did not live the sheltered life of the ivory tower. From his early student years in Leipzig and Strasbourg to the last days in Weimar he experienced the deepest joys and sorrows of life. He did not remain a spectator but participated in a way few men have in as many of the active and creative pursuits as human limitations allow. He showed less inclination toward philosophy than did most prominent Germans—among them his friend Friedrich Schiller—but he was unequalled among Germans in the breadth of his poetic genius, and his creative power did not weaken with the advance of old age.

He was profoundly interested in science and devoted much thought and observation to the understanding of the mysterious forms of nature and the laws of their growth. He even naively overestimated the value of his scientific work. On August 2, 1830, a visitor found the octogenarian deeply moved by the latest news from Paris. But this news did not concern the July revolution, which ended the Bourbon monarchy and shook Europe, but a meeting of the Academy of Science in which Geoffroy Saint-Hilaire presented an interpretation of nature similar to the one put forward by Goethe. "I have had this on my mind for fifty years," Goethe said. "At first I was alone, then I found support, and now at last, to my great joy, I am surpassed by congenial minds. This occurrence is of incredible importance to me: and I rejoice that I have at last seen the victory of an idea to which I have devoted my life, and which, moreover, is my own par excellence."

But Goethe dedicated as much of his life to the study of art and archeology as to science. He drew and painted, collected *objets d'art,* and had a deep and abiding interest in all forms of art. His capacity for work was tremendous. Much of his old age was spent editing periodicals dealing with science and the history of art. He also published many translations from foreign languages. Yet these intellectual pursuits did not exhaust him. For many years he was Minister of State in the duchy of Saxony-Weimar and though the state was small, the various aspects of administration with which he had to deal—the budget, the operation of mines, the development of agriculture, and the supervision of education—demanded attention to minute and prosaic details. For twenty-seven years he was also director and stage manager of the Weimar Theatre. In his official capacity he did good though not exceptionally outstanding work, but in all these many-sided activities he acquired a knowledge of the world which found its expression in the wisdom of his poetic creations and in many recorded conversations and surviving letters. In all his practical and official activities he preserved his fullest independence as a poet and artist. "Never, in my vocation as an author," Goethe said on October 20, 1830, "have I asked what would the people like and how I could (through my poetry) serve the whole. I have always striven to improve myself, to raise the standard of my personality, and to express only that which I recognized as good and true." Among his last utterances, in March, 1832, he sounded a warning against "committed literature." A poet, he said, who writes political poetry, "is lost as a poet; he must bid farewell to his free spirit, his unbiased views, and draw over his ears the cap of bigotry and hatred." Goethe served his prince and his state and cared for the cultural progress and the welfare of the people, but in his mind and in his work he remained the free individual.

We know nothing or very little of the life of men of similar genius—Homer, Dante, Shakespeare. Their work alone testifies to their greatness. Goethe's life and his opinions are unusually well documented. Even were his work lost, his life would form a human document of the first order. In his appearance, both as a youth and as an old man, Goethe must have been unusually attractive. He won the love, friendship, and devotion of men and women alike. He lived a life rich in passion and in wisdom, replete with hard work, great achievements, and magic enchantment, almost inexhaustible in its human interest, a unique and yet an exemplary life. No wonder that Goethe regarded himself, and was regarded by his contemporaries, as "a favorite of the gods," (*ein Liebling der Gotter*). He used this phrase himself when he told, in his autobiography, the fairy-tale *The New Paris.* But beyond his work and his life, which are both of universal interest, there is a third dimension in which Goethe is of fundamental importance, especially for the Germans. At the very time that Germany surrendered to antiwestern Germanophilism, he firmly upheld the values of the universal civilization of the West, its cosmopolitan freedom of the mind, and the wisdom of moderation and tolerance.

Goethe and Schiller

IN THIS ENDEAVOR Goethe found the support of another great German poet, Friedrich Schiller, with whom he maintained for over ten years a close friendship and working alliance such as had hardly been known between two men of almost equal stature and of opposite temperament. Schiller was ten years younger than Goethe and lived only forty-five years, few of them happy ones. Whereas Goethe came from a well-to-do family of the middle class, Schiller had to struggle for a long time against bitter poverty. As a human being he was less complex and more perfect than Goethe. It was Schiller's character more than his work which evoked Goethe's deepest respect. In immortal lines he expressed his respect for this man to whom he owed a new spring of life and a new moral resolve:

> . . . *hinter ihm, im wesenlosen Scheine,*
> *Lag, was uns alle bändigt, das Gemeine.*

> (Far behind he left that vulgar meanness
> that dominates our lives)

When Schiller died, Goethe wrote to his friend Zelter on June 1, 1805: "I lose a friend, and with him half my existence." More than a quarter of a century later, the old man remarked to Eckermann what good fortune it had been for him to have been favored by Schiller's friendship. "For though our nature was entirely different, we were directed toward the same goal, which made our relationship so intimate that one could not live without the other. . . . We lived so closely together that we could never decide whether our thoughts originated with one or the other." Even more moving are passages in the generally much restrained letters of the older man to the younger. "Continue," Goethe wrote Schiller on March 6, 1799, "to assist me, in good and in bad hours, with the strength of your mind and heart." "We are so intimate," a letter of October 26, 1799 assured Schiller, "that whatever happens to you might have happened to me." And Goethe's gratitude found expression in the famous words, written on January 6, 1798: "You have given me a second youth and have made me a poet again, which I had practically ceased to be."

After Goethe's initial distrust of the younger man, in whose early
works he recognized the immoderate passions of his own rejected
'Storm and Stress" period, the two became close friends when
Schiller invited Goethe to collaborate with him in his new review
Die Horen Announcing this publication, Schiller wrote: "At a
time when the approaching sounds of war frighten the Fatherland,
when the struggle of political opinions and interest renews this war
in almost every circle and much too often drives the muses and
graces away, when the discussions and writings of the day offer no
refuge from this all-haunting demon of political criticism, it may
appear at once audacious and meritorious to invite the reader to an
entertainment of an entirely different nature. In fact the climate of
the time seems to promise hardly any chance for a periodical which
will keep strictly silent about the favorite topic of the day, and will
seek its glory in trying to please with something different from that
which is now used to please." Schiller determined to turn his
readers' minds away from politics to universal human interests and
thus "reunite the politically divided world under the banner of
Truth and Beauty."

It would be a mistake to regard the two friends as men dedicated
only to pure art, unconcerned with social obligations. They felt no
contempt for political life or for the people. After all, Goethe spent
years of his life as a civil servant. He wrote to Herder on March 20,
1783, that even the patronage of arts and sciences, which otherwise
confer upon the state the greatest glory, could not earn so beautiful
and lasting a laurel for a prince as close and continuous attention
to the needs of the common people. Yet neither Goethe nor Schiller
made much of the state, in that sense the example of antiquity did
not prevail. Both passionately preferred peace to war and would
have considered it unthinkable to subordinate the individual to the
state or nation. The individual of whom they thought was not
primarily the heroic or great man. Goethe, though he was a prince's
friend and a member of court society, was always close to simple
people. His wife Christiane and Zelter, the closest friend of his last
decades, came from the lower ranks, as did the poetical figures he
most loved, Faust's Margaret, Egmont's Klärchen, and Hermann
and Dorothea.

What Goethe and Schiller could not tolerate was the emphasis
upon, or idealization of, national self-interest and the lack of moderation and good sense which in their time German intellectuals and
youth began to show in the pursuit of political goals. Schiller's
famous and often misinterpreted play, *Wilhelm Tell*, did not praise
a revolutionary struggle for liberation as such. Its praise was meant

only for a people which, even in the midst of its struggle, honored the universal values of humanitarianism and was humble in its hour of victory. When revolutionary and nationalistic passions threatened the civilization of Europe, Goethe and Schiller, horrified by the demons that had been set free, prayed that moderation might prevail. They were not "escapists" longing for a far off island of blessed dreams Both faced the human problem—that of the individual and that of the community—with all its dangerous potentialities. Yet they were convinced that this problem would be more serious if universal values did not restrain the personal and nationalistic ambitions that were bringing such deep anxiety to the modern world. However, they were as one in their optimistic humanism. Aware of the tragic element in life they rejected the modern fear of life and of death on the strength of their faith in human values.

In his lifetime Schiller's works were more popular than those of Goethe. He expressed the sentiments of the German educated classes before the rise of nationalism. Later generations have misinterpreted his message in a nationalistic sense and this misunderstanding preserved his popularity in the nineteenth century. In 1859, at the celebration of the centennial of Schiller's birth—the year in which Sardinia's war for Italian unification kindled similar aspirations among the Germans—Schiller was officially consecrated as the herald of the German nation-state. Nothing could have been farther from the mind of Kant's disciple. In the center of his intellectual world stood the dignity of the individual and the oneness of mankind. "The state is a creature of accident, but man is a being of necessity," Schiller wrote on November 27, 1788, to Caroline von Beulwitz, his sister-in-law. "The state is only a result of human forces, only a work of our thoughts, but man is the source of the force itself and the creator of the thought." How different was the intellectual and moral climate of the Germany of Schiller and Goethe from that of Hegel, Ranke, and Treitschke. "The first law of decency," Schiller wrote, "is to preserve the liberty of others; the second, to show one's own freedom." In *Don Carlos* Schiller spoke "as the deputy of all humanity" through the mouth of Posa. Posa's heart beat

> For all mankind; his passion was
> The world and future generations.

As Professor Jakob Minor pointed out, "Never have the slogans of cosmopolitanism, of universal philanthropy, and of liberty of thought and faith found a more eloquent and powerful expression than in

this play." As guardians of these supreme values Schiller saw the
creative artists, not the statesmen or the people.

> O sons of art! into your hands consigned
> (O heed the trust, O heed it and revere!)
> The liberal dignity of humankind!

When Schiller delivered his inaugural address as professor of
history at the University of Jena he spoke on the subject, "What
does universal history mean, and for what purpose do we study it?"
His lecture culminated in the statement, "All thinking minds are
now united by a cosmopolitan bond of friendship." He thought the
Germans better prepared for this new cosmopolitan age because they
lived, at the end of the eighteenth century, under a constitution
which allowed the greatest possible diversity and freedom. Its lack
of unity and centralization made any plans for conquest or dominion impossible. Therein Germany differed from such seats of
power as Sparta or Rome. Contrasting the legislations of Lycurgus
in Sparta and of Solon in Athens, Schiller wrote, "A single virtue
was practiced in Sparta at the expense of all others. patriotism. To
this artificial sentiment the most natural and beautiful sentiments of
mankind were sacrificed." On the other hand, "It was wise of Solon
never to sacrifice the individual to the state, the end to the means;
instead he made the state subservient to man. His laws were not so
binding that citizens did not feel free to move freely and easily in
all directions . . . The laws of Lycurgus were iron fetters, which by
their oppressive weight dragged down the spirit." Sparta could produce warriors and heroes but there was no place in Schiller's scale
of values for them; he saw the end of human development in the
freely creative individual and in the citizen of the world.

In the two apparently patriotic plays of Schiller, *The Maid of
Orleans* and *Wilhelm Tell*, he chose as the embodiment of enlightened patriotism not German figures but a French national heroine
and a Swiss peasant who helped establish the independence of
Switzerland from Germany. What he honored in Joan of Arc and in
Tell was neither military exploits nor their—historically non-existent
—nationalism, but their Rousseauistic simplicity of life and heart.
The message of the two plays was the rejection of the spirit of conquest and pride, a glorification of idyllic peace, of the dignity of man,
and of modesty and moderation in victory. Anticipating what
Goethe told Eckermann about nationalism forty years later, Schiller
wrote his friend Christian Gottfried Körner on October 13, 1789,
that "It is a poor and trifling thing to write for one nation; such a

limitation is totally unbearable for a philosophical mind. Such a mind cannot find satisfaction in such a changing, accidental and arbitrary form of mankind, a mere fragment—and what else is even the most important nation?" If one people could stand for the ideal of humanity, it was, thought Goethe and Schiller, Ancient Greece. Schiller, a professor of modern history in his last years, conveyed his classical message in plays on modern themes; Goethe nowhere proclaimed the same faith in the human and the humane so beautifully as in his *Iphigenia in Tauris,* adapted from Euripides.

Iphigenia's Message

THE FIRST VERSION OF *Iphigenia* was published in the very year in which Lessing brought out *Nathan the Wise,* a drama that Goethe declared a "supreme masterwork of poetry." Both plays were charged with the idealism of the Enlightenment. Lessing's hero was a wise old Jew who transcended the traditional limitations of his faith and tribe; Goethe spoke his message through a Greek woman who in a supreme moment of crisis transcended her Greek inheritance. His Iphigenia, Agamemnon's daughter and a descendant of the cursed family of Atreus, had been suffering for many years from frightful loneliness on the forsaken, barbaric island of Tauris. There the goddess Artemis had brought her to haven from the altar on which her father planned to sacrifice her to the gods. Her longing to be reunited with her family in Greece was intensified by the sight of two Greeks who had just landed on the island. One she recognized as her brother Orestes, the murderer of their mother. Apollo, the brother of Artemis, had promised him deliverance from his torments if he succeeded in carrying off the image of the goddess from Tauris to the mainland. In Euripides' drama, Orestes easily got his way and freed his sister: his ally was Apollo who obligingly imposed the will of the Greeks on the barbarians.

A solution so external and nationalistic was unacceptable to Goethe. His Iphigenia saved the Greeks, not by the help of a god who interceded for them, but by her own humaneness. She found that she could not share in the plan which would save the Greeks at the price of deceiving the barbarians. She was reminded that those whom she "was willing to forsake were also men." By her humaneness she had changed the ways of the barbarians and had won the

heart of their king Thoas. She could not betray them and thereby
herself, but this stand threatened her brother's rescue and en-
tangled her in the apparently hopeless coils of fate. It was then that
she decided to take the risk and to meet the Taurians on the level
of pure humanity. She revealed the plot to the king, entrusting her
own and her brother's lives to the barbarians' humanity. To the
question of the king:

> And dost thou think
> That the uncultured Scythian will attend
> The voice of truth and of humanity
> Which Atreus, the Greek, heard not?

Iphigenia answered:

> 'Tis heard
> By every one, born 'neath whatever clime,
> Within whose bosom flows the stream of life
> Pure and unhindered.

The king hesitated. Too easily he recalled the wiles of the Greeks:

> The Greeks are wont to cast a longing eye
> Upon the treasure of barbarians,
> The Golden Fleece, good steeds, or daughters fair;
> But force and guile not always have availed
> To lead them, with their booty, safely home.

But force and guile were not at work this time between Greeks
and barbarians. Iphigenia pointed to a path out of hopelessness. By so
doing, Professor R. M. Browning writes, "Iphigenia died as a Greek
to become something more than a Greek."

When the king gave his grudging consent to the departure of the
Greeks, Iphigenia could not part from him without relieving his
disappointment. She had longed to leave for the sake of her family,
for the purification of her cursed house But now the barbarian
king was of her family too. "Honored and beloved as mine own
father was," Iphigenia told the king, "art thou to me; and this impression in my soul abides."

Iphigenia did more than soothe the passions in the hearts of
Orestes and Thoas: she also bridged the deeper abyss between
hostile nations and civilizations. As Professor Oskar Seidlin has
pointed out in his essay on "Iphigenia and the Humane Idea,"
Iphigenia, solving her most personal crisis by a courageous moral
decision, helped to redeem the relationship between Greeks and
barbarians from a self-centered nationalism. Her influence had

changed the barbarian king into a civilized ruler who abolished human sacrifice. But Tauris remained an isolated island, rejecting all intercourse with foreigners. The Greeks on their part believed in barriers too. Thanks to Iphigenia a world separated by hatred and suspicion became one bound by friendship. In the last words with the king, she promised to do her share.

> Let but the least among thy people bring
> Back to my ear the tones I heard from thee,
> Or should I on the humblest see thy garb,
> I will with joy receive him like a god,
> Prepare his couch myself, beside our hearth
> Invite him to a seat, and only ask
> Touching thy fate and thee.

So the play ended on a note of universal peace and tolerance. Goethe was no easy optimist. He knew that demonic restlessness, overreaching aspirations and boasting forcefulness are ever ready to threaten and confuse the human mind. He regarded them as a heritage of the primitive past. But he did not think its impact inescapable. *"Des Ungestümen wilden Ausdruck lieb ich nicht,"* (I do not like the expression of raging passions) he wrote in 1807. "For wherever a tiny human spark glints, I am happy to approve. The world's spirit is more tolerant than people think."

It was in Italy that Goethe completed the final version of *Iphigenia*. Like Jacob Burckhardt, he identified darkness and impetuosity with the Germanic North, and brightness and serenity with the Mediterranean. He would have been the first to appreciate Burckhardt's exultant cry of 1847:

> *O nimm, du heissgeliebter Süden,*
> *Den Fremdling auf, . . .*
> *Erfülle seine Seele ganz*
> *Mit deinem heitern Sonnenglanz!*
>
> *Lass rings um ihn den Wunderreigen*
> *Der alten Götter leuchtend steigen!*
> *Zeig ihm aus alt und neuer Zeit*
> *Gestalten voll Unsterblichkeit!*
>
> (Receive, O dearly beloved Southland
> The Northerner's prayer . . .
> Pour full his soul 'til it o'er runs
> With joyful radiance of thy sun.

Let round him dancing magic rise,
Let gods and heroes leap before his eyes
And let arise within his view
Immortal figures old and new.)

It was the sun of Homer, not the Germanic past, which brought Goethe and Schiller the comforting message of humanity.

Und die Sonne Homers, siehe, sie lachelt
auch uns.

See, the Sun of Homer, smiles upon us too.

Goethe and Napoleon

GOETHE REMAINED FAITHFUL to what he preached even in the critical decade of German history when the intellectual climate around him rapidly changed. Between 1806 and 1817 many Germans of the educated classes became the champions of a fervent German nationalism. However, the patriotic fervor at that time was not so general as German historians and publicists later wished to make it appear. Much of the population remained untouched by it. In a recent study of the rise of national consciousness in northwestern Germany between 1790 and 1830, Wolfgang von Groote found the northwestern Germans equally remote, in their sobriety, from the patriotic enthusiasm of Prussia and from the Napoleonic cult so widespread in western and southern Germany. "In the majority of the population no national enthusiasm was felt." The people disliked the foreigners but they did not feel humiliated or offended by the occupation. Only a few intellectuals tried, without any appreciable result, to arouse hatred of the French among the people. One such intellectual was the Principal of the Gymnasium in Oldenburg, Reinhard Ricklefs, who launched the review *Germania*, in 1814, which soon failed for lack of readers. Said Ricklefs: "The spirit of the old Germans must again awaken. . . . Each German must be ready at any moment to sacrifice everything, goods and life, for freedom and hearth. He must close his ears to all the falsehoods and insinuations of his faithless neighbors across the Rhine, and must, with a truly German mind and a truly German heart, love his Fatherland above all other things (*uber alles*), so that all danger and oppression disappear." In his commencement address to the graduating class in the same year Ricklefs bitterly lamented the fact that the Germans had been morally weakened by alien cultural influences.

For the fears of men like Ricklefs Goethe showed no sympathy. He was too deeply concerned with the spiritual growth of the German people and the perfection of German art and letters. The Heidelberg philosopher Reichlin-Meldegg well expressed Goethe's attitude in 1853, when, in his biography of H. E. G. Paulus, his predecessor in the Heidelberg chair, he wrote that "Goethe gave much serious thought to the German character (*das Deutschsein*), but none to Germany's growth . . . into a unified Reich." In 1796 Goethe and Schiller warned, in a famous distich, that the Germans hoped in vain to form a nation; instead they should develop into free individuals, a goal more easily attainable.

> *Zur* Nation *euch zu bilden, ihr hoffet es,*
>   *Deutsche, vergebens,*
> *Bildet, ihr könnt es, dafur freier zu*
>   *Menschen euch aus!*

The Germans, Goethe was convinced, could best fulfill their real task in history without creating a nation-state. He willingly accepted for them a future like that of the Jews, surviving as a people, preserving their character and accomplishing great things without a common Fatherland. Like the Jews, the Germans seemed to Goethe valuable as individuals but rather miserable as a people. In his conversations throughout the years he returned to this analogy several times. "The German nation is nothing," he told his friend Friedrich von Müller on December 14, 1808, "but the individual German is something, and yet they imagine the opposite to be true. The Germans should be dispersed throughout the world, like the Jews, in order fully to develop all the good that is in them for the benefit of mankind."

Even at the height of nationalist excitement, when the defeat of Napoleon was imminent and the patriotic youth hopefully discussed the problem of building a new German Reich, Goethe remained aloof. To a publicist, Franz Bernhard von Bucholtz, who had asked for his approval of a patriotic pamphlet, Goethe answered on February 14, 1814: "If I am to be perfectly sincere I must say that I believe that the greatest service I can render my country is to continue . . . to point out fairly and calmly the changes in our moral, aesthetic and philosophic culture which I witnessed. . . . As regards unification and pacification of the German Reich, we should leave this to the men in power and to those possessed of political wisdom." In a monograph on Goethe's political views Professor Wilhelm Mommsen showed that Goethe did not in the least care for a German Reich and never thought about a renovation of the defunct Reich. Nor did the Prussian State, the importance of which loomed so large in the thoughts of nineteenth century German political writers, hold any attraction for him. Goethe regarded the diversity and plurality of German states and independent German centers as a positive good. He expressed his deepest conviction when he wrote to Johann Jakob Hottinger on March 15, 1799: "At a time when everyone is busy creating new Fatherlands, the Fatherland of the man who thinks without prejudice and can rise above his time is nowhere and everywhere." He remained true to this faith amidst the patriotic fervor which gripped many Germans fifteen years later. He did not participate in the then fashionable rejection of cosmopolitanism (*Weltburgertum*) and in the glorification of the nation-state

At the turn of the nineteenth century Goethe's attitude had been widely shared all over Europe, and especially in Germany. Few German intellectuals were then nationalists; many admired Napoleon and saw in him the "prince of peace." Goethe, however, continued even after 1812 to revere Napoleon and refused to feel any hostility toward the French. As long as it was possible, he counseled submission to French domination over Germany. With all his love of classical antiquity he was opposed to the narrow Greco-Roman patriotism and warned the German teachers and writers not to use the example of ancient patriotism to arouse similar feelings among the modern Germans against the French. "Our life does not lead us to segregation and separation from other peoples," he told his friend Zelter, "on the contrary, it leads to the closest interchange. Our civic life is not that of the ancients. We are living, on the one hand, in much greater liberty and without their narrow limitations, and on the other hand, without such claims of the state upon us. To defy a conqueror because we have been imbued with Greek and Latin, would be childish." An appeal to ancient patriotism among modern men seemed, to Goethe, to degenerate all too easily into a travesty. The depth of Germany's national misery after 1806 did not move Goethe; the height of the nation's rise after 1812 did not arouse him.

Wilhelm von Humboldt reported in January, 1809, that Goethe never went out without wearing the Cross of the French Legion of

Honor and that he always used to call the man from whom he had received it, "my Emperor." In October, 1813, after the defeat of Napoleon in the Battle of Leipzig, the victorious Prussians and Austrians entered Weimar. The Austrian Field-Marshal, Count Wenzel Joseph Colloredo, was billeted in Goethe's house, and his host received him decorated with the French Legion of Honor. A few days later he explained to Humboldt that he could not remove the distinction which the French Emperor had bestowed upon him simply because this Emperor had lost a battle.

Goethe's refusal to write patriotic poetry during the War of Liberation was based not only on his dislike of all war poetry, but especially on his sympathy for Napoleon. He was indifferent to the war, not because he did not believe in the possibility of its success, but because he did not think it worth waging. German cultural life seemed to him to thrive under Napoleon as well as, if not better than, it had under German princes. Until 1813 he did not abandon the hope that Napoleon would bring peace to the world. It was not out of any dislike for Napoleon or for French control, but out of his deep desire for peace, that Goethe viewed Napoleon's attempts at renewing the war in 1814 and 1815 with disfavor. His veneration for Napoleon did not diminish with the latter's defeat. When Napoleon died on May 5, 1821, the news shook Goethe as profoundly as it did many other Europeans He was the first German to translate Manzoni's famous ode on the death of Napoleon, "Il Cinque Maggio." Manzoni, like Goethe, was a man of peace who detested war. His immortalization of Napoleon, in spite of the Emperor's conquests, expressed Goethe's feelings. The spirit of the poem is evident in these two stanzas in the translation of Edward, Earl of Derby:

> Was this true glory? let succeeding time
> That arduous question ask;
> Ours be the simpler task
> Before the mighty Maker's throne to bow,
> Who in that towering genius deigned to show
> Of His Creator Spirit an image, how sublime!
>
> From foul reproach, angelic friend,
> Do thou this weary dust defend;
> Since on that lonely couch and suffering breast
> He Who alone hath power the soul
> To raise, depress, afflict, console,
> The mighty God hath deigned to rest.

Goethe read his own translation of the poem to the Court at Weimar on August 8, 1822. "What a reading!" wrote one of those present. "Goethe seemed transfigured . . . his eyes were burning with an inner fire."

In 1814 Humboldt expressed his surprise that neither Goethe's nor Schiller's sons were eager to volunteer for the War of Liberation, as did many other young Germans of good family. Goethe was most anxious for his son not to join the forces fighting the French. In this respect he acted not only as a father, but on principle. He was bitterly opposed to the formation of patriotic volunteer corps composed of students. "Our young people," he wrote to Friedrich von Trebra on January 5, 1814, "find it most convenient to join the forces and thus become as much of a nuisance to other honest people as these people have been to us. It is a very enticing occupation, especially as it allows one to gain the reputation of being an accomplished patriot." Frau von Stein commented in a letter to her son Fritz on April 24, 1814: "Everybody says that Goethe does not wish to allow his son to join the volunteers, and so he is the only young man of the upper classes who has stayed at home. His father does not seem to share our present enthusiasm at all; one is not allowed to speak of political matters in his house." When young Goethe finally volunteered, he did it against the expressed will of his father who used all his influence to keep his son out of active service in the field.

Goethe, the Nation and the World

AFTER THE DEFEAT of the French Goethe never equated German victory in arms with moral or cultural superiority. He did not indulge in the widespread German intellectual arrogance that contrasted French superficiality and immorality with German depth and spirituality. During the following seventeen years, Goethe emphasized again and again how much he owed to the French in the development of his mind and readily acknowledged their moral and intellectual leadership. In his mature years he always felt close to the West and could not think of Germany as anything but an integral part of it. When, on December 13, 1813, the nationalist historian, Heinrich Luden, asked him to contribute to his new patriotic review, significantly named *Nemesis,* Goethe coolly hinted that he expected the threat to Germany's cultural life to come not from the West but from the East. When, in the following year, an official invitation induced him to write a festival play to be performed on the stage of the Berlin Court Theatre in honor of the victorious monarchs his work, *Des Epimenides Erwachen,* was free of all patriotic jubilation. Its last stanza, suppressed at the time, was characteristic of Goethe. It cursed the Germans who set out to imitate Napoleon's conquering spirit.

> *Verflucht sei, wer nach falschem Rat,*
> *Mit überfrechem Mut,*
> *Das was der Korse-Franke tat*
> *Nun als ein Deutscher tut!*
> *Er fuhle spat, er fühle früh:*
> *Es sei ein dauernd Recht;*
> *Ihm geh es, trotz Gewalt und Müh,*
> *Ihm und den Seinen schlecht!*

> (A curse on the misguided man
> Who, void of ruth or shame,
> Does just as did the Corsican
> Under a German name
> Let him protest both soon and late
> Unto a lasting right,
> His force and toil prepare a fate
> Him and his kin to blight.)

In 1817 the tercentenary of the Reformation was celebrated in a nationalistic spirit by patriotic German students and intellectuals. For some of the orators the spirit of Luther's religious reformation and of the "War of Liberation" was one and the same. Goethe interpreted the Reformation in an equally a-historical though diametrically opposed spirit. He insisted on viewing the celebration only as a festival of the purest humanity *("ein Fest der reinsten Humanität")*. He remained faithful to his ideal to the end. In 1829, in his *Studien zur Weltliteratur,* Goethe called the French the most stimulating nation on earth. "I would love to say more," he continued with his typical reticence, knowing himself very much alone among his German contemporaries, "but one would have to discuss it at great length to make oneself understood. . . ." In his conversations with Eckermann Goethe repeatedly emphasized his love and respect for France, his praise for Paris and his indebtedness to the French Enlightenment. "Conceive of a city like Paris," he told the younger man on May 3, 1827, "this metropolis of the world, where . . . men like Molière, Voltaire, Diderot and the like have kept up a current of intellectual life which cannot be found anywhere else on the whole earth." Two years before his death, in discussing the growing German animosity toward France, he asked, "How can I . . . hate a nation which is among the most cultivated of the earth and to which I owe so much of my own cultivation?" From this particular case Goethe rose to a general consideration of the nature of chauvinism which, as the nineteenth century advanced, had begun to darken the intellectual and moral skies of Europe: "You will always find it rampant where culture is at the lowest level. But there is a stage of civilization in which it is not possible to hate one's neighbors, where one stands, so to speak, above nations, and feels the weal or woe of a neighboring people as if it were one's own. This is the stage of civilization that I long for."

Goethe's scorn was quickly aroused by all efforts at cultural self-sufficiency. In the nineteenth century, the Germans—and following in their wake many others in Europe and Asia—began to praise and overvalue their own spiritual roots and to glorify their particular autochthonous culture, their *Eigenart*, grown in the native soil. Writing to Johann Heinrich Mayer, Goethe spoke of the "foolishness of patriotic Germans," who thought they could exist in a cultural vacuum and at the same time appropriate the virtues of all other peoples. "There is no patriotic art and no patriotic scholarship," we read in *Wilhelm Meisters Wanderjahre*, "both belong, like everything else of great value, to the whole of mankind. Art and scholarship can be promoted only by the free and general intercourse of all contemporaries building on what has come down to them from the past." In the same vein Goethe rejected the often fanatical cult of the national tongue which became characteristic of the Age of Nationalism. To Goethe, the greatest master of the German word, German was dear and important as a cultural not as a national language. But it was not more important than other languages. In an article "The German Language," published in 1817 in the review *On Art and Antiquity,* he praised the German poets who had written in Latin He quoted with approval a passage from Count Sergei Uvarov. This Russian scholar and future Minister of Education had just published a work in German on a fifth century Greco-Egyptian Christian poet. In his preface Uvarov explained that he had written in German because the rebirth of classical studies was due to German scholarship. "I very much hope," said Uvarov, "that we have abandoned the mistaken idea of attributing political rank to a language in the world of scholarship. It is high time for each one among us to select that language which seems most appropriate to him for the treatment of the ideas he wishes to discuss." In his article Goethe quoted Uvarov's words with full approval and was happy to find a talented and intelligent man who had raised himself far above the miserable limitations of a linguistic patriotism (*die kümmerliche Beschrankung eines erkaltenden Sprachpatriotismus*). "I wish," Goethe continued, "that all educated Germans would gratefully remember these honorable and instructive words, and that intelligent young men would be inspired by them to become capable of using several languages according to the varying needs of scholarship and life."

In the same article, referring to the time when scholars and poets made use of universal languages, Goethe complained of the curious conceit of Germans who deliberately narrowed their speculations to their own culture. In a long letter to Carlyle on July 20, 1827, he pleaded for world-wide cultural intercourse, looking forward to the progress in tolerance and in mildness of manners found to occur wherever the horizon was broadened. He did not turn to the Middle Ages for inspiration as did the German romantics; to him, as to the men of the French Enlightenment, the Middle Ages remained an age of barbarism between antiquity and modern times He dismissed it as a period dominated by knights and priests (*"dunkelste Pfaffen- und Ritterzeit"*). While studying this era, he noted in his diary on August 4, 1816, "Anarchic. Absurd."

His friend Henriette von Knebel reported on November 16, 1808 that Goethe after reading the *Nibelungenlied* to his friends told them that those old Germanic times, though officially Christian, were, in reality, pagan. While Homer was truly in touch with the Gods, no reflection of the Divine was to be found in the *Nibelungenlied*. In his essay on the German language, Goethe wrote: "The Germans were on the right path and will find it again as soon as they abandon the harmful practice of comparing the Nibelungen with the Iliad." In his *Maxims and Reflections* he insisted that if "we have something good to say, we should say it in French, as the Romans said it in Greek."

Goethe's main interest centered on the literatures of the Latin and Germanic peoples as they had developed, since Renaissance and Humanism, out of the common Greco-Roman heritage. With advancing age his horizon widened until it embraced the literatures of the entire world. Though he feared the prospect of a Russian advance into Europe after Napoleon's defeat he followed Slavic thought with the greatest interest. His many visits to his favorite

Bohemian spas aroused his sympathy for the nascent Czech literature. In a long review of the first scholarly patriotic Bohemian
monthly, which the Czech historian František Palacký began editing
in 1827, Goethe stressed the close relationship of Czech and German
writers in their common homeland of Bohemia. In 1814, in the
midst of the unhappiness which the war against Napoleon brought
to him, he discovered Hafiz, the Persian poet of the fourteenth
century, and was delighted with the points they had in common.
The fruit of the meeting between the two poets from West and East
was Goethe's great book of poems, *Western-Eastern Divan,* which
contained the well-known lines

> Unto God the Orient
> Unto God the Occident.
> Northern lands and Southern lands
> Rest in the peace of His great hands

On January 21, 1827, Eckermann found Goethe reading and praising a Chinese novel. "The Chinese have thousands of them," Goethe
said, "and had them when our forefathers were still living in the
woods." After discussing the merits of Chinese literature Goethe
went on to say, "National literature has now become a meaningless
term. The era of world literature is fast approaching and everyone
must strive to hasten its progress."

Goethe and the Nineteenth Century

AS THE LAST GREAT MAN of the German Enlightenment, Goethe was
one of the few Europeans of the nineteenth century who praised and
cherished the United States of America and believed in its future.
In the second half of the eighteenth century, in Goethe's younger
years, his sentiment had been shared by many Europeans; Americans were idealized. With the turn of the century the attitude of
the European intellectuals changed. With few exceptions, they became disinterested in the New World or belittled it as the home of a
primitive and uncouth people lacking the refinement of civilization
and the depth of a great past.

Goethe's attitude was radically different. The older he grew the
more confident he became of America's future and of the importance of its civilization. Perhaps no other great European of his

time so keenly felt America's significance and was so deeply in sympathy with its destiny as was Goethe. His vision was in accord with the self-awareness expressed by many Americans. In his old age, at a time when most people are no longer open to new interests, Goethe was eager to read as much as possible of the new American literature and to study the geography and living conditions of the United States. Joseph Green Cogswell, a New England scholar and educator, reported his impressions of Goethe in a letter of April 17, 1817: "Soon after being introduced to him, with the politeness of a real gentleman, he turned the conversation to America, and spoke of its hopes and promises, in a manner that showed it had been the subject of his inquiries, and made more just and rational observations upon its literary pretensions and character, than I ever heard from any man in Europe." Even George Bancroft, who had little love for Goethe because of the latter's "immorality," wrote in a letter of November 20, 1819, to John Thornton Kirkland, President of Harvard, that "Goethe received me with unusual kindness and spoke of America as if our country was one of the objects that most interested him in his old age."

Though such a comparison may seem far fetched to European readers, some Americans liked to compare Goethe to Benjamin Franklin. Franklin was the first American intellectual whom eighteenth century Europe met and admired. He and Goethe belonged to two entirely different orders of greatness yet they shared a love for science, for practical wisdom, for minute attention to details, and a concern for the good of man and society. In his *Hyperion* (1839), Henry Wadsworth Longfellow asked: "Did it ever occur to you that he was in some points like Ben Franklin—a kind of rhymed Ben Franklin? The practical tendency of his mind was the same; his love of science was the same; his benign, philosophic spirit was the same; and the vast number of his little political maxims and soothsayings seem nothing more than the worldly wisdom of Poor Richard, versified." In his later years Goethe, who had read Franklin's autobiography in the 1790's, reread it three times—in 1810, 1817, and in 1828. In his own autobiography, *Poetry and Truth,* Goethe compared Justus Möser, a man whom he highly esteemed, with Benjamin Franklin and praised both of them for their "selection of genuinely useful topics, deep insight, open mind, felicitous style, and profound humor."

Goethe was fascinated by the pioneering technological spirit of the United States. When Duke Bernhard, the second son of the Grand Duke of Weimar, visited the United States to gather information about Mexican silver mines in which he and his father were interested, Goethe read his report with the greatest attention. On September 15, 1826, Goethe welcomed the Duke, his fellow Mason in the Lodge Amelia, as "a man happily enriched" by America. In his poem on the occasion, Goethe celebrated American industriousness:

> There it hums like a bee hive
> They build and gather.
> In the morning it was poor and empty,
> In the evening it has grown full and rich
> The rivers' course is being regulated
> Across hardly settled lands,
> Out of rocks, houses emerge,
> And gardens flower in the sand.

The scene resembles the end of the second part of *Faust*. But what a difference. The colonizing enterprise of the aged Faust, so often misinterpreted, is a work of evil magic and sinful violence. Ultimately it is shown to be nothing but an empty dream in which Faust mistakes the digging of his grave by the infernal hosts for the clatter of shovels and spades building dams. But in the United States colonization was beneficial, carried on with ceaseless eagerness by free men.

A year later, on February 21, 1827, Goethe discussed the possibility of a canal through the isthmus of Panama with Eckermann. "I should be surprised," he said, "if the United States let the opportunity escape of carrying out such work themselves. It can be foreseen that this young state, with its decided love of the West, will, in thirty or forty years, have occupied and peopled the vast lands beyond the Rocky Mountains. And it may also be foreseen that along the whole coast of the Pacific, important commercial cities will gradually arise and help to promote trade between China, the East Indies and the United States. In such a case it would not only be desirable, but even necessary to establish a more rapid communication between the eastern and western shores of North America, both for merchant ships and men of war, than has hitherto been possible with the tedious, unpleasant and expensive voyage around Cape Horn. I therefore repeat that it is absolutely indispensable for the United States to effect a passage from the Mexican Gulf to the Pacific Ocean, and I am certain that they will do it."

But it was not the economic and social activity of free individuals that aroused Goethe's main interest in the United States. Johannes

Urzidil, who years ago wrote the best study of Goethe's debt to Bohemia, has recently analyzed in *Das Glück der Gegenwart* (The Happiness of the Present), Goethe's relationship to the United States. According to Urzidil Goethe's loving admiration of the United States had less to do with its technological achievements than with its moral foundation and its climate of individual liberty, equal opportunity, and broad tolerance. Here again Goethe spoke for the enlightened humanitarianism of the eighteenth century. Greeting Duke Bernhard, he praised him for entering into the life of America:

> *Er fuhlt des edlen Landes Glück*
> *Ihm eignet er sich an . . .*
>
> (He feels the happiness of the noble land;
> He is at home in it . . .)
>
> *Die Erde wird durch Liebe frei,*
> *Durch Taten wird sie gross.*
>
> (The earth is set free through love,
> Through deeds it grows great)

Goethe was deeply impressed by American tolerance. "In New York," he noted at the time of Duke Bernhard's return, "there are ninety different Christian denominations, each one of which worships its God and Master in its own way without feeling disturbed by the fact. We must advance to a similar freedom in science and scholarship. We talk a lot about liberalism and yet, with us, everyone wishes to hinder his fellow-man from thinking and expressing himself in his own way." Three years later Goethe returned to this subject: "The loveliest sight today is to be found in a North American city, in which, as I recently read, there are about sixty churches, each one of which preaches a different creed. There people can receive their edification from a different denomination each week."

Goethe accented the benefits of liberty and tolerance in *Wilhelm Meisters Wanderjahre*. The uncle in the novel, whose father had lived happily in America but who, to spite his father, returned to Europe, continued to propagate American social and religious ideas. His younger European friends felt the urge to emigrate to the United States where, apparently, man could find the fulfillment of his individual life and could at the same time participate in the building of a new society. Equally important for Goethe was the

fact that life in the United States meant liberation from the bonds
of the past. He expressed it at the beginning of the novel when he
wrote: *"Das Leben gehört den Lebendigen an und wer lebt, muss
auf Wechsel gefasst sein."* (Life belongs to the living, and whoever
lives must be prepared for change.)

In the famous short poem "To the United States," which Goethe
wrote in 1827, after reading a critical review of Fenimore Cooper's
works, he rejoiced that America was unencumbered by memories
of the past in its enjoyment of the present. At a time when intellectual Germany devoted itself to romantic historicism Goethe
stressed the importance of the contemporary world. Europeans,
Goethe felt, were hindered in their development by too many
memories. Americans could face the present—*"lebendige Zeit"*—
without being encumbered by the past. In another poem, written
in his sixties, Goethe expressed his own optimistic individualism
which he, not without reason, thought closely akin to that of the
Americans.

> *Willst du dir ein gut Leben zimmern,*
> *Musst ums Vergangene dich nicht bekummern,*
> *Und wäre dir auch was verloren,*
> *Erweise dich wie neugeboren.*
> *Was jeder Tag will? sollst du fragen.*
> *Was jeder Tag will, wird er sagen.*
> *Musst dich an eignem Tun ergotzen;*
> *Was andre tun, nicht überschätzen;*
> *Besonders keinen Menschen hassen*
> *Und das übrige Gott überlassen.*

(If you wish to build a good life for yourself, you must not worry
about the past, and even if you have been hurt, behave as though
you were born yesterday. Ask what each day demands. Each day will
tell you. You must find delight in your own activities; you should
not overestimate what others do; above all hate no one, and leave the
rest to God.)

His confidence in America liberalized Goethe's conservatism and
strengthened his faith in the future, at a time when many conservative intellectuals succumbed to a profound pessimism. Characteristic of this mood were the words of the historian Barthold
Niebuhr in the introduction to his *Roman History* in 1830: "If God
does not provide a miracle, we face a disaster like that which the
Roman world experienced in the third century of the Christian era."
Even stronger were the words Niebuhr used at the time in private

letters. He wrote to Karl Friedrich von Savigny on November 16, 1830, about his firm conviction that, "especially in Germany, we are advancing rapidly toward barbarism, and the situation is not much better in France. I am equally convinced that we are threatened by wars as devastating as they were two centuries ago. The end of it all will be despotism amidst the ruins. In fifty years, and probably much earlier, free institutions and a free press will have completely disappeared in the whole of Europe, at least in the continental countries." On the 22nd of the same month Niebuhr wrote to Moltke: "We are living in a situation like that of Rome after the time of the Gracchi, with all its horrors Whoever does not see this is blind, whoever believes that the present unrest has anything to do with liberty is a fool. . . . We shall finally bless a despotism, if it saves our lives, just as the Romans blessed the despotism of Augustus." Goethe never shared this excessive pessimism which anticipated that of Spengler, nor did he refuse to recognize the regenerative forces in the modern West. But occasionally he worried about the days to come. "Wealth and speed," he wrote in a well-known letter to Zelter on June 7, 1825, "are what the world admires and everyone strives for; railways, fast mails, steamships and all possible facilities for communication are the areas in which the civilized world is intent upon outdoing and out-training itself, thereby persisting in mediocrity. And it is of course the result of such commonness that a culture of the mean becomes general. . . . Ours is . . . the century for . . . quick, grasping practical men who . . . feel their superiority to the crowd, even if they themselves are not on the highest level. . . . Let us be faithful as far as possible to the world that formed us. We shall be, with perhaps a few others, the last of an epoch which will not recur soon again."

But Goethe did not yearn for the past. He looked with confidence upon man and his future. Like Burckhardt, he distrusted many aspects of the approaching modern time. The poet in Weimar and the scholar in Basle were residents of quiet oligarchic towns and feared that the rise of the masses might threaten civilization and liberty. They could not foresee that liberal democracy as it was developing in the English-speaking countries could broaden and strengthen liberty while ensuring the well-being of the masses.

Goethe knew that either excessive enthusiasm or excessive pessimism endangered civilization. He was far removed from any glorification of the state. Like Burckhardt, he distrusted power. This attitude pervades the second part of *Faust*. Even the famous colonizing enterprise at its end is the work of devilish magic and not a political message. In contemplating it the idyllic old couple, Philemon and Baucis, in their innocence clearly saw through it and described it with horror.

> *Menschenopfer mussten bluten,*
> *Nachts erscholl des Jammers Qual,*
> *Meerab flossen Feuergluten,*
> *Morgens war es ein Kanal.*

(Human lives were sacrificed; Nightly one heard cries of anguish and pain; Glowing fires were streaming toward the sea; In the morning a new canal was there.)

In his Prologue in the Theater which opened the first part of *Faust,* Goethe announced:

> Thus in our narrow booth today
> Creation's ample scope display,
> And wander swiftly yet observing well,
> From heaven through the world to hell.

But in the end Goethe refused to condemn. For him history was not a road that led to hell. Faust, rejecting magic, was saved. Goethe in his later years showed no enthusiasm for the Faustian man whom Oswald Spengler identified with western man. The phantom of Spengler's imagination was a German romanticist unmindful of the limits which common sense and common humanity have set to make possible a tolerable existence. There is a Faustian element in modern western civilization, but it is not the only element. It is checked by a sense of ethical moderation and empirical wisdom, by a confidence in human life, as that which Goethe expressed, at the conclusion of his *Faust,* in the final blessing sung by Lynceus, the watchman in the tower:

> Eyes happily ranging,
> All that you have seen,
> Though fortune was changing,
> How fair has it been.

Chapter Three

ROMANTICISM

AND THE GERMAN MIND

The Character of German Romanticism

THE ENLIGHTENMENT WAS the first intellectual movement to sweep Europe as a whole. The Romantic Movement, which in many ways represented a revolt against the Enlightenment, was the second. Everywhere the restraints imposed by classicism were rejected, the free play of the imagination was exalted, the unusual made a fetish and the genius a demigod. But in Germany as nowhere else romantic poets and thinkers influenced political and social thought. German romanticism, however apolitical it may have been at the beginning, encouraged the development of German nationalism after 1800 and influenced it as much as the Enlightenment shaped the form of nationalism in Western Europe. Originally romanticism was an aesthetic revolution, a resort to imagination almost feminine in its sensibility. It was poetry closer to the spirit of music than that of the eighteenth century, rich in emotional depth, and potent in the art of magic evocation.

"Romantic poetry," wrote Friedrich Schlegel in 1798, "alone is infinite, because it alone is free and recognizes as its only law that the poet's license tolerates no law." German romanticism began but did not end in poetry. It was an interpretation of life, nature, and history and this philosophic character distinguished it from romanticism in other lands. Disdainful of the rationalism of the eighteenth century, it mobilized the fascination of the national, even the primitive, past to lower the prestige of the principles of 1789. In this in-

49

direct fashion romanticism came to concern itself with political and
social life and with the state. It did its best to poeticize and roman-
ticize the German concept of the state. It never developed a program
for a modern German nation-state; however with its emphasis on
the great depth of the German mind it led to a growth of a consciousness of German uniqueness and to the belief that a nation
may be a law unto itself.

The intellectuals who launched the romantic movement were
the spiritual children of the Storm and Stress of the 1770's. They
were in ardent opposition to Goethe who had long outgrown his
brief Storm and Stress period. They admired him as a creative man
of letters, as an embodiment of the princely artist, but they rejected
his ideal of the well-rounded harmonious individual. Goethe's ideal
personality willingly subordinated itself to universal form and law,
rejoiced in measure and proportion, acknowledged the limits of the
human and the humane. The romantic individual, on the other
hand, regarded himself not as a representative of universal order
but as a unique being and demanded complete freedom, in life and
in work, for his creative genius. At the same time the romantics,
for all their revolt against society, did not accept the titanic loneliness of the Storm and Stress. They longed for a community of
like-minded individuals who would live a full life according to
their innermost emotions and convictions. The complexity and anguish of their search for this community were heightened by their
underlying subjectivism. The unique individual longed for a full
gratification of all his desires and yet felt the need for fulfillment in
the miracle of a true harmonious union in which all the conflicting
opposites of life would be reconciled.

Yearning for the miraculous the romantics quite naturally found
the rationalism of the eighteenth century insipid. The more passionate man was the more completely he lived. Passion was the
prerogative of the artist, the poet, or the seer who obeyed his impulses. This discovery of the irrational enriched poetry and added
to our understanding of man, but, as Goethe recognized, it would
have fatal results if it meant the loss of self-control. The desired
object could easily appear to poetic imagination as something indispensable which had to be achieved at any cost. The ideal community refused to accept the limitations imposed in the interests of
fellow men; it promised to unite all in an organic way in which
everybody would be fully himself and yet also fully part of the
whole without conflict or friction. In such a perfect community
individual and society no longer were in need of legal or constitu-

tional protection; they became two sides of the one perfect life. The anarchic individualism found its complement in the total community. In the imagination of the romantics both these extremes led a pure life and existed outside the real society with its necessary adjustments and compromises.

French rationalism had glanced with contempt at the Middle Ages. The German romantics found in this very period the wonderland they could not discover in the present. Repelled by the contemporary world, they sought for inspiration in history. Time and time again, they confused poetry with history and politics. All this had its influence on German political thinking.

On the road to the past the romantics followed Justus Moeser and Johann Gottfried Herder, the forerunners of German nationalism, but rejected the fundamental values of these older men. Moeser was a practical statesman, and his love of the rural freeholders of the Middle Ages was rooted in his personal experience. Herder's vision was infinitely broader. Like the romantics, he saw creative forces at work in every phenomenon of nature and history yet he held fast to the humanitarianism of the Enlightenment No matter how intensely Moeser and Herder studied the past they lived in the present. The romantics, however, attempted to enrich the present by reviving the past. They were so completely under the spell of its poetry, its legends, and its prophecies that they could not gaze upon it with rational detachment.

Though they had no factual foundation for their opinion the romantics believed that national characteristics were never so pronounced as in the Middle Ages. The ideals of the knights and guilds seemed in their eyes to express the true national soul, its creative forces as yet unvitiated by a rationalism that led to lifeless uniformity. The national past set a standard valid only for the one national community. The concept of individuality, unique and self-contained, was transferred from the individual to the national community. The nation was no longer, as in the West, a legal compact entered into by individuals for mutual benefits; it was an original phenomenon of nature and history. Civilization and law were no longer universal and rational; they were now the creative achievements of the irrational force of the people. National individuality, alive and striving, was a divine manifestation with a special mission to fulfill.

The national community or the state—the romantics did not establish clear distinctions—became the source of all aesthetic and even political and ethical creativeness. The realtionship of man to the state became highly personal, a matter of love and devotion. Such a state resembled the ideal feudal patriarchal state: a great family held together by love and mutual responsibility, hostile to the spirit of rational capitalism but willing to submit to semi-socialist measures of control and protection of the citizens. This was not a return to the past; it was a poetic dream transfiguring a legendary past into a golden age.

Novalis and the Schlegels

ONE OF THOSE WHO IDEALIZED the past was Friedrich Freiherr von Hardenberg, who wrote under the name of Novalis. It was his ambition to fuse poetry and politics, science and religion, life and magic. Closer to the Coleridge of *Kubla Khan* and *Christabel* than any of his contemporaries, he proved he was one of the great explorers of the dream world in his unfinished romance *Heinrich von Ofterdingen,* and one of the great lyric poets in his *Hymns to the Night.* In 1798 Novalis' close friend and contemporary Karl Friedrich Schlegel defined their poetic ideal. Poetry "can be fathomed by no theory, and only intuitive criticism could presume to characterize its ideal."

Schlegel's older brother August Wilhelm complained bitterly about the unpoetic character of the age. "The times when a poet by the presentation of great events of antiquity could become the preserver of folk sagas, the beloved teacher of his nation, are perhaps gone forever. It seems almost impossible today to write a national heroic poem. The word Fatherland has lost its magic power; the place of patriotism has been taken by a more general but therefore also colder interest for mankind. With the destruction of the folk religions the old saga perished too."

Though Novalis endowed the state with an unprecedented importance, he did not conceive of a German nation-state. In his famous *Fragments*—jottings that were too evanescent to form the basis of a politico-philosophical system—he expressed his conviction that the state should be omnipresent. "It is a great mistake of our states, that one sees the state too little. The state should be visible everywhere and every man should be characterized as a citizen. Could one not introduce everywhere marks of distinction and uniforms? Whoever regards this as insignificant disregards an essential part of our nation. . . . The state is too little known to us. There should be heralds of the state, preachers of patriotism. At present most citizens are on a rather indifferent, almost hostile, footing with the state. . . . The state is a person like the individual. What man is to himself, the state is to men. The states will remain different as long as men are different. Essentially the state like man remains always the same. . . . The perfect citizen lives entirely in the state; he has no property outside the state." This all-embracing state was, however, not a political concept; it was a poetic creation, the embodiment of that perfection to which man aspires. "A state with intense spiritual and intellectual life will of itself be political. The more spiritual the state is the more it approaches the poetical, the more joyfully will every citizen, out of love for the beautiful great individual, limit his demand and be ready to make the necessary sacrifices, the less will the state need it, the more similar will the spirit of the state become to the spirit of a single exemplary man who has expressed forever one law only: be as good and as poetical as possible."

The ideal state was for Novalis a divine work of art. "A true prince is the artist of artists. Every man should become an artist. Everything can become beautiful art." As every man should become an artist and king the "true" monarchy was compatible with a "true" republic; in fact they were complementary, for the republic demanded the identification of every citizen with the state. Novalis complained that in Germany only small local events were discussed while great issues aroused no interest. "They manage things better in republics, where the state is the principal concern of everyone and everyone forgets his selfish interests in those of the community." Man was not meant to be a utilitarian, he went on to argue. "The greatest of the kings of France wanted to make his subjects so prosperous that every peasant would have a chicken with rice on the table every Sunday. But would not a government be preferable under which a peasant would rather have a slice of moldy bread than a roast in another country, and yet thank God for the good luck of having been born in his native land?"

⌐ Novalis could never be considered a nationalist. "The European," he wrote, "is as superior to the German as the German is to the Saxon and the Saxon to the inhabitant of Leipzig. The cosmopolitan is superior to the European." Again: "Our old nationality was truly Roman. The instinctive universality of the Romans is shared by the Germans." He saw in Germany the best hope for a new world. "Germany," he wrote, "forges slowly but surely ahead of all Euro-

pean lands While they are preoccupied by war, commercial speculation, and party conflicts the Germans are training for the oppor-
tunities of a new cultural epoch, and this training must give
them in the course of time a great superiority over all other nations."

Though Novalis hinted, in his mysterious way, at the future cultural greatness of the Germans his vision did not encompass the
Age of Nationalism; instead he cast a backward glance at the
spiritual unity of medieval Europe under Christianity. His hope
was for a new Jerusalem, a world capital where Christianity would
once again establish its spiritual dominion. "Europe will be drenched
in blood," he wrote, ". . . until the nations realize the horror of
their madness . . . until the nations, moved by divine music, return to the altars of yesterday, and there take up the tasks of peace.
. . . The time has come for a 'feast of love' to be celebrated on the
smoking battlefields. . . . Religion alone can revive Europe." Such
was the message of Novalis's essay "Christianity or Europe" which
he submitted in 1799 to the review *Das Athenaum*. It was declined
by the editors—the Schlegels—on the ground that it was too arbitrary. Though Novalis, the descendant of Protestant Pietists, never
embraced Catholicism, his praise for the medieval Christian hier-
archy was too strong for his Protestant friends, many of whom
later turned Catholic. But the essay, for all its mingling of poetry
with religious fervor, introduced an interpretation of history that
ran counter to that of the eighteenth century. Like the French
traditionalists, Bonald and de Maistre, Novalis had no patience
with reason and progress. The Reformation, rationalism, the revolutionary spirit—all these were deviations in his eyes from the true
tradition of Europe. For him the Golden Age was Europe in the
thirteenth century. "Those were the great days," he decided, "when
Europe was a Christian land, inhabited by one Christianity; one
great common interest united the most distant provinces of this
vast spiritual realm."

The Romantics and the Middle Ages

FOR NOVALIS THE MIDDLE AGES was still a universal period. Soon however the romantics were to reinterpret it as a fountainhead of national culture. Through romanticism history established its impact

over nationalism. Novalis himself was partly responsible for this since he had overstressed the influence of history. "We bear the burdens of our fathers," he said, "and we actually live in the past and the future and are nowhere less at home than in the present." And again: "The historian must often turn orator. For he intones the gospels; all of history is nothing but a gospel." Statements such as these inspired the new scholarship. Within a decade the literature of the Middle Ages was collected and edited, the poetry of the courts as well as the contributions of the common man.

The romantics made much of the Swiss historian Johannes Müller whose passion for medieval history was matched by his skill as a writer and his eagerness to revel in local color. His rhetorical style—his grasp of facts was none too firm—won him a vast audience from the generation that had come under the spell of Rousseau's sentimentalism. His fondness for old chronicles endeared him to the romantics, as did his insistence that a historian needs a "soul." His evocation of Switzerland in the Middle Ages confirmed the conviction that this was the era of true patriotism and heroic manhood Yet Müller could not pass for a German romantic. He was a Swiss enthusiast for the rights of man. Later he idolized Napoleon, and was rebuked by his former admirers for his lack of patriotism. What the romantics could not forgive was Johannes Muller's impartiality. This was all very well when discussing domestic policies, but was intolerable when dealing with foreign affairs. "Every hero—and this includes the scholar-hero—needs a fatherland, a firm foundation on which to build his army camp," commented the romantic critic Adam Müller in 1808. A cosmopolitan mentality in a historian was now regarded as contrary to true humanity and true scholarship.

Though Johannes Müller and the romantics parted company as early as 1806, the latter could not forget that he had been the first to emphasize the importance of the *Nibelungenlied*. This saga had been published in 1782 after having been neglected for centuries. Müller believed, and August Wilhelm Schlegel came to agree with him, that the *Nibelungenlied* could serve as the German *Iliad*. Indeed Schlegel went so far in 1812 as to demand that it be introduced as the chief classic in the German curriculum in order to endow German history with a great poetic background. This wish quickly came true. Friedrich Heinrich Freiherr von der Hagen, one of the popularizers of medieval poetry, brought out a translation into modern German. So did August Zeume, the founder, in 1814, of the Society for the German Language. Zeume even prepared a special edition for Germans off to the wars against Napoleon to use in the field.

The *Nibelungenlied* was not the only medieval classic to be rediscovered. In 1803 Ludwig Tieck, who had been a close friend of Novalis and the Schlegel brothers, published his *Minnelieder aus dem Schwäbischen Zeitalter*. "If we look back," he wrote in the introduction to this collection of love songs from the Swabian age— the age of the Hohenstaufen—"to the immediate past, when we were so indifferent to letters and to the arts, we shall be surprised by the change that has occurred in so short a time, for today we appreciate the relics of our past." At a time when German political fortunes seemed at as low an ebb as in the Thirty Years War, when French occupation was willingly accepted, and when an active national sentiment could be found hardly anywhere, the romantics called upon the past to kindle the spirits of the living; they went back to the treasures which they believed buried and yet alive in the minds of the people, in the true German *Volksgemüt* which had not yet been influenced by the universal rational civilization of the eighteenth century. Two years after Tieck's love songs, there appeared a collection of folk songs, *Des Knaben Wunderhorn*. This was the work of younger romantics, the Prussian Junker Achim von Arnim and the Rhinelander Clemens Brentano. In 1807 their friend Joseph Görres published the results of his investigations of almanacs and old story-books. In the next decade came the *Fairy Tales* and *German Sagas* edited by the brothers Grimm.

In 1808, as editor of the *Zeitung für Einsiedler* (*Journal for Hermits*), Arnim prepared his subscribers for a new birth of German patriotism. At the very mention of "my poor, poor Fatherland," he wrote, "tears flow from my eyes and from those of my readers." Jacob Grimm was equally sentimental when he thought of what had been accomplished by preserving the folk songs of the German people. "The evergrowing appreciation of the true nature of history and poetry has aroused the desire to save from oblivion what previously seemed contemptible, and this at the very last moment when such material could be collected." To the romantics this literature of the common people was truly national and hence superior to modern art-literature. "Only folk poetry is perfect," declared Wilhelm Grimm. "God himself wrote it as he did the ten commandments; it was not pieced together like the mere work of man."

The Grimm brothers and their friends were positive that a nation could never be based upon a constitution protecting individual rights but only upon indigenous customs. For them there existed no culture worthy of the word outside the true folk spirit of *Volksgeist.* Folk traditions were grounded in history and had stood the test of time, while the liberal principles of 1789 were conceived without respect for history Even if the French Revolution should succeed in establishing a democratic regime of freedom suitable for France such a regime would be bound to fail elsewhere, because it would be alien to national character. History alone could safeguard the destiny of a nation.

According to the romantics the historical *Volksgeist* should determine not only the constitution but even the laws. Any departure from this, such as the famous Prussian legal code of 1794—conceived in the rational spirit of the Enlightenment, though with many concessions to the backward Prussian social structure—filled these partisans with disgust. In May, 1805, Jacob Grimm wrote his brother Wilhelm the sad news of the new code in Hesse "Must everything that sprouts in the level sands of Prussia be imitated?" he asked. In another letter he expressed his conviction that the new code would mean the end of all judicial scholarship. For true law could only be customary law rooted in the remote past, the living record of the aspiration of untold generations. He and his followers had nothing but contempt for law codified according to new-found modern principles. And since natural law was founded on reason it, too, was suspect.

When Anton Friedrich Justus Thibaut, one of the leading jurists of the period, pleaded, after Napoleon's defeat, for the introduction of a civil law code common to all German lands—in hope of putting an end to an incredible confusion—he was taken to task by Friedrich Karl von Savigny, professor of law at the newly founded University of Berlin. True law, thought Savigny, was an emanation of the semimystical *Volksgeist,* and the courts should lay down their decisions accordingly, not as the exponents of rational legislation. One of those who agreed with Savigny was Karl Friedrich Eichhorn, author of a history of German public and private law, the first volume of which appeared in 1808. Eichhorn taught the history of German law to ensure the continuity of German legal development to fit the national character and the folk traditions. And so romantic historical scholarship came into its own: everything could be explained and, if need be, excused by appealing to the newly discovered mystically creative forces of the folk.

The Career of Friedrich Schlegel

FRIEDRICH SCHLEGEL WAS one of the first German writers to turn from rational universalism to mystical nationalism. In 1796, while still under the influence of Kant's essay on perpetual peace, he wrote an "Essay on the Concept of Republicanism," in which he claimed that political liberty and equality were the indispensable conditions of the good state. He even, with the enthusiasm of a young man of twenty-four, wrote his brother that "divine republicanism is still a little closer to my heart than divine criticism or even the most divine poetry." Like many of his French contemporaries, he looked to classical antiquity for the ideal political form—which could be nothing but republican. But at this very moment he was discovering the greatness of the German national character. "Not much attention has been paid as yet to the German character," he wrote his brother on November 8, 1791. "Recently I think I have discovered that our people has a very great character." Referring to Frederick the Great, Goethe, Klopstock, Winckelmann, and Kant he decided that men of this stamp were rare—"they are endowed as are the representatives of almost no other nation. I see in all the achievements of the Germans, especially in the field of scholarship, only an indication of great things to come. . . . Ceaseless activity, profound penetration, instinctive reverence for morality and liberty, all this I find in our nation. Everywhere I see traces of development and expansion."

Friedrich Schlegel made this observation the theme of his poem *"An die Deutschen"* (To the Germans)* written early in 1800. He called upon the Germans to remember their spiritual mission and to surpass in religion, philosophy and poetry the civilizations of Greece and India. The rest of Europe was decadent; only in Germany was there hope for the future: German heroes would spread over the continent, arousing the French and Italians. Rome would live again

---

* *Europas Geist erlosch: In Deutschland fliesst*
  Der Quell der neuen Zeit Die aus ihm tranken
  Sind wahrhaft deutsch· Die Heldenschar ergiesst
  Sich überall Erhebt den raschen Franken,
  Den Italiener zur Natur, und Rom
  Wird wach.

So Schlegel was converted to nationalism—for the moment a purely cultural nationalism. Had not the Greeks, without desiring or achieving national statehood, won the leadership of mankind, and had not their great works borne the stamp of their national character? Could not the Germans follow their example and become the Greeks of the new age? This was the time when Schiller expressed similar hopes in his fragmentary poem *"Deutsche Grösse"* (German Greatness). As Schiller saw it, the Germans were the universal people whose destiny it was to fulfill the aspirations of all mankind.

Schlegel turned into a political nationalist while on his way to Paris in 1802. He was particularly impressed by the ruins of the Thuringian castle of Wartburg near Eisenach, where the famous medieval contests of the Minnesingers were held, and where Luther completed his version of the New Testament. "At such a sight," he wrote, "one cannot help thinking what Germans once were. . . . Since those days, men have settled in the valleys and along the highways, eager for alien customs and alien money, and the castles on the heights stand deserted." The ruins of the Middle Ages spelled an epoch in which moral standards were high, quite unlike the present, when the people living in cities succumbed to alien gold and immorality.

To Schlegel German nationalism owes not only the symbol of the Thuringian Wartburg—which like the Thuringian Kyffhäuser recalled the glorious Middle Ages—but also the symbolic value of the Rhine which soon was to become the rallying point of the German struggle against France. The Rhine impressed Schlegel as much as the Wartburg, as a symbol of German nature and history. His poem *"Am Rheine"* (1802) marked the beginning of the glorification of the river which he called "the all too faithful image of our fatherland, our history and our character. . . . The old patriotic stream appears to us like a mighty stream of nature-inspired poetry." These nationalist sentiments found their theoretical expression in his "Philosophical Lectures in the Years 1804 to 1806" in which he for the first time expressed his political philosophy. Now he decided that republicanism was no better than a meteor that left in its wake confusion and destruction. Only a truly Germanic monarchy met his approval; his ideal was the medieval monarchy under the moral guidance of the church. But Schlegel went far beyond Novalis in the importance he placed on nationality within Christian universality. Mankind or Christendom was no longer one; the nation alone was one, the highest unity attainable. "The concept of the nation requires that all its members should form, as it were, only one individual."

Of course such a nation could not be based primarily on political allegiance, upon loyalty to a common constitution, upon dedication to individual liberty and the welfare of the people. In a true nation—and this meant a community resembling a closely knit family—citizens, he reasoned, should be bound to one another by their very blood. The antiquity and purity of the bloodstream would guarantee the persistence of and loyalty to traditional customs, and militate against alien influences.

A true nation could tolerate only one language, argued Schlegel. For reasons difficult to understand because they contradict all historical evidence he saw in a comomn language "the indisputable testimony of common descent." He then went on to say that "it is much more appropriate for the human race to be strictly separated into nations than for several nations to be united, as has happened in recent times. . . . Each state is an independent individual, existing for itself; it is unconditionally its own master . . . governed by its own laws, habits, and customs."

Inevitably, Schlegel opposed the assimilation of backward nations. "That would be highly immoral. The original moral character of a people, its customs, its peculiarities, must be regarded as sacred." A subject nationality should be maintained as a separate entity, but it could be educated by the victor, even forcibly, if the education was compatible with its character. Schlegel believed that was the German method of dealing with Magyars and other peoples on the Eastern frontier. The French, however, Schlegel thought, were abusing their cultural superiority by destroying the nationality of other peoples. He violently rejected the French thesis of cultural assimilation as immoral. Such an attitude on the part of the French justified, in Schlegel's opinion, the union of all peoples threatened by the French in a war which should end in the "total annihilation" of this "corrupt nation." Here for the first time, was a clear call to the Germans, from a thinker of renown for German nationality and for a sacred war on its behalf against the French.

Although at first Schlegel wrote patriotic poetry calling the Germans to fight against Napoleon, he abandoned this task, in later years, to bards like Arndt, Schenkendorf, and Rückert who soon surpassed him in popularity. During these years Schlegel joined the Roman Catholic Church; although a native of Hanover, he placed his hopes for the regeneration of Germany in Austria, and in 1809 became an official propagandist in Vienna. Schlegel appealed to the Germans outside Austria to stand by her and to brave all dangers in unity and courage, but the German states were still far removed from any deep-felt nationalism. None joined Austria in the war against France; Austria was quickly defeated, Napoleon entered Vienna and imposed the crushing peace treaty of Schönbrunn. Schlegel's appeals were in vain. They found their most poetic expression in the deeply felt poem *"Gelübde"* (The Vow),* in which he dedicated his heart and blood to the salvation of the fatherland and called upon all Germans to disregard with typical German loyalty all danger when Liberty called.

Though "The Vow" was the last of Schlegel's patriotic poems he went on to elaborate his theory of nationalism in the lectures he delivered on modern history, and on ancient and modern literature. His favorite heroes were the Habsburg princes Rudolf I, Ferdinand II, and Charles V. "If one does not overemphasize minutiae, there is no better way of putting the present into perspective than recalling a great past. For that reason I thought of adding to our knowledge of the three great world-shaking events—the migration of the Germanic tribes, the Crusades, and the Reformation. I painted a picture of the Germany of old in colors as bright as I could make them. I described Germany in early times when its liberty and its original character were untrammeled, as well as its cultural development in the Middle Ages. This meant that I had to pay especial attention to the medieval state, to the unity of Christianity, to the Holy Roman Empire, and to the spirit of knighthood." For all his nationalism Schlegel longed for the days when the concept of the Reich—which he thought the Germans alone could appreciate— and the universalism of the church maintained the appearance of unity among the nations of western Christendom. As a Catholic he could scarcely glorify the secularized state and its moral self-sufficiency.**

---

* *Es sei mein Herz und Blut geweiht*
Dich Vaterland zu retten . . .

Der deutsche Stamm ist alt und stark,
Voll Hochgefuhl und Glauben;
Die Treue ist der Ehre Mark,
Wankt nicht, wenn Sturme schnauben . . .

So spotte jeder der Gefahr,
Die Freiheit ruft uns allen. . . .

** It remained for Friedrich Meinecke, the greatest German historian of the twentieth century, to reject both the Christian political ethos of the romantics and the universalism of the Enlightenment as unsuitable for a

Schlegel's lectures of 1812—and the review *Deutsches Museum* which he was editing at that time—were devoted to the thesis that "every literature must and should be national." The same standard was applied to music, painting, and philosophy, but Schlegel thought that poetry was the most essential of all the arts. The spiritual growth of a nation was dependent on a store of great national memories "often lost in the darkness of time, but preserved and enhanced by poets. Such national memories, the most wonderful heritage that a people can have, are an advantage which nothing else can replace; and if a people finds itself in its own feelings elated and, so to speak, ennobled by the possession of a great past, of memories from prehistoric times, in brief by the possession of poetry, it will be raised by this very fact in our judgment to a higher plane. Memorable deeds, great events, and destinies alone are not sufficient to keep our admiration and to determine the judgment of posterity; a people must also gain a clear consciousness of its own deeds and destinies. This self-consciousness of a nation which expresses itself in reflective and descriptive works is its history."

Again and again the romantics pointed to Shakespeare's historical plays as the model for any dramatist who wished to revive the national past, and it was August Wilhelm Schlegel and his friend Tieck who provided the great translations of Shakespeare's works. Since the theater, in the eyes of the romantics, was the most national of all the arts they dreamed of the day when national epics would transform the German stage. In this they were disappointed. Henrich von Kleist, the greatest of the romantic dramatists, never reached the popularity of the humanitarian Schiller in spite of the fact that he was devoured by patriotic zeal and hatred of the French.

modern power state. Writing in 1907, Meinecke argued that these movements dismissed as a mere lust for power what is essentially part of the nature of the state, the result of its self-preservation and self-determination. He believed at the time that in addition to universal morality for individuals there existed an individual morality for the state, that this justified the apparent immorality of the state. "There can be nothing immoral about what grows out of the deepest nature of an individual." Such a "Wagnerian" attitude would, of course, allow every powerful state or powerful individual to establish "natural longing" as a categorical imperative. Years later Meinecke came to understand that this sort of thinking led directly to the catastrophe of 1933.

The Romantics and the State

TO THE ROMANTICS the state was too miraculous to be the work of mere man. It was the creation of the elemental forces of nature and of the unfathomable will of God. The state was an individual like man himself, only infinitely greater and more powerful. Joseph Freiherr von Eichendorff, one of the Catholic members of the Romantic Movement, declared that the state was "a spiritual community. Its aim was to make life as perfect as possible by developing strength of mind and soul." Another Catholic romantic, Zacharias Werner, originally a follower of the Enlightenment, defined the state as "a society organized to make it possible for human beings to fulfill their highest aims, a group isolated in order to return nobly transformed to humanity."

For all their adoration of the state, the romantics were artists and could scarcely dream of imposing a deadly uniformity. According to their ideal the citizen should serve the state with all his heart and soul, and yet remain a free individual. In Eichendorff's novel *Ahnung und Gegenwart* (Premonition and the Present), Leontin did not hesitate to cry "Long live liberty," but by this he did not mean the universal liberty of 1789, but *jene uralte, lebendige Freiheit* (that ancient pulsating freedom) he found in the proud but simple life of mountain dwellers.

The romantic concept of the patriarchal state—union by means of nonpolitical and nonlegal ties—was compatible with the existence of aristocratic individuals conscious of their privileges. But it had nothing in common with the new age of individualism, economic rationalism, and equality before the law. This dismissal of the values of western civilization had its influence on German thought in the decades to come. The romantics opposed capitalism, commerce, and the "influence of money." Schlegel went so far as to oppose taxes because they might give to the moneyed classes the power to influence the state. He suggested that the state should receive its income from the ownership of land and from the monopoly of all foreign trade.

Novalis and Eichendorff were poets, the brothers Schlegel were literary historians and critics; Adam Müller was the political philosopher of romanticism. He was practically unknown in the second half of the nineteenth century until the German neo-romantics of the twentieth century rediscovered him. With characteristic romantic vagueness the limits between poetry and scholarship were not clearly drawn in Adam Muller's work. Yet amid its contradictions romantic political philosophy held fast to the thesis that the state was not established for the benefit of the individual; on the other hand the individual was indissolubly part of the state and inevitably determined by its past. "Man," said Müller, "cannot be imagined outside of the state . . . the state . . . is the totality of all human concerns." To this philosopher and his friends western capitalism was "the most general manifestation of that antisocial spirit, that arrogant egotism, that immoral enthusiasm for false reasoning" which led to the French Revolution. They regarded capitalism's claim of having introduced liberty and equality as a mask to cover the change from rural serfdom to wage slavery and found the latter infinitely worse; they had no doubt that the capitalistic system was incompatible with the divine order of things. To the optimism of the eighteenth century, which looked toward the future, Müller opposed an equally fervent optimism regarding the past. While both forms of optimism might be equally unfounded the past was known to the memory of men and accessible to historical research; the future was known to God alone, and this may explain why utopias, which place the golden age in the future—especially in the distant future—often exercise a greater attraction than those placing it in the past—especially a not-too-distant past.

Müller's revolt against the Enlightenment represented a revolt against his own youth. The son of a Prussian official, he was born in the Berlin of Frederick the Great. While a student at Göttingen, he came under the influence of Adam Smith. Only later did he fall under the spell of Burke and of Burke's translator Friedrich Gentz. "If one regards the state as a great individual encompassing the individuality of lesser men," he wrote, "then one understands that society cannot be conceived except as a complete personality. . . . Its construction cannot be subjected to arbitrary speculation." In 1805 Muller joined the Catholic Church; he remained for a few years longer in Dresden and Berlin in close touch with Prussian conservative circles before he found in Austria his political and spiritual home. From this time on he shared the fate of Friedrich Schlegel, becoming, after 1817, progressively more traditionalist and removed from the main stream of German intellectual and political life, bent exclusively upon the praise of the past and the vain hope for its return. But between 1806 and 1810, years of decisive importance in the development of the German mind, he helped to arouse national resistance to western ideas and to strengthen German confidence in its mission.

In 1806, when the German cause seemed lost, Muller delivered a series of lectures, in Dresden, on scholarship and literature in which he proclaimed: "The development of the scholarly mind in Germany is the most important event in modern intellectual history. . . . Just as the German tribes founded the political order of Europe, so the German mind will eventually dominate the continent." To Müller the German mind more than any other was a universal mind in which other cultures found their consummation, a mind tolerant of all others and infinite in its longing. "We find," he said, "our happiness not in the suppression but in the flowering of the civilization of our neighbors, and thus Germany, the fortunate heartland, will respect the achievements of those beyond the borders."

Müller warned his listeners against liberal reforms. Rational innovations were inorganic, he maintained, and he summoned the spirits of the dead to his aid when he spoke of the necessity for continuity. In this subordination of the present to the past, he claimed to follow Burke . . . "the greatest, most profound, most powerful, and most human statesman" of all time, who, Muller claimed, belonged to Germany since the British never fully understood him. In his eyes Burke was "the representative of the invisible England . . . in whom the sacred eloquence of this century has found its only mouth." But of the practical wisdom of Burke, of his respect for individual liberty and constitutional rights, of his understanding of the living forces of history and of natural law, Muller and the German romantics knew little and cared less.

Like Fichte in his famous addresses to the German nation, Müller wished to call the Germans to a fatherland of the mind, to be aroused first in some awakened hearts. Through some miraculous transformation this new fatherland would not only triumph over the enemy but finally be blessed by the grandchildren of this enemy. The victorious state which would emerge was hardly defined as a state of the German nation—Müller was little concerned with the problems of German unification—it was a state opposed in every way to the ideas of 1789 and to economic liberalism, a theocratic state much less inspired by Burke than by the Vicomte de Bonald. The latter's *Théorie du Pouvoir Politique et Religieux dans la Société Civile* was obviously the model for the lectures Müller delivered in the winter of 1808–9 on the elements of statecraft. In these lectures he developed the theory that "the state is the union of many families, not only those living at the same time but those that follow each other in time—a union not only infinite in space but immortal." Depressed by the emphasis on the present and on the pursuit of happiness, he stressed eternity and duty. As a devout monarchist he chanted the praises of the one "immortal" family, the royal family.

Müller believed that the tragic errors of the French Revolution were the inevitable consequence of the belief that the state was designed to assure the security and prosperity of the citizens. If that were true every generation would be free to begin anew. But the truth, as he saw it, was that we could not take such liberties; the state was so inextricably linked with every human activity that at no time could one hear or see, think or feel without the aid of the state. Nor could science or scholarship lead an existence independent of the state.

The greatest blessing of a nation, thought Muller, was that which made it different from all others. A world in which there was only one government, one law, and one system of weights and measures would be without the incentive that springs from conflict. To Müller Kant's perpetual peace, whether assured by a universal monarchy or by a league of constitutional nations, would be a misfortune that would bring human development to a standstill. Nothing could unite a nation more firmly than a "true" war. Nothing else could give the citizen a true understanding of the state This notion was borrowed from Ruhle von Lihenstern's *Vom Kriege,* in which both the nationalization of armies and the militarization of nations were advocated. At the time this book was given slight notice. Half a century later the historian Heinrich von Treitschke gave Lilienstern his due. "Nowhere else," he wrote, "did the acute political idealism of the War of Liberation find a nobler expression." It proved, positively, "the indestructible and blissful necessity of war." Muller himself did not go quite so far. In his time, before Bismarck's triumph, German nationalism was still far from the idolatry of naked power. "The concept of the fatherland," Muller wrote, "no matter how deep an impression it may make is not sufficient; there is a superior world-ideal, forming the center of all order because it is the idea of world-order itself—the Christian religion."

After these lectures in Dresden Müller wandered back to Berlin. There, in the company of like-minded noblemen and romantic poets, he noted with satisfaction that "the better ones among us have been fortunately cured of cosmopolitanism; it was a phase of our history through which we had to pass." Understandably, he found much to criticize in Frederick the Great who had rationalized the administration of the nation under the influence of the French Enlightenment. In the lectures he delivered in Berlin, in 1810, on the king and on the nature of the Prussian monarchy, he stressed the point that every man must have a fatherland; to say that one has none, or that one belongs to a cosmopolitan society of independent rational minds is as stupid as to proclaim that one has no sex, or no honor. As for a European community, he believed that it could be realized only under the influence of Germany. "I, too, dreamed of unification of that great nation of which we are but a fragment," he declared, "I, too, expected revolutions, the coming of heroes, and changes in the mentality of peoples that would make my dream come true. The great confederation of European nations will one day be a reality and, as sure as I am alive, will fly the German flag, for everything that is great, everything that is thorough, every-thing that is enduring in European institutions is German—that is what I have held on to, when all my hopes were dashed."

Muller caught something of the fervor of his contemporary Fichte, and in one of the eight lectures he delivered in Berlin, he stated: "To be able to feel and to understand the future clearly one first has to feel and understand national life. What the private individual refers to as the future is only a number of incidents, unintelligible to the individual heart for the very reason that it is an isolated, private heart, unable to conceive the infinity of God and to understand his laws. Only if one identifies oneself with the nation can one con-ceive the future accurately, because only then does one take the fatherland, meaning God and his laws, into account. It follows that the private individual cannot qualify as an educator—only a citizen of a nation-state can so qualify: nationality is the *conditio sine qua non* of all education. How could anyone pretend to be an educator without having understood that there must be an altar, a sanctuary, a patriotic ideal to be our guide in the centuries to come? Without such a national-religious focus, one will only succeed in educating private individuals and continuing the old misery."

In time Müller followed the Schlegels to Austria, but whether in Berlin or Vienna, whether idolizing the Hohenzollern or the Habs-burgs, he did not alter his fundamental conviction that war to the end must be waged on western ideas. After 1813 he was happy to observe that—partly through his own efforts—the tide in Germany had turned. He was especially pleased to note that intellectuals in the better nations were afflicted with "a tremendous longing for the discredited barbarians of the Middle Ages. Burke and certain of the Germans had guessed that a jewel would come to light if the Middle Ages were re-examined. The ideals of nobility have been rediscovered." But with them also appeared the new theories of an anti-western Germanophilism, steeped in a misunderstanding of history. In the early part of the nineteenth century this kind of thought remained confined to a narrow circle, but beneath the surface it continued to influence Germany's intellectual life. A century later, under a different leadership and with a different emphasis, it inspired a mass movement. The uniting link of these trends was "the war against the West."

Chapter Four

FATHER JAHN AND THE
WAR AGAINST THE WEST

On the Eve of German Nationalism

THE CONCERN OF THE German romanticists was not with politics and national power, but with the national mind and poetic character. In that regard they still belonged to Goethe's time. This age drew to its end during the poet's life. The turning point was the year 1806, which concluded Germany's eighteenth century.

Before 1806 Germany knew hardly any nationalism or political activity. The people lived peacefully, unmoved by French revolutionary appeals, without any understanding of western aspirations. The rights of the many princes were not questioned by their subjects who were proud of their orderly discipline and their trust in authority. The horizon of the rural population and of the burghers of the many somnolent free cities was strictly parochial. The German intellectuals, well informed about what went on in the West, were earnest men dedicated to ideas but did not dream of submitting them to the test of reality. With daring ingenuity they proposed metaphysical or poetic systems; they explored new branches of scholarship; they created immortal musical or literary works. Their paternalistic governments protected them against an application of their theories, so that their intellectual revolution did not influence the people who met it with the same indifference as they met the western political revolution. Even the liberals did not demand participation in government but only freedom of the mind and the insulation of society from the state.

69

At the turn of the century practically no one thought of German honor or of German power. The statesmen did their best to keep their principalities out of war, though making the most of all the changes war brought about, without regard for the interests of the German Reich or of a nation which few believed in or desired. German poets did not call for patriotic resistance or voice the wrath of an outraged nation; they moaned over the devastation of the peaceful countryside and the suffering of peasants and burghers; they expressed their longing for peace and for the undisturbed flow of tranquil and unheroic days. Even men who later became fervent patriots felt no concern for Germany's future. In 1792 Friedrich Perthes, the great publisher, then a young man of twenty in Hamburg, greeted the French victories over the German armies: "As a man and a citizen of the world I rejoice over the progress of the French armies; as a German I wish to weep, for it will be an eternal shame for the Germans to have yielded to the good cause only by force."

When some Germans opposed the French revolutionary wars of conquest, they did it as eighteenth century humanitarians not as German nationalists. The most patriotic of the older poets, Friedrich Gottfried Klopstock, who had celebrated Bastille Day in Hamburg in 1790 by donning the tricolor, five years later was writing a poem in which he reminded the French of their sacred promise never to wage a war of conquest. Not as a German but as a lover of peace and mankind he was distressed to see the French desire military glory. He warned them that should they rise to dizzy heights the fall might be disastrous. Three years later another German poet, Johann Gottfried Herder, sounded a new note: "Germany, are you slumbering on? Look what happens around you, what has happened to yourself. Feel it, wake up. . . . See your neighbor Poland, formerly so powerful and proud, kneeling dishonored and disheveled before three victors. Look at the giant in the east; you yourself taught him to brandish his sword and his club. Look westward: there relying on might and luck another fighter faces you, full of agility and enthusiasm. And you, you still tarry to stand up like a man and wisely unite? . . . Should your name be gone with the wind? Will you too kneel before strangers and be partitioned by them? Do none of your ancestors, does not your own heart, does not your language mean anything to you? . . . Courts will not protect you nor princely priests. . . . Who does not protect himself does he deserve liberty?" But in his time Herder was almost alone in his zeal to awaken Germany.

Few German states proved as immune to German nationalism at the turn of the century as Prussia. The policy of Frederick II had been anti-German, both politically and culturally· he weakened the German Reich and felt no sympathy for German culture. Under his two successors Frederick William II and Frederick William III the Prussian monarchy failed to live up to its military tradition. The public opinion of the educated classes, whom Frederick II had hardly noticed, began to assert itself. As elsewhere in Germany it desired a peaceful and undisturbed life. The war against France in 1793 was unpopular. Feeling of hostility toward a foreign country was directed against Austria; the idea of a community of interests with Austria and other German states against France was at that time alien to Prussia's statesmen and people. The separate peace which Prussia and France concluded at Basel in 1795 abandoned the left bank of the Rhine to France and declared Prussia's neutrality in the wars between France and the German Reich. The Prussians welcomed this treaty with enthusiasm.

In the following ten years, while Napoleon conquered and disposed of southern Germany, the Prussians enjoyed peace and prosperity. "They had no feeling whatsoever against the French oppression [in Germany] and no sympathy for the distress of the Reich, its honor mortally wounded, its fortune at the lowest ebb, so long as they flattered themselves that Prussia would get her share, and that they were the chosen people of the new God," wrote Barthold Georg Niebuhr, the famous historian of Ancient Rome who became one of the first supporters of Prussia's claim to German leadership; "They only became alarmed when they noticed that their own existence was threatened; they then realized that they had been deceived." In these years of peace "without honor or glory" Prussia grew richer and letters and the arts began to flourish. Most people were highly satisfied. With the same self-satisfaction which characterized the middle class the Prussian minister Karl Gustav von Struensee declared to the French chargé d'affaires in August, 1799: "The salutary revolution which you have made from below will occur in Prussia but slowly and from on high. The king is a demagogue in his own way; he labors day in day out to curtail the privileges of the nobility. In a few years there will no longer be any privileged class in Prussia." Needless to say nothing of the kind happened. The necessary energy and incentive were equally lacking.

The few German intellectuals who comprehended the importance of power and of the state were not nationalists. They failed to grasp the significance of the people's participation in government

brought about by the French Revolution. In 1801 Georg Friedrich
Wilhelm Hegel demanded a reform of the German Imperial constitution. He stressed for the first time his theory that the state is
power. Without power no state could exist, and therefore, as he
pointed out in his first sentence, Germany was no longer a state.
In marked contrast to the other German political scientists of the
period he inserted a discussion of the armed forces of the Reich
at the beginning of his treatise, and insisted that here was the core
of the problem. He saw the essence of the state as its power over
the individual citizen and as its ability to defend itself against other
states. He showed no understanding of the vitality which civic spirit
and widespread cultural activity could infuse into a state. The test
of war was, for him, the true criterion of the strength of national
life. He demanded a powerful Germany not a national Germany;
the reform of the Reich was not to come from the people but from
forceful leadership.

Like Fichte a few years later, Hegel called for a *"Zwingherr,"*
a hero who would impose unity and greatness upon the Germans.
He did not at that time expect leadership from Prussia. As between
her and Austria all his sympathies were on the side of the latter. In
his eyes Prussia was a soulless despotism totally lacking in scientific
or artistic genius, and he warned against an overestimation of
Prussian strength. Like Fichte, Hegel was led by the study of
Machiavelli to abandon the eighteenth century humanitarian concepts. Hegel's prince was no longer the first servant of the state,
as the eighteenth century had understood him. His power was no
longer based on the social contract which the citizens concluded of
their own free will. The prince was now the great man whom
others obey even against their will, not only on account of his over-
powering personality but because he represents the unconscious will
of the people. Hegel never named the hero whom he expected to
bring about German regeneration. Some commentators saw the
Austrian Archduke Charles, others Bonaparte as the man on whom
he set his hopes. As for Hegel's concept of the state it owed next
to nothing to the ideas of 1789 and the nationalism which the
French Revolution originally aroused It was a reflection of Napoleon and his doctrines which the march of history seemed to
confirm.

Hegel was not alone among the Germans of his time in admiring
the French general and in expecting from his hands the salvation
of Germany and of Europe. Karl Theodor von Dalberg, the last
Imperial Elector of Mainz and later the prince primate of the Con-

federation of the Rhine, was one of the enlightened administrators
of the time, a highly cultivated patron of German letters, and himself a scholar of note. In 1802 he voiced the opinion of many educated Germans when he wrote of Napoleon: "This extraordinary
man, who brought order out of the anarchy in France . . . has the
greatness of soul that is needed to rise above being merely the
benefactor of a single nation to become the benefactor of mankind." At the beginning of the century most German statesmen and
writers hailed Napoleon either as the prince of peace or as the re-
generator of Germany; the masses welcomed the progressive reforms
where French administration introduced them or remained indifferent. The disenchantment with Napoleon among the educated classes
began to spread only after 1808; but even then many remained loyal
either to his political leadership or to the spirit of greatness which
he seemed to embody.

When the Holy Roman Empire came to an end, in 1806, only
the romantics looked back with longing on its ancient traditions;
many regarded the Confederation of the Rhine which Napoleon
founded as the basis for a better Germany. It brought all the German states, outside of half-Slavic Prussia and ethnically mixed Austria, into a loose union which leaned geographically and in its ad-
ministrative organization toward the West. The Confederation never
had a chance to realize its promise. Napoleon's unprincipled and
restless ambition constantly undid his political concepts. The German princes did not wish to abandon their sovereignty to the Confederation. Yet many Germans welcomed its creation.

The medieval empire was dead. In contrast to the old Reich, the
new Confederation seemed turned toward the future. It was founded
on the progressive ideas of the new age. It was inspired by the
greatest personality of the time, who restored the unity of western
civilization on a rational basis and revived the empire of Charlemagne, thus ending almost one thousand years of hostility among
French, Germans, and Italians. Did not Napoleon himself in assum-
ing the protection of the Confederation declare as his goal the end
of dissention and disorder? "Having thus provided," his chargé
d'affaires explained, "for the dearest interests of his people and of
his neighbors, and having assured, as far as lay in his power, the
future peace of Europe and that of Germany in particular, hereto-
fore constantly the theater of war, . . . he hopes that the nations of
Europe will at last close their ears to the insinuations of those who
would maintain an eternal war on the continent of Europe. He
trusts the French armies that have crossed the Rhine have done so

for the last time, and that the German people will no longer witness, except in the annals of the past, the terrible pictures of chaos, devastation, and carnage, which war invariably brings with it."

Austria's and Prussia's wars against Napoleon in 1805 and 1806 hardly evoked any sympathy in other German lands. While Napoleon went from victory to victory the progressiveness of his administration and the never-before-encountered power of his personality created a legend to which the greatest minds of Germany succumbed the more willingly because national sentiment was unknown to them. On October 13, 1806, the day before the battle of Jena in which the Prussian army was ignominiously defeated, Hegel wrote from the city—then occupied by French forces—"Just as I did in former times, now everybody prays for the success of the French army." Three months later Hegel saw in the French victory the proof that "education and intelligence had defeated crude efficiency." In the years to come he worked in Bavaria, the leading state of the Confederation, and his loyalty to the Emperor remained unshaken. Even in 1813 he treated the liberation movement with irony and the liberators with contempt. In April, 1814, he declared that Napoleon's downfall meant that a great man had been defeated by the mediocrity of the multitude.

Many German intellectuals shared Hegel's attitude of admiration for Napoleon. Most of them saw in Napoleon not the embodiment of power which fascinated Hegel, but the prince of peace, the *Friedensfürst*. Later these intellectuals became disillusioned by Napoleon's failure to bring peace to Europe. Jean Paul Richter was typical of these intellectuals, a man famous in his generation for the novels he published under the name Jean Paul. He too saw in Napoleon one of the greatest geniuses of mankind. When he finally turned away from him, it was not from motives of nationalism but of pacifism and liberalism. He had desired Napoleon's victory over England because he believed that in that event Napoleon and a confederation of German princes under his protectorate would guarantee a long-lasting peace. "Do we not since the last wars again gladly share," he wrote, "the common name of Franks, and do we not remember from history that the majority in France are not Gauls but transplanted Germans?" As late as 1809 he was rejoicing in the rebirth of Charlemagne's empire and was convinced that Napoleon would settle down after having built a new Europe and perhaps a new Asia. In that very year when the publisher Perthes asked him to contribute to his new review, *Vaterländisches Museum,* Jean Paul found fault with the use of the word *"unterjocht"* (subjected) as applied to the German people. This, he felt, was far from the truth, and in his contribution to Perthes' first issue he made it plain that he saw no reason for German self-pity. "Let us remember," he wrote, "that with the French invasion of Germany, we did not exchange republican liberty—which we did not have—for despotical serfdom—which cannot come from a country where it does not exist—but only more or less moderate rulers for more or less moderate rulers."

Jean Paul's vision was inspired by his faith in liberty and peace. "We live," he wrote in December, 1812, "in a period without precedent; not countries but three continents are laboring to transform themselves and to become more similar. The olive tree of peace can no longer strike its roots in one garden, but only in the whole globe The compass needle and the pen, the ship and the printing press have abolished the isolation of nations. . . . At present our laws spread liberty to colonies, to Negroes, to Jews, and to the serfs; the antagonism between the various classes gives way to a common patriotic attraction since all classes fight together on the battlefield." By this time Jean Paul was deeply disappointed with Napoleon in whom he no longer saw a humanitarian and a force for peace.

German Nationalism: Arndt

AFTER 1806 NATIONALISM BEGAN to spread among German intellectuals. This was a nationalism inspired by resistance against alien rule. The French were identified with the eighteenth century, with the Enlightenment, with the ideas of 1789, and with the liberal West: forces that now were regarded as wholly alien and un-German. Jean Paul had rejected Napoleon because he had revealed himself to be a man of war and a betrayer of the generous message of 1789. The new German nationalists turned against Napoleon for the very reason that he claimed to embody a new universal order of peace. They did not strive for a regeneration based upon the individual, as the eighteenth century had done; their concept of regeneration centered upon the self-willed and self-contained national group. They believed in the regenerative power of war, above all national wars. One of their earliest spokesmen, Ernst Moritz Arndt, complained in a letter of 1812 that most people looked frightened or dumbstruck on being told that the Germans must continue to fight the French for at least five years if they wished to become really free.

Though the new nationalism did not overlook the need for the moral regeneration of Germany it was first and foremost a call to arms against the alien. "The highest form of religion," Arndt wrote, "is to love the fatherland more passionately than laws and princes, fathers and mothers, wives and children." This love was inextricably linked with hatred of the foreign enemy and of all those who supported him at home. Arndt never ceased to stress his rejection of universality. Rationalism and enlightenment hoped for an end to the hatreds and divisions inherited from the past In his "Address of Hope of the Year 1810," Arndt did not deny that something might be said in favor of such a hope but only by the contemplative mind. He and his generation believed that the hour had struck for the man of action

"The man of action," Arndt insisted, "will be guided by something else and will be guided by something else through all eternity; he will be guided by the dark forces of the age, and by a darker love for his people, its way of life, its language which from childhood has become an inseparable part of the innermost recesses of his being." It was nature's wonderful secret, Arndt believed, that these dark forces remained the same through the centuries however outward forms might change. Against the enlightened hopes for a united humanity the dark forces of the past prevailed and determined man. Man could think or dream of a united mankind; but he could only act and live impelled by his own national past. This nationalism of deep and dark forces was later to influence many other movements when the Age of Nationalism spread outside western Europe.

For this nationalism common descent and common language became the most powerful symbols of national life. These two elements united all Germans and constituted the German nation. In these two respects, Arndt was happy to point out, the Germans excelled all other nations. They were the purest race; they spoke the purest language. This twofold purity guaranteed their superiority. "The Germans have not been bastardized," Arndt wrote in 1815, "they have retained their original purity and have been able to develop slowly but surely according to the everlasting laws of time; the fortunate Germans are an original people." He went on to quote Tacitus, "that extraordinary man who penetrated with his prophetic glance not only the depths of the human heart but also the depths of nature." Long ago Tacitus had prophesied the splendid future of the Germans. "But of all things, he realized how important it was for their future greatness and majesty that they preserved the purity of their blood and resembled only themselves; he saw his Italy, once the mistress of the world, a bastardized canaille, . . . and the proud Roman soul bled and writhed because there were no longer any true Romans."

More important than purity of race was a language pure and undefiled. Language seemed to Arndt the best guarantee of the differentiation among nations. The fact that more than one nation might speak the same tongue and yet maintain a separate nationality apparently did not enter his mind. Like Herder, he believed that there was no greater tragedy for a people than to abandon its native language. Differences in language, Arndt believed, helped to keep alive those prejudices and dislikes which protect the independence of a people far better than unsheathed swords or fortified cities. Otherwise peoples might be in danger of becoming *"solche Allerweltmenschen, die man Sklaven und Juden nennt,"* cosmopolitans the like of slaves and Jews.

Arndt went far beyond Herder In the latter's eyes a small, peaceful, and pastoral people could have a wonderful language; its beauty or its worth were independent of political power. Arndt, however, was convinced that only a unified powerful people conscious of its destiny could have a worthwhile language. Like Fichte, Arndt believed that of all the European peoples only the Germans could boast of an original and undefiled language, an *Ursprache,* not a mongrel language as did the others. The purity of language and race established the superiority of the Germans over the French and the Italians, the Englishmen and the Spaniards. All creative power originated with the people and depended on their purity. "All great things which a man does, forms, thinks, and invents as a hero, an artist, a lawgiver, or an inventor—all that comes to him only from the nation."

Arndt was finally convinced that God had willed the diversity of languages to the end that mankind should not sink to the level of a "good-for-nothing gang of slaves." Here his interpretation of God's will differed from that of the Bible, which tells us that God instituted the diversity of languages not to improve men but to punish them for building the Tower of Babel. What appeared to Arndt a blessing was regarded in the Bible as a curse. But Arndt proudly claimed that "what God plans in the mighty and secret court of times is not hidden from us, not even for a minute." It was apparent that what God willed was nationalism. What He could

not countenance was cosmopolitanism. "Cursed be the humanitarianism and the cosmopolitanism you brag about," Arndt cried out,
"cursed be that Jewish one-worldism which you hail as the summit
of human education."

Arndt was the most influential pamphleteer of the first explosion
of German nationalism, the first *Aufbruch*, the setting-out and
bursting forth of the German people, the *Volk*, on the new dynamic
pursuit of its destiny. He was also a poet: one of his many patriotic
songs *"Was ist des Deutschen Vaterland?"* (What is the German's
Fatherland?) called upon the Germans to build their fatherland
out of all the lands where German was spoken. In this new fatherland truth and loyalty would be cherished. It would be a land "where
wrath would annihilate French trumpery and in which every
Frenchman would be an enemy." For two generations this was the
most popular national song until it was replaced by the equally
Francophobic *"Wacht am Rhein."*

Arndt could scarcely sympathize with the notion, advanced by
Goethe in *Wilhelm Meisters Wanderjahre*, that a man might be
justified in leaving his native land in pursuit of happiness and individual freedom. To Arndt freedom meant something else. the right
to follow in one's ancestors' footsteps uncorrupted by alien influences.
In his famous *Catechism*—to give the full title, *Catechism for a
German warrior, in which the Christian soldier is told how to
deserve that title, and how to go into battle with God on his side,*—
Arndt defined liberty as a condition in which "no foreign menials
rule over us, and no foreign slave drivers crack their whips over us."
Thus a German could lead a full life only in a German state. Apparently freedom existed where one's own slavedrivers and execu-
tioners were in power.

To Arndt nationalism was not primarily a practical political
program or the basis for the broadening of government, but a religious experience, the immersion of the individual into the security
and ecstacy of mass-comradeship. In 1813 he wrote: "I have known
misfortune; I have suffered; it has scarcely moved me to tears. But
when I have thought of the *Volk* I have always had to weep in the
depth of my soul. When a great crowd moves before me, when a
band of warriors passes by with flowing banners and sounding
trumpets and drums, then I realize that my feelings and my actions
are not an empty illusion, then it is that I feel the indestructible life,
the eternal spirit, and eternal God . . . Like other men I am
egoistic and sinful but in my exaltation I am freed at once from all
my sins, I am no longer a single suffering individual, I am one with

the *Volk* and God. In such a moment any doubts about my life and work vanish."

Arndt believed that once the German was united with the *Volk*, he would overcome his egoism, feel his way into the infinite and the sublime, into God himself. The eighteenth century, Arndt complained, had made too much of the individual; the new nationalism outgrew egoism and thus became an ethical force. As if group-egoism could be superior to individual egoism! On the contrary it can be much more dangerous. For experience has shown that in most cases the individual indulges his egoism with a bad conscience, whereas the *sacro egoismo* of the *Volk* is free of qualms; it is an egoism above criticism; its strength is that of the pseudo-religious experience which Arndt so movingly described when his heart overflowed.

Arndt believed in constitutional limitation of a truly national monarchy; he, like Bismarck, maintained the need for a strong monarchy which was superior to a parliament with which it shared the legislative power. In 1850 Arndt, then eighty-one, wrote an article in the periodical *Germania*, in which he insisted that the German people "was so monarchical by education and national preference that even the inhabitants of the two great capitals of Germany [Vienna and Berlin], who at the beginning of the German revolution [1848] raised arms against their governments, have reverted to their monarchical loyalties. The real desires of our people seem to demand only that measure of freedom in the constitution of the state that is in harmony with the monarchy, and not more; what goes beyond these limits is something alien [to us]."

In his long life—he died in 1860 at the age of ninety-one—Arndt lived through all the early stages of German nationalism, from its rejection of the humanism and universalism of the eighteenth century almost to its self-centered assertion of power under Bismarck. He was a truly representative *Erwecker zur Deutschheit* (awakener to Germandom), a concept introduced by his generation into the history of nationalism. He was a man of great power and sincerity. He preserved enough rational clarity and intellectual responsibility not to succumb to the blind adoration of the people. He even paid his respects to the humanism of the German classicists. "In the midst of terrifying revolutions that unhinged the world they hoped that the enlightened spirit of the times would bring to the fore the noblest elements of European culture. This would put an end to the old pernicious struggles and would revive all that had been good and beautiful in the Ancient World in even more glorious forms. From the heights on which they lived the political events—the overthrow of old thrones and constitutions, destructive wars, annihilation of nations—appeared to them as of only minor importance, nay, even perhaps as helpful for the sublime purpose of the age as they understood it." But to Arndt such a point of view was impractical. The age of blood and iron had arrived and the Germans had to master it. In the second volume of his *Geist der Zeit* (1809) from which we have just been quoting, he published his first four German war poems, among them the famous *"Lob des Eisens"* ("In Praise of Iron").

> *Gold schreit die feige Welt,*
> *Und Gold macht feige Knechte, . . .*
> *Drum preis' ich das Metall,*
> *Das schlechte, schwarze Eisen.*

> Gold! shrieks the cowardly world
> And gold makes cowards of us all . . .
> And so I praise another metal
> Iron, evil and black.

To him Germany seemed "the sacred heart of old Europe." Without drawing on its strength there was no salvation for Europe. Geographically, Germany was the meeting ground and the synthesis of north and south; historically, most European peoples descended from tribes that had migrated from the German heartland; hence the Germans could feel they were the parents of all the European peoples and could understand them; intellectually the Germans had absorbed all that was best of the cultures of all other nations and thus developed a more universal humanity. In that sense, the nationalist Arndt could join with the classical humanists in proclaiming a universalism, but it was a German universalism with the German as the representative pan-human being. In 1843 he wrote: "The German is a universal man (*Allerweltmensch*), to whom God has given the whole world as his home. The more he has discovered and explored this home the more he will love his own smaller fatherland and the better he will build it." And on January 9, 1853, one of the last utterances of the patriarch summed up his creed: "The idea of unity and might of the greatest world-nation of the present world will and must finally through the will of God and the course of nature assert itself, and all those who know and all those who think must not cease to uphold such prophecy."

Father Jahn

EVEN MORE INFLUENTIAL than Arndt was Friedrich Ludwig Jahn, or Father Jahn as he was generally called. While Arndt was born in Rügen, a German-speaking island in the Baltic, then part of Sweden, and bore throughout his life the imprint of Swedish (and even English) constitutional ideas, Jahn was one of the very few leaders of early German nationalism born in the Mark Brandenburg, the heartland of Prussia. He was also one of the very first to fuse Prussianism and Germanism. From his youth, he was a fervent Prussian patriot. His first book, which he wrote in 1799 at the age of twenty-one, was a proposal for strengthening Prussian patriotism. He opened the book with a motto from a poem which glorified the patriot. "Of all the heroes who shine upon the world as eternal stars," the motto read, "through all regions to the end of the world, you, oh patriot, are my hero: you who are often misunderstood by men give yourself entirely to the fatherland, feel only its sorrows, think only of its greatness, live and die for the fatherland." What the poem expressed as an imaginative exercise in the sentimental style of the period became an all-pervasive reality in Jahn's life. Originally his was a merely Prussian patriotism, a deep-seated loyalty to the Prussian dynasty and army. After 1806 this feeling changed into an equally strong German nationalism which distinguished itself from that of the romanticists or that of Arndt by its organic unity with Prussianism.

"History," Jahn wrote toward the end of his career, "was my first playmate when I was a child, and she has remained my friend and companion throughout my life." But the history which fired his imagination at the outset was not German history but the great deeds of the Hohenzollern monarchs. The first book which he published showed no trace of German nationalism; it was entirely devoted to a glorification of Prussia. In its naive and often coarse boastfulness which Jahn and his followers thought essentially patriotic and German it anticipated the more mature nationalism of his later years. "The uneducated peasant," Jahn wrote in 1799, "in the German states of the Prussian Reich (as distinct from its Polish states) always shows his pride in his fatherland. A fight starts quickly at the country fairs in the frontier towns when the superiority of the Prussians is not recognized. Almost always the

Prussians win, and even if they are in a minority, never tolerate the taunts of their adversaries. Often did I hear it said on such occasions: one Prussian can take care of three Saxons, Hannoverians, Mecklenburgians or Swedes."

Jahn was convinced that a traveler through Germany would immediately notice a great difference the second he set foot on Prussian soil. The Prussians, he felt, were distinguished by their manly aggressive stride, their firm and courageous glance, and by the spontaneity of their salutations. The Prussians could hardly avoid recognizing their natural superiority, for non-Prussians stopped to stare in admiration as if they were men from another world. Thinking upon these things, Jahn reached the conclusion that here, as nowhere else, was pride of the fatherland rooted in men's hearts. "Even little boys at play are already filled with this patriotic spirit. They play more warlike games than elsewhere, and if a playmate runs away from a fight, they say: "That's no true Prussian."

Thus young Jahn glorified his native Prussia without any consciousness of German national community or destiny. Within the next decade he changed, but he carried over into his German nationalism much of the Prussian attitude and the lasting conviction that "the history of the Prussian States under the rulers of the house of Zollern is a magnificent column in the temple of the history of mankind." In 1800 he met Arndt and his experiences in the following years shifted his attention and his enthusiasm from the Prussian state to the German folk. In 1806 he wrote the first draft of his *Deutsches Volkstum* which appeared in 1810. This is one of the essential books for an understanding of the new nationalism. In it the influence of romanticism combined with that of the French Revolution and of the Prussian traditions; of the three elements the romantic prevailed: the emphasis was no longer on the citizen in a society founded on law nor on the loyalty of the subject to his hereditary monarch, but on the originality of a deeply rooted creative force, the German *Volk*.

Here was an almost mystical force that transcended mere history; it became for Jahn one of the central and elemental forces of nature and a supreme part of God's own creative effort. Jahn did not confine himself to developing the theory of folkdom; during the crucial years of the formation of German nationalism he became its indefatigable propagandist. Most important was his influence on three movements which were not only characteristic of German nationalism but models as well for similar trends in central and eastern Europe: free corps of patriotic volunteers; gymnastic associations for the training of patriotic fighters; and student fraternities aflame with nationalistic zeal. Each of these three movements stood in its own peculiar way for freedom—but a freedom overcharged with nationalistic emotionalism and stressing the disciplined dedication to national service, a freedom which had little in common with the Western concepts of individual liberty.

Jahn's influence on the free corps can scarcely be separated from his concern for a reform of the Prussian army. Here he found himself in agreement with General Gerhard Johann David von Scharnhorst, the reformer of the Prussian army after 1807: both men were anxious to imbue the army with the spirit of conscious nationalism. In 1806, in his first project of a national militia, Scharnhorst wished to exclude from it not only foreigners but even Prussian subjects of Polish antecedents. "In France as well as in England," he wrote, "the formation of the national militia, and that alone, aroused the military spirit of the nation and created an enthusiasm for the independence of the fatherland which does not appear as strong in other countries." Scharnhorst only partly succeeded. He made the Prussian army more efficient; he did not render it more democratic The old spirit remained, though now equipped with new weapons. The élan of Frederick's army was preserved and so, the historian Treitschke noted with approval, was the caste spirit among the officers.

Jahn wished to go farther than Scharnhorst; he desired a democratization of the Prussian army. Both men were in favor of universal military service, access for everyone to the commissioned ranks, the introduction of examinations for officers, and the abolition of corporal punishment. But Jahn opposed standing armies; he sought to base the military strength of the fatherland on a national militia in which the soldiers would elect the noncommissioned officers and these in turn would choose subaltern commissioned officers, while the colonels and generals would be appointed by the king. He believed in an army of volunteers driven to great deeds by a burning patriotism. To a small extent the war of liberation realized his hopes In February, 1813, Scharnhorst authorized the formation of a free corps, a band of patriotic volunteers, mostly students, under the command of a Prussian officer, Adolf Freiherr von Lützow. This was a truly national legion Its purpose was to gather Germans from outside Prussia for the war against Napoleon and to fight as a German corps, not as part of the Prussian army. In 1813 no German army existed. Austrian, Prussian, Saxon, or Württemberg armies fought, some against France, some on France's side. The free corps was the only armed embodiment of the new German nationalism.

In that respect it differed from the free corps of Major Ferdinand von Schill, who in 1807 had won fame as a Prussian army officer in the defense of the Prussian fortress of Kolberg, a port on the Gulf of Pomerania, and in 1809 had led his regiment of Prussian hussars, without the authorization of his king, into independent action against Napoleon on Austria's side Ultimately, in May, 1809, he was defeated and fell in the defense of another Pomeranian seaport, Stralsund. Though his expedition, like the uprising of the Tyrolese peasants in the same year, served as inspiration to the rising German nationalism he and his soldiers fought as Prussians not as Germans. On the other hand, Lützow's free corps, though it originated in Prussia, served the German cause. In its black uniforms—known therefore as *die Schwarze Schar* or as Lützow's *Wilde Jagd* (Wild Huntsmen)—the free corps, consisting of infantry, chasseurs, and cavalry, made a deeper impression on the imagination of Germany in later years than it did on the French army at the time. Designed for guerilla warfare in the enemy's rear, Lützow's free corps was practically annihilated when, in June, 1813, it was ambushed near Kitzen by German troops of the Rhenish Confederation under the command of a Wurttemberg general Yet the spirit of the free corps lived on in many nationalist legions: probably the most famous was Garibaldi's expeditionary corps to Sicily. In Germany proper the free corps disappeared Prussia imposed its discipline which was hardly favorable to the free spirit of enthusiasm and adventure. As to the free corps which mushroomed in Germany after 1918, they had little in common with the spirit of 1813 except its nationalism. They were debased by the twentieth century cult of violence which, however, was foreshadowed by some utterances of Father Jahn and of his contemporary, the great poet Heinrich von Kleist.

The *Turnerschaft*

JAHN AND HIS YOUNG FRIEND Friedrich Friesen formed the link between the free corps and the German gymnastic movement. Like Jahn, Friesen was proud of his Prussian birth. As a student he was deeply affected by Fichte's *Addresses to the German Nation,* and by 1810, when he and Jahn were teaching at Dr. Plamann's Institute in Berlin, they felt the time had come to spread the education advocated in the *Addresses.* They founded the nucleus of the fast growing *Turnerschaft.*

At this time Jahn was also an instructor in the classical high school (*Gymnasium*) in Berlin-Kölln, the famous Graue Kloster, founded in 1574, where he had been a student himself. Gathering the pupils around him, he led them to the open spaces of the Hasenheide in the southern part of the city, and began instructing them in games, gymnastic drill, and other athletics. There, in the beginning of June, 1811, he opened the first gymnastic ground (*Turnplatz*). The word *turnen* was selected because it derived from the medieval tournaments, symbolic of the ancient German spirit. The movement grew rapidly, its various branches were ever more perfected, and a new discipline, the *Turnkunst,* was worked out with typical Germanic earnestness. Its purpose was from the beginning primarily nationalistic education: young men were trained to be able, ready, and willing to fight for the fatherland and to form the core of the armies of tomorrow.

The *Turnerschaft* was consciously German. It inspired loyalty to the nation waiting to be created by the willpower, the disciplined unity, and the vigilant preparedness of the gymnasts and their leaders. Physical education or health (though the *mens sana in corpore sano* was often quoted) was not the primary goal. Nor did the movement have anything in common with sport in the English sense of the word. The ideals of fair play, of the good loser, of the gentleman did not attract Jahn at all. The *Turnerschaft,* though civilian in appearance, was military in spirit and purpose. It was a potential army trained for the ardently desired day of the battle against the enemy.

The gymnastic movement did not disguise its ambition to shape history. Jahn rejected the secrecy that shrouded the activities of many societies with similar nationalist and revolutionary goals. In a letter to a gymnastic instructor years later he denied the widespread assumption that the *Turnerschaft* originated in the secret *Tugendbund* "It has always been a public association, and so it must remain," he claimed. "The time has now come when everything must come into daylight that was formerly hidden in darkness. The soul of the gymnastic association (*Turnwesen*) is the life of the people itself (*das Volksleben*), and this thrives only in the open, in light and air."

Jahn's gymnasts had no hesitation about manifesting what they conceived to be their truly German character—their *Deutschheit*. They wore their own peculiar dress, they used the familiar thou in addressing everyone, and they spoke a German which was consciously coarse. They believed that polished speech was used only to conceal the truth—for such a purpose French, the language of diplomacy and civilized society, seemed especially fit—whereas German was the tongue of those who were forthright and sincere. Jahn himself, who despised all words of foreign origin, was nothing if not forthright and sincere.

In a letter written in 1809 he defined the difference between the humanism of Goethe and Schiller and the new nationalism. "We seek the same goal," he wrote, "but in Germanity instead of humanity. This seeming limitation is really an enhancement." He added that "Every attempt to redeem the people, every revolution and renaissance has been the work of a few enthusiasts. The chain of serfdom had to be rattled by fanatics before liberty could brandish in victory its sword of vengeance." Jahn believed that the zealot who fought for his holy cause could be forgiven any sins that he happened to commit. "Every people," he wrote in 1814, "venerates as a savior the hero who by fanaticism and fury creates national unity." For nothing should stand in the way of the fulfillment of the one ultimate goal· the folk must establish its state, a true *Volksstaat*, a nation in the democratic sense of the word, in which all the members are united in equality and all class distinctions abolished.

The outbreak of the war of liberation led most of the young gymnasts to join the free corps as volunteers. Jahn himself was no success as a soldier: modern weapons and the discipline of a modern army were not to his taste; he would have preferred to fight with a sabre and an ax. His friend Friesen, however, became Lützow's aide de camp, and fell in France in March, 1814. Friesen and his close friend, the young poet Theodor Körner, who also fell in battle, became the ideal representatives of the younger nationalist generation. Their nationalism was characterized by religious enthusiasm and by bitter hatred of the French. Friesen shared with Jahn the sponsorship of the *Burschenschaft* for the dissemination of nationalism in the academic world.

The *Burschenschaft*

WHEN THE PHILOSOPHER Fichte, rector of the University of Berlin, turned down the project of Jahn and Friesen in 1812 for the reorganization of student life in the universities, pronouncing the plan un-German, the two confederates were undismayed. Jahn turned to Jena, reasoning that in such a small principality German nationalism could triumph more easily over the patriotism of the several German states. Moreover, Heinrich Luden, a popular professor of history at the university, had already prepared the way for Jahn's message.

When the first *Burschenschaft* was founded at Jena on June 12, 1815, Jahn's contribution was manifest. Intended to replace the traditional German student organizations formed of small groups of friends, often from the same territory, the *Burschenschaft* was to become the only organization of all Christian German students in all German universities, united irrespective of class, caste, state, or province. Following Jahn's example, the students emphasized their Teutonism by their dress and speech, and their Christian seriousness by rejecting overindulgence in beer drinking and dueling. A more practical application of the Christian character was exclusion of Jews from participation in the *Burschenschaft*.

At Jahn's suggestion the *Burschenschaft* hoisted black, red, and gold as the colors of German unity. The origin of this tricolor is unknown; it may have been inspired by the colors of the Jena student corps Vandalia or by those of Lützow's free corps, which had its black uniforms set off with red and gold. Symbolically, the colors represented the struggle out of the black night of slavery through the red blood of battle to the golden day of liberty.

So Jahn set all his hopes on youth. The older generation was corrupted in his eyes; it was that very corruption that explained the decline of German power and the victory of France. Germany had to be reborn, and the true German character of old restored in the hearts of the Germans of tomorrow. How was all this to come to pass? In England and France the nation was founded on a political association, the state; its regeneration had been accomplished by political and social revolutions, transforming the state and reinvigorating the nation. No similar political association existed in

Germany. If the Germans were to build a united nation on a firm foundation, they must look back to what was more ancient and more essential than the state—to the mystical force of *Volkstum*. What was *Volkstum* but the inner creative life of the *Volk*, which was itself a manifestation of God's eternal creation? The *Volk* existed before the state; it was its foundation. All true history was the history of *Volker*. This discovery led Jahn to the conclusion that scholarship must develop a new discipline, the study of the *Volk* and all folkish life. His book *Deutsches Volkstum* laid the foundation for what he hoped would be a new science.

All this while, Jahn's Prussian patriotism was far from dead. To him Austria was "too much a mixture of races, where the happiness of the ruler is prayed for in seven languages." In Prussia the overwhelming majority of the people were German. "I expect," he wrote in 1810, "to observe in Prussia a timely rejuvenation of the venerable German Reich." He went on to indicate that "if Germany developed its immense but unused strength it could establish eternal peace in Europe and become the guardian angel of mankind" But to assume leadership Prussia would have to undergo a profound change. Frederick the Great created a state, but the state could not endure because it was not based on *Volkstum*. "A state without *Volk* is nothing, a soulless artifice; a *Volk* without a state is nothing, a bodiless airy phantom, like the gypsies and the Jews Only state and *Volk* together can form a Reich, and such a Reich cannot be preserved without *Volkstum*." It was high time for the Germans to rehabilitate the word *Volk* in all its glory and to look to it for guidance. Germany, Jahn decided, can find salvation only in herself. "We are not yet lost! We can still be saved, but only through ourselves!"

Jahn's Concept of *Volkstum*

JAHN APPEALED TO READERS for whom the lofty triad "Volk, Deutsch-. heit, und Vaterland"—the precedence of Volk and Germanity over Fatherland is characteristic—was a reality. He reminded them that for two thousand years honesty and straightforwardness, loyalty and seriousness, truthfulness and industry, had been part of the German folk character, but that lately the name German was no longer held in high regard. The Germans, the most populous nation of Europe, must now begin to understand what was their true character. While Rome was a never-satisfied people's hell—*eine nimmersatte Volkerholle*—Germany was truly representative of humanity—a pan-human people (In later years Dostoevsky and the Slavophiles were to speak in the same way of the Russians.) Jahn called the Germans *"ein menschheitliches Volkstum, das alte ehrwurdige Mittelvolk Europas"*—"an humane Volk, the ancient and honorable mediator of Europe." But the Germans had been ruined by the peace of Westphalia at the end of the Thirty Years War. Under the terms of the treaty Germany was separated from the Netherlands and Switzerland. The Rhine ceased at that time to be the old protective stream of Germany, though at its source (in Switzerland) and at its mouth (in the Netherlands) lived German half-brothers. Such were the harsh terms dictated by non-German nations. A century later, the National Socialists, too, wished above all to undo the treaty of Westphalia.

Herder had been the first to develop the concept of the folk, but to him all the *Völker* were true manifestations of the universal divine force, all equally near and dear to God. He rejected the idea of the superiority of any one people, and of any special God-given mission. Jahn—and later Dostoevsky—singled out one people as representing in its universality the whole of humanity, as mankind's holy people. And to such a people a sublime fate was reserved, to bring salvation and happiness to mankind. "The holy task of the people which has to make the world happy, is difficult to learn, and even more difficult to master," Jahn wrote, "but there can be no greater aim than to implant in the nations of the world the seeds of true humanity. . . . There is still the stuff for great deeds on earth. There are still holy wars of mankind to be waged, the whole earth is a promised land, still unconquered by justice, happiness, and virtue." An immense civilizing task lay waiting for the people which was the highest representative of humanity.

For this high purpose the peoples must preserve themselves pure and undefiled. Jahn was convinced that the eternal laws of nature doomed every intermingling of the races. Rome fell for that very reason. "The purer a people the better. The day on which a universal monarchy is established will be the last day of mankind." Peoples were different and these differences had to be maintained. There could not exist, and there should not exist, a universal model for mankind. The concept of a world government, a world language, a world religion was wrong, for it contradicted the supreme ethical and creative spirit, the originality of each people. True, Jahn glorified man's longing for unity. But this desire for unity was not intended to stretch beyond the frontier of the fatherland, or rather, of the *Volk*. For to Jahn the source of all creativity lay in folklife. Naturally he railed against ethnically mixed marriages, labeling them animal copulation. He solved the conflict between his German nationalism and Christian universality in much the same manner as Dostoevsky when faced with a similar problem. "Which of all the existing folkdoms corresponds most closely to pure Christianity?" Jahn asked. His answer carried the force of conviction. "The final judgment cannot possibly point to any other but to the genuine panhuman German folkdom"

Jahn was positive that Germany had reached a pitiable plight by abandoning its folkdom and by imitating foreign peoples and speaking foreign languages. He never tired of calling upon the Germans to safeguard their minds against all alien influences. He was more than coarse when he spoke of the French language. "It has fooled your men," he told the Germans, "enticed your youth, dishonored your wives. Germans! remember your noble language. Draw from its never drying resources, and leave Lutetia's stagnant pool alone!" In the teachers of foreign languages Jahn saw dangerous spies, in the foreign languages a hidden poison.

According to Jahn the Germans would be much happier if only they rid themselves of their greatest failing, the low esteem of themselves, and swelled with pride like their neighbors. But hope was not lost. The Germans might experience a true rebirth through the rediscovery of their folkdom. "In the whole history of a people, its most sacred moment arrives when it awakens from its torpor, becomes for the first time conscious of itself, thinks of its sacred rights and of the eternal duty of preserving them. . . . The new period of creation begins when a people . . . acknowledges freely and without reservation, how it fell into humiliating serfdom by imitating foreign models. A people which learns again to love its folkdom can look forward to its rebirth." For that purpose a new education had to reshape the nation.

Jahn developed a detailed plan of national education. He placed in its center the study of patriotic history, the writing of popular literature, and the training in manual work, in gymnastics, and in military sports for every young German—the sons of laborers as well as those of princes. National festivals, monuments, and public funerals of men who had merited well of the nation should arouse the public spirit. These suggestions were influenced by the French Revolution but the emphasis had shifted from the initial generous universal message to a narrower and more self-centered nationalism. In this form nationalism spread to other peoples. People's armies, nationalistic gymnastic organizations, patriotic and highly political student activity, emphasis on the sacredness of nationality, on the originality and uniqueness of the folk-language and indigenous civilization—all influenced the awakening of many national entities in central and eastern Europe and later in Asia.

Jahn was convinced that "the effects of such a German national education will be infinite; like everything good they will spread beyond the frontiers of the state. The citizen will feel, think and act with the state, through it, for it, and in it; he will be one with it and the people in life, woe, and love. Through all the changing times, the folkdom and its sacredly treasured originality (*heilig bewahrte Ursprunglichkeit*) will mirror itself from generation to generation with ever increasing beauty." This folkstate would be a national democracy where the people would collaborate through its representatives in the work of legislation and through its military preparedness be ever ready to defend the fatherland. Jahn demanded a parliament which would not be "an institution for the deaf and dumb." For Jahn had learned enough from the West to realize that no government was more secure than one founded on the free participation of its citizens. Nor did he approve of standing armies. He demanded the strength of a *Friedensvolk*, of a peaceful nation, which would efficiently prepare its youth for a defensive war and thus in case of necessity have ready a nation of warriors against which any conqueror would be powerless.

Jahn's Last Years

DURING THE WARS OF LIBERATION, Jahn pleaded for the creation of a greater Germany including Switzerland (which he called *Oberland*), the Low Countries, Denmark (which he called *Nordreich*), Prussia, and Austria. Only then would Germany be able to fulfill its high humanitarian mission of universal mediator. This new Germany should build a new capital for which Jahn suggested the name Teutona, situated on the Elbe river, approximately in the center of the roads which would connect the frontier cities of the Reich, Geneva and Memel, Fiume and Copenhagen. Jahn naturally desired a powerful Germany. Weak nations that lacked the

will to power appeared to him afflicted with the gravest malady, and
he recommended for them what Hippocrates advised against cancer: "What medicine does not heal, steel heals; what steel does not
heal, fire does." Since then this ferocious medicine of fire and blood
has inspired many a struggle for the supreme good of national independence and glory, and certainly not only in Germany. Max von
Schenkendorf, one of the popular poets of the War of Liberation,
proclaimed a similar faith in his poem *"Das Eiserne Kreuz"* (The
Iron Cross):

> *Denn nur Eisen kann uns retten,*
> *Nur erlosen kann uns Blut*

> Only iron can rescue us,
> Only blood can redeem us.

Bismarck made the road to salvation through fire and sword even
better known when he wrote on May 12, 1859, to Alexander Graf
von Schleinitz, the Prussian Minister of Foreign Affairs, who
hesitated to break with Austria over the reform of the German
Confederation· "I see in our federal relations an affliction of Prussia
which we shall have sooner or later to cure, *fero et igne."* And he
repeated Schenkendorf's advice of "iron and blood" in his famous
speech of September 20, 1862, before the Budget Commission of the
Prussian Chamber of Deputies.

The War of Liberation did not fulfill Jahn's hopes. It was a
European war, not a German war. The Peace settlements were
characterized by a sense of rational moderation; they did not realize
the German nationalistic dreams. Jahn was convinced that Germany
needed a war of her own to consummate the national awakening
and to create a true German nation, and he remained faithful to
this conviction for the rest of his life. In a letter of October 2, 1831,
he wrote: "May God soon grant to Germany what I wrote in the
guest book of the Wartburg in 1815 after my return from Paris:
Germany needs a war of her own and through her own means to
feel her strength. She needs a war against Frankdom (*Franzo-
sentum*) to form herself in the fullness of her own folkdom." It
must be a truly German war. "Germans can be helped only by
Germans; Latin and Slav allies (*welsche und wendische Helfer*)
drag us even deeper into perdition. Recently the whole world has
been called up, from the Ural and Caucasian mountains to the
columns of Hercules, to defeat the French. God has given the
victory to the Germans, but all the useless allies (*Mitgeher und*

Mitesser) want to act as guardians for Germany. Germany needs her own war. . . . This time will come; for no people can be born without passing through the pangs of birth." As time went on Jahn became ever more nationalist and aggressive. The French liberal revolutions of 1830 and 1848 aroused in him only reactions of extreme hostility; he threatened Belgium, Poland, and Denmark with aggression and devoted most of his energy to the fight against liberalism. He now saw in it the greatest misfortune for Germany. The angry old man who died in 1852 summed up his life work in the inscription which he wished put on his tombstone: "German, you who pass by, and have not yet forgotten your mother tongue for French and Polish, hear my motto · shame, misery, curses, destruction, and death on you if you expect a savior from abroad."

The War Against the West

JAHN REPRESENTED the antiwestern trend of the new German nationalism At that time there was hardly any anti-German sentiment among the French. Under the influence of *Burschenschaft* and *Turnerschaft*, however, many Germans saw France and French civilization as the enemy. Christian Friedrich Ruhs, who, after 1810, held the chair for history at the newly founded University of Berlin and later became the official historian of the Prussian state, published in 1815 his book *Historische Entwicklung des Einflusses Frankreichs und der Franzosen auf Deutschland und die Deutschen (Historical Development of the Influence of France and the French upon Germany and the Germans)* which he dedicated to General Count Gneisenau, Blücher's chief of staff in the wars of 1814 and 1815. In the book, Rühs wished to prove to the German patriots that their hatred of France was historically well-founded: since the Renaissance, the French, "the villainous and odious race" (*das verruchte und abscheuliche Geschlecht*), had always opposed every German interest. The French language and French cultural influence must therefore disappear from German education, courts, and diplomatic usage. France, Rühs maintained, was the enemy not only of the Germans but of all peoples; there were only two peoples to whom France was friendly, the Turks and the Jews. The Turks, of course, hardly played a role in early nineteenth century German thought or policy; it was different with the German Jews, some of whom actively participated in influential German intellectual circles and were among the foremost admirers of Goethe, Beethoven, and Hegel.

The hostility to the West also explained Ruhs' strong anti-Jewish attitude. His *Die Anspruche der Juden an das deutsche Bürgerrecht* (*The Jews' Claim to German Citizenship*), appeared in the same year as his attack upon France. The emancipation and assimilation of the Jews into German life was rejected as a typical manifestation of the western spirit of liberalism; this was incompatible with German nationalism, for the Jews, Rühs maintained, were a nation of their own. Therefore Jews could not be at home in Germany. They should form only a tolerated alien group, excluded from public offices and the army, from guilds and corporations. To make it easier for the Germans to recognize immediately the "Hebrew enemy," Rühs proposed that the Jews should wear a yellow patch on their dress.

Leading members of the University of Jena agreed with Rühs' position against the Jews. Among those professors, highly regarded by the *Burschenschaft* as intellectual guides, were the historian Luden and the philosopher Jakob Friedrich Fries, who in 1816 published his *Über die Gefährdung des Wohlstands und Charakters der Teutschen durch die Juden* (*How the Jews Endanger the Welfare and the Character of the Germans*). The close affinity of the rising German nationalism to romanticism and its glorification of the Middle Ages and the past in general, the corresponding rejection of the western Enlightenment and its corollaries of emancipation and tolerance, the insistence upon the desirability of the development and intensification of inherited national character traits—real or imagined ones—and their uncritical praise: all these factors explain the fact that from the early nineteenth century on Germany became, "the fatherland of [modern] Anti-Semitism, where its theories were evolved and its slogans coined." In the last (eleventh) volume of the *Geschichte der Juden von den ältesten Zeiten bis zur Gegenwart* (*History of the Jews from the Oldest Time to the Present, 1853–1875*) the historian Heinrich Graetz wrote that German literature was the richest in defamatory writings against the Jews. "Since the Latin language has ceased to be the language of literature the great majority of the invectives against the Jewish race (*Stamm*) and against Judaism, and by far the most important ones, have been written in German."

The war against the West was fanned by the leading literary critic of the period, Wolfgang Menzel. A young historian, Erwin

Schuppe, in 1952, devoted to him a discerning study (*Der Burschen-schafter W. Menzel*) which is characteristic of the better under-standing of the past by German historians since 1945. Born in 1798, Menzel was too young to participate in the war of 1813; as a student in Breslau he became, however, an enthusiastic *Turner* and later a member of the Jena *Burschenschaft*. Jahn's ideas and personality deeply influenced him. From 1825 to 1849 he edited the *Literatur-blatt* of the Stuttgart *Morgenblatt für gebildete Stände* (*Morning Journal for the Educated Classes*), a paper founded in 1807 by Johann Friedrich Cotta, who was Goethe's and Schiller's publisher. After a brief interruption Menzel edited the *Literaturblatt* under his own imprint until 1869—in all for a period of forty-two years. In addition he wrote many books, some of them multi-volumed, on German literature, history, and politics. Not without justification was he called the pope of German literature. His judgments were *ex cathedra* pronouncements on political and personal ethics.

Menzel grew up in the atmosphere of the war of liberation and lived to witness the wars of unification; 1871 was to him the glorious fulfillment of what the beautiful dawn of 1813 had promised. His whole outlook was shaped by his rejection of modern western civilization and of the classical humanitarian ideal; he dared to ex-press openly what many Germans felt; his personally unimpeach-able life and his deep moral seriousness helped him to exercise a tremendous influence upon the educated German middle classes.

During his high school days in Breslau Menzel and his friends studied old German literature. "This was in accordance with the trends of the time," he wrote later in his memoirs, published after his death. "Even then I could not agree with many things which the moderns praised. Now I found a starting point enabling me to compare the moral and intellectual climates of the two periods [the modern and the old-Germanic] and to understand what some patriotic poets had meant or vaguely foreseen when they expected that the great national rising of 1813 would produce a rebirth of the nation." Zealous absorption in old German literature led Menzel, as he himself stated, to join the Breslau *Turner;* throughout his life he shared their enthusiasm for physical valor and rough manli-ness, their excessive hatred of the enemy, their uncritical enthusiasm for true Germanism.

In 1817 in Breslau some conservative patriots, especially the his-torian Karl Adolf Menzel and the natural scientist and philosopher Heinrich Steffens, protested against the *Turners'* semireligious adoration of Germanism. "This fury," Karl Adolf Menzel warned them in his *Über die Undeutschheit des neueren Deutschtums (On the non-Germanic Character of the New Germanism)*, "with which you strive in the midst of peace to excite the heart of youth against a whole people, these truly cannibalistic war-songs which you make the youth sing, this lamentable doctrine that God will not abandon his Germans . . . all this is not Christian and German, but pagan and Jewish, Jewish in the worst sense of the word, in spite of the haughtiness with which you look down from your German superiority upon Jews and Judaism."

Hatred of the enemy after liberation and victory was no longer a perhaps inevitable but passing element of wartime emotionalism; it became an ethical counterpart of the love of one's nation. Love and hatred were both cultivated with an utmost moral earnestness, an all-consuming devotion, which Jahn and his disciples proudly contrasted with the coolness, the measured balance, the rational humanitarianism of German classicism. Their nationalism was no longer concerned with human rights and individual liberty—it became a supreme value and a semireligious force in contradiction to the universal character of Christianity. There was still much talk of true Christianity, there was much enthusiasm and moral vigor among these young men, but all these qualities were put into the exclusive service of nationalism.

The same spirit animated the original *Burschenschaft* when Menzel joined it. In the 1820's, it is true, the *Burschenschaft* changed. A liberal spirit prevailed. Early in March, 1848, when the news of the Paris February revolution reached Jena, the *Burschenschaft* marched in a parade, carrying the French tricolor and singing the Marseillaise. By then, however, Menzel had taken a sharp position against any concession to the "spirit of the time," to liberalism, or to any co-operation with the French. As editor of the *Literaturblatt* he demanded the absolute primacy of the national interest in thought and art. Poetry, he taught in his *Die Deutsche Dichtung von den ältesten Zeiten bis auf die neueste Zeit (German Poetry from Ancient to Modern Times)*, must bow before the majesty of the nation whose inalienable property it is. The new historiography must oppose the false doctrine that Greco-Roman antiquity was the high watermark of history; in truth this honor belonged to the Germanic-Christian Middle Ages.

Sometimes the Christian element appeared of lesser importance; in his book *On German Mythology* (1855) Menzel proclaimed Odin as the "innermost spirit of the German people, the personification of that driving power which made the German people supreme in world history." When the Germans accepted the new religion, Menzel insisted, they saved Christianity from inevitable corruption by the physically and morally decadent Romans; the Germans understood the real depth of the Christian message and their moral character was further ennobled by the new religion. So Menzel rejected everything for which Goethe stood. Most Germans continued to pay homage to Goethe, and many regarded him as a national asset; later the National Socialists and the Communists tried to interpret him as their forerunner. Menzel was more sincere. his attacks against Goethe were often ridiculed as extreme, though they only drew the consequences from an attitude shared by the disciples of Arndt and Jahn.

Goethe represented to Menzel the three fundamental evils: an irresponsible individualism, a demoralizing classicism, and an effeminate sensualism and estheticism. Goethe, Menzel complained bitterly, showed neither understanding for, nor interest in, the Germanic-Christian Middle Ages and national honor. To Goethe cultural values were universal; to Menzel and to his many followers —not only among the Germans—the national originality was the supreme value. The greatest evil in the eyes of nationalists, not only in Germany but elsewhere as well, was what the Germans called *Überfremdung* (alienation). Goethe represented this alienation of the truly German by classic and western influences and thereby weakened and undermined the German mind and character as the nationalists interpreted it.

Menzel saw history as a sequence of plots to weaken or to destroy the Germans. Even the Renaissance with its reawakening of sensuous estheticism was interpreted as such a plot to undermine the Christian-German empire of the Middle Ages. Menzel believed that the Latins were always hostile to Germany. They had corrupted generations of German intellectuals, who in the name of civilization debilitated Germany's vital energies.

Situated in the center of Europe, open to influences and incursions from all sides, deprived by historical fate and enemy envy of their national unity and world-historical rank, the Germans felt that they had been ill-treated by history. Therefore they had a right— and even a moral obligation—to take recourse to exceptional measures in order to remedy this intolerable situation. The supposed uniqueness of their historical fate led many Germans to justify actions which they themselves regarded as immoral if other nations resorted to them. German intellectuals and historians appealed to Germany's historical needs to distinguish German *Lebensrecht* (rights imposed by the necessities of life) from the rights and obliga-tions of other historically more privileged or normal nations. Did German history not present a tragedy and did not this tragic fate demand that the Germans put the achievement of their national goals ahead of universal rights or of consideration for other peo-ples? Thus Menzel could write in his book *Die deutsche Literatur* (1836): "The hero and statesman, who subjects everything to his tyrannical will and tramples upon justice can be excused, if his-torical situations [*gebieterische Ereignisse*] demand his terrorism or if the greatness of his deeds forces us to admire him." "Only the winning of a great war," Menzel wrote in the first issue of his *Literaturblatt* for 1849, "can bring to Germany fulfillment of all her hopes."

In his innumerable articles and books, Menzel represented the link between Father Jahn and the generation which greeted Bis-marck's success in the war against France. But the very violence of Menzel's language in his polemical writings against other Ger-mans proves that in the four decades between 1825 and 1866 very many Germans held views contrary to those propagated by him. Some Germans remained faithful to older German traditions and to the universal values of Christianity or humanism. Others strove for a rapprochement with France, on the basis of a common enlightened liberalism, for the full integration of German intellectual life into the mainstream of modern western civilization. The war against the West and the idealization of the nation were in no way shared by all Germans. One of the German patriots who resisted the anti-French trend was Heinrich Heine, a native of the Rhineland which historically formed a bridge uniting Germany and the West.

Chapter Five

HEINRICH HEINE:
POET AND PATRIOT

Heine, the Rhinelander

HEINRICH HEINE WAS BORN in 1797 in Düsseldorf on the Rhine where he went to school while the Rhineland was under French rule. Like many of his compatriots he preserved a deep attachment to the memory of Napoleon and to the progressive character of the French administration. This attachment was heightened by the contrast which political and social life in most of Germany offered in the years following the War of Liberation. Liberated Germany knew less freedom than it had known under the French rule or than France enjoyed under Louis XVIII. The Rhineland had become part of Prussia and Prussia co-operated closely with Austria and Russia to keep liberty confined to the West. The nationalist temper aroused by the struggle against Napoleon; romantic historical thought glorifying the nonwestern national traditions; the feeling of moral and spiritual superiority over the French and their Revolution, of which only the failures and extremes were recognized—all these at this time turned even many German liberals against France. If they looked to the West during those years, they preferred Germanic England, the roots of whose traditional liberty were believed to be firmly implanted in old Saxon soil. In Germany, where constitutional rights were hardly known and little fought for, Johann Friedrich Benzenberg, a physicist in Düsseldorf, could smugly write that "in France one finds freedom and representative government only on paper and in words. The thing itself is never there."

Heine, as a Rhinelander, found himself, in 1814, a subject of Prussia. The territorial settlement of the Congress of Vienna unwittingly helped Prussia's claim to German leadership by giving it the Rhineland with its Catholic population There, until the opening years of the nineteenth century, the ecclesiastical principalities of Cologne and Trier—cities and bishoprics dating from Roman times —had shut off the people from modern life. Their secularization as part of the French Empire or of the Rhenish Confederation opened them up to the liberating influences of the West. Thus when Prussian rule was imposed upon the Rhinelanders in 1814 they accepted it only with greatest reluctance.

Originally Prussia did not wish to annex the Rhineland. Anxious to consolidate its hold upon central and eastern Germany, Prussia demanded Saxony which would have assured Prussia a homogeneous population and a contiguous area from the Baltic Sea to the Sudeten Mountains The Catholic ruling house of Saxony would have been compensated by part of the Rhineland. In this case the course of European history would have been changed. Prussia would not have mounted the watch on the Rhine nor felt the need for annexing Hannover and Hessen-Nassau in order to join its new western provinces with its possessions on and beyond the Elbe river. Ironically, Talleyrand, the French representative to the Congress, following his country's traditional policy, was more afraid of Austria on the Rhine than of Prussia; at his suggestion the Rhineland became a Prussian province.

Heinrich von Treitschke, a fervently pro-Prussian historian, stressed in his *German History in the Nineteenth Century* the hostility with which the Catholic Rhinelanders received the Prussian administration. They complained as bitterly as did the Poles in the eastern provinces of Prussia about the "hordes of foreign intruders (the Prussians) who overrun their (the Rhinelanders') homeland." They felt no affinity for the "cold and rigid Prussianism." Proud and happy about their fertile country and their one-thousand-years-older civilization, the Rhinelanders who—to quote Treitschke—were then entirely unfamiliar with the German world beyond Frankfurt, were firmly convinced of their superiority over everything Prussian.

Joseph Gorres, the famous patriotic publicist whose *Rheinischer Merkur* had aroused the Rhinelanders against French rule in 1814, now turned against the Prussians. To him they were no better than Lithuanians, eastern barbarians. In February, 1816, the Prussian administration suppressed the *Rheinischer Merkur* and three years later Gorres had to take refuge in French Strasbourg. His deep resentiment at the incorporation of his native land into Prussia made him in his later years, when he became professor of history at the University of Munich, the leading spokesman against Prussia and Protestantism. The Prussian system caused the Rhinelanders to forget what they had suffered under Napoleon. "They remembered only the blessings of the French administration," Treitschke wrote. "They raved about the glorious ideas of 1789, they preferred to read French or Belgian newspapers, and were convinced that the sun over Europe would rise in the West." From the Rhineland the Prussian agrarian expert Schwerz reported to the Chancellor Prince Hardenberg in August, 1816, that "There is no one who would not thank God on his knees, if the land came again under French domination."

After 1830 western and southwestern Germany bordering on France—the Rhineland, the Palatinate, Frankfurt, and Baden—assumed for two decades a historical importance which it regained only after 1945. The people there looked to France and Belgium where the liberal cause had triumphed. The university students who joined their provincial fraternities (*Landsmannschaften*) called "Rhenania" wore not the Germanic colors of black, red and gold, but the blue, white, and red of the French tricolor. With a determination which grew with time, the Rhinelanders clung to the Napoleonic Code. Treitschke wondered why the liberators of 1814 allowed the laws of the foreign conqueror to continue. In fact, in the Prussian Rhineland, in the Bavarian Rhenish Palatinate, and in Baden the Code Napoleon remained in force until 1901. A quarter of a century after the liberation of the Rhineland the French laws were regarded as almost sacrosanct, "so completely," wrote Treitschke, "had French and Belgian ideas captivated the minds in western Germany." The Prussian government, "intimidated by the obstinate defiance of Rhenish particularism" ordered an official translation of the five Napoleonic Codes, and this small stout book with the blue, white, and red stripes on the cover, "remained the political Bible of all true Rhinelanders." If the Prussian monarchy insisted on establishing unity of legal systems throughout its territories, the Rhinelanders argued, the backward East should follow the advanced West, and the French laws should be introduced in the eastern provinces, too. Catholics and liberals in the Rhineland were equally in favor of the four freedoms of the Belgian constitution of 1831 which was admired as a model—the freedom of church, school, press, and associations. The public opinion of all German lands in the west and the south backed the Rhinelanders.

Heine, German Jew

HEINE FELT A DEEPER AFFECTION for Germany than most Rhine-landers. Two circumstances complicated Heine's relations with his fatherland—his French wit or *esprit*, in which serious-minded Germans suspected a lack of depth or sincerity, and his Jewish ancestry. This ancestry did not prevent most of his relatives from doing well in the European society of their time. Of his paternal uncles one died a prosperous business man in Bordeaux, and two others gained great wealth and influence as bankers and merchants in Hamburg. Of his two brothers one became a rich newspaper owner in Vienna and was ennobled, the other had a lucrative medical practice in St. Petersburg. But Heine's case was different; he was a highly sensitive poet and, with all his alert intelligence and sharp wit, a romantic dreamer. In 1819 he entered the Rhineland University of Bonn which the Prussians had reopened the year before to counter the prevailing French influence. There Arndt taught history and the romantic critic. August Wilhelm Schlegel, literature. As their student, Heine was enraptured by the glories of the newly discovered German middle ages. He joined the *Burschenschaft* and when he was later expelled it was not for lack of patriotism but for lack of chastity.

At the beginning of the nineteenth century it was more difficult for a German poet of Jewish ancestry to feel himself at one with his native land than for his confreres in western Europe. In the German speaking lands the integration of the Jews to whom, as to other sections of the people, the French Revolution had brought the promise of emancipation, produced greater tensions and yet was intellectually more fertile than elsewhere. In its Jewish problem too, Germany occupied, culturally and politically, a middle position between East and West: backward compared with the West, far advanced seen from the East. In eastern Europe even the late nineteenth century brought no steps toward Jewish emancipation. There the Jews remained an unassimilated minority with their own language and civilization, leading their own separate life. In western Europe and in North America, on the other hand, the integration of the Jews into existing political and cultural communities was facilitated by the prevailing liberal climate. Central Europe, in the first half of the nineteenth century, lacked both an accepted political form and a strong liberal tradition. No framework existed into which the Jews who eagerly sought to participate in the new exhilarating experience of European culture and free society could be integrated.

Heine believed in a spiritual kinship of Germans and Jews. Such a kinship explained, for him, the virulence of German anti-Semitism. "The affinity which prevails between the two ethical peoples (*den beiden Völkern der Sittlichkeit*), the Jews and the Germans, is indeed remarkable," Heine wrote in his analysis of Shakespeare's Jessica (1838). "This elective affinity did not originate in historical facts, though the Bible, the great Jewish family chronicle, became the educational manual of the whole Germanic world, and Jews and Germans faced from early times the same implacable enemy, the Romans, and thus were allies. The affinity has a deeper root: both peoples are fundamentally so much alike that one might regard ancient Palestine as an oriental Germany, just as one might regard today's Germany as the house of the Holy Word, the mother soil of prophetdom, the citadel of the pure Spirit."

Heine's loyalty, in spite of all his misfortunes in the Germany of his time, belonged to Germany, this house of the Holy Word, the mother soil of the language which he loved and mastered as few Germans ever did. "I know that I am one of the most German animals that exists," he wrote to a friend in 1824. "At heart I love everything German more than anything else in the world. It fills me with pride and joy; and my breast is a register of German feelings just as my books are archives of German songs." Thirty years later, nearing death, Heine added a concluding remark to a moving memorial which he had written in 1844 for Ludwig Marcus, a friend of his young years in Berlin when they had struggled together for Jewish emancipation in their fatherland. Looking back upon those years Heine warned that the Jews must finally realize that they would achieve their emancipation only when the emancipation of all Germans should be fully won and secure. The cause of the German Jews, Heine insisted, was identical with that of the German people. "The Jews must not demand as Jews what has long been due them as Germans."

Heine was born and brought up in the Jewish faith. The political and social conditions in Germany during his lifetime forced him to remain conscious of his Jewish descent long after he abandoned the faith. His attitude toward Jews and Judaism was as ambivalent and ambiguous as his attitude toward democracy and other popular causes. As a young man he had a short period of pride in his Jewishness as he lived through a similar period of priding himself in being a soldier in the cause of democracy. But in his mature years he could never bring himself to accept his Jewishness as an obvious part of his being or to learn how to live with it It appeared to him as a misfortune, thousands of years old, worse than poverty or physical suffering, a burden which the Jews carried with them from the Nile valley, an unhealthy old-Egyptian faith:

> Das tausendjahrige Familienubel,
> Die aus dem Niltal mitgeschleppte Plage,
> Der altagyptisch ungesunde Glauben.

No medical art could heal this "incurably deep affliction," Heine went on. "Will time, the eternal goddess, one day lift this somber woe, which passes down from father to son,—will ever the grandson recover and be sane and joyful?" With astonishment Heine noted Börne's attitude whenever his critics mentioned his Jewish descent. "He was even amused, when, given the spotless conduct of his life, his enemies had nothing worse to say of him than the fact that he descended from a tribe which had once filled the world with its fame and which, in spite of all degradation, had not yet entirely lost its ancient consecration. He often even gloried in all this although in a facetious way, and once, in a parody of Mirabeau's words, he told a Frenchman: *"Jésus Christ—qui en parenthèse était mon cousin—a prêché l'égalité."* Heine never could achieve this acceptance of the misfortune of being a Jew.

This misfortune caught up with him while he was rotting in his mattress tomb In April, 1849, he confessed that he was no longer a pleasure loving rather corpulent Hellene, but only a poor deadly sick Jew, an emaciated picture of misery, an unhappy man. But the miracle was not Heine's much discussed conversion to God who sometimes appeared to him in a Jewish but equally often in a Protestant or Catholic manifestation. The miracle was that a helpless paralytic, racked with agonizing pain for over eight years, heroically preserved his serene wit. His poetic genius did not weaken or falter. He never allowed hopeless apathy to gain hold of his mind. To the very last, as poet, charmer, and lover he retained his passionate imagination and his creative power.

No believer ever has spoken with such irreverence of God while being on such an intimate footing with Him as the dying Heine.

The well known poem "Disputation" between a Rabbi and a Fran-
ciscan Friar before Donna Blanca is full of blasphemies. Heine's
Mephistophelian nature asserts itself in Donna Blanca's judgment
that she has no idea which of the two disputants is right, but that
both stink equally. To quote Professor Butler, if religion did not
console Heine it always exhilarated him greatly. "The good God
experiments with me," he told a visitor shortly before his death,
"but I wish he had chosen someone else for that purpose." In his
last "Lazarus" poems Heine faced the problem of Job but with a
gruesome irony.

> *Woran liegt die Schuld? Ist etwa*
> *Unser Herr nicht ganz allmachtig?*
> *Oder treibt er selbst den Unfug?*
> *Ach, das wäre niedertrachtig.*
> *Also fragen wir bestandig,*
> *Bis man uns mit einer Handvoll*
> *Erde endlich stopft die Mauler—*
> *Aber ist das eine Antwort?*

> Whose is the responsibility? Is perhaps
> Our Lord not fully all-powerful?
> Or does He Himself play these mischievous tricks?
> Oh, that would be beastly.
> Thus we ask incessantly,
> Until one stops our mouths
> With a handful of earth.
> But is this a reply?

Heine's dazzling vitality and his genuine high spirits again and
again surprised those who came to mourn the suffering poet in his
airless and cheerless sick room. His love for the Greek Gods survived to the end. *The Gods in Exile* was hailed, when it appeared in
1853, as his masterpiece in prose. Nowhere in European literature
have the ancient Gods in their downfall and degradation come so
alive as through the deep love and compassion bestowed upon them
by a suffering Jew. The Greek Gods no longer represented, as they
did for Goethe, measured loveliness but the ecstasy of life, and Dionysus emerged among them more and more as the leading figure. No
wonder that Nietzsche loved Heine. Goethe and his generation of
classical humanists had reverently imitated the Greeks. Heine, and
Nietzsche after him, brought them to life in the modern world.

Heine, Poet of Young Germany

EVEN MORE THAN NIETZSCHE in his mountain solitude, Heine in his mattress tomb was the singer of exuberant life defying stark tragedy. He had not the purity and strength of Nietzsche's personal conduct; in spite of his all-too-human failings, his accomplishment was the greater. In Heine modernity triumphed over classicism and romanticism, quietism and provincialism. In this respect Heine's prose was as important as his poetry in artistic value and lasting influence. No previous German poetry or prose was so immediate as his. The technical achievement of his first poems, Professor Butler writes, "lies in the skill with which he made magic with plain speech, so simple and direct that his vocabulary has all the soul and savor of ordinary life miraculously melting into music."

Heine was the first German poet to deny implicitly the existence of unpoetical themes and words. His mastery grew with time and reached its zenith in his last years. His poetical imagination radiates through many morally reprehensible statements and makes controversies of a long dead past interesting even to today's readers. The French critic Barbey d'Aurevilly, a writer often as aggressive as Heine but in his political convictions an uncompromising Catholic, said of Heine: "He is always a poet. He is a poet in poetry and in prose. He is a poet everywhere, even in the most erroneous ideas which he sometimes has, this man of his time! He was a poet (I myself saw it once) and he could not help being one, even when he spoke of a piece of cheese. . . . Whether he praises or vilifies men or causes, whether he is mistaken or whether he is right, Heine is as naturally a poet as others breathe."

With Heine German poetry and prose came closer to life than they had ever been before. In that sense he was a true liberator at a time when Young Germany longed to break through the confinements of tradition.

Young Germany was a short-lived literary movement of revolt, similar to the Storm and Stress of sixty years before. The Young Germans felt themselves at one with Young Europe in their preoccupation with political and social problems. They appealed to youth and demanded not only social but sexual emancipation; they spoke out for rationalism and democracy; they had neither a clear political plan nor were they great writers; but they succeeded in shocking the authorities and the reading public. Their leaders were the critic Ludof Wienbarg and the novelist and playwright Karl Ferdinand Gutzkow. In 1835 they wrote to Heine as the *princeps iuventutis* to help them found their new organ *Deutsche Revue*.

One year before this, Ludof Wienbarg dedicated his *Aesthetische Feldzuge (Esthetic Campaigns)* to Young Germany. In his protest against legitimacy hallowed by history, against romanticism, against Metternich and Hegel, Wienbarg appealed to Luther whom he misinterpreted, as did Heine, as a fighter for liberty. Wienbarg opposed the orthodoxy of the Church and the estheticism of the German classics. His great slogan was Life. "Life is life's greatest and highest purpose," he wrote. "Out of our ashes a new European Hellenism will rise," he proclaimed, a Hellenism inspired by Heine's sensuality not by Goethe's love of the perfect form. The Young Germans demanded the untrammeled expression of the senses. Heinrich Laube edited the works of Johann Jakob Wilhelm Heinse, the great eroticist of the preceding generation, and wrote a novel, *Das junge Europa (Young Europe)*, which appeared in three volumes between 1833 and 1837. In 1834, after Schleiermacher's death, Gutzkow republished the great theologian's defense of Friedrich Schlegel's erotic novel *Lucinde* (1799) and proclaimed that love and marriage needed as urgently to be reformed as other social disorders of the time. The next year his *Wally, the Doubter* attacked conventional matrimony and religion and became, to quote Walter Höllerer, "the most discussed and shocking German novel of the nineteenth century."

Treitschke blamed the new literature and its often wild and diffuse language, which was so alien to Heine's wit, for its alleged lack of patriotism and contrasted it with the *Teutschtümelei* of the patriots of 1814. "What distance," he exclaimed, "between Jahn's Teutonism and this new literary generation. There everything is strength to the point of coarse brutality; here—affected and farfetched; there is faith, here is sneering; instead of the patriotic zeal of linguistic purifiers there is an ostentatious use of alien words which even surpasses that of the liberals in the south German parliaments. The tremendous power of our language to take over alien words has always been a sign of our strength, because the German as a born conqueror takes his property wherever he finds it; but like every great talent, this power of assimilation has been often abused and never more than in these days. Out of pure vanity, because they thought everything French more distinguished and because they wished to create the impression that they were at home in Paris, the Young German writers burdened their style, which was artifical to begin with, with a mass of tasteless and sumptuous French."

In the same spirit Wolfgang Menzel denounced the writings of Gutzkow and other Young Germans for immorality, irreligion, and lack of patriotism. He wrote in his *Literaturblatt* on September 11, 1835, about Gutzkow's novel *Wally*: "I find here a novel by Mr. Gutzkow which is puffed up with impudence and obscenity, and now I must perform my duty . . . Such mentality can grow only out of the deepest mire of demoralization, out of a brothel. . . . Mr. Gutzkow has taken it upon himself to transplant this wicked French shame (*Affenschande*), which, in the arms of harlots, slanders God, to Germany." Two months later Menzel wrote of Wienbarg that "this new Frankfurt school of slander and vice (*Frankfurter Laster- und Lasterschule*) smuggles [into Germany] a horrible lewdness under the mask of French republicanism." The modern reader who, because of Menzel's indignation, expects to find some daring eroti- cism in *Wally* will be disappointed. The novel ponders the chang- ing position of women, or rather of the new woman, in the light of literary and human events which were then causing a great stir in Germany.

In 1834 Varnhagen von Ense published a book in memory of his wife Rahel who had died the year before. Her daring thoughts about women's rights and child education, her brilliant insights into litera- ture, politics, and the human heart had won her many admirers, among them Heine. In the same year, Bettina von Arnim (Bettina Brentano) published *Goethe's Correspondence with a Child*, in which she saw Goethe, with greater clarity than anyone before her, not as the master or the Olympian but as the liberator who through his life and example encouraged men and artists to live and to create out of their innermost free nature.

Stronger than the impact of these printed words was the impres- sion caused at the end of 1834 by the suicide of Charlotte Stieglitz, the young wife of a mediocre but ambitious writer, who killed her- self in the vain hope that a great grief would mature her husband both as a man and as a poet. Alexander von Humboldt praised Charlotte as a new Alcestis: she appeared as a strong personality who was not satisfied with pale ideals and half-hearted deeds but was faithful to herself unto death and whose sacrifice breathed the spirit of the new vital era. Men have "world-hearts (*Weltherzen*) at present," she wrote her husband shortly before her death. "That is the heavenly character of our epoch: that is the young generation;

therein lies the courage to live. Join the young generation . . . then you will find in their world-wide and world-open interests, the right subject matter for your work. . . . You don't need to talk much about the new age and about liberty, your whole work will breathe the spirit of liberty."

In the same vein a literary critic, Gustav Schlesier, called upon Gutzkow in 1833 to be modern, to live in his own time and out of his own life. "You must show your heart's blood," he wrote, "fit the character of the present time! You must tear open your breast! The writer of today must be only 'modern,' specifically 'modern.' German literature must follow the road which George Sand has traced for all European literatures." *Life* was the great slogan. A few years later Georg Herwegh characteristically called his poems *Gedichte eines Lebendigen (Poems of a Man Alive)*. Outside the demand for a new literature quickened by zest for life and responsive to all demands of the time, the modern feeling found in the 1840's its strongest expression in a new earth-bound religiosity. Herwegh called upon the Germans to tear the iron crosses out of the earth and to transform them into swords. Gottfried Kinkel, who started life as an orthodox theologian before he became a poet and an art historian, wrote in 1846 his *"Männerlied"* whose most characteristic lines read:

Lasst die alten Weiber sich
Um den Himmel schelten!
Aber freie Manner wir
Lassen das nicht gelten.
Gegen dich, o Vaterland,
Sind uns nichts als eitler Tand
Alle Sternenwelten.
Denket alle denn zuerst
An die grune Erde . .

(Let old women scold each other about Heaven!
For us free men this has no validity.
Compared with Thee, oh Fatherland,
All the starry worlds are for us nothing
      but vain trumpery . .
Therefore all of you think first and foremost
      of this green Earth . . .)

Menzel's articles drew the attention of the German governments to the dangers of a supposed Young German conspiracy. The works of the leading Young German writers were placed under perpetual

ban and the name of Heinrich Heine was added to the list. In reality
the Young German writers were as deeply patriotic as those of
Young Italy or Young Poland. The Germany of their dreams was
a proud and great nation, rejuvenated and strengthened by the new
European forces of liberation which would end the oppression of the
creative personality and the misery of the suffering masses.

Heine and the Revolution

HEINE WAS AS LITTLE A REVOLUTIONARY as were the Young Germans.
His enemies suspected him of being a cosmopolitan exile fighting
in the service of the international revolution. Heine himself in his
younger years loved to present himself as a soldier in the cause of
human liberty. On his travels through Italy when he passed the
battlefield of Marengo his heart lept with joy. Napolean's victory
over the Austrians recalled to him the great struggle for emancipation going on in Europe after Waterloo. At that moment Heine had
no greater wish than to be engaged all his life in that struggle for
emancipation. "I really do not know," he wrote, "whether I deserve
that one day my coffin should be adorned with a wreath of laurel.
Poetry, however much I have loved it, has always been only a sacred
plaything for me or a consecrated means to heavenly ends. I have
never attached great value to poetic fame. I am very little concerned
whether people praise or blame my songs. But you must lay a sword
on my coffin, for I was a worthy soldier in the war for the liberation
of mankind."

For obvious reasons Heine favored emancipation. "What is the
great task of our time?" he asked on the battlefield of Marengo. "It
is emancipation. Not only that of the Irish, the Greeks, the Jews of
Frankfurt, the Negro in the West Indies, and similar oppressed peoples, but the emancipation of the whole world, especially of Europe,
which has grown to maturity and which tears itself away from the
iron leading-strings of the privileged, the aristocracy." Heine after
all was the subject of a country which granted Jewish emancipation
only thirteen years after his death and where the prerogatives of the
aristocracy as well as certain limitations on Jewish rights persisted
for half a century longer. Thus self-interest dictated that Heine be
a soldier in the cause of emancipation, but his heart was rarely in it.

The image which Heine drew of himself as a soldier in the service of liberty was hardly shared by his contemporaries, among whom were many who certainly sacrificed for what they conceived to be the liberation of mankind. They were dedicated men, he was an artist. By nature and intention he was too complex a personality to be able to serve any cause but his own. He had no party line and not even a consistent personal line. He contradicted himself according to the needs of the situation, the mood of the hour, often for the mere playful pleasure of mask and pretense. The lucidity of his intelligence and his hedonistic self-indulgence made it impossible for him to share the deep convictions of a Ludwig Börne or a Georg Büchner. In spite of his lucidity he inclined—as individuals and groups often do—to identify his personal cause and interest with that of human liberty.

Heine's greatness as a writer stems from a unique blend of highly sensitive poet and romantic dreamer with a hardly surpassed sharp wit in his analysis of men and trends. This blend was his weakness too. It was responsible for the many lines which unexpectedly and painfully shock the reader. Yet among the bewildering dissonances of Heine's life and work there persisted throughout a two-fold loyalty: his dedication as a poet and his faithful love of his fatherland. For these causes the man Heine lived, not as a soldier yet with every fiber of his heart. Rightfully he asked to have engraved on his tombstone the words, "Here lies a German poet." The accent falls with equal weight on both words, German and poet.

Heine spoke the truth when he wrote from Paris to Heinrich Laube in November, 1835. "I stayed away from all the agitations of Jacobinism." When he came to Paris a deep gulf separated him from his German fellow-exiles. They were republicans and democrats. He was a convinced monarchist. He warned against the revolutionaries "who in their logical frenzy seek to eradicate by their arguments from the depth of our hearts all the reverence which is ordained by the ancient sacrament of monarchy." From the beginning he opposed the republican movement in France. "A royalist by innate inclination I am becoming one from conviction in France." As an artist he disliked the bourgeoisie and he feared the proletariat. "Though Communism," he wrote in 1842, "is at present yearning away its life in forgotten garrets on wretched straw pallets, it is still the gloomy hero to whom a great if transitory part is assigned in the modern tragedy, and which only awaits its cue to enter the stage." The victory of communism, he was convinced, will threaten "our whole modern civilization, the laborious achievements of so many centuries, the fruit of the noblest efforts of our predecessors."

As a poet Heine felt "a mysterious horror" at the thought that the great crude mass which some called the People and others called the Mob would establish its rule. "We would willingly sacrifice ourselves for the people," he wrote, not entirely truthfully as far as he was concerned, "for self-sacrifice is among our most refined pleasures, but the pure and sensitive part of the poet shrinks from any close personal association with the people and even more are we horrified at the thought of its caresses from which God may preserve us." He shuddered at the thought of the coming mass-civilization. "Democratic hatred of poetry," one manuscript note reads, "Parnassus is to be leveled, macadamized, and where once an idle poet climbed and listened to the nightingales, there will soon be a flat highway, a railroad where the locomotive roars and rushes past the busy crowd."

Heine disliked the middle class as much as he distrusted the masses. In his *Letters on the French Stage* he complained that tragedy was unthinkable without the heroic faith which the bourgeoisie had destroyed by overthrowing the aristocracy. A society with a free press and parliamentary institutions could not develop, Heine wrote, great personalities indispensible to great art. "I do not even wish to mention that the republicans in France use the freedom of the press to debase all conspicuous greatness by sneer and slander." It meant the end of the poetic universe when the world was guided by the calculating mind of the middle class instead of by "the man of genius, by beauty, by love, and by strength." In words like these Heine sounded like a typical romantic German poet.

The revolution of 1848 meant little to Heine. He had always distrusted barricades and the enthusiasm of the people manning them. He paid hardly any attention to the revolution. The last time he ventured out before being entombed in his mattress grave—it was in May, 1848—he dragged himself to the Louvre where he lay for a long time at the feet of the goddess of beauty, of Our dear Lady of Milo. In April, 1848, when all European liberals celebrated the Spring of the People, he wrote to Alfred Meissner: "You can easily understand my feelings when I saw the revolution taking place before my very eyes. You know that I was not a republican, and you will not be surprised that I did not become one. The world's present doings and hopes are foreign to my heart. . . . Gladly would I flee the turmoil of public life that so oppresses me to the imperishable springtime of poetry and imperishable things, if only I could walk better and were not so sick." He no longer claimed to be a worthy soldier in the struggle for the liberation of mankind. He was proud of being a poet. "It is a great thing," he wrote in his Confessions in 1853, "to be a poet, and above all to be a great lyrical poet in Germany, which, in the two fields of philosophy and song, has surpassed all other nations."

His dislike of the Paris revolution was so great that he wrote in March, 1848, to his mother that the spectacle of the revolution had depressed him so much, physically and morally, that he thought of leaving revolutionary France, where liberty had triumphed, for tranquil Germany, either with or without his French wife. "My wife is behaving very well," he continued in his typical satirical way. "If she were not behaving well, I would now give her her liberty as all kings give now liberty to their peoples; she would then see what comes of liberty. You have no idea of the misery now prevailing here. The whole world is going to be free and bankrupt." But soon he abandoned any thought of leaving Paris without his wife. She was indispensible to him. His staying in France did not increase his sympathy for French democracy or republican liberty. He pinned all his hopes on Louis Napolean, the authority of whose name he expected to counteract the great evil of republican liberty. "Like Louis Philippe [in 1830]," Heine wrote, "Louis Bonaparte is [in 1848] a miracle which a kind fate has granted the French."

Heine felt an even deeper distrust of republican democracy in Germany When the democratic revolution of 1848 swept Germany, Heine observed the elemental popular forces behind the revolution. "The news which I received from my country," he wrote in August, 1848 to a French friend, "increases my anxiety. . . . Our enemies have gotten the upper hand in Germany. The so-called national parties, the fanatics of Germanism, are strutting about in their overbearing conceit, as ridiculous as they are coarse. Their boastful rantings are incredible. They dream that their turn at playing the leading role in world history has arrived and that they will gather all the lost German tribes from east and west to the fold of German nationalism." Heine was full of pride in being a German and he cherished a vague idea of a universal brotherhood in which Germany would lead the world; therefore he was even more apprehensive of the destructive potentialities of the Germans than of those of the French and other peoples.

Heine, who is so often regarded as a liberal or even a radical, shared with the conservative Swiss historian Jakob Burckhardt an extreme distaste for democratic republicanism and nationalism. Both were convinced that the triumph of the people would destroy cultural values. Both saw demons lurking in the lower orders of society, above all in the great cities, ready to break out and submerge the achievements of civilization. Heine lived for more than a quarter of a century in Paris, yet the great mysterious city left hardly a trace in his poems although it was then the unchallenged center of the civilized world and inspired the modernity of Baudelaire's poetry.

Heine the Patriot

HEINE'S GERMAN PATRIOTISM made him feel grateful to Prussia, he wrote in 1838, for Germanizing the Rhineland. He found Prussian measures against the Rhenish Catholics "much too mild." If Prussia did not make use of the present tranquil period to proceed with due severity the Rhineland might be lost to Germany in critical times. "What do the pious Catholics in Munich care," Heine wrote, "whether the people on the Rhine talk German or French; to them it is sufficient that the Mass be sung there in Latin." Heine cared very much that the people in the Rhineland should speak German.

It was not a cosmopolitan enthusiasm for liberty which brought Heine to Paris in 1831. He went there because Germany offered him no desirable position. "If I cannot find one," he wrote to Varnhagen von Ense, "then I shall go to Paris, where I unfortunately have to play a role in which all of my artistic and poetic capacities will be destroyed." Heine was convinced that he could be creative only in Germany. After his return from a journey to Germany he wrote his publisher in December, 1843: "I have written many verses on my trip. They come with great ease when I breathe German air."

Although he was received with great warmth and friendliness by the French, he never ceased to feel an exile in Paris. Here he differed from Goethe and Nietzsche. In his later years Goethe regarded the French language and civilization as the most refined in Europe. Nietzsche preferred French to German and Rainer Maria Rilke spent his last years writing French poetry. Nietzsche and Rilke lived voluntarily and gladly in exile.

Such an unpatriotic attitude was unthinkable to Heine. "He felt exiled in spirit where German was not spoken," Hugo Bieber wrote. "This feeling overwhelmed him in England and in Italy, and it did not leave him even in France. For a long while he was convinced that German philosophy was superior to the thought of all other peoples and that it alone adequately comprehended the development of world history and the spirit of the age. On this point Heine changed his mind in the last years of his life. But to the end he insisted that the poetry of no other people attained the artistic heights of German song and that German song alone was true poetry. During the quarter of a century in which he lived in France, the French language as a poetic medium and French cultural life left him cool."

As a young man Heine adored German antiquities and glorified the *Nibelungenlied,* the great national epic of the Middle Ages. In the conclusion of his essay on Poland he deeply regretted the neglect of "our most sacred and important concern," the study of ancient German monuments. "May the time soon come," he wrote, "when the Middle Ages will receive its full due and when no silly apostle of the shallow Enlightenment will produce an inventory of the shadows of the great [Medieval] picture in order to flatter his dear period of light; when no learned schoolboy will draw a comparison between the Cologne Cathedral and the Pantheon, between the *Nibelungenlied* and the *Odyssey,* when one will recognize the splendors of the Middle Ages in their organic context, compare them only with themselves, and call the *Nibelungenlied* a versified cathedral and the Cologne Cathedral a stony *Nibelungenlied."*

No romantic poet could have pleaded more eloquently for the German Middle Ages or disagreed more fully with Hegel, who in his *Vorlesungen über die Aesthetik* sharply repudiated the romantic Teutomania which thirty years later triumphed in Wagner's *Ring der Nibelungen.* "The Burgundians, the vengeance of Chriemhilde, the deeds of Siegfried, the whole condition of life, the fate of the whole declining clan, the Nordic spirit, King Etzel, etc. . . . all that no longer has any kind of living connection with our domestic, civic, and legal life, with our private and public institutions. The history of Christ, Jerusalem, Bethlehem, the Roman law, even the Trojan War, hold much more of the present for us than the adventure of the Nibelungs, which are for the national consciousness past history, a past completely swept away. To insist upon making something national—a popular bible—of such material is utterly stale and inane."

Heine, however, remained faithful to the German Middle Ages even in exile. Upon his arrival in France he did not seek out the glorious monuments of French history or letters. He went first to the Royal Library and asked to see the famous Manesse manuscript of the German Minnesinger which the French had carried away from Heidelberg in the seventeenth century. "For years," Heine wrote, "I have longed to see with my own eyes those precious pages which have preserved for us, among others, the poems of Walther von der Vogelweide, the greatest German lyric poet." He never ceased to long for German poetry and its inspiration. Thus, in 1840, he complained that only those who lived in exile knew what one's love for the fatherland is, "love of one's fatherland with all its sweet terrors and its wistful woes " But among all those exiled, Heine cried, none was unhappier than the poet. "Happy are those who quietly rot in the jails of their fatherland . . . for those jails are a *home* with iron bars, and German air blows through them and the jailer speaks German unless he is entirely mute. . . . Perhaps you know what bodily exile means, but only a German poet can imagine spiritual exile,—a poet forced to speak and write in French all day and even during the night to sigh in French at the bosom of his beloved. My thoughts, too, are exiled, exiled into a foreign language."

Since he was so loyal we can understand why Heine, in the quarter century he lived in France, never became a French citizen. Leading Frenchmen urged him to become naturalized and promised him in return anything his heart desired. "It was the foolish pride of the German poet," he wrote in August, 1854, two years before his death, "which kept me from becoming a Frenchman even *pro forma*. It was an idealistic whim from which I could not free myself . . . I could never free myself from a certain dread that I should do anything which might seem, even only half-way, to be breaking loose from my native land . . . It would be a horrible and mad thought for me to have to say that I am a German poet and also a naturalized Frenchman. . . . When I study that so-called *poésie lyrique* of the French, then I recognize the grandeur and glory of German poetry, and then I dare imagine that I may boast of having gained my laurels in this field." In his angry arraignment of the denunciator Wolfgang Menzel, which he wrote in 1839, Heine declared that "whoever has lived his days in exile—the damp cold days and the long black nights—whoever has gone up and down the hard stairs of a foreign land, will repudiate any aspersions against [his] patriotism." Few German exiles remained as faithful to their fatherland, few resented as steadfastly exile in Paris as did Heine.

Heine did not participate in the nationalistic fervor which brought Prussia and France to the brink of war in 1840. Max Schneckenburger wrote his famous "Wacht am Rhein" then, and Nikolaus Becker challenged the French in a poem which proclaimed that "they shall not have the free German Rhine." Musset and Lamartine answered the challenge on behalf of the French, the latter in a pacifist spirit, calling his poem, "La Marseillaise de la Paix." In the same year Hoffmann von Fallersleben wrote the German anthem, "Deutschland, Deutschland über alles." Heine referred to this agitation in the preface to *Germany: A Winter's Tale.* "I love the Fatherland as well as you," he wrote. "Because of this love I have spent thirteen years of my life in exile, and because of this love I return to exile, perhaps forever. I am the friend of the French as I am the friend of all men if they are good and reasonable men. I myself am not so stupid or so evil as to wish that my own Germans and the French, both the chosen peoples of humanity, should break each others' necks to the advantage of England and Russia . . . I will never yield the Rhine to the French for the very simple reason that the Rhine belongs to me. Yes, it belongs to me by my inalienable birthright. I am the free son of the free Rhine; my cradle stood upon its banks, and I see no reason why the Rhine should belong to others than the children of its own country."

Heine's patriotism made him recognize with great clarity the dangers lurking in German nationalism. The last chapter of his *De l'Allemagne* culminates in an apocalyptic vision which throws light on the hidden Germany of Heine's time, a Germany which one hundred years later for a brief period became fully visible to an incredulous world. "German philosophy is a serious matter, of concern to all mankind," Heine wrote. "Our remotest descendants alone will be able to judge whether we are to be blamed or praised for having first produced our philosophy and then our revolution. But it seems to me that a methodical people like the Germans had to commence with the Reformation. Thereafter they could occupy themselves with philosophy, and only when they had completed that task, were they in a position to pass on to a political revolution. I find this sequence very reasonable. The heads which philosophy used for reflection could later be chopped off by the revolution for its own purposes. But philosophy could never have used these heads if the revolution had first chopped them off. Don't worry, German republicans—your German revolution will be no gentler or milder because it has been preceded by the *Critique* of Kant, the transcendental idealism of Fichte, and even the philosophy of nature. These doctrines give birth to revolutionary forces which only wait for the day to erupt and fill the world with terror and amazement . . .

"Most terrifying will be the philosophers of nature . . . because they have allies in the primitive forces of nature, able to invoke the demoniac energies of old German pantheism, that ancient love of war of the old Germans which makes them fight for the sake of fighting. Christianity—and that is its greatest merit—has mitigated

that German love of war, but it could not destroy it. Should that
subduing talisman, the cross, be shattered, the frenzied madness of
the ancient warriors, of which Nordic bards have spoken and sung
so often, will once more burst into flames. That talisman is rotting,
and the day will come when it will break into miserable fragments.
The old stone gods will arise from long forgotten ruins and rub the
dust of a thousand years from their eyes, and Thor will leap to life
with his giant hammer and smash the Gothic cathedrals¹ . . ."

Heine warned the French to beware of the Germans. "What it is
that you are being reproached with I don't know. Once, in a beer-
hall in Göttingen, I heard a young Pan-German declare that Germany must avenge Konradin von Hohenstaufen on the French,
who beheaded him in Naples. You have surely forgotten about that
long long ago. We, however, forget nothing. . . . No matter what
happens in Germany, whether the Crown Prince of Prussia or Dr.
Wirth comes to power, always be on the alert."

"Whether the Crown Prince of Prussia or Dr. Wirth comes to
power"—these are perhaps the most startling words in Heine's
vision. For the Dr. Wirth of whom he spoke was the bitter foe of
Prussian princes. He was a Bavarian journalist who became a leader
of the radical left; one year before Heine wrote his warning (in
1832) he helped to organize the famous "National Festival of the
Germans" in Hambach in the Bavarian Rhenish Palatinate. Under
the impact of the Paris July Revolution and the Polish rising against
the Russians, German liberal patriots met on May 27, 1832, in the ruins
of the Hambach castle. The meeting was greeted as the German
May, the dawn of a free Germany, of the people's rights and liberties.
High above the castle flew a black, red, and gold flag with the inscription, "Germany's Rebirth." More than 30,000 people listened
for three days to many orators, some of whom demanded the immediate proclamation of a German Republic. The meeting ended
without any practical results; most of its leaders, among them Wirth,
were arrested and sentenced to imprisonment. Later on, many, Wirth
among them, went into exile, some forever.

In his address, Wirth violently attacked the German princes as
traitors to the German cause. His attack upon France was equally
violent. Though Wirth acknowledged that the "present government of France wished to maintain peace at any price," he feared
lest France might help Germany gain unity at the expense of the
Rhineland. He warned "that any attempt on France's part to conquer even one clod of German soil would immediately silence all
opposition within Germany and the whole of Germany would

rise against France; all Germans were unanimous that the liberation of our Fatherland would mean the reunion of Alsace and Lorraine with Germany." Germany must never buy political liberty at
the expense of territorial integrity. Unity was more important than
liberty. Wirth concluded his speech with a reference to a federated
republican Europe; he was convinced that a free Germany must
lead this Europe. He cheered the "God-inspired struggle for the
Fatherland, for our adored, thrice magnificent (*herrlich*) Germany."
    It would be wrong to judge the Hambach festival in the light of
Wirth's nationalistic fervor. Many orators disagreed with his anti-
French outburst. The Germans in the Palatinate were conscious
of their close link with western liberal ideas. Heine himself, in
his essay on Ludwig Börne, stressed the great difference between
the political mood at Hambach in 1832 and that at the Wartburg
Festival in 1817. He regarded the latter as a manifestation of narrow
nationalist, religious, and racial obscurantism, whereas, "at Hambach the modern era jubilantly sang its songs of dawn and there
was a feeling in the air of fraternization with the whole of mankind." But Hambach lacked a clear political line. Most of the leading
personalities followed opposite and complex impulses. A rational
cosmopolitanism was mixed, sometimes in the same person, with a
nationalist exclusivism. The liberals who accepted the principles of
French liberty were in the majority but there was, according to
Heine, a minority of Teutomaniacs who gained strength from their
semireligious fanaticism. Their slogans of "Fatherland" and "Faith
of our Fathers" electrified the masses more than "Humanity, Reason, and Truth." All the future trends of German nationalism
intermingled at Hambach; the hopes of liberalism and of close
co-operation with the West, as well as the pride of a superior national destiny. Heine himself, and even the radical Börne, inclined
often to an outspoken German nationalism. When someone proposed to strengthen France, the "natural representative of the revolution," through the reacquisition of the Rhineland so that France
could better resist aristocratic absolutist Europe, Börne, according
to Heine, exclaimed that he would not even cede a German chamber-
pot to France.
    Heine feared that revolutionary leftist German mass leaders, after
their victory over monarchy and traditional religion, might appeal
to the masses with the "dark magic invocations of the Middle Ages
and these invocations, a mixture of ancient superstitions and of
demoniac forces, would be stronger than all the arguments of
reason." This explains his uncanny foresight in placing side by side

in his warning to the French the reactionary Prussian prince and the
leading radical and profoundly antimonarchist Hambach orator. In
his letters from Paris Heine wrote in 1832 that Emperor Barbarossa
sent the black, red, and gold flag to the German liberals from the
Kyffhäuser where he slept, as a sign that the old imperial dream
lived on and that he himself would soon come with his sceptre and
his crown. In his patriotism, too, Heine showed an ambiguous attitude—the heritage of romanticism and of the Enlightenment, the
attraction of the modern West and of medieval traditions mingling
and conflicting in his complex personality. His attitude toward
France was equally ambiguous.

Heine and France

IN HIS PARISIAN EXILE Heine became ever more conscious of his
Germanism. But two aspects of French life fascinated him in contrast to conditions in his native land: the freedom of thought and
discussion, and the participation of intellectuals in public life. One
century before, Voltaire, coming from absolutist France to free England, had been struck by a similar contrast and his *Lettres Philo-
sophiques sur les Anglais* had tried to communicate something of
this air of liberty, of true intellectual activity, of social mobility to
his countrymen. When Voltaire's book appeared (1734), it was condemned by the French government, copies were seized and burned,
and Voltaire escaped arrest only because he was abroad, living in
the then independent Duchy of Lorraine. One hundred years later
France was as advanced in relationship to Germany as England had
been in relation to the France of Louis XV. In the France of the
July monarchy orators and writers were free to voice the most varied
and original opinions and their words were listened to. Poets like
Lamartine and Victor Hugo were political men; scholars like
Cousin, Guizot and Thiers occupied leading cabinet posts. What a
contrast to nineteenth century Germany!
   Heine filled an important function in his effort to acquaint the
Germans with the realities of French life and to make the French
understand the conditions of German society. He did not always
correctly evaluate the events and trends of the day, but he viewed
them with the power of his creative and penetrating imagination

and he clothed them with the sparkling imagery of his language. In his testament Heine wrote on November 13, 1851, that "it has been the greatest task of my life to work for a cordial understanding between Germany and France, and to frustrate the plots of the enemies of democracy who exploit the national prejudices and animosities for their own use. I believe that I have deserved well of my fellow countrymen and of the French and the claims which I have on their gratitude are no doubt the most valuable legacy which I can bequeath to my heirs."

The French accepted Heine from the beginning as an intermediary between the two nations. *Le Globe*, the Saint-Simonian newspaper, welcomed the young German poet who was at that time deeply attracted by Saint-Simonianism. "If, as we believe," the editor wrote on December 25, 1831, "the time is near when Germany and France will join hands to realize the Holy Alliance of the Peoples, a beautiful part is reserved in this great work for M. Heine." Balzac, as Friedrich Hirth tells in his book on *Heinrich Heine and his French Friends*, dedicated his tale *"Un Prince de la Bohême"* to Heine, *"à vous qui représentez à Paris l'esprit et la poésie de l'Allemagne comme en Allemagne vous représentez la vive et spirituelle critique française."* Sainte-Beuve wrote in 1833 that Heine *"est des nôtres, autant que le spirituel Melchior Grimm l'a jamais été . . . M. Heine sera davantage encore à notre niveau de Français quand il aura un peu moins d'esprit. Au milieu de ses qualités françaises, M. Heine est au fond poète et poète de son pays."*

Most French intellectuals, from 1815 to 1870, loved and admired Germany. Victor Hugo believed that Europe's only salvation was a union between France and Germany. France would be able to force England back into the Ocean, Germany to expel Russia into Asia. In the preface to his romantic trilogy *Les Burgraves* he expressed the hope that the "glorious military Messiah whom Germany still expects," Frederick Barbarossa, would rise up from the deep down in the mountain where he slept. In January, 1843, Hugo confessed a "filial sentiment for this noble and holy fatherland of all thinkers. If he were not a Frenchman, he would wish to be a German." Gérard de Nerval, Heine's friend and the translator of Goethe's *Faust*, upon the first visit to the Rhine in 1836 greeted "Germany, the old Germany, mother of us all, Teutonia!" No political or ideological antagonism between the two nations was anticipated by French students of German letters. Saint-René Taillandier, who published a history of Young Germany in 1848, was convinced that the Germans were enthusiastically following in the wake of liberal France and desired to co-operate with the French in building the Holy Alliance of the Peoples.

Few German intellectuals of the 1830's and 1840's showed a similar love and admiration for France. One of the outstanding friends of France among the poets of the period was August Count Platen-Hallermunde. This scion of an old though impoverished aristocratic family was the target of one of Heine's most objectionable egocentric outbursts. Yet politically Platen was much more of a liberal and a cosmopolitan than was Heine Both were opposed to Prussia; more naively than Heine, Platen hoped for a truly free, united Germany under Austria's leadership, which would join a new and free France in a brotherly embrace "over the sacred tomb in Aix-la-Chapelle,"—Charlemagne's tomb in the city which was his favorite residence and throughout the Middle Ages the coronation city of the Holy Roman Empire. He dreamt of a new Carolingian Empire, separated according to nationalities but united in the spirit of liberty.

Platen shared Heine's admiration for Napoleon. In his "Ode to Napoleon" (1825) he called the Emperor "an immortal hero," "a shepherd of the peoples, girded by glory, who never thought of himself, who always thought of the world." He praised Napoleon for his intention of giving liberty to the globe he had conquered. To him, Napoleon was no tyrant; on the contrary, he "had destroyed what threatened Europe with ancient violence, he who had stormed England's insular arrogance and Russia's devilish bulwark." Five years later, after the July revolution of 1830, in a poem to Charles X, Platen joyfully greeted the tricolor once more flying over France, the "bulwark of liberty, Europe's splendid jewel."

Many French intellectuals, while friendly to Germany, felt a deep hostility for Britain. They could not forget Waterloo. To the French historian Jules Michelet the "war of all wars" was that between Britain and France: "the rest are episodes." Britain was rich but, Michelet claimed, without a soul or an idea. Her greatness was sterile. Heine shared on the whole this anti-British attitude. His carping strictures on British political and social life even gained him the short-lived sympathy of some German nationalists during the war of 1914. In his edition of Heine's letters Friedrich Hirth remarked in 1916 that Heine's "excellent portrayal of the English and their brutal political methods gained him appreciation and recognition in circles that had formerly been indifferent to him." The widespread continental prejudices against England, which even Nietzsche and Rilke shared, were brilliantly expressed by Heine in an article which he wrote in 1841 against Guizot who, as French ambassador to London, had failed to understand British "perfidy." Heine thought the English people were profoundly corrupted by a long domestic peace—for the wars which they fought abroad they fought through mercenaries—, by excessive wealth and misery, by the corruption inherent in a representative constitution, by their mercenary spirit and their religious hypocrisy.

In his essay on Shakespeare's female characters Heine mentioned a Christian acquaintance of his in Hamburg who could never accept the fact that Jesus was born "among as repulsive a people" as the Jews. Heine felt the same way about the English—how, he asked, could Shakespeare belong to "the most loathsome people which God created in his wrath." His dislike of the English extended also to the Americans. On Heligoland on July 1, 1830, Heine dismissed not only the thought of going to "infernal England, where I would not even wish to hang in effigy, much less live in person," but also of going to America, "that monstrous prison of freedom where the invisible chains would oppress me even more heavily than the visible ones do at home, and where the most repulsive of tyrants, the populace, holds vulgar sway."

Heine's typically German approach to the concept of liberty received an almost grotesque expression in his *Travel Pictures* where he compared liberty in England with that which he believed existed in Russia. "In England liberty sprang from historical precedents, in Russia from principles. Like the precedents themselves, the intellectual results bear the stamp of the Middle Ages; the whole of England is frozen in medieval institutions which are incapable of rejuvenation and behind which the aristocracy is entrenched to await the stroke of death. On the other hand, the principles from which Russian liberty is daily emerging are the liberal ideas of the present age; the Russian government is permeated with these ideas, its unrestricted absolutism is rather a dictatorship for the direct introduction of these ideas . . . Russia is a democratic state, and I would even call it a Christian state if I might employ this much abused term in its most delectable and cosmopolitan sense, for the Russians are exempt by the very extent of their empire from the narrow-mindedness of pagan nationalism. They are cosmopolitans, or at least a sixth cosmopolitan, since Russia comprises almost a sixth of the inhabited world."

Heine shared the anti-British prejudices of most Frenchmen and Germans of his time. But he also shared fully the prejudice of

the average German against French immorality and frivolity as contrasted with German virtue In his *Letters on the French Stage* there
are passages which Richard Wagner could have written though with
less wit. Heine insisted that no one with a German soul and heart
could enjoy French comedy. Turning from the inherent weaknesses
of French art to a more general reflection Heine called it "the secret
curse of exile, that we never really feel at home in the foreign land.
With our own way of thinking and feeling which we have brought
with us from our homeland, we always remain isolated among a
people which feels and thinks quite differently In Paris we Germans are perpetually hurt by moral, or rather immoral, sights to
which the native has long become accustomed, which through habit
he notices as little as he does the natural sights of his land. . . . Ah,
the moral and intellectual climate in a foreign land is for us as in-
hospitable as the physical climate; nay, it is easier to accept the latter; for only the body suffers from it, not the soul."

Heine's distrust of the common people and his views on France
made him at first struggle violently against the strongest passion of
his life, his love for Mathilde. She was a scantily educated girl from
the lower classes who could neither understand nor appreciate him
as a German poet but who was singularly devoted to him for more
than two decades, cheerfully nursing the paralytic, and remaining
faithful to him after his death. "For eight years," Heine wrote to
his brother in April, 1843, "I have loved her with a tenderness and
passion which borders on the fabulous." Eight years later, in 1851,
he wrote to his mother and sister: "Without her, life would have no
interest at all for me; she has helped me bear the painful burden
which I should certainly cast off if I were alone." Yet Ignaz Kuranda,
a liberal German publicist of Jewish descent, reported after his
visit to Heine in 1840 that: "He [Heine] is married to the often
mentioned Mathilde—a pleasant stoutish French woman. A German
poet needs a German wife; what German women are, one learns
only in Paris. The concept of family life as we know it cannot be
translated at all into French."

Heine, Germany, and the World

IN HIS POETRY and in his prose, Heine inaugurated a new epoch of
German literature. Of the half century between Goethe's death and

the German cultural resurgence after 1890, Nietzsche rightly wrote in a letter that "Wagner is and remains a capital fact in the history of the European mind and of the modern soul, precisely as Heinrich Heine was such a fact. Wagner and Heine are the last great men whom Germany has bestowed on Europe." Yet what a difference between these two great Germans and Europeans! Wagner's style and thought were turgid and his passions sultry; he had none of Heine's mocking lightness and severe self-analysis. Nowhere was Wagner's turgidity so obvious as in his German nationalism. Nowhere did Heine preserve as balanced a lucidity as in his dedicated German patriotism. The two men were similar in one respect: both thought of themselves often as soldiers in a popular cause and yet were above all aristocratic artists of supreme vitality and egocentricity, striking out for new forms of expresssion.

In the last analysis it would be too restrictive to stress Heine as the great poet or the patriotic German. He was above all a human being intensely alive, in love with all aspects of life to the very last day of his agony in the mattress tomb. Goethe, a man of infinitely greater wisdom and much higher creative rank than Heine, had an even greater vitality; but Goethe was a favorite of the gods, a *Götter-liebling,* endowed by nature with all its gifts. He had never to suffer as Heine did from what Heine himself called the triple sorrow, the three-fold heavy burden—crippling disease, oppressive poverty, and Jewishness. Heine remained faithful to life with a courageous wit and a Dionysian exuberance under the most trying circumstances. In his life he outgrew the limitations of the man and the artist. He never could have written of himself and of the reality of life in the way in which Rilke wrote to Lou Andreas-Salomé in 1903: "There is much more reality in a poem which I succeed in writing than in any relationship or affection which I feel. I wish I could find the strength to base my life entirely on this truth." Heine, on the other hand, found reality in the fulness of life. He was supremely real himself. His complex personality will always allow many and contradictory appreciations and judgments.

Heine's political thought was without great originality or depth. He was a publicist and a journalist—a profession never highly esteemed in Germany Yet in German history he was not without significance. He was completely of his own time and had an insight into its complexities. He tried to open Germany to the modern West, to break down the wall which some of his compatriots were then building. He was equally instrumental in introducing Germany to the West.

When his essays on the German Romantic School were published in an English translation in 1836, a reviewer in *The American Monthly Magazine* wrote: "We took up the book with a strong prejudice against Heinrich Heine. We read at first with distaste, then with distaste mingled with pleasure, then with pleasure mingled with admiration. . . . We rejoice to see among us symptoms of a growing interest in German literature, having some time been convinced that this is the very culture we want to counterpoise the natural influences which, amid all our so-called prosperity, are threatening to blight every poetic bud, and turn the American mind into a spiritual spinning jenny, set in motion by no higher impulse than that of utility, understood in its lowest sense. . . . To whom, then, can we look with more propriety than to the true-hearted Germans for the idealism we require to balance our utilitarianism? The Germans have their faults, but those faults, pointed out with so much acuteness by Heine, the 'progress-man,' are as good as virtues to us, since, being the exact opposites of our own faults, they may teach us the most important lessons . . . Heine has brought some excellent materials for the bridge between Germany and us."

In 1863, Matthew Arnold regarded Heine as "the most important German successor and continuator of Goethe. . . . The wit and ardent modern spirit of France, Heine joined to the culture, the sentiment, the thought of Germany. This is what makes him so remarkable, this wonderful clearness, lightness, and freedom, united with such power of feeling and width of range. . . . Such as he is, he is (and posterity, too, I am quite sure, will say this), in the European literature of that quarter of a century which follows the death of Goethe, incomparably the most important figure."

The quarter of a century which followed the death of Goethe marked a turning point in German history. Heine hoped that Germany would repeat the experience of the West, in entering the modern age, in fusing nationalism and liberalism. Such a possibility existed in the 1830's. But Heine feared that the prestige and social structure of Prussia, combined with an antiwestern Germanophilism, might create a Germany hostile to liberalism—a German nationalism convinced that Germanophilism and Prussianism supplied stronger and more enduring foundations of national life than individual liberty, representative democracy and tolerant diversity.

The four decades between 1830 and 1870 were crucial in European history: Western Europe from England to Switzerland grew more liberal and the belief in the final triumph of liberalism all over Europe became widespread. Even Russia entered hopefully into a brief period of liberalism At that very moment, Germany reversed the trend. By so doing, she broke not only with the West, but with many of her own traditions. Symbolically, the center of gravity in Germany shifted from the west to the east. In 1848, the center of German political life was in southwest Germany, in Baden, in Württemberg, and in the free city of Frankfurt on the Main, the history of which goes back to Roman times and to Charlemagne. After the partition of Charlemagne's empire, Frankfurt became the capital of the East Frankish Kingdom. Within its walls Frederick I Barbarossa was elected German King in 1152, and in 1356 the Golden Bull made the city the perpetual seat for the imperial elections. From 1562 on, the emperors were crowned there. In continuation of this tradition the city became, in 1816, the seat of the German Confederation, and from May 16, 1848, to May 31, 1849, the first freely elected German National Assembly held its sessions there in the Church of St. Paul. But in 1866 Prussia annexed Frankfurt and put an end to its freedom and its traditions. The Consul General of the United States reported from Frankfurt on October 15, 1866, that the event "spread a very gloomy feeling amongst the population of Frankfurt which are from all their heart opposed to the Prussian administration. Even the female part of the population is expressing its disgust by appearing on the public walks, opera, etc only dressed or decorated in red and white, the Frankfurt colors." Frankfurt and western Germany lost the position which they had held through many centuries of German history. When, a few years later, a German parliament met again, it was no longer in the Free City, but in Prussia's capital, in the eastern marches of Germany. It met in an entirely different moral and intellectual climate.

Chapter Six

THE WITHERING OF
LIBERALISM

Hohenstaufen and Hohenzollern

HEINRICH HEINE DIED IN 1856—in the midst of a profound change in
the political and moral climate of Germany. As late as 1840 liberals
were influencing major decisions, but by 1870 most of the liberals
had turned into nationalists To the historian Friedrich Sell this
was a tragedy. Tragic indeed were the consequences, but the word
tragedy is misleading, for it implies that the German liberals were
unwittingly tangled in events outside their control. The truth is that
most liberals were convinced that they had to choose between a free
society and a unified power state. Wittingly and willingly they preferred national power to individual liberty.

The turning point meant a break not only with the West but also
with most of Germany's past. For Goethe the small town and principality of Weimar set the stage for a wide-open world of cultural
intercourse and for the intensity of fruitful daily work. For the generation of 1870 the Prussian power-state alone seemed to guarantee
a worthwhile national and personal life. Goethe as we have seen had
no use for the Middle Ages. Now the Prussian dynasty of the Hohenzollern was greeted as the legitimate successor of the Hohenstaufen.

The interest in their empire was revived in the 1820's by a number
of historical and poetical works. Friedrich von Raumer, Professor
at the University of Berlin, began publication in 1823 of a six-volume
"History of the Hohenstaufen and their Times." It presented the
Hohenstaufen Reich not only as the first European power of its

128

times, but also as a much more centralized national state than was actually the case. Under the influence of Raumer's widely read work, Karl Leberecht Immermann wrote a tragedy, "Kaiser Friedrich II," in 1828, and Ernst Benjamin Raupach wrote a cycle of not less than sixteen plays called "Die Hohenstaufen," which in spite of the fact that today his name has long been forgotten, were very popular in their day, so popular that in 1832 young Richard Wagner wrote an overture on this subject More talented than Raupach was Christian Dietrich Grabbe; his two plays on the same subject may be read even today. In 1849 Raumer was a member of the delegation which on behalf of the German National Assembly offered the imperial crown to the Hohenzollern King. He lived long enough to witness, as a nonagenarian in 1871, the assumption by the Hohenzollern of the imperial title which popular imagination confounded with that of the Hohenstaufen. But the two had nothing in common. The Hohenstaufen Reich was rooted in southern Germany; in its religion it was Catholic; in its concept it was universal; and many of the Hohenstaufen felt more Mediterranean than German.

In the mid-nineteenth century the Prussian historian, Heinrich von Sybel, proposed a new interpretation of German history, which, under the impact of the Prussian victories was soon generally accepted. The new interpretation shifted the center of German history to the northeast, made Protestantism its dominant and creative religion, and based this religion upon a strictly nation-centered concept. Its outlook was not only anti-Roman and anti-Mediterranean, but antiwestern. It saw German history after the fall of the Hohenstaufen reaching its first climax in the War of Liberation fought under Prussia's leadership against France, and finding its fulfillment in Prussia's victory over France in 1871.

Such were the forces that brought about the close co-operation of most German liberal intellectuals with the Prussian authoritarian monarchy. The co-operation was originally not sought by either of the two sides. They neither loved nor trusted each other. But Prussia, which had little liking for modern liberalism, seemed the only country to offer what so many liberals desired, power to achieve national greatness and to restore Germany, as in the time of the Hohenstaufen, to the imperial leadership in Europe. In the end, after some resistance, but not too unwillingly or ungraciously, most liberals capitulated to Prussia. In return, the latter made minor concessions to the liberals, concessions without which a modern power-state could not have existed but which did not go far enough to transform Prussia into a durable and viable modern society.

There was nothing traditional or hallowed about the Prussian monarchy. The kingdom came into existence on January 18, 1701, when the Elector of Brandenburg assumed the title of king in Prussia. This took place in Königsberg, a city in the extreme northeast of Germany, then politically and spiritually outside Germany proper. It was a German outpost surrounded on all sides by Slav and Lithuanian populations which had been subjugated in the late Middle Ages by the Teutonic Knights. From its original domain, the March of Brandenburg, itself a frontier territory occupying former Slav lands east of the Elbe River, the power of the House of Hohenzollern had spread over many territorially disconnected possessions, which were united only by two factors: the dynasty and the need of defending long frontiers in a shapeless plain, a landscape much more characteristic of eastern than of western Europe. From the end of the seventeenth century Brandenburg, until then a minor German state, was bent upon glory and expansion. It lacked natural resources and its soil was poor; thus, it could achieve military strength only by the most efficient and economical administration and by giving full precedence to the military.

Life in eighteenth century Prussia was dominated by a stern sense of duty and service, by frugality and cultural insensibility. The emphasis was on efficiency, self-reliance, and thrift, not, as in the middle-class world of puritanism, for the sake of the individual and of religion but for the sake of the authoritarian state and of military power. Its own historians praised the Prussian state as the personification of political power. The state became the fountainhead of ethical life and the center of devotion.

In the eighteenth century Prussia was alien to the German mind and suspect to the German intellectuals who hated its garrison-spirit. The princes who founded Prussian greatness in that century, the dedicated soldier-king Frederick William I and his more complex and famous son Frederick II, had no regard or understanding for German cultural life. Prussia owed little to Germany and gave little. Its astonishing growth was dominated by only one goal—power—and only one norm—Prussia.

During the Napoleonic period a generation of great reformers, almost all of them born outside Prussia, tried to infuse Prussian power with a German spirit and to liberalize the monarchy. Their efforts saved Prussia and made victory in the war of 1813 possible. After that, reforms were halted. The University of Berlin, founded in 1810 as a part of the reform movement, became in many ways a model of scholarship and efficiency, but its professors accepted the authority of the state so willingly that one of the leading scholars there could call himself and his colleagues "the intellectual body-guard of the Hohenzollern." This description was intended by the author and received by his colleagues as high praise. It was to this unreformed Prussia, the openly acknowledged bulwark of author-itarianism and conservative militarism, that most German liberals turned for guidance and inspiration.

The German Liberals before 1848

THIS CHANGE IN THE ATTITUDE of the German liberals can best be followed in the writing of the German historians, from Johann Gus-tav Droysen, born in 1808, to Heinrich von Treitschke who died in 1896. Leopold von Ranke, whom they acknowledged as their master, belonged to an older generation. He never was a liberal. Nevertheless, his political thought influenced many of those who called them-selves liberal. "Ranke asserted the right of any state to follow its own logic of politics, its right to be different from the strict standard of liberalism," writes Professor Theodore H. von Laue in his study of Ranke's formative years. "The consequences of this assertion were momentous. It implied a break with the political development in France, England, and the United States. Under its guidance Prussia preserved the absolutist state of the eighteenth century instead of fol-lowing the western trend toward democracy, and the more pacifist evaluation of international relations. The philosophy which Ranke so clearly stated was one of the landmarks in the revolt against the West, upholding against the advocates of western liberalism a new Prussophilism, which in time grew into a Germanophilism."

What separated Ranke from his successors was not merely his conservatism. Like Hegel, Ranke was no nationalist. He accepted the Europe of his time and believed in the concert of nations, whereas an historian like Droysen demanded the pre-eminence of the one nation clearly marked out for leadership. Ranke believed in the authoritarian monarchical state; Droysen believed in the German nation-state. Ranke still participated in the open world of Goethe, and in the balanced Europe of Metternich. Droysen finally embraced nothing except Germany and its national self-interest.

German historians and the German people ultimately accepted the idealization of state and power which Ranke held in common with Hegel, and as time went on oversimplified and vulgarized it. Perhaps the most generous judgment on Ranke's influence on nineteenth century German thought was expressed in 1886, on the occasion of Ranke's ninetieth birthday, by a Dutch historian, Robert Fruin, a master of the critical method himself and a liberal in the western sense of the word. "To us, who find more in the history of mankind than just the impact of power, and who care for other interests besides those of the State, Ranke's writings, however beautiful, will always appear lacking in something and unsatisfying. . . . Is it an injustice to our German neighbors to suggest that it is this characteristic attitude which has earned for Ranke the position of the historian *par excellence* of present-day Germany? Or is it not true that to the rulers and leaders of opinion in that country the power of the State is the overriding consideration? That to it everything else must give way and is, if need be, sacrificed? Prosperity, trade, and industry, are not promoted in accordance with their own needs and the laws of political economy, but are managed with an eye to the demands of State power, in the interests of the unity and efficiency of the Reich. Everything is regarded as lawful in these, and alas in other, respects, whenever German unity and German ascendancy in Europe might otherwise be thought to suffer."

With Hegel and Ranke the liberal historians felt some fundamental affinity; a world separated them from Goethe and classical humanism. Of this opposition they were fully conscious and they gloried in it. When an acquaintance of Droysen decided to move from Berlin to Weimar, Droysen was almost sickened by this decision. On October 29, 1853, he wrote to a mutual friend: "I strongly resent [his] departure for Weimar. How can one leave a great state and allow oneself and one's children to become stunted and degenerate?" He compared the atmosphere of Weimar with the "stagnant air in a room full of spinsters prattling about art. (*diese aesthetische Altjungfern-Stubenluft*").

To move from tiny Weimar to vast Prussia meant narrowing the intellectual horizon of the German elite, to an outsider a saddening and frightening change, for these were men of character and scholarly distinction. Yet in discussing matters of state, they became quaintly provincial and irresponsibly vague. Whenever they mentioned a constitution they emphasized that it must be a constitution which originated in, and corresponded to, the true German folk-spirit (*dem ureigensten Geiste des Volkes*). Nobody was ever able to define this true folk-spirit, which meant that cries for constitutional reforms were easily silenced. The liberals' goal was not mere political liberties in the Anglo-American sense but the inner freedom of man, not the protection of the individual against the nation-state but his willing co-operation with it, and subordination to it. For these men the citizen was no longer the individual strong in his independence, the individual envisaged by Milton and Locke, by Jefferson and Kant In the name of a higher idealism they conceived of men as "a willing organ of the national whole." They immersed themselves in the study of their own people; alien influences were either neglected or rejected. National evolution appeared an organic whole with its own inherent law of growth And the goal of the growth was national greatness expressed in the power and majesty of the state.

Schiller's ideal was embodied in the simple democratic life of the peasants and shepherds of diminutive Swiss republics; Goethe could absorb the whole breadth of human life in the tiny town and duchy of Weimar; but for Droysen and Treitschke only the monarchical power-state afforded adequate scope for human development. Against all historical evidence Treitschke insisted that the existence of a mighty state was indispensable to develop and protect the flowering of a worthwhile cultural and intellectual life. In Germany Prussia alone appeared to offer this opportunity. These German liberals were not disturbed by their growing separation from the West. Elaborating lofty theories to justify their abandonment of liberalism, they early coined a name for their new creed—national liberalism—which had as little in common with western liberalism as national socialism had with western socialism. They cultivated a serious virile moralism and regarded everything purely artistic as effeminate. Droysen wrote to Theodor von Schoen on March 7, 1851, that he felt in the depth of his heart very far removed from the shallow Enlightenment which had prevailed in Germany toward the end of the eighteenth century.

Looking back to the War of Liberation, the liberals of this generation rejoiced in the recollection of the high moral standard maintained by the German people in their struggle against the French. Droysen's colleague Friedrich Christoph Dahlmann could not conceal his disgust for French frivolity when, in 1815, he came to deliver an academic address celebrating the victory over Napoleon. "Any one of us in the future who considers the French and the Germans merely as two hostile nations fighting with equal right on each side, anyone of us who goes on believing that he would act in the same way if he were born a Frenchman, any one of us who compares this people who have so ignominiously degenerated, this rapacious people who commit perjury and deny God, with the noble and self-sacrificing Germans, he, wherever he be born, is really French and deserves so to be regarded in Germany." On behalf of the University Dahlmann stressed that all scholarship was meaningless if it did not enrich society and that scholars more than anyone else were called to preserve the scared flame of the love of the Fatherland.

Before 1848 this dedication to an exclusive patriotism and this emphasis on the power-state were in no way characteristic of German liberals. In southwestern Germany and in the Rhineland the desire to follow western ways prevailed. The year 1819 saw the introduction of parliamentary institutions in Bavaria, Baden, and Württemberg. The leader of the liberal opposition in Baden was Karl von Rotteck who taught history and political science at the University of his native town, Freiburg. In his time his influence on the educated middle class in southern Germany was very great. His multi-voluminous *Universal History* reached its 25th printing twenty-six years after his death. His *Encyclopedia of Political Science (Staatslexikon)* which he edited with his young colleague, Karl Theodor Welcker, was, in the 1830's, a powerful vehicle for spreading western liberal ideas. The Chamber of Deputies in Baden, originally modeled after that of the French Charte of 1814, became after 1831, with the growing influence of French liberalism, the first school of parliamentary life in Germany.

Rotteck's spiritual home was not the War of Liberation but the Enlightenment. The state to him was primarily the embodiment not of might, but of right. Like so many other eighteenth century Germans, he lavished no praise on great conquerors and least of all on Frederick II of Prussia. Like most German liberals of 1830 he demanded the restoration of Poland's independence. In his *History* he called the partition of Poland "the most horrible violation of international law and of the sacred right of mankind in modern times, infinitely more terrible than the horrors of the Huns and the Vandals." Rotteck believed in natural law, which the Germans called *Vernunftrecht,* rational law. He also admired the United States. "There no secret police, no censorship, no suspension of personal liberty, no closing of the borders, no terrorist measures were needed to maintain public tranquility and the respect for authority." Rotteck was neither a revolutionary nor a republican. He sought to transform Baden and southwestern Germany into a bulwark of western liberty rivaling England, France, and Belgium. "For Rotteck," writes Professor Sell, "liberty unquestionably took precedence over nationalism. In the Napoleonic period he proved himself a patriot; Napoleon as he saw it had suppressed liberty." But he was reluctant to sacrifice the liberty acquired in a small German state for the nation at large if that were less liberal. He preferred being the citizen of a constitutional free state to being the subject of a great power. After the German Festival of Hambach in 1832 he delivered a speech in Badenweiler in which he exclaimed: "I do not desire [national] unity without [political] liberty, and I prefer liberty without unity to unity without liberty. I reject unity under the wings of the Prussian or Austrian eagle." When war between liberal France and reactionary Prussia threatened to break out Rotteck was of the opinion that in such a case liberal Germany should side with France.

His fellow liberal Gervinus was thirty years younger than Rotteck. Born in Darmstadt, Hessen, he lived most of his life in nearby Heidelberg. As a student there he came under the influence of the historian Friedrich Christoph Schlosser, who, like Rotteck, was an historian of the old school, not a scholar like Ranke but, thanks to his background, a man with a "just conception of the breadth and scope of history." Like his contemporaries, Dahlmann and Droysen, Gervinus was a fervent patriot. He too believed that the contemplative period of German history was over and that the active period of German political life must begin. His *Geschichte der Poetischen Nationalliteratur der Deutschen (History of the Poetical National Literature of the Germans)*, published in five volumes between 1835 and 1842, was "the first comprehensive history of German literature, written both with scholarly erudition and literary skill." In this work, dedicated to Dahlmann and the Brothers Grimm, Gervinus proved he could learn from the past and plan for the future. "Why should this people situated in the center of the universe," he asked in the conclusion of the last volume, "not play the moral and political role in the council of nations which geography has attributed to it?" He refused to believe that "this nation which could reach the highest achievements in the fields of art, religion, and scholarship could not do the same in the realm of politics."

Gervinus had what Dahlmann and Droysen lacked, an understanding of constitutional liberalism and of western ways. In his *Introduction to the History of the Nineteenth Century* he praised the British constitution, in which 'the elements are so thoroughly blended that History stands up and points to the English Commonwealth as her masterpiece." With even greater love he regarded the development of the English Constitution in the United States which appeared to him as the true embodiment and interpretation of the

Zeitgeist. "The American Declaration of Independence has become the creed of liberals the world over. The North American Republic is not one great nation but a federal union, in which each separate state strives to obtain the sovereign power, while within these states individuals claim the utmost independence. . . . The state exists far more for the individual than the individual for the state. The institutions of the state are at the service of personal liberty. The freedom of man is more important than his duties as a citizen. . . . This new state, by its astonishing achievements in fortune and power, has suddenly surpassed all of us, and the boldest political ventures have succeeded, in spite of all the sceptics." Gervinus was longing for a similar development in Germany. The Anglo-Americans and the Germans appeared to him, through their common descent and common Protestant faith, equally destined for individual liberty. Germany should become a federal union like the United States.

In the days before 1848 Gervinus shared the faith of Dahlmann and Droysen that German liberty and unity would come from Prussia. In 1847 a new liberal spirit originating in Switzerland and Italy began to influence Central Europe. Eager to meet in his own way some liberal demands, the Prussian king established the United Estates by his decree of February 3, 1847. Gervinus was deeply disappointed. He not only attacked the reactionary character of this act but deplored Prussia's repeated failure to follow the trend toward liberalism. "Prussia was given a constitution but it does not deserve the name." In the spring of 1847, in an effort to clear the atmosphere, he founded the *Deutsche Zeitung* in Heidelberg. He also participated in the planning for the National Assembly in the following year and became one of its members. But very soon the rabid nationalism and feeble liberalism of most of the members disgusted him. He left Frankfurt for Italy in July. He had lost any hope of a regeneration of Germany through a regenerated Prussia.

Events bore him out even in his own southwestern Germany. There, too, in Baden, Württemberg, and the Palatinate, democracy failed. It was finally suppressed by Prussian arms. In September, 1847, a mass meeting held at Offenburg in Baden, under the leadership of Friedrich Hecker, called for democratic reforms, and seven months later Hecker and his friends proclaimed a republic in Baden. The poet Georg Herwegh set out from Paris with a legion of German volunteers but the republic was poorly organized and poorly led, and the army gained the upper hand. More important was the attempt one year later to preserve the democratic constitution of the Frankfurt National Assembly in spite of the opposition of the German monarchies. Most of the members of the Assembly meekly capitulated before the authorities, but its radical members gathered in Stuttgart in Württemberg. One of their leaders, Ludwig Simon, a lawyer from Trier in the Rhineland, warned his compatriots that "if you allow yourselves to be conquered by Prussia, you will preserve in Germany the peace of the grave and the order of the churchyard. If you stand by the South German liberals, you will create the peace and order that liberty brings with her."

When the Prussian army under Prince William, the future William I, moved southward to suppress democracy in Germany, it found the stiffest resistance in Baden. There Lorenz Brentano, a lawyer from Mannheim, proclaimed a republic with the support of the majority of the population. The people fought well. The Swiss poet Gottfried Keller, who was then in Heidelberg and could observe the war at close range, wrote: "The Prussians paid dearly for their victory though they had superior forces. Especially the Baden artillerymen showed great heroism. As it was very hot, they worked at their guns in shirtsleeves as bakers do in front of the oven, and yet they were in high spirits. They shot their own wounded comrades to death to prevent them from falling into Prussian hands." The superior equipment and numbers of the Prussian army rendered resistance hopeless.

What the Russian troops did at about the same time in Hungary, Prussian soldiers accomplished in south-western Germany. German liberty was extinguished in a reign of terror. Nearly a thousand men were sentenced to long terms of hard labor, and over forty were executed. Out of a population of nearly one and one half million, eighty thousand citizens left Baden for Switzerland, England, and the United States. Almost equally great was the number who fled the Palatinate and the Rhineland. The revolutions of 1849 in Baden and the Palatinate were the last attempt to introduce democracy into Germany. An authoritarian exclusive nationalism triumphed in 1848 and carried Germany along a road far removed from that traced by Rotteck and Gervinus.

German Liberalism in 1848

BEFORE 1848 GERMAN LIBERALS hoped to achieve both national unity and political liberty. In the nineteenth century in western Europe nationalism and democratic liberalism supported and strengthened each other. The same process took place during the century in most Germanic lands—in Switzerland, in the Netherlands, and in Scandinavia. The Germans, however, did not succeed in uniting the two forces. The great majority of them desired national power even above liberty.

There were those who hoped that liberty would come after the creation of a strong nation-state. Recalling Periclean Athens and Elizabethan England, they insisted that great civilizations flourish under a strong government. But history exhibits many examples of artistic activity under weak governments, to mention only the Italian Renaissance and the ferment of Germany in Goethe's generation. But whatever might have been the hopes and illusions of the German national liberals, they preferred nationalism, and their liberalism was short-lived. Two critical years in the surrender of liberalism were 1848 and 1866. In both cases few Germans could resist the lure of power, a power embodied in the Prussian military monarchy.

After the Revolution of 1848 in Paris fanned the hopes of democracy in central Europe, the German liberals had to choose one of two alternatives. One was to reform the governments in the various German states, to call democratic assemblies in each, and thus to replace the absolutist authorities by popular institutions. Later on, the new democratic German states could have formed, by democratic means, a closer and more perfect union. In their haste to establish national unity, the German liberals proceeded otherwise. Instead of reforming and democratizing the various individual states—as the Swiss did in their cantons after 1831—and thus laying the foundations for German democracy, they ignored local institutions, traditional seats of loyalty and power, and called a democratically elected National Assembly to Frankfurt-am-Main, an assembly which rested on no real foundations and was not supported by any existing political structure. It was an overly ambitious project. For that very reason it achieved neither liberty nor unity. During the many months that it took to work out a democratic constitution for the whole of Germany the authoritarian governments of the various German lands, which in the spring of 1848 had briefly lost control of the situation, reasserted themselves, and the democratic constitution was doomed. Unity was achieved twenty years later by a determined adversary of liberal democracy, by Bismarck.

The National Assembly went further in predetermining the course of German history. No German prince of the time stood in as sharp an opposition to all western concepts of liberty and parliamentarism as did King Frederick William IV of Prussia. When he opened, on

April 11, 1847, the first session of the United Estates (*Vereinigte Landtag*) representing the various provinces of his kingdom, he warned the assembly against the un-Germanic and impractical illusion that it might be possible to realize in Germany parliamentary institutions. No power on earth, he solemnly professed, would ever succeed in making him change the natural relation between prince and people into a constitutional one. He swore that he would never allow a constitution, a piece of paper, to come between our Lord in Heaven and his (the king's) country, "to govern us with its articles and to replace old and sacred loyalties." He was convinced that his people would resist the wiles of seduction, that they did not wish to share in the government through their representatives and to break the plenitude of power entrusted by God to their kings. "I and my House, we wish to serve the Lord."

At the time this medieval approach aroused general consternation. Only Ranke was so naive as to believe that since King David no king had uttered more beautiful words. "I say definitely," he wrote, "that I know nothing since the psalms where the idea of a religious monarchy has been expressed more powerfully and more nobly. It has great passages of historical truth." Though the national liberals in Frankfurt did not share Ranke's profound devotion and put their hope instead in a liberal Prussia, they were so fascinated by Prussian power that in April, 1849, they offered the imperial crown of Germany to King Frederick William IV. The king, more faithful to his principles than the majority of liberals in the National Assembly were to theirs, rejected the crown offered to him by the democratically elected representatives of the nation. The Prussian ruling class had no faith in nation or people, in democracy or parliament. They expected the regeneration of Prussia from Prussia's traditional pillar of strength, the army. *"Gegen Demokraten helfen nur Soldaten"*— Only soldiers are of help against democrats—expressed the then prevailing mood in Berlin. After the failure of the Frankfurt Assembly to achieve German unity, many of the national liberals came to share their faith in Prussia's mission and in Prussia's army.

Before 1848 the national liberals expected Prussia to be absorbed in Germany. In an article published in the *Deutsche Zeitung* on January 1, 1848, Dahlmann pleaded for an hereditary imperial monarchy under the Hohenzollern. But he rejected the idea of Prussian domination over Germany and insisted that the German parliament must not meet in Berlin. On the contrary, he demanded, "the German Reichstag should have its seat anywhere but on Prussian soil. . . . In a short time there must be no Prussian region which has not

felt the rejuvenating breath of free German life." Piussia was to be
Germanized, not Germany Prussianized There was widespread
hope among the liberals that Prussia could be dissolved into its various provinces which would become in their own right part of the
united Germany. Thus the threat presented to German liberty and
cultural life by Prussia's overwhelming power and tradition might
be averted. This seemed not impossible in 1847. Most Prussian provinces were still corporate personalities with their own traditions,
their own Estates, and their own administrations. In March, 1848,
a strong separatist movement made itself felt in the Prussian Rhineland.

The experience of the year 1848-49 changed the outlook of the
national liberals. In a recent book, *Liberal Thought at the Time of
the Frankfurt Assembly*, the young German historian Wolfgang
Hock has carefully followed the progress of many German intellectuals from an initial clear distinction between national might and
self-interest on the one hand and right and morality on the other,
to their harmonization and identification. Gustav Rümelin took
this to be the mission which "our German people received from
history," to make morality ever more political and politics ever more
moral. Such an attempt at the harmonization of might and morality
was facilitated by several factors: the educated German middle class
lacked political experience It had not shared in the political life of
the country or in the administration of the state, which was reserved
for the closed caste of professional bureaucrats. German thought had
been predominantly philosophical and poetical and had neglected
the realities of state and power as well as the task of responsible self-
government and political education of the citizen.

Now the intellectuals seized upon the revelation of power—from the
exercise of which they remained excluded—with typical German
thoroughness, and with the enthusiasm of converts to a new faith.
They over-estimated and idealized power and the state as much as
they had formerly underestimated them. They overlooked the necessary limits and inherent dangers of power. They were convinced that
these dangers did not exist when power was in the right hands, in
the hands of a morally superior and better educated governing class
or nation. The new vision of power and national greatness was
intoxicating. The danger was all the greater the more sincerely
these educated Germans were convinced of their own morality and
rationality. They lacked even a slight—and often healthy—dash of
humor, of cynicism, or of self-criticism. They were deeply in earnest.
Thus they easily succumbed to temptation without even being

aware of it. Jacob Burckhardt saw this clearly. On August 23, 1848, he wrote to his German friend, Hermann Schaumburg· "Do what you wish or must do, only don't imagine that you are free while in reality the darkest elemental spirits dwell in you and drive you on *(die dunkelsten Elementargeister ihr Wesen mit Euch treiben)."*

An understandable desire for action, for a new fulness of life, animated the educated German middle class. They no longer wished to be a people of thinkers, poets, and dreamers. Impatiently they longed for great deeds on the world stage. The pettier the present appeared to them the mightier was their vision of the future. They knew that German classical literature was great. In their eyes it represented a unique re-embodiment of the heritage of Greece. But now its task was fulfilled. The time had come to assert German political leadership as Luther had three centuries before established German religious leadership. A man like Luther was needed, not in the field of religion but in the realm of politics. How could such a great destiny be realized without the help of those in power?

Dahlmann, in the speech of January 22, 1849, in which he proposed the imperial crown for Prussia, voiced the growing conviction that power was more important than liberty. "The path of power," he declared, "is the only one which can satisfy and satiate our urge for liberty. For this urge does not primarily aspire to liberty; to a greater degree it lusts for power which has so far been denied to it. This can be accomplished only through Prussia. Prussia can not thrive *(genesen)* without Germany nor Germany without Prussia." The same shift to a preference for state-power over liberty can be traced, as Professor Felix Gilbert has shown, in the thought of another great liberal historian, Droysen. In 1847 he had written that history teaches us everywhere that the longing for power and glory deludes nations and states, for it overstimulates and finally brutalizes and debilitates them. But at the end of 1848, in the midst of the popular uprisings, he confessed that he saw in the [Prussian] army a great moral force, and that power alone could save Germany. "The State is Power," he proclaimed as did Treitschke later. Droysen now abandoned the hope that Prussia would become Germanized and a part of Germany; on the contrary, Prussia in its full power and armed with the Prussian tradition appeared as the political savior of Germany. In a revolutionary year men and movements travel rapidly a long road, some forward to liberty, others backward to the apparent security of great power.

The desire to establish unity before securing liberty, had another and even more fateful consequence. The Frankfurt Assembly took the lead in the disputes over imperial frontiers. The question of the territorial size of the state, the precedence given to all its national rights and needs overshadowed the concern for liberty and obliterated the former liberal principle of equal rights of all nationalities. This insistence on the vague concept of integrity of the Reich frontiers—an insistence in which historical rights and ethnographic claims were used whenever necessary—was as dangerous to liberal democracy in 1848–49 as it was in 1918–19. In 1848 the national liberals developed the system of double entry bookkeeping which is so widely characteristic of modern nationalism everywhere. They established a twofold scale of political and moral judgment, defining the same action as wrong when done by the other people and regarding it as right when one's own national advantage seemed to justify it.

The three frontiers where historical and ethnic principles were invoked, depending upon national aggrandizement and self-interest, were Schleswig, Polish Poznan, and Alsace. The desire to annex Schleswig which had been historically united with Denmark for centuries and where Danish and German elements intermingled, led to a further demand which—in spite of its novelty—acquired a sudden popularity, the demand for the creation of a German navy to re-establish the long forgotten glory of the days of Hanseatic supremacy. The thought of a German navy sailing the seven seas was tempting. Everywhere navy clubs were organized and money was collected. All this was utterly impractical. At that time Germany was entirely unprepared for such a task. Yet for many weeks the representatives of the German people devoted their energies to vague dreams of expansion at the risk of losing whatever opportunity they had to establish liberty at home.

In 1830 the German liberals had not dreamed of a German fleet but of the restoration of Polish liberty. What a contrast eighteen years later! The National Assembly was no longer willing to restore Poland. It was, on the contrary, eager to incorporate into Germany the Poles of the Grand Duchy of Poznan which in 1815 at the Congress of Vienna had been given to Prussia as an autonomous province, preserving its Polish character. Some members of the National Assembly—Robert Blum, Arnold Ruge, Wilhelm Michael Schaffrath—were faithful to the liberal European tradition of condemning the Polish partitions. They held it was the duty of the German people to plan for the restoration of an independent Poland. The majority of the National Assembly, however, agreed with Wilhelm Jordan, a liberal from East Prussia who appealed to the right of conquest by plough and sword and called all those who saw some justice in the Polish point of view "traitors to their own people." "An iron ruthlessness, a delight in German strength and greatness found its expression in this speech, often almost with a deliberate rudeness," wrote Veit Valentin, the leading historian of the Frankfurt Assembly. "The discussion concerning Poland in July, 1848, was one of the most important turning points in the history of the German National Assembly." The majority voted against the very principles which the movement of 1848 had professed. In four months most of the liberals in Frankfurt were converted from liberalism to nationalism. In March, 1848, the principle of self-determination was proclaimed as universally valid. Four months later it was applied to Germans only whenever German claims conflicted with other peoples' rights. Yet the national liberals were convinced that they did not assert a desire for dominion but fulfilled a sacred national duty. No people, their spokesmen declared, could be expected to sacrifice its rights and interests for another people.

This change in the intellectual climate was not confined to Germany. Throughout central and eastern Europe the year 1848 marked a transition from liberalism to nationalism, from humanitarian considerations to self-assertion, from a faith in harmony to an affirmation of power and violence. Historians and scholars of all nationalities put their ingenuity into the service of nationalist claims and causes. But the Germans who so easily succumbed to the seduction of ideas went farther astray than other peoples. They took greater pride in it. Their greater power and their greater abilities made their vagaries more dangerous to themselves and to other people.

The Germans of the Age of Nationalism had no liberal statesman, no Gladstone, not even a Cavour, Clemenceau, or Masaryk, to direct their national energies into democratic channels. Instead, they had Bismarck. What the revolution of 1848 failed to do, his revolution of 1866 accomplished. It laid the foundations of a unified German nation-state. Bismarck put the Hohenzollern into the position which the Hohenstaufen once occupied. But the foundations laid by Bismarck seemed stronger at that time than they were shown to be a few decades later. Solitary voices crying in the wilderness of national self-satisfaction warned Bismarck's admirers in vain against overestimating power and underestimating liberty. For 1866 failed even more disastrously than 1848 in securing liberty and infusing nationalism with the spirit of democracy.

Chapter Seven

1866: ANNUS MIRABILIS

The Revival of Nationalism

AFTER THE FAILURE of the Frankfurt National Assembly to establish German national unity and political liberty, the old order was secure for a decade. Frederick William IV was its typical representative. He and his advisors were archconservatives. The king was not ungifted; he was simply devoid of common sense. But as a conservative he was neither a militarist nor an expansionist. He did not enlarge the Prussian army nor did he dream of depriving fellow monarchs of their lands. For romantic-historical reasons he identified the German imperial crown with the Habsburgs. He followed his father Frederick William III who had lived in the tradition of the Holy Alliance and had insisted upon the concert of powers. In his testament the old king admonished his successor never to separate Prussia from Russia and Austria. "Their co-operation should be regarded as the cornerstone of the European alliance," intended to maintain a peaceful and conservative international order.

The year 1859 brought a revival of the political aspirations of 1848. Germany was not, like Italy, merely a cultural unit. Nor did it consist only of small and weak states, many of them ruled by foreigners. After all, two of the five great European powers were German in their character. In addition, most of Germany, in the customs union founded by Prussia, formed an economic unit. The German Confederation provided a loose political tie among the German lands, an internationally recognized representation of Germany as a whole. Yet growing public opinion demanded a closer and more perfect union. No agreement, however, existed about the means of reaching this goal. Many Germans wished to maintain the Con-

144

federation with its federal character strengthened. They believed that neither Prussia nor Austria should form the center of this reformed confederation, but that a third Germany, a third force between the two great powers, should be the core—a core consisting of the smaller states of the South and the Southwest which seemed, not without justification, to be the historical and cultural heart of Germany. The national liberals, however, were opposed to the federal principle. They demanded a unified state under Prussia's leadership. Their hopes that a reformed Prussia would unify Germany, by moral conquests or by the sword, were revived at the end of 1858 when Frederick William IV became insane and was succeeded by his brother William. The new regent, the future King William I, was then sixty-one years old. He was a much less complex personality than his brother. He had only one main interest, the Prussian army. Nevertheless, at the beginning, he seemed to be ready to break with the extreme ideological conservatism of his brother and to make some concessions to liberalism.

The German desire for closer unity was also stimulated in 1859 by the war which France and Sardinia started against Austria on behalf of Italian nationalism and its desire for political unity. The war marked the beginning of the rapid unification of Italy under the Sardinian dynasty. Cavour's daring policy was actively supported by the National Association, *Società nazionale italiana,* which represented the educated middle class in several of the Italian states. It was founded in 1857 under the auspices of Daniel Manin and had as its motto *"Italia e Vittorio Emanuele,"* Italy and the King of Sardinia. The Italian example stirred the Germans in various ways. The national liberals founded in 1859 their national association (*Nationalverein*) which had its center in Frankfurt. It was staunchly pro-Prussian and Protestant. Understandably it aroused violent opposition in Catholic southern Germany. Prussia was unwilling to come to the help of Austria in 1859; on the other hand, most south Germans were eager to support Catholic Austria in the struggle with Napoleon III. They accused Prussia of betraying the German cause, as she had done in two previous wars against France—in 1795 and 1805. But the willingness to support the German cause by preserving Austria's position in Italy—a position in the tradition of the medieval Germanic Empire—was in no way confined to Catholics.

In 1859, the Protestant historian Felix Dahn, who grew up in Munich and became a fervent follower of Bismarck, declared in a poem that Austria's struggle for Italy was Germany's opportunity to restore the Hohenstaufen glory and to avenge Konradin's death.

"I know of a black day," a stanza of the poem read, "when a glorious German dynasty fell, fell by the blow of a French executioner, fell in Italy, fell against all right. A blond youth cried out, 'Before I die, I throw down the glove of vengeance.' Arise, Austria, heir of the Hohenstaufen!—Konradin still waits for vengeance." *

Most German nationalists, however, favored Sardinia. The Prussian socialist Ferdinand Lassalle called upon Prussia to follow Sardinia's example. Napoleon III apparently was out to revise the map of Europe according to the principle of nationality. Prussia should do the same in the north by taking Schleswig-Holstein from Denmark. The young socialist leader enthusiastically embraced the nationalist goals of 1848 "Let the Prussian government begin this national war quickly, alone and of its own volition," Lassalle's fiery argument may be summed up, "Let it appear before the world with the fact accompli of a declared war," and the German people will readily follow it. "This war is just as vital for the German people as for Prussia. German democracy itself will carry Prussia's standard and will cast down all obstacles with an expansive force which will be created by the intoxicated outbreak of national emotion." Only by such deeds, Lassalle proclaimed, will German national sentiment become strong, proud, and secure.

In this respect Lassalle's sentiments were shared by the most determined opponent of socialism and of the working class, Heinrich von Treitschke, who wrote in a letter on November 26, 1860. "I wish Prussia to take an intelligent and honest step and to start now the war, which will in any case break out within a few years. Prussia should—at the risk of a terrible struggle—finally, finally demand that Denmark pay its debt of honor to Germany. Should the war with Napoleon then follow, let it come. Our hands are clean, and the struggle will be a popular war which will bring Prussia immeasurable moral gains if not the German crown." Treitschke was convinced of the close affinity between Sardinia and Prussia. "Both cherish the ambition of conquest. . . . Both are the sword of their nations. . . . Both earn by their deeds of arms the irreconcilable

---

* *Ich weiss von einem schwarzen Tage,*
Da fiel ein herrlich deutsch Geschlecht,
Fiel von franzos'schem Henkerschlage,
In Welschland fiel's, fiel wider Recht
Ein blonder Knab' rief: Eh ich sterbe,
Werf' ich den Rachehandschuh hin.—
Auf, Östreich, Hohenstaufenerbe—
Noch harrt der Rache Konradin!

hatred of radicalism (by radicalism Treitschke always meant democracy). In both countries the dream of the Piedmontese aristocracy has come true· A king who rules, a nobility at his side, a people that obeys."

The Socialist Lassalle and the extreme nationalist Treitschke agreed upon the military spirit of Prussia. They both welcomed it, as the liberal Gustav Freytag had done as far back as 1848· "If in order to bring about (German) unity, we must march against Germans, which God forbid, Prussia will march. Perhaps this is what fundamentally distinguishes us Prussians from other Germans. We are ready to shed our last drop of blood to have our way. We have an object in view, a great idea for which we live. Our opponents have no such idea. What have we to fear? Are we not a nation of warriors?"

Lassalle and Freytag were both Prussians, natives of Prussia's eastern border lands. Treitschke was by birth not a Prussian, but a Saxon. His father, a general, remained throughout his life loyal to his king and country. He suffered grievously when his beloved and gifted son turned against his native land and extolled its most relentless enemy, Prussia. Young Treitschke studied in 1851 at the Prussian University of Bonn where many years before Heine's fervent love of Germany had been awakened. There Treitschke was inspired by two history teachers, typical national liberals of the older generation. Ernst Moritz Arndt, then eighty-two years old, filled him with pride in the German race and with confidence in German greatness. From Dahlmann Treitschke received the vision of an approaching great struggle which would decide "whether our European continent will be able in the future to defend its position against America which is developing in such a different direction." In this struggle, Dahlmann was convinced, Europe's salvation would depend upon a strong Germany led by Prussia. To this goal Treitschke devoted his life. Reading Machiavelli in 1856, he wrote his father that the Renaissance historian sacrificed abstract justice for a greater ideal, the might and unity of his nation. "The fundamental idea of the book—the fiery patriotism and the conviction that even the most oppressive despotism must be welcomed if the might and unity of the fatherland demand it—this is what reconciles me to the many objectionable and terrible opinions of the great Florentine."

When a young man, Treitschke called himself a liberal. The conservatives of his day defended the status quo—the petty princely courts and stagnant police regimes. Treitschke realized that these obsolete regimes were unable to assure national greatness and power, to inaugurate an era of dynamic growth, and to give scope to the ambitions of the rising middle class. But he was opposed to what the West called liberalism. He did not realize that modern nations draw their strength from individual liberty and universal ideas. From these ideas, and not from the nation-state, flow the vital forces and the inspiration which endow western society with a cohesion and resilience unknown to authoritarian regimes. In an essay, *"Die Frei-heit"* (1861), he took issue with John Stuart Mill's "On Liberty" and Edouard Laboulaye's *L'état et ses limites*. He objected to the point of view that led the Englishman to proclaim the political development of the United States as a desirable end, and the Frenchman to regard the nineteenth century as an epoch in which the Christian ideal of the dignity of the individual would be realized. Unlike these men Treitschke demanded not liberty from the state but only liberty within the state, liberty limited by the state's own aims. He clearly distinguished the ideal of authoritarian German society from the liberal society of the West.

In its fundamental opposition to western liberalism the Prussian monarchy had only one rival in Europe: the Russian monarchy. Lord Acton defined the character of the two governments in the last lecture on modern history he delivered at Cambridge at the end of the nineteenth century. He stressed the fact that the two governments of St. Petersburg and Berlin were fundamentally different from those of London and Washington. In the two eastern monarchies, the government was "the intellectual guide of the nation, the promotor of wealth, the teacher of knowledge, the guardian of morality, the mainspring of the ascending movement of man." He warned that the tremendous power, supported by millions of bayonets which grew up in the eighteenth century in Petersburg and was later developed by much abler minds in Berlin, was "the greatest danger that remains to be encountered by the Anglo-Saxon race." The development of such a power in Germany was due to the extremely able mind of Bismarck. But he could not have succeeded if writers and historians had not prepared the public mind. In 1886 Lord Acton spoke of a phalanx of scholars, "the first classics of imperialism, a garrison of distinguished historians, that prepared the Prussian supremacy together with their own and now hold Berlin like a fortress." In those days it seemed an impregnable fortress, but like all fortresses, it limited the view of the outside world and distorted perspective.

Prussia and Liberalism

THE HOPES FOR A LIBERALIZATION of Prussia under William did not outlast 1859. In that year Germany celebrated the centennial of Schiller's birth. He was then seen as a powerful voice awakening the dormant German people to a high idealism devoted to nation-hood and independence. His popular plays were interpreted as calls to action; the war of liberation, the fiftieth anniversary of which was celebrated in 1863, was strangely regarded as Schiller's spiritual child. In Vienna Grillparzer thought of protesting Schiller's degra-dation into a patriotic bard, but his friend Heinrich Laube, director of the Burgtheater, dissuaded him from doing so. But even this misinterpretation of Schiller—whose supposed patriotic élan was extolled against Goethe's indifference—could not conceal the passion for individual liberty that inspired all of Schiller's works. In 1859 this cry for liberty was taken up by the nationalists. Was not Prussia herself on the road to liberalism? The evidence for such a develop-ment was not lacking. The Prussian Chamber of Deputies, though composed only of members of the upper classes, rejected the king's demands for the expansion and strengthening of the Prussian army. More than the size or equipment of the armed forces was involved in the struggle between king and parliament. The king insisted on an army under his personal command, exempt from all civilian or parliamentary control. The soldiers were to serve for long periods and to be trained in a spirit which would make them a reliable bul-wark against democracy and parliamentarism. To accept the king's demand would thus have meant the capitulation of the middle class to militarism and junkerism. In this constitutional struggle the char-acter of the Prussian state and the future of Germany were at stake. The fears which animated the middle class were well founded. Dis-turbed by the unexpected resistance of the Chamber, King William resolutely turned away from the incipient liberalization of the re-gime. The Diet was dissolved. In the new elections the administra-tion used all its power to have a conservative majority returned. In spite of open pressure and interference, the opposition emerged strengthened from the elections; it received more than two thirds of the seats. A liberal future seemed assured for Prussia. Many men of high rank favored it Even devoted royalists spoke of the need of introducing a parliamentary regime and of asserting the power of public opinion over an obsolete divine-right monarchy.

In these months the future of Prussia was in the balance. King William, who could not imagine himself as king if he were not in absolute control of the armed forces, wished to abdicate. But the crown prince, a more liberal and modern man than his father, refused the throne, partly out of the delicacy of scruples, partly out of the conviction that his father was an old man and that his turn would soon come. History decided otherwise. His father lived to be niney-one years old, and when the crown prince followed him, at the age of fifty-seven, he was dying of cancer of the throat. In the twenty-six intervening years the man whom the crown prince soon learned to hate, Otto von Bismarck, decided the fate of Prussia, of Germany, and of Europe. For almost a century German liberalism was crippled, after Bismarck broke its backbone. Without his long reign Prussia and Germany would in all probability have developed along more western lines. So much in history often depends on personal decisions and biological accidents.

Dismayed by the strength of the liberal opposition in the country, the king turned in September, 1862 to Bismarck as the one man able to destroy the opposition and to carry through the program of junkerism and militarism. Bismarck's success surpassed William's hopes. Without abolishing the constitution Bismarck completely disregarded it. With a strong hand he restored the police state with its censorship and its use of the courts and bureaucracy to suppress popular opposition. But the new police state no longer was conservative and peaceful; it became in Bismarck's mastermind the instrument of a dynamic and aggressive policy. The middle classes did not at first understand these implications. They were indignant and regarded Bismarck as an old-fashioned reactionary. Max von Forckenbeck, a national liberal, a member of the Prussian Chamber of Deputies and its president from 1866 to 1873, wrote on September 24, 1862: "Bismarck stands for a government without an approved budget, a regime of the sabre at home and a war abroad. I regard him as the most dangerous minister for Prussia's liberty and well-being." Five days later Treitschke himself wrote to his brother-in-law: "You know how passionately I love Prussia but when I hear a shallow Junker like this Bismarck boast of the iron and blood by which he intends to dominate Germany, I can only say it is hard to tell whether he is more vulgar or ridiculous."

But dislike for Bismarck was in no way confined to the educated middle class, for whom spoke men like Forckenbeck and Treitschke. It was equally strong at the court and among Prussian diplomats Not only the crown prince but his wife, Victoria, oldest daughter of Queen Victoria, were and remained Bismarck's opponents. The Queen of Prussia herself shared the aversion to the powerful Prime Minister and his policy. Augusta was born and educated in Goethe's Weimar, the grand-daughter of Karl August, Goethe's patron. She was deeply interested in music, in the arts and in humanitarian causes. Bismarck, who was a passionate hater, did everything in his power to make life difficult not only for the crown prince, but for the wife of his sovereign. Out of the depth of his nature he despised in Augusta the spirit of Weimar and everything Weimar stood for. It is difficult to say whether his growing dislike for Augusta increased his innate disgust of Weimar, as Friedrich Gundolf assumes, or whether the reverse was the case.* But supremely unmindful of all the opposition, whether from the liberals or from the court, Bismarck unflinchingly and with supreme intelligence carried through his policy. It represented—from the conservative as well as from the liberal point of view—a break with Prussian and German traditions, a true revolution.

Bismarck even considered embarrassing his liberal opponents by introducing general suffrage in Prussia. Napoleon III had shown that this instrument of democracy could be harmless in the hands of a popular authoritarian regime. Bismarck was convinced that the grant of the vote to the farmers and rural workers would weaken the liberals; the masses who depended upon their landlords and were susceptible to pressure from the authorities could be relied upon to vote for the government. Bismarck toyed with this idea and discussed it with Lassalle; he later introduced democratic suffrage in

---

* In almost untranslatable German Friedrich Gundolf, professor of German literature at Heidelberg, described Bismarck's antipathy to Augusta and Weimar, to the arts, to humanitarianism, to what had been regarded as German culture: *"Seine angeborene Fremdheit gegen den Geist von Weimar und dessen Sinnbilder, gegen das Apollinische, Hellenistische, Olympische, Idealische, Humanitare mag noch gesteigert worden sein durch den Widerwillen gegen die Frau seines Herrn und Gonners Wilhelm Schon als Prinzessin von Preussen, dann als Königin und Kaiserin hat diese feinsinnige, geistreiche, ehrgeizig ahnungslose, ränkesuchtig gepflegte Dame dem gewaltigen Mann auf Schritt und Tritt seine Arbeit gestört, und da er nicht in Prinzipien, sondern in Menschen, Kraften, Dünsten dachte und fühlte, so warf ihm diese Widersacherin mit dem abgestandenen bissigsubtilen Bildungsgetue, mit dem unverantwortlichen Geschmäckern, mit ihrem Gezisch und Geschleiche, mit dem huldvollen Geraschel und Gehüstel ihren grünlichen Giftschein zuruck auf den ganzen Bereich ihrer Herkunft, auf das spatgoethische Weimar."*

the new Reichstag, though not in Prussia, where it was not realized before 1919; the means, however, by which he carried through his revolution was not the vote but the sword. Napoleon III and Cavour relied on plebiscites, on the expression of the will of the people. Bismarck trusted in arms and in diplomacy. He crushed the liberal opposition not by parliamentary majorities but by a successful foreign policy based upon "iron and blood" In 1862, in the same speech in which he first used this famous phrase, Bismarck confidently claimed that "Germany does not look to Prussia for liberalism, but for power." He was right, and not only for his own day. Even under his successors, down to the year 1945, German life bore the indelible imprint of his spirit. "There can be no question," Professor Hajo Holborn recently wrote, "that the traditions of the Bismarckian Empire were the principal factor in the destruction of the Weimar Republic."

The Polish uprising against Russia in 1863 offered Bismarck the first opportunity for his new policy. Denying the tradition of liberalism and the principle of national self-determination Bismarck openly supported the tsarist regime in its suppression of the Polish struggle for liberty. At the same time he played with more far-reaching projects in case Russia should decide to withdraw from Poland. He was determined that in that event Prussia should gain control of Poland. He had no doubt the Germans would be able "to Germanize Poland in three years." He thus anticipated, to quote Professor Sell, the plan carried out by Hitler eighty years later.

In all likelihood, however, the Germanization of Poland would have been less popular with German liberals than the subjugation of the Schleswig-Holsteiners to Prussia, a step which could be presented as their liberation from Danish domination. In 1864 as in 1848, this issue fanned the flames of German nationalism. Bismarck went to war against Denmark, ostensibly to help the prince Friedrich von Augustenburg whom the Schleswig-Holsteiners and the German Confederation regarded as the lawful pretender for the duchies. As soon as victory was won, however, Bismarck—who as a monarchist was supposed to support the legitimate rights of princes—repudiated the legitimate German dynasty. In the conquered land he established a Prussian administration which the Schleswig-Holsteiners violently opposed and which German public opinion denounced. Both demanded the recognition of the right of the Germans of Schleswig-Holstein to self-determination, a right which Bismarck denied for the sake of Prussian self-interest.

In that conflict leading German historians—Droysen, Sybel,

Mommsen, and Treitschke—came to Bismarck's support. They maintained that it was more important to strengthen Prussia than to uphold either the lawful claims of the Prince of Augustenburg and of the German Confederation or the right of the inhabitants of Schleswig-Holstein to self-determination. It was a fateful step. For these scholars were counted liberals. Yet they were willing to abandon the foundations of law and justice, indispensable even for authoritarian states, and to sanctify the principle of naked power and self-interest. Bismarck felt fortified in his policy, but in spite of this incipient liberal support, he made no concessions to constitutionalism. Domestic repression was even intensified. Prussian courts were openly turned into instruments of governmental policy, and in spite of Bismarck's victory against Denmark, the distrust and dislike of him became general throughout Germany. In this situation he seized the initiative by bringing about a war in which Prussia allied itself with Italy against Austria and the German Confederation.

During the war Bismarck began to inflame Magyar and Czech nationalism against Austria. For the sake of Prussia, he was willing to gamble with the revolutionary principle of national self-determination among Italians, Hungarians, and Slavs. The monarchist Junker was ready to align himself with revolution against legitimacy. Other Prussian conservatives, advisors of the late King Frederick William IV, saw him following in the footsteps of Napoleon III, and warned him against an unprincipled power policy. But they misjudged Bismarck as much as the liberals did. The complexity of his personality escaped all of them. He stood above party and principle. The means which he employed appeared objectionable and revolutionary at different times to all parties. His success brought about a complete revolution in both conservative and liberal thought. After 1866 Germany knew neither a true conservatism nor a true liberalism. For Germany Burke and Disraeli were as unthinkable as Gladstone and Mill.

The Revolution of 1866

AT THE BEGINNING Bismarck's war met hostility throughout the German lands. Even in Prussia it was highly unpopular. Few Protestants favored it. The Catholics unanimously opposed it. The liberals were convinced that Bismarck's victory would deal the last blow to liberalism. The king himself had to be maneuvered into accepting the war. He played the same role which Hindenburg, so like the king in many respects. performed at a later period. In 1928 the German historian Hans Delbruck, an admirer of Bismarck, wrote of the war: "Bismarck willed it, deeply convinced of its necessity, but he carried it through against the will of the king, the will of the people, and even the will of the army." In its consequences the war represented a revolution in German history and thought. This revolution could not have happened without Bismarck just as the revolution of 1933 could not have happened without Hitler. In both cases it was the work of one man who accomplished it against much opposition and many doubts, in the case of Bismarck even more than in the case of Hitler. In both cases once the revolutions were successful opposition rapidly dissolved and the doubts were stilled.

In a letter written on May 18th, the eve of the war of 1866, the Prussian liberal Franz Ziegler, then a member of the Diet and a former Lord Mayor of Brandenburg, described the general distrust of Bismarck, shared by almost all Prussians: "One would gladly accept Caesarism, if there were a Caesar. A Caesar enjoys the confidence of the masses, while Bismarck has none. You can't imagine how much this man is being hated or, what is even worse, is being ridiculed. . . . Everything is going to pieces: if you heard the army reservists talk and saw how they behave, you could not understand how the officers could lead them. I hardly believe in revolution, but should we have reverses, we must expect an uprising, and Bismarck will be unable to show himself anywhere in this country. The people hate the feudal class, and they count Bismarck irrevocably a member of it. They are offended at the thought that a man of this type should be in charge." This opinion was shared by high conservative officials. Albrecht Count Bernstorff, the Prussian ambassador to London, wrote on June 26, 1866, to Count Robert von der Goltz, the Prussian ambassador to Paris: "I have often considered whether there was a way to avert the misfortune which Bismarck has brought on us, and whether I could intervene with the king. But I had to tell myself that His Majesty undoubtedly knew my point of view and that many important persons around him urged him to keep the peace without being able to draw him away from the unfortunate influence of the Prime Minister. How shall we be able to enter upon such a war, without backing in our own country, against the will of the immense majority of our own people, with the army reserves recalcitrant?"

Sir Robert Morier, for many years a British diplomatic agent at German courts, rightly foresaw, however, that Bismarck's success might revolutionize public opinion. "The one thing," he wrote to Lady Salisbury on June 24, 1866, "for which, . . . above all other things, I conceive Bismarck ought to be execrated, is his having by the impress of his own detestable individuality on the political canvas now unrolling before Europe so utterly disfigured the true outlines of the picture, that not only public opinion, but the judgment of wise and thoughtful men is almost sure to go wrong. I say this quite deliberately, knowing that if Bismarck succeeds, the world will clap its hands and say he was the only man who knew how to bring about what the world, which always worships success, will say was a consummation it always desired. Whereas that which will be really proved is that Prussia was so strong and so really the heart and head and lungs of Germany, that she could, by her mere natural development *with* instead of *against* the liberal and national forces of Germany, have effected what required to be done by peaceful means and without bloodshed."

Sir Robert would have agreed with the character sketch of Bismarck which the British minister to the German Diet in Frankfurt, Sir Alexander Malet, drew in a report of May 28, 1862. He called him first a Prussian, second a through and through Prussian, and third a German by being Prussian. Sir Alexander insisted on Bismarck's measureless contempt for public opinion, and for German liberalism. Without hesitation he would do anything, if opportunity offered itself, to accomplish a greater Prussia which remained the goal of his life and of his political ambition.

The war of 1866 brought this opportunity. Prussia won it in a few weeks with astonishing ease. The German Confederation, the only existing political tie of the German lands, was dissolved. Prussia annexed German territory with equal disregard of the rights of hereditary monarchs, of the wishes of the population, and of centuries-old German traditions. The kingdom of Hanover, ruled by a dynasty older and more famous than the Hohenzollern, was incorporated into Prussia, as was the free city of Frankfurt which had been for so long Germany's capital and the symbol of its democratic hopes. For that very reason it was hated by Bismarck and, though it did not participate in the war, suffered more cruel depradation than any other of the German territories occupied by the Prussians. Frankfurt lost its historical significance. The memory of the National Assembly of 1848 was wiped out by the new revolution.*

---

* Frankfurt became a Prussian provincial town. The same fate was later to befall Vienna. In a letter of October 2, 1869 Treitschke wrote to his

More important, however, than the aggrandizement of Prussia and its now undisputed leading role in Germany was the revolution in German public opinion. The outcome of one battle—near König-grätz on July 3—decided the war. Immediately after the victory the population of Berlin, which, according to Professor Ziekursch, had only a few months before regretted that an attempt on Bismarck's life miscarried, turned jubilantly to Bismarck. It was as if the German people had witnessed a miracle. Nothing was any longer as it had been. Insoluble problems seemed solved. National unity seemed within reach. In June most Germans dreaded a long and costly war of Germans against Germans. In mid-July one of the few who proved completely immune to the general intoxication, the socialist leader, Wilhelm Liebknecht, wrote that in a sudden change yesterday's oppressors were greeted as today's saviors; what was right had become wrong, and what was wrong had become right. The angel of darkness, whom the Germans only yesterday stigmatized as the destroyer of constitutional life, had by the mystic power of bloodshed been transformed into an angel of light, crowned with a laurel wreath, before whom the people prostrated themselves. Many years later, looking back upon the year 1866, a Baltic German journalist, Julius von Eckardt, wrote in his memoirs· "I never breathed in my life a more invigorating air than the one which blew in the fall of 1866 through north Germany. It cast an incomparable spell over us. One felt as if one were standing at the threshold of a new period, a period which promised miracles. One lived under the impression of a surprise which had come so suddenly and with such overwhelming fulness that the patriots who a short while before had been full of fears and sombre premonitions suddenly felt like dreamers."

German history was reinterpreted in the wake of the revolution. Southern and western Germany now appeared far less German than Prussia. They were regarded as the home of two un-Germanic forces, Western democracy and Roman Catholicism, which threatened and weakened Germany and prevented her political and cul-

---

wife that he met Wilhelm Scherer, a native of Austria, who was then professor of German literature at the University of Vienna and later became professor in Strasbourg and Berlin. The Austrian passionately insisted that Vienna could become a decent place only as a Prussian provincial city. Treitschke did not share his opinion for he could not see where Prussia could find the immense strength needed for such a tremendous task. Seventy years later Vienna became a Prussian provincial city. Another Austrian, Hitler, was confident that Prussia was strong enough to make Vienna a decent place (ein anständiger Ort).

tural strength. Even more astonishing was the sudden discovery that Frederick II of Prussia represented the true Germany. Schiller's warning was forgotten:

> *Die grossen schnellen Taten der Gewalt,*
> *Des Augenblicks erstaunenswerte Wunder,*
> *Die sind es nicht, die das Begluckerde,*
> *Das ruhig, mächtig Dauernde erzeugen.*

(The great and rapid deeds of force
The awe-inspiring miracles of the moment,
These do not create lasting values
Which thrive in stillness and enrich man.)

The Surrender of Liberalism

AN ESSAY, *"Der Deutsche Liberalismus. Eine Selbstkritik,"* by the German historian Hermann Baumgarten, provides a curious commentary on the Revolution of 1866. A typical liberal in his reaction to the revolution, this disciple of Gervinus, who joined the faculty of the University of Karlsruhe in Baden, and played his part in the political life of that liberal state, was a specialist in Spanish history. He explained Spain's downfall by pointing out that she "had lived for over one hundred years in a dangerous dream, as if she had the ability and the moral obligation of determining the fate of mankind. Perhaps nothing has done greater harm to Spain than her squandering so much of her best strength on this phantom."

Yet when it came to a similar problem in German history, Baumgarten was blind to its implications. His analysis of German liberalism that appeared at the end of 1866 in *Preussische Jahrbücher,* a periodical edited by Treitschke, is one of the most remarkable—though today largely forgotten—documents in the history of German liberalism. It proclaimed its capitulation before the victorious forces of Prussian militarism. Like most liberals, Baumgarten had opposed Bismarck and the king. Now he was convinced that he and his fellow-scholars had been wrong. The military program of the king, which the majority of the Prussian Chamber and nation had opposed, had been necessary, because Prussia, as Baumgarten now discovered, was in the 1860's in danger of being encircled by the smaller German states. Prussia could only save herself by arming for a quick offensive. But how could the civilian middle class understand the situation? Baumgarten asked. Even at the outbreak of the war of 1866 it doubted the wisdom of the king and attacked Bismarck. Only to the hands of monarchs and their chosen leaders could foreign and military affairs be safely entrusted.

Thus the German liberals were ready to adore what, a few weeks before they had condemned. Baumgarten, a mild, learned, and good man, spoke in lyrical terms of victorious Prussia. She had proved herself not only healthy, but also highly civilized, whereas her enemies—Austria and the other German states—were not only sickly, but even barbaric. "The astonished world," he went on, "did not know what to admire more, the unique organization of Prussia's armed forces or the ethical dedication of its people, the incomparable health of its economy or the solidity of its general education, the greatness of its victories or the modesty of its victory bulletins, the courage of its young soldiers or the devotion to duty of its aged king. . . . This peoples in arms stormed forward with irrepressible force . . . and yet remained a people of peace, entirely untouched by the intoxication of military glory, . . . mourning over those who had died rather than jubilant over victory."

In this panegyric the historian was a poor witness to truth, for most of the people, like most of the scholars, were intoxicated with and jubilant over victory. More important was the fact that Baumgarten and his colleagues were unable to see Prussia's victory in a long-range perspective. They attributed the victory to Prussia's innate and therefore enduring superiority, instead of to circumstances of capable leadership and thorough preparation, circumstances which were subject to change.

Equally ominous was the self-abasement of the liberals and the middle class before the Junker aristocracy and the military experts. Baumgarten did not confine himself to the statement that he and his friends had been wrong in their opposition to the king and to Bismarck. He immediately drew sweeping conclusions from the fact that success had apparently proven Bismarck right. Denying the general ability of himself and his class to understand, even less to direct, national policy, he concluded that "the citizen is born to work, but not to be a statesman." The best among the nonaristocratic citizens had to forge their way from relative poverty to success and esteem, and such a preparation did not, in the opinion of the educated German middle class in the second half of the nineteenth century, qualify them for political life. The citizen simply lacked the knowledge necessary to understand politics. "It is one of the most ruinous errors to believe that a good scholar, lawyer, merchant, or civil servant, who is interested in public affairs and reads the newspapers assiduously, is able to participate actually in political life," wrote Baumgarten. The educated middle class in the Chamber of Deputies certainly had shown good qualities, because otherwise they would not have gained the confidence of their voters, Baumgarten conceded, speaking of his own class, but how, he asked, could such people decide matters beyond their horizon and about which they had no independent judgment and no profound knowledge?

These passages written with so much sincerity must be pondered if we are to understand the deep gulf which separated the educated and professional Germans from their counterparts in the West. A whole class of learned and well-meaning men professed their immaturity in political affairs. Such an attitude explains the disaster which overcame liberty and civic dignity not only in Bismarckian Germany but in the Weimar Republic. The educated middle classes conceded that only the traditional upper class could govern.

Looking back upon the liberal opposition to militarism and junkerism which characterized the early 1860's, Baumgarten was relieved at being able to point out that all this was now changed. The liberals, he wrote, had seen that the much maligned Junkers knew how to fight and to die for the fatherland—as if workers and farmers had not fought and died too—and therefore the liberals must resign themselves to occupying a secondary though still honorable place. "We thought that by our agitation we could transform Germany. But the tremendous events which we have witnessed have taught us how frail those premises were on which . . . we have built our national liberal policy in the last years. Almost all the elements of our political system have been shown erroneous by the facts themselves. It would be difficult for us to accept this new insight if it were accompanied by our misfortune. But we have experienced a miracle almost without parallel. The victory of our principles would have brought upon us misery, whereas the defeat of our principles has brought us boundless salvation (*uberschwangliches Heil*). Truly we could not be conscientious, altruistic, and pure"—Baumgarten spoke of himself and his fellow-liberals in these terms—"if we did not respond to such a celestial blessing by sincere self-criticism and by the unshakable determination, to start life anew with unassuming dedication and faithful obedience to the great revelation which this year has brought us." The revelation of the annus mirabilis was the superiority of Bismarck, junkerism, and militarism in political wisdom and ethical guidance.

Even before 1866 Baumgarten had combined a naive nationalism with his liberalism. Celebrating the fiftieth anniversary of the battle of Leipzig on October 18, 1863, he declared that German disunity and stress on diversity were her greatest vice and the cause of all her misfortune. But in the war of liberation Germany proved that she could rise from deepest shame to highest glory. Going far beyond the limits allowed to popular oratory, the scholarly historian exclaimed that "no people has ever emerged from so difficult a trial with greater glory than the German people; no people has ever made greater efforts with greater enthusiasm and at the same time . . . has shown in victory a more noble moderation. No people has ever had better generals and soldiers than we had then in Blücher, Scharnhorst, Gneisenau, in our veterans and volunteers; no people has ever had nobler men than we had then in Stein, Fichte, Arndt." When he delivered his address, Baumgarten was still a liberal, strongly opposed to Bismarck, Prussian junkerism and militarism. Yet in his inordinate glorification of men like Blücher and Arndt, in his entirely unhistorical emphasis on the noble moderation of the Germans after the victory of 1814, Baumgarten prepared the way for the abdication of liberal principles and of historical understanding which he and so many others condoned after the miracle of 1866.

Baumgarten's point of view was more succinctly expressed by an older fellow-historian, Droysen. When the citizens of Kolberg intended to nominate him as their liberal candidate, he wrote to them in January, 1867: "If you ask what I am and how I shall vote, then I will tell you that I shall vote neither liberal nor conservative. I am a Prussian, and that means a German. I am a German, and that means a Prussian. The war of 1866 has finally made it possible for us to launch a truly national German power policy. The German nation which has been politically dead since the fall of the Hohenstaufen, has now the opportunity of making its national greatness politically effective." The conviction became general, to quote Treitschke's words, that "it does not become the German to repeat the commonplaces of the apostles of peace and of the priests of mammon or to shut his eyes to the cruel truth that we live in an age of war." Every success in foreign policy led to ever greater demands. Initial assurances of the peaceful character of the new state grew into ever more threatening and aggressive claims in which any understanding of political realities vanished. Were not Prussia's victories proof of her superiority—in actual strength as much as in moral valor? That the strong prevails over the weak was accepted as an indisputable law of life, and this law was praised as ethically good. But whatever the law or its ethical character, where was the guarantee that the strong would always remain the strong? Bismarck's victories in 1866 and in 1870 did not express an enduring reality. They were due to temporary superiority in military training and to Bismarck's diplomatic wiles for which the mediocre Francis Joseph and the unstable and vainglorious Napoleon III were no match Under the impact of Prussia's victory, other nations reformed their military establishments. The German statesmen of the age of William II and of Hitler were no match for Lloyd George and Clemenceau, for Churchill and Franklin D. Roosevelt. The Prussian victories of the 1860's, the transformation which they wrought in the mind of most Germans, laid the foundations for the defeats of 1918 and 1945.

The New Reich

THE WAR WHICH BISMARCK STARTED in 1870 against France was the logical outcome of the revolution of 1866. It achieved what the Frankfurt Assembly had failed to do; it bestowed the Imperial German crown upon the Prussian monarchy. On January 18, 1871, the 170th anniversary of the assumption by the Hohenzollern of the royal title in Prussia, the king of Prussia was acclaimed German Emperor by the assembled German princes in the palace of Versailles. No representatives of the German people, no civilians took part in that ceremony of glittering uniforms. But the people, in their overwhelming majority, welcomed it with enthusiasm. By a curious non sequitur the new nation-state of the late nineteenth century was identified with the medieval Reich, the heir of the Roman Empire and the imperial crown of Charlemagne. Thus, Treitschke in his article *"Unser Reich"* (1866) arrived at the astonishing statement that "the imperial crown (*das Kaisertum*) of the Hohenzollern is the oldest and noblest in the world."

This imperial intoxication did not escape the attention of foreign observers. In *The Adventures of Harry Richmond* (1871) George Meredith introduced Prince Herrmann, who contrasted the littleness of Europe with the greatness of Germany: "Mistress of the Baltic, of the North Sea and the East, as eventually she must be, Germany would claim to take India as a matter of course, and find an outlet for the energies of the most prolific and the toughest of the races of mankind—the purest, in fact, the only true race, properly so called, out of India (an allusion to the then fashionable "Aryan" or "Indo-European" racial theory), to which it would return as to its source, and there create an empire, magnificent in force and solidity, the actual wedding of East and West; an empire, firm on the ground and in the blood of the people, instead of an empire as with the English of aliens."

The vision of Felix Dahn, a professor of jurisprudence and history who was one of the most popular and prolific authors in the Bismarckian empire, was equally grandiose. He did not look to India but to the pre-Christian Nordic gods. Next to Odin or Wotan hammer-throwing Thor was his favorite, whom one of Dahn's most widely quoted poems celebrated:

> Thor stood at the world's northern end.
> He threw his heavy battle axe
> "As far as a whizzing hammer falls
> Are mine the land and the seas."

> And the hammer flew out of his hand,
> Flew over the whole earth,
> Fell down in the farthest South,
> So that everything became his.

> Since then it has been the joyful right of the Germans,
> With their hammer to acquire land;
> We belong to the race of the hammer-god,
> And we wish to inherit his world-wide Reich

The war of 1870 marked a further stage in the self-imposed decline of German liberalism and scholarship. The war was seen as a milestone in history, the settlement of centuries-old accounts with the French and at the same time as the beginning of an entirely new era. It was an awe-inspiring spectacle: a new leading power stepped forth on the world stage. Such a change always moves and impresses the spectators. "Yet it will be twice as magnificent when it happens with such dramatic splendor, in such terrific blows, as a punishment of an unheard-of arrogance and infatuation, as the victory of the still and unappreciated force, as a divine judgment which has been written into the books of history more unmistakably than any other event."

In 1870 Treitschke wondered who could be so blind as not to see in the miraculous events of the Franco-Prussian War the working of divine reason. The fact that God was supposed to have assumed responsibility for Bismarck's deeds and wars absolved the individual from responsibility. "That is the glorious character of this great time," Treitschke wrote after the surrender of the French army at Sedan, "that it allows Reason in History to speak with overwhelming eloquence. From now on German policy can hardly commit any serious mistakes." Was it not clear that God and History themselves had decided against liberalism? The Germans went farther: they were convinced that the divine judgment was true not only for Germany, but for mankind as a whole.

This conviction explains German indifference to the opinion of Europe, their unlimited confidence in the righteousness of their case. Treitschke saw in Europe's condemnation of the German annexation of Alsace the best proof that this annexation was right. Instead of trying to understand the West, the Germans took its negative judgment as the justification for disregarding it. Thus they could never understand why Europe distrusted the new Germany. The fault could not be theirs. The Germans were deeply sincere in their rejection of Europe's criticism and fears. They felt themselves misunderstood and unjustly treated. Such a feeling of undeserved distrust and discrimination was, of course, not confined to the Germans. The Russian Slavophiles and Pan-Slavs similarly resented European attitudes toward Russia. Both German and Russian nationalists loved to adduce western criticism as proof for the existence of a deep and unbridgeable conflict between western thought on the one hand and German or Russian on the other. Western criticism could be disregarded; it was motivated by jealousy and self-interest which excluded the critics from that objective and unprejudiced view of which the Germans, or the Russians, were capable. "No nation in the world," Treitschke wrote, "can think so greatly and so humanly of its state as can Germany. None strives as seriously as the Germans to reconcile the ancient contrasts in the life of the peoples, the power of the state and the liberty of the people, well-being and armed strength, science and faith. And because the foreigners know it, they hate us."

In 1866 Prussia had annexed the Germans of Schleswig-Holstein, Hannover, and Frankfurt against their will; in 1870 Bismarck annexed the "Germans" of Alsace. As soon as he heard of this intention, Gladstone was so deeply concerned that he issued a warning. As he was then Prime Minister, he could not sign the article which appeared in the *Edinburgh Review* for October, 1870. "Are we to revert to that old practice," annexation without consent of the people, he asked. "Will its revival be in harmony with the feeling, the best feeling, of Europe? Will it conduce to future peace? Can Germany afford, and does she mean, to set herself up above European opinion? . . . Certain it is that the new law of nations is gradually taking hold of the mind, and coming to sway the practice, of the world. . . . The greatest triumph of our time, a triumph in a region loftier than that of electricity and steam, will be the enthronement of this idea of Public Right as a governing idea of European policy; as a common and precious inheritance of all lands, but superior to the passing opinion of any." Neither Bismarck nor the large majority of the German educated class understood Gladstone or took him seriously His reasoning was to them either meaningless or represented typical English cant.

In a pamphlet, "What We Demand from France," Treitschke expressed the belief that all Germans, all people who had in the past been Germans, must be, whatever their wishes, ingathered into the new Reich. "In view of our obligation to secure the peace of the world, who dares object that the people of Alsace and Lorraine do not wish to belong to us?" he asked. "In face of the sacred necessity of these great days, the doctrine of the right of self-determination for all branches of the German race—that alluring solution proposed by demagogues without a country—becomes a pitiable and a shameful thing. These provinces are ours by the right of the sword, and we shall dispose of them by a higher right—the right of the German nation, which cannot allow its lost children to remain forever alien to the German Empire. We Germans, knowing Germany and France, know better than these unfortunates themselves what is to the advantage of the people of Alsace, who, because of the misleading influence of the French, have no knowledge of the new Germany. Against their will we shall restore them to their true selves. With joyful wonder, we have watched the immortal progress of the moral forces of history in the awful changes of these days, and we have done so too often to be capable of belief in the unconditional value of mere popular disinclination. The spirit of a nation embraces not only contemporary generations, but those also who are before and behind it! We appeal from the misguided wills of those who now live in Alsace to the desires of those who lived there before them."

How far the new German border should reach, Treitschke refused to discuss. In a letter of September 23, 1871 he showed for the time being some sobriety. He hoped that a kind fate would preserve Germany from being obliged to make Warsaw again a German city. Warsaw had been Prussian for a very short time after the third partition of Poland. But Treitschke felt that, at least in 1871, the German world ended in Poznan, which was by the way a Polish city too. The appetite for Warsaw came later. In 1870 Treitschke concentrated on the French city of Metz. As soon as the Prussian general staff thought Metz strategically necessary, Treitschke insisted that it was "the patriotic duty of the German press to make short shrift of secondary considerations and to support like one man Prussian demands on the enemy." Before the victorious outcome of the war of 1866, Treitschke had insisted that "a civilized nation cannot abandon its independent judgment even in questions of foreign policy," that the press and public had to stand up for their convictions. Now the former liberal conviction against the annexation of non-German lands had become a secondary consideration. What counted was the will of the army. It had to be accepted unquestioningly. "Treitschke," Professor Walter Bussmann writes, "in no way represented an individual case. His attitude was only one example of a general trend." Another former liberal, the political economist Bernhard Oppenheim, who had spent eleven years in exile, in 1870 asked the editor of the *Kölnische Zeitung*, Heinrich Kruse, to abandon his opposition to the annexation of Metz or at least not to express in public an opinion which went against the national temper. Kruse was a courageous man. In 1866 he protested the annexation of the Danish-speaking part of Schleswig and opposed treating the Danes as second-class citizens. Such treatment, he wrote, would demoralize the Germans even more than it would harm the Danes. But Kruse's attitude was an exception. In general, public opinion followed with astonishing rapidity the miraculously swift progress of German arms. On August 11, 1870, Hermann Baumgarten advised leaving Alsace to the French since the people were fanatically anti-German, but at the end of the month, after the first German victories, he changed his mind. He suddenly insisted on the necessity of annexing Alsace and even parts of Lorraine and Metz. His fellow historian, Alfred Dove, praised German scholarship for supplying the historical arguments which would help to gather each and every German splinter into the new Reich.

In vain Ernest Renan warned in September, 1871, that this abuse of scholarship in support of historical rights might one day be used against the Germans. "You have erected in the world a standard of ethnographical and archaeological policy, instead of a liberal policy," Renan wrote. "This policy will be fatal to you. . . . The Slavs will wax enthusiastic over it. How can you believe that the Slavs will not do to you what you are doing to others? Every affirmation of Germanism is an affirmation of Slavism. . . . Think only how much it will weigh in the balance of the world when one day the Bohemians,

. . . all the Slav peoples of the Ottoman Empire, certainly destined
for emancipation . . . will group themselves around the great Mus-
covite aggregation which already comprises so many diverse elements. . . . What will you say if one day the Slavs come and vindicate Prussia proper, Pomerania, Silesia, Berlin, because their names
are Slavic; if they do on the banks of the Oder what you are doing
on the banks of the Moselle; if they point out, on the map, villages
which once were inhabited by Slavic tribes? . . . By abandoning herself to the statesmen and warriors of Prussia," Renan wrote, "Germany
has mounted a frisky horse, which will lead her where she does not
wish to go. You play for too high stakes."

Exactly one year before, Karl Marx had sounded a similar warning. He predicted that the annexation of Alsace-Lorraine would not
secure German freedom and peace but would drive France into Russia's arms. "The military clique, the professors and the politicizing
middle class pretend that the annexation of Alsace-Lorraine is the
best way of protecting Germany forever against a war with France.
In reality, it will achieve the opposite end: it is the most certain
means of transforming this present war into an European institution.
It will without fail change the coming peace into a mere armistice
until the time when France feels strong enough to reclaim her lost
territory. . . . Even the most extreme German nationalist does not
dare to affirm that the people of Lorraine and Alsace desire the blessings of German government. The proclamation of the principles of
Pan-Germanism and of strategically 'secure' frontiers must bring
evil results upon Germany and Europe in the future when these same
principles will be invoked and used by Germany's eastern neighbors."

Marx was a Rhinelander and a socialist. Another German, Julius
von Eckardt, born in a Baltic family, was a moderate liberal. Yet
he arrived at similar conclusions. Looking back in his memoirs
upon 1871, he wrote: "Whatever the value of regaining (for Germany) the frontierline of the Vosges might have been, the price
we had to pay for it seemed to me too high. A man who believed in
a moral idea for the Germans and in human progress could not accept the erection of an irreparable barrier between the two leading
cultural nations of the European continent. It meant the beginning
of a policy of oppression which by necessity was an evil influence
upon the development of the new Reich, the continuity of armaments and the expansion of Russian influence upon Europe." Eckardt knew of the consequences of the policy of Russification in the
western provinces of the Russian empire. He shuddered at the

thought that Germany might follow in the footsteps of this Russian nationalist despotism. Yet under Bismarck Germany did this very thing both in Prussian Poland and in Alsace-Lorraine, which, after 1870, became the Poland of the West.

It is understandable that these and similar warnings were not heeded in the Germany of 1871. The miraculous fulfilment of fervent national hopes made dispassionate and moderate reflections impossible. As Renan and Marx foresaw, the Prussian victories changed the course not only of German but of European history. They contained the germs of the wars of 1914 and of 1939. Bismarck's triumph vindicated the ideal of the Prussian state and the traditionalism of German scholarship against the western ideals of the rights of men and the peace of peoples. In foreign and domestic relations the authoritarian power-state seemed to confirm by its success Hegel's sanctification of an instinctive and naive Machiavellianism. Bismarck's domestic policy of regarding all his adversaries as "enemies of the state" undermined the sense for due process of law and for moderation among the Germans. His example made it difficult for the nation to adapt itself to the need of a modern society in which all its members could find their place; instead religious and class divisions were sharpened. Bismarck's contempt for humanitarian liberalism confirmed the dangerous trends which had begun to daze and dazzle German thought in the nineteenth century.

So it was, as Professor Franz Schnabel has noted, that the conscience of the individual was silenced and force and injustice were no longer felt as such. Even religion became the handmaiden of the state. Bismarck was a Christian, but Christianity did not enter into his concept of the state. "Bismarck's whole intellectual development," wrote Professor Paul Joachimsen in 1922, "was a liberation from the Christian concept of the state." The annus mirabilis accelerated the de-Christianization and dewesternization of Germany that Heine had dreaded.

Chapter Eight

MIRACLE OR MISFORTUNE?

Voices of Protest

Bismarck's triumphs of 1866 and 1871 were generally acclaimed in Germany, but there were a few people who regarded the annus mirabilis as a year of misfortune and even of guilt and not as proof of God's miraculous working in history. Others who had welcomed the events ultimately became disillusioned. But Bismarck's hold over the German mind lasted for over seven decades; as history is always written by the victors, the voices of protest and warning raised in Germany after 1866 had been largely forgotten. Among them were many who had fervently desired German unification and believed in Prussian leadership.

The politician Heinrich von Gagern, the historian Georg Gottfried Gervinus, and the poet Georg Herwegh were in their younger days famous German patriots. Long before they died they had dropped out of the public eye, lonely and forlorn men. Their contemporaries were convinced that they had become embittered and quarrelsome malcontents who were unable to understand the new times, and had been proven wrong by the course of events.

Gagern was a true national liberal with a deep faith in Prussia. In 1848 he was the most renowned and popular leader in the movement for German unity. In the parliament of his native state, Hessen, he had shown great courage in opposing reactionary trends and in defending the idea of German unity. In 1847 he helped Gervinus to found the *Deutsche Zeitung* which became the rallying point of German nationalism. From the very beginning he was the driving force behind the convocation of the Frankfurt National Assembly. There he became the leader of the party which wished to bestow the hereditary imperial crown of Germany upon the Prussian royal house. The *German Dictionary of National Biography*, published before the First World War, praised his vigorous faith in Germany and the courage with which, in spite of all the weaknesses and errors of Prussia, he clung to that state and its mission. He was elected president of the National Assembly and the following year became Prime Minister of the Reich government based upon the new Frankfurt constitution. Even Prussia's rejection of the Frankfurt Constitution and of the German crown offered by the Assembly could not shake his devotion to the Hohenzollern. But from 1862 on Prussia's increasingly anticonstitutional and militaristic policy drove Gagern into opposition. Bismarck's success did not convince Gagern of the righteousness of Prussia's policy. He remained faithful to principle. When he died, in 1880, the man who thirty years before had been the idol of the national movement was completely forgotten. The German press of the day took almost no note of his passing. The hero of 1848 found no biographer, not even in the Weimar Republic. Only after the Second World War did the *Biographical Dictionary of German History* concede that though he was not a creative statesman he represented the spirit of 1848 at its best.

Like Gagern, Gervinus had worked for many years for German unity under Prussia's leadership In the spring of 1848 he wrote in the *Deutsche Zeitung:* "The hour has come for Prussia to take over the supreme guidance of the German cause." Gervinus fervently desired German unity, but the means were as important to him as the end. He knew that if the foundations were wrongly laid, the German state might not long endure After 1862 he opposed not only Bismarck's militarism, which seemed to him to run counter to the spirit of the times, but also the national liberal drive for a unitarian Germany which negated the German federal tradition. "Continuity and durability," wrote Gervinus in reference to Germany and to Italy, "will be better assured by federation in a country and among a people in whose nature and history particularism is deeply founded." Gervinus' opinion was diametrically opposed to that of Treitschke who regarded particularism as the sin and shame of Germany and the centralized power-state as the only desirable goal. Though the large majority of educated Germans sided in the 1860's with Treitschke, Gervinus showed a better understanding of the needs and trends of the nineteenth century and of the forces at work in Bismarck's victories. "The envy of the gods has always punished overweening arrogance," Gervinus warned. "A dangerous conceit can lead to an intoxication which makes us regard what was caused by good luck and temporary circumstances, as the work of a higher reason."

But even when he rejected Bismarck's policy Gervinus did not lose his faith in the Prussian royal house. He knew that many of its members had shown a sense of moderation. It was to this sense he appealed when he asked them to abandon the obsolete concept of monarchy by divine right. "It seems more in conformity with the history of the Hohenzollern to renounce a power which men and God no longer wish to bear and not to challenge the forces of earth and heaven." After her victory over Austria, however, Prussia became unfaithful to her mission by the unlawful annexation of German lands. Instead, she should have united all German states in a truly free federation "Even the dazzling glory (of the victories of 1870) and the enhanced external power of the Prussian state will not silence the violated rights of the smaller German lands." Before he died Gervinus submitted in 1870 to the Prussian royal house a moving Memorandum on Peace which his widow published posthumously. Its sober warning, unheeded then, has been revealed as a true prophecy:

"Europe has watched over the ambition of Germany for a thousand years because this land and its people have by their strong central position an immeasurable advantage in planning for a warlike policy. The expansionism of the great German imperial dynasties of the Middle Ages with their lust for conquest has produced nothing but hatred and discord, uprisings and wars, defeat and decline in both domestic and foreign policy. Since the seventeenth century it has been a principle of European policy that the organization of the Germanies must be federal; the German Confederation has been created for the very purpose of forming in the center of Europe a neutral state which would by its federal organization guarantee peace. By the disruption of the Confederation in 1866, two-thirds of the German territory have been transformed into a warrior-state ever ready for aggression, in which one can see, without being an enemy of Prussia and Germany, a permanent threat to the peace of the continent and to the security of the neighboring states.

"Prussia has been reproached with having by its war and its methods transformed the whole of Europe into one armed camp; it would be impossible to regard as a malevolent phrase in the mouth of an enemy what can be simply proved by facts. It is not wise to overlook out of patriotism the fact that the events of 1866 have revived for the continent and for our age the dangers of a system gen-

erally held to be in decline, and to have immeasurably magnified
them. After the hopes and labors of half a century to outgrow the
military systems of former times, there has been here created a
permanent military power of such tremendous superiority as the
world has not known even in the iron age of the Napoleonic wars
    "This interpretation of the situation created by the war of 1866,"
Gervinus went on, "could have been regarded as exaggerated before
the events of 1870. They have further strengthened military power
and increased self-assurance. Whatever the first reaction to these
miraculous deeds, they will end by making us even more distrusted."
    Gervinus made several concrete proposals to avoid the tragic con-
sequences of Bismarck's victories. He implored the Prussian dynasty
to restore peace at home by freeing the German lands annexed in
1866, so that after the "defeat of the external enemy [France] all
could share in the general jubilation over victory and peace." He
suggested making not Berlin but one of the free and more typically
German cities the national capital. Hamburg seemed to him ideally
suited for that role. It could become, he wrote, a German London,
a world-open citadel of freedom and trade, endowed with a much
wider hinterland and situated on a mightier river. "Such a capital
would lead Germany on the road to a peaceful and civilized policy
which alone becomes the German character. . . . It would be a woe-
ful perversion if Germany turned from a people dedicated to culture
to a people trusting in power, and thus become involved in war after
war."
    Some Germans, Gervinus continued, liked to point to the good
nature and the peaceful traditions of their people as a guarantee that
any German plans of conquest were impossible. But Gervinus insisted
that temptations could prove stronger than the best principles and
that recent Prussian history did not bear out the optimism of his
fellow-citizens regarding German love of peace. Only the abandonment of the military dictatorship which Prussia—after 1862—had
imposed upon Germany would insure the nation against the temptations of power.
    During the many years of his work as a historian and publicist,
Gervinus had not always been consistent or farsighted. Like so
many other German liberals, he had wishfully projected his own
liberalism into Prussia and had hoped that in some miraculous way
she would transform herself from a noble-ridden and military caste
state into a liberal civilian society after the English model. His limitations as a liberal were clearly shown in his treatment of Catholic
and Latin civilizations. Yet with all these shortcomings he had suf-

ficient historical understanding to plead for moderation in the decisive hours of victory and to oppose the defection of his friends
from the camp of liberalism to that of Bismarck. Feeling himself
almost alone in the sweeping acceptance of military triumph and
national glory as standards of conduct and history, he wrote, addressing himself:

> Im ungeheuren Abfall dieser Tage
> Bist du dem echten Glauben treu geblieben,
> Dem ew'gen A und O der Weltgeschichte.
> Wer nicht an's Mass sich bindet, wird zunichte.

> (In the monstrous defection of these days
> You have remained faithful to the true principle,
> The eternal Alpha and Omega of world history
> Whoever does not hold to moderation will perish.)

The leading German historians were certain that the national
triumph would endure. When Gervinus died in 1871, they blamed
him for his lack of understanding. Treitschke paid him the com-
pliment that he had helped educate the German people for the new
national state, but added "that he completely lacked political foresight, and that of his numerous prophecies hardly any were fulfilled.
The constitutional forms of the internal life of the state seemed more
important to him than the great relationships of power in the society
of nations, relationships to which Ranke preferred to devote his attention. In truth, Gervinus never got far beyond the outlook of the
South German liberal parliamentarian."

"A South German liberal parliamentarian"—that was in Treitschke's and his colleagues' judgment almost the worst that could be
said of a political thinker. Treitschke never realized that domestic
constitutional forms might be more important than the power relationships among states emphasized by Ranke, an attitude which
went far to distort modern German historical and political thought.
Ranke himself wrote an obituary notice of Gervinus in the *Historische Zeitschrift*. As was his way, he wrote in measured terms.
He was confident that Gervinus' liberalism was out of date. In his
opinion the hereditary imperial dignity bestowed upon the Prussian
crown offered a guarantee for German unity in the future such as
had never existed before. *"Das gesammelte Nationalgefühl kann der
Zukunft ruhig entgegen sehen,"* the now united national sentiment
can confidently look toward the future, Ranke felt able to assure his
fellow-historians, most of them his disciples and admirers. Much

more violent in his criticism of Gervinus was Karl Hillebrand, one of the most brilliant and cosmopolitan German essayists of the time. As a student in Heidelberg he participated in the Baden revolutionary movement. Afterwards he lived abroad, first in France and after 1870 in Florence. His strictures on Gervinus' literary style and lack of artistic sensitivity were well founded. But he took also issue with his liberalism and his political views. He could not forgive Gervinus for having held up the United States as a model of liberty, and he repeated the assertion—popular in 1873—that the United States was a disgrace to liberty. His most fundamental disagreement with Gervinus concerned the evaluation of the *annus mirabilis*. Hillebrand called the war of 1866 "the greatest revolution since Luther," and complained that a liberal like Gervinus could not understand its true nature because it was a revolution "in uniform, carried out by trained officers and statesmen." In another essay Hillebrand called the war of 1866 "the nineteenth century deed fraught with the greatest consequences" (*die genialste, kuhnste, und folgenreichste Tat des neunzehnten Jahrhunderts*). Gervinus agreed with his critic about the great consequences of 1866, but he did not share the optimism and self-assurance of Ranke, Treitschke and Hillebrand.

More pessimistic and outspoken than Gervinus was Georg Herwegh In 1841 he was a minor poet from Württemberg who captured the mood of the German youth and knew a brief wave of immense popularity. He then proclaimed Germany as the greatest people on earth; he called upon the Prussian king to defend Germany and the Rhine against France; he demanded the creation of a German navy which would dominate the seas. For twenty-five years he lived as an exile in Paris and in Switzerland, until in 1866 he returned to Germany where he spent his last years in Baden-Baden. The poetry which he then wrote was a most bitter denunciation of Bismarck's Germany. To Herwegh who remained faithful to the ideals of 1848, unity was worthless without liberty. Liberty, however, could not be confined to Germans alone. Again, faithful to the ideals of the 1830's and 1840's, Herwegh demanded the independence of all peoples— Czechs and Poles, Italians or Germans. But national independence was no absolute ideal for him· he had no use for it when achieved at the expense of the rights or interests of other peoples. He condemned the methods and results of 1866 and 1870. "The watch on the Rhine will not suffice," he wrote in 1871. "The worst enemy [of Germany] stands on the Spree"—the river on which Berlin is situated.

He was a lonely figure when he wrote:

Du bist im ruhmgekrönten Morden
Das erste Land der Welt geworden
Germania· mir graut vor dir!

(By glory-crowned killings you have
Become the first country of the world·
Germany, I shudder before you!)

In his dream the poet heard the Sun address the Germans: "I suffer deeply in my sun-soul that you are so inane as to adore primitive idols, the prophets of steel and blood. . . . O, could I put an end to the victory marches and to the foolish conceit of world domination in Berlin upon which I never have liked to shine." * When Herwegh died in 1875 he wished to be buried in the Swiss canton of Basle Land of which he had become a citizen during his exile. "Here lies, as he had wished, in his homeland's free earth . . ." the inscription on his tombstone runs. Before his death he begged his son to put the words "Rejoice father, Prussia no longer exists" on his tomb after Prussia had ceased to exist.

Of course Gagern, Gervinus, and Herwegh were not the only critics of the new Germany. Many lesser known Germans criticized for ethical reasons. In 1872 the theologian Martin Kaehler published a pamphlet against Treitschke, "The Firm Roots of Our Strength," in which he denied that it was "more ethical to found a state than to fulfill the simplest duty in a hidden life. This principle alone can form the firm foundation of true humanity. It must not be abandoned for a political absolutism which belongs to pagan antiquity and not to Christian humanity. Success does not decide the question whether a man is allowed to achieve his people's goals if this goal can be achieved only through means which in every other case would be suspect." Another critic was the Swabian philosopher Karl Christian Planck who died in 1880. He bitterly regretted in his posthumous *Testament of a German* that "our people has now entered, like the Jews of biblical times, into a period of selfish national Messianism." Like an Old Testament prophet, he saw the heav-

---

* *In meiner Sonnenseele leid*
Tut mir's, dass ihr so töricht seid,
Die plumpsten Götzen anzubeten,
Die Eisen-und die Blutpropheten—
O dürft ich . .
Dem Mordgebrüll, den Siegesmarschen
Ein Ende machen und dem narr'schen
Weltherrschaftsdünkel in Berlin,
Das ich von je nicht gern beschien

ily armed nation-state as a terrifying distortion and perversion of the true German character. "If such a universalist people, situated in the heart of Europe, forms in sharp contrast to all its preceding history a centralized nation-state and sets before its neighbor nations an example of increased armaments, what can result in an age of acute nationalism but total conflict?"

The Imperial Crown

PLANCK WAS CONVINCED that Bismarck's Reich had no foundation in German history. In the Prussian government itself, as Professor Franz Schnabel has pointed out, the tradition of Frederick the Great died out before Bismarck's rise to power. It was Germany's and Europe's misfortune (*Verhängnis*) that at that time when all possibilities still seemed open Bismarck's genius willed what seemed least constructive for Germany and for Europe. As the new Prussian imperial crown had no roots in history, a scholarly legend had to provide them. Sober Germans, among them King William of Prussia, did not welcome the imperial dignity. But historians, poets, and publicists provided a halo for the new crown by proclaiming Bismarck's empire, in spite of its imitation of Bonapartism, as the legitimate heir of the Holy Roman Empire—the Second Reich. This romantic mystique of the Reich concept inflamed the imagination of the man who succeeded Bismarck in directing the fate of the Reich, Emperor William II. The first Emperor, William I, knew that Bismarck and not he had created the Reich. The old man recognized his Chancellor's intellectual superiority. But William II could not accept the situation. The bearer of the imperial crown, the real Kaiser, had to be the only master and man of genius. According to this point of view, Bismarck could have achieved what he had achieved only as a counselor and servant [*Handlanger des allerhöchsten, erhabenen Willens*] of the first German Emperor, who was now officially elevated to become William the Great. When William II brusquely dismissed Bismarck in 1890, many Germans, accustomed to Byzantinism through Bismarck himself, willingly accepted this degradation of the man who a few years before had been the adored national hero.

In September, 1898, only a few weeks after Bismarck's death, William II explained in a letter to his mother that his ascension to the throne had imposed upon him the task of saving the crown from the overwhelming shadow of its minister, and thereby saving the honor and the future of the Hohenzollern from the pernicious influence of the man who had stolen the heart of the German people. "I clearly felt what my duty was and thanks be to God that He helped me. . . . I felied him [Bismarck] for the salvation of my crown and of our house! Since that terrible year [1890] I had to suffer . . . the lowest intrigues of the enraged and passionate Bismarck! . . . Where is Bismarck now? The storm has abated; my standard waves high in the wind, a comfort for everyone who seeks help from above. The crown sends its rays, by God's grace, into palaces and huts, and—excuse me for saying it—Europe and the whole world listens to hear, 'What does the German Kaiser say and think?' and not what is the will of his Chancellor! . . . For ever and ever I am convinced that there is only *one real Kaiser* in the world, and that is the *German* Kaiser, not through his personality or his special qualifications, but through the right of the millenary tradition; and his Chancellor has to *obey!*" The medieval mystique of Reich and Kaiser which Bismarck implanted in a perverted form into the ninteenth century, turned not only against Bismarck. In the bearer of the imperial crown at the turn of the twentieth century, it revealed its absurdity and its perils.

As early as January, 1871, two poets went into raptures over the new imperial throne. Emanuel Geibel saw it circled by Barbarossa's ravens. Richard Wagner, addressing the German army before Paris, insisted that only a German could be Emperor; the army should consecrate him on French soil; thus, the noblest of all earthly crowns of which the Germans had been robbed, would again rest on a German head and would reward the sacred deeds of German loyalty:

> Drum soll ein Deutscher auch nur Kaiser sein,
> In welschem Lande solltet ihr ihn weihn:—
> Die uns geraubt,
> Die würdevollste aller Erdenkronen,
> Auf seinem Haupt
> Soll sie der Treue heil'ge Taten lohnen.

Not all Germans, however, welcomed the new imperial crown. The strongest opposition came from the Bavarian patriotic party. Forty-eight of its members voted in the Bavarian Chamber on January 21, 1871, against the ratification of the Treaty of Versailles which incorporated Bavaria into the new empire. Their arguments sound familiar today; some of their predictions have come true. All of them complained that the new Reich was not a federation in the German tradition It gave to the Hohenzollern dynasty greater power in a centralized Germany than any emperor in the first Reich had possessed. In that connection Dr. Jörg, the leader of the party, recalled Bismarck's words in the North German Reichstag on February 24, 1870, when Bavaria and the other southern German states were still independent—united with the North German Confederation only by a military alliance and a customs union. Nevertheless, Bismarck could then say that "the head of the North German Confederation [the king of Prussia] exercised in South Germany an imperial power greater than that which the German emperors had exercised for five hundred years, since the time of Emperor Barbarossa. Even Barbarossa exercised such a power only intermittently, when his sword was victorious, and not on the strength of a generally recognized treaty." Another speaker, Dr. Josef Pfahler, regretted that after the defeat of Napoleonic France the victor imitated its shortcomings and mistakes, above all, Napoleon's Caesarism, supported by a nationalist principle which belonged, after all, to pagan antiquity.

The Bavarian patriots did not oppose German unification. Many had actively fought for it. But they wished to preserve Bavaria's independence and autonomous development within the German nation. They feared that Bavaria's integration into a Prussia-dominated Germany would destroy the country's freedom and bring the Bavarian people new burdens and new suffering. "Our Bavarian people and the whole people of south Germany has no military past which could be compared to that of the north German people, of the Prussian people for the last one hundred years. Our people has been born for peace, it has been accustomed to peace, and it will bitterly resent becoming a member serving a great military nation." Another Bavarian patriot, August Wiesnet, called the federation proposed by Bismarck a sham federation under Prussia's undisputable leadership. Prussia's hegemonic position was based upon her annexations of 1866. True, Wiesnet conceded, Prussia accepted the Reichstag as a constitutional balance, but no weaker parliament could be found in Europe than the Reichstag. Turning to the national liberals who favored Bavaria's entrance into the new Reich, the speaker protested against the assumption that they alone represented the national idea. "We too are animated by the national idea. I have served it since the days of my youth. But we think the national idea is not served if we divide Germany as you do, and subject a part of it to Prussian hegemony. Our immediate goal on the road to the realization of the national idea should be to preserve an independent Bavaria as the nucleus of a future Germany, for the reunion of all German lands on the basis of freedom and equality. We do not stand alone. Our brothers, even in the farthest north of Germany, in Schleswig-Holstein, in the Hanseatic cities, in Hannover, in Mecklenburg, pin their last hope on us Bavarians. But there is another difference between us and you national liberals. We do not kowtow before success. We do not regard the creation of the new Prussian empire as something to endure. It is only the continuation of the temporary situation created in 1866." To those who maintained that Bavaria could preserve her national security and existence only as part of the new empire Wiesnet replied that Bavaria felt threatened neither by Austria nor by Britain or Russia. "If we have an enemy who threatens our independence, I can see him only in Prussia."

Another Bavarian who had his doubts was Georg Friedrich Kolb, who stood up in the Chamber of Deputies and declared that the new Constitution did not offer a sufficient guarantee of the rights of the people. He warned against the illusion that liberty would flourish once national unity was established. "This is a premise contradicted by history. No people has ever been given liberty as a gift. It had always to fight for it. The present constitution makes such a fight more difficult. Some people say that the German nation will never tolerate absolutism. But, gentlemen, how much has the German nation and every other nation tolerated? One can easily underestimate the tremendous power of organization, and this constitution creates an organization which serves absolutism and militarism but certainly not liberty." The men of 1848 would never have accepted such a constitution, the speaker continued.

Still another Bavarian, Dr. Anton Ruland, protested the fact that the treaties which established the new Reich were discussed and signed in wartime, in an enemy country, and in a highly charged nationalistic atmosphere. Would not the imperial title fan the flames of passion? "The crown of Charlemagne belongs to the past, and to revive past glory will have unfortunate consequences." The Reformation and the Peace of Westphalia buried forever the old universal imperial idea. Even in ancient times there was no hereditary emperor. The Germans had always insisted on the right to elect their own kings. Now they were to be burdened with an imperial crown, which was to go down from generation to generation in the Prussian dynasty.

The Bavarian patriots who protested against the Prussian Reich were Catholics. Protestants joined them. Perhaps the most distinguished was Heinrich Ewald. Born in Göttingen, the site of the famous university of the kingdom of Hannover, he studied oriental languages there and became professor of theology. In 1837, when King Ernst August abolished the liberal constitution of 1833, Ewald protested, together with six other professors—among them Dahlmann, Gervinus, and the brothers Grimm—and was dismissed. With the restoration of the constitution in 1847 he was able to return from Tübingen to his Alma Mater. He was the greatest Protestant scholar of his time He took an important part in founding the Protestant Association (*Protestantenverein*) in September of 1863. He was equally famous as a teacher and as a prolific scholar. His *Hebrew Grammar* and his *History of Israel,* which marked the beginning of a new epoch in research and interpretation, are "a storehouse of learning and increasingly recognized as works of rare genius."

Ewald's sturdy independence and fearlessness of character singled him out among scholars. When Prussia annexed Hannover in 1866, he remained loyal to King George V. In 1868 he lost his *venia legendi,* or permission to lecture, for publishing his *Lob des Königs und des Volkes* (Praise of King and People), in which he called upon the Germans to consider that "from the present beginnings, if Prussia persists, nothing but evil can ensue, and eventually the total disintegration of Germany. The ancient peoples felt, and rightly, that every serious transgression for which the people did not atone must be effaced like a blood stain with the greatest awe and care. The unatoned guilt of Germany created the indescribable misery in which we find ourselves today. If this misery is not righted and if this transgression is not atoned for, then the German Reich and the German people must perish."

It took almost eighty years to pay for what Ewald called the great transgression. During the last years of his life, he represented the city of Hannover as a member first of the North German, then of the German Reichstag. In 1874 the septogenarian was sent to prison for comparing Bismarck to Frederick II in having waged an unrighteous war against Austria and ruined religion and morality, and to Napoleon III for "picking out the best possible time for robbery and plunder."

The assumption of the imperial crown with its romantic connotations was also resented by some Prussian conservatives. It changed the character of Prussia. An unassuming sobriety had been traditional there. Now a grandiloquent ostentation became the fashion. With it the consciousness of limitations disappeared. A world-

encompassing march of German ideas and German power was envisaged. Suddenly England, this new Carthage, as Treitschke called
her, appeared as the chief obstacle to German ambition. The conviction grew that in view of the apparent decay of the West through
liberalism and individualism only the German mind with its deeper
insight and its higher morality could regenerate the world. Germany's mission demanded German expansion across the seas which,
against all "historical justice," the British Empire hindered. The
world-wide influence of England and English liberal ideas was
possible only as long as Germany was not unified and there was no
German leadership in Europe. Now this situation had to change.
"The world position of Germany," Treitschke wrote, "depends
upon the number of German-speaking millions in the future. Therefore, we must see to it that the outcome of our next successsful war
is the acquisition of colonies by all possible means." Otherwise,
Treitschke foresaw "the appalling prospects" of a division of the
world between the English-speaking nations and Russia. "In such
a case," he continued, "it is hard to say whether the Russian knout
or English moneybags would be the worse alternative." That the
Russian knout meant the loss of freedom, whereas freedom pros-
pered with English moneybags, made no difference to the most popular German political scientist of the day.

Voices of Disillusionment

THE VICTORY OF 1870 filled Friedrich Nietzsche with many misgivings. "Public opinion," he wrote in 1873 in his *Thoughts Out of
Season*, "practically forbids mentioning the evil consequences of war,
especially of a victorious war. With the greatest willingness those
writers are listened to who compete in praising war and in exploring
its powerful influence on morality, culture, and art. Nevertheless,
a great victory is a great danger. It is more difficult for human nature
to bear than a defeat. A victory is more easily achieved than borne
in such a way as not to turn into a serious defeat. Of all the evil
consequences of the last war with France, perhaps the worst is the
widespread error that German culture too has been victorious and
that it must be adorned with laurel wreaths befitting such unusual
success. This illusion is highly pernicious, not only because it is an
illusion—for there are healthy and blissful illusions—but because

it can pervert our victory into a total defeat, into the defeat, nay even into the extirpation of the German mind (*Geist*) for the benefit of the German Reich

Intellectual standards declined in the new Reich. As time went on, more and more Germans were flushed with the successes of the army, and with the immense prosperity the nation enjoyed under the Kaiser. Yet there were a few men who became disappointed. Compared with the Germany of the early nineteenth century, much had been gained, but had not much more been lost? The first to express disillusionment were Germans living outside the Reich. In 1870 most Germans who had settled in the United States after 1848 enthusiastically supported Bismarck and the war against France. As an example, Professor Helmut Hirsch quotes the editor of the *Illinois Staats-Zeitung,* then one of the leading German papers in the United States, who called upon a German-American meeting in Chicago, "to feel themselves at the moment as Germans and only as Germans, as the people to whom the future of Europe belongs, the people to whose brothers across the ocean America's future will belong." One sentiment only was becoming to the German-American then, "to shake his fist against the French hereditary enemy." The French were "a barbarian people who in the interests of mankind had to be rendered harmless for all time to come." Five years later the same newspaper complained bitterly that the Reich was founded upon a mortal human being—Bismarck—and not upon liberty. The latter alone could have provided a cornerstone for an enduring building. "Four years ago," the editor wrote, "the Germans abroad jubilantly greeted the victories of their fellow-Germans (*Stammesgenossen*) over the French hereditary enemy [this time the editor put the words, 'French hereditary enemy,' into quotation marks]. Then they were deeply enthusiastic over the greatness, might and glory of the new German Reich. Yet what is happening there now goes a long way to cool this enthusiasm."

Disillusionment was also evident among the Austrian Germans. The poet Ferdnand von Saar wrote that he had once loved Germany when she dreamt of unity and of Barbarossa's awakening in the Kyffhäuser. Now with Germany united, victorious, and heavily armed, people praise and fear the power of the Reich, but they no longer bow in reverence before the German mind (*Geist*). Nobody praises any longer—even Germans themselves do not do it—German love and the German heart.* Another Austrian poet, Moritz Hart-

* *O wie liebt ich dich einst, jetzt so gewaltiges Volk.*
  Als uneinig du noch träumtest von Einigung—

mann, warned that Germany might regret her triumph; she had sacrificed her ideals for military glory and conquests, and this would only result in making her hated by her neighbors. *"Am Siege stirbt der Sieger mit."*

Even conservative Germans like the novelist Wilhelm Raabe could not hide their disappointment in the Reich. In his aphorisms he told some telling truths. "The horizon of the generation which came after 1870 has not become wider," he wrote. "We don't go to Canossa, instead we go every day to Byzantium. In the long run that becomes boring too. . . . We are now asked to become Romans and to surrender everything to the state, and yet we are a different kind of people with highly developed individual needs and sentiments." But more indicative of a growing uneasiness was the case of liberals who had enthusiastically supported Bismarck and had confidently expected that the unification of Germany, by whatever means achieved, would ultimately promote liberty and cultural growth Now among the multitudes of their fellow-countrymen who continued undisturbed in their triumphant self-confidence, they found themselves disillusioned, isolated, and embittered. Their case was different from that of the Bavarian or Hannoverian patriots, of the few upright liberals and the few presistent conservatives, who from the beginning had rejected Bismarck's domestic and foreign policies and had seen misfortune rather than a miracle in the events of 1866. But the men who had deeply believed in the miracle, and sacrificed their liberal principles to it, lived their last years in the Reich which they had helped to create among deep and dark forebodings. They did not understand the new Germany and the new Germany did not understand them. To their smug contemporaries, they seemed odd indeed.

One of these disillusioned men was Hermann Baumgarten. From 1866 to 1870 he had been very close to Treitschke. Both regarded nationalism as the supreme end to which men must dedicate all their energies. "Unity, power of the state, national independence are the highest of all political goods. They are the foundation and beginning of all earthly welfare," Baumgarten wrote in his *"Was*

Und von Rotbarts Erwachen
Der da still im Kyffhäuser schlief.

Ja, man fürchtet und preist weithin des Reiches Macht,
Doch man beugt sich nicht mehr willig dem deutschen Geist—
Und wer preist noch—du selbst nicht!—
Deutsche Liebe und deutsches Herz?

wir in diesem Kriege wollen" ("What We Want in this War") on
July 17, 1870. But soon he became appalled at the excessive nationalism, monarchism, and militarism which he found among his people.
He pleaded for moderation and reason against the overestimation of
one's strength. Nothing seemed more dangerous for the Germans
than their moral self-righteousness combined with the conviction
of a superior strength. With such opinions Baumgarten found himself isolated at the University and among his fellow-historians.
When the second volume of Treitschke's *German History in the
Nineteenth Century* appeared in 1882, he subjected it to a sharp criticism. The break between the two former friends was now complete.
Whereas Treitschke from his chair in Berlin infected German youth
with his ever-growing and ever-blinder faith in Bismarck and the
miraculous deeds of unification, Baumgarten wrote in 1881 to Sybel
that Bismarck "will bequeath to us a frightful chaos and we shall
have to atone terribly for our blindness."

Baumgarten was one of the minor liberal historians. Few people
remember him today. The position of Theodor Mommsen was different. He was, after Ranke, the greatest German historian. His
Roman History made him famous throughout the world. Few national liberals had gone so far to support Bismarck's policy. Few
were so disappointed by the consequences of what they had helped
to create. Even in his last years he did not understand that it was
his nationalism and his adoration of power which were responsible
for the consequences which he deplored. He continued to live in the
illusion, typical of a German national liberal, that Germany's unification through Bismarck's Prussia could have established a free
society. So he turned in the 1880's against the German nation which
had followed his own precepts. He sat in judgment over the nation.
He never sat in judgment over his own nationalism, over the dangerous aspirations and illusions of his younger years. In that sense
he was in his old age one of the most tragic figures of nineteenth
century Germany.

From his early years in his native Schleswig up until the creation
of Bismarck's Reich, Mommsen conceived of the unification of Germany as the ultimate goal, to be achieved by any and every means.
He found that the Frankfurt Constitution was too democratic and
not sufficiently centralized. Political liberties without national power
were meaningless to him. The National Assembly "should reunite
Germany, and should establish a state which every German must
obey and before which every foreigner must tremble." Should such
power be qualified? Mommsen never asked himself this question.

Liberty was a word for him; national power was the only reality for which he longed. Against the wishes of most German liberals and those of his fellow Schleswig-Holsteiners he endorsed Prussia's annexation of Schleswig-Holstein. "Our South German friends," he wrote in 1865, "speak of the Prussian lust for conquest, but anyone who knows the Prussians knows that we cannot speak of their lustful conquest but only of duty. . . . If the great dream of 1848 [their love of unity] should come true, then every means, including force, will be justified. Necessity and the nation both speak in the categorical imperative, and as the nation-state can heal every wound, it is also entitled to inflict every wound." Mommsen's use of the categorical imperative would have perplexed Kant, but it would have had Treitschke's unqualified approval. Mommsen fully shared Droysen's and Treitschke's conviction of the absolute primacy of the omnipotent nation-state as the enduring ethical goal of history. In 1866 he wrote to his brother Tycho: "It is a wonderful feeling to be present when world history turns a corner. It is no longer a hope but a fact that Germany has a future and that this future will be determined by Prussia This is a prodigious fact for all time to come." Even in 1881 he saw in Bismarck the man whom the nation "rightly called its saviour and in a certain sense its creator."

In later years Mommsen accused the German people of having betrayed the ideals which were his from the 1840's to the 1870's. That the people were less to blame than the ideals which he himself had proclaimed apparently never occurred to him. Or did it? This may perhaps explain the violence with which he turned, in the 1880's, against the German nation. From Rome he wrote in 1885 to his wife: "Frequently I regret that I have not years ago settled in Italy. . . . I tell you now, and you will obey me when I am no longer here: put on my tomb neither an image nor a word, not even my name. I wish to be forgotten by this spineless nation as quickly as possible, and I do not regard it as an honor to be remembered by it." Fourteen years later, in his eighty-third year, he added a codicil to his testament, which was published for the first time in 1948. He asked his family to prevent as far as possible the writing of a biography. Looking back on his life, he felt that it had been a failure. "I never had and never desired a political position and political influence. But true to myself, and to what I think is the best in me, I have always been an animal politicum and wished to be a citizen. That is impossible in our nation, for even the best of the individuals cannot go beyond serving in his assigned place. This inner estrangement from my people accounts for my not wishing to appear before the public which I do not esteem."

There are innumerable other private utterances in which Mommsen expressed his disgust with the new Reich. Thus, in 1893, he wrote to his son-in-law: "To speak seriously, what drove me away [from Germany] was my despair at our public and moral conditions." Three years later, when he heard of Treitschke's sudden death, Mommsen wrote: "I did not love him, and I esteemed only his talent, not his character, but even the passing of such an adversary is a blow. Probably we shall live to see very difficult times politically. It seems likely that the insane and criminal will (*der wahnwitzige und verbrecherische Eigenwille*) of the man who unfortunately rules Germany will provoke a crisis and that all the most evil passions and lusts will flame high in this abyss. We poor Germans!" In 1956, two German historians, Alfred Heuss and Albert Wucher, published outstanding studies of Mommsen emphasizing his achievement not only as an historian of Roman antiquity but as a citizen of nineteenth century Germany. Their effort forms an important part of the reappraisal of the recent past which set in with the catastrophe of 1945. The two books offer to the student of modern German history a surprising insight into one of the great Germans of the period. Yet both authors curiously underplay Mommsen's fundamentally antiliberal nationalism and thus lessen the tragic implications of his disillusionment and despair.

Heuss and Wucher stress the close connection between Mommsen the Roman historian and Mommsen the German nationalist. In both cases Mommsen the man was entirely absorbed in the powerful nation-state as the supreme achievement of man. Disillusioned by the failure of the Frankfurt Assembly Mommsen turned to the composition of the first three volumes of his *History*. Written with passionate brilliance, they were to bear out his fundamental political faith. "I put my innermost self and my best in this book," he wrote in 1856, after having finished the third volume. Mommsen viewed the history of the Roman Republic as the story of the unification of Italy into a nation-state by Rome's military power, culminating in Caesar whom Mommsen glorified as the only creative genius produced by Rome. "Hellas was the prototype of a purely human development," Mommsen wrote. "Latium was no less for all time the prototype of national development." Goethe and Burckhardt had turned to Greece. For them the state meant little; for Mommsen it meant everything. Purely human development was of little significance to him. He turned from Greek philosophy and art to Roman politics, from Cicero's humanism, which he despised, to Caesar's realistic dictatorship. Under the influence of Hegel, to which all national liberals succumbed, he glorified the *res publica*, in which alone the individual, as a servant of the whole, could win liberty. "Even if the individual perished in this subjection, . . . he gained in return a fatherland." The growth of powerful centralized nation-states was, for him, a law of nature and of history, and he interpreted the first seven centuries of Roman history as an illustration of this supposedly universal law.

Mommsen saw in Caesar the perfect statesman, at once passionate and sober, free from all ideological prejudices who ruthlessly and intelligently realized the trend of the age. He appeared the ideal for whom Germany longed after 1848, a man similar to Napoleon but working with better human material. Having met the French Emperor in 1863 Mommsen wrote to his wife that Napoleon impressed him as a personality "such as we might wish for our own nation. . . . I confess that I left with a feeling of envy that fate does not once throw to us such a *grand criminel*. What could such a man do with a healthy nation like ours?" Fate was soon to be so unkind as to fulfill Mommsen's wish. Almost half a century after Caesar's glorification Mommsen bitterly complained to his liberal fellow-scholar, Lujo Brentano in Munich, "of the pseudo-constitutional absolutism, under which we live and which our spineless people has inwardly accepted. . . . Bismarck has broken the nation's backbone."

For an article which appeared at the end of 1902, less than one year before his death, Mommsen chose the alarming title *"Was uns noch retten kann" (What alone can still save us)*. Here he proposed an unheard-of demand for that time, co-operation between "those liberals who are still entitled to call themselves liberals" and the workers. He rejected the tenets of the Social Democratic Party but, he continued, "it is unfortunately true that at present it is the only great party which can command political respect. It is not necessary to speak of talent. Everybody in Germany knows that one head like Bebel's [leader of the Social Democrats] divided among a dozen Junkers would be sufficient to make each one of them appear brilliant in his own class." To avert the approaching catastrophe Mommsen demanded united action by all nonreactionary parties, "naturally excluding the one which has disgraced the name of liberalism and the name of the nation," but including the Social Democrats. "We must make an end to the false and perfidious superstition that the nation is divided into loyal parties and subversive parties and that it is the first political duty of every loyal citizen to avoid the millions of the workers' party as if they had the plague and to fight them as enemies of the state." Mommsen's words showed that the old man had learned much. Thirty years before he had supported Bismarck's fight against the Catholic Party and had seen in it a subversive force, as many liberals later saw the Social Democratic Party. In 1874 he himself, in his inaugural address as Rector of Berlin University, had called Social-Democracy "the mean enemy of all noble human kind, the gospel of the necessary abolition of all civilization, the oligarchy of the mob." That a modern nation could continue to exist only as an open democratic society which tried to integrate all faiths and classes as equal partners, went far beyond the national foundations of the Bismarckian Reich.

In the 1860's Treitschke and Mommsen had fought shoulder to shoulder for common ideals. Twenty years later Treitschke appeared to Mommsen as "the true representative [*der rechte Ausdruck*] of that moral brutalization which threatens our civilization, and as its mightiest literary spokesman." The two historians disagreed more and more on all issues of domestic and foreign policy. Mommsen, no friend of Judaism, openly opposed Treitschke's anti-Semitism; he turned violently against German conservatives and began to think of co-operation with socialists; he was friendly toward Britain and the United States; in his last years he stressed international co-operation and the ideals of peace. But the overwhelming majority of educated Germans followed Treitschke. They regarded all opposition to Bismarck and the regime as national felony. "Most of the younger generation," Professor Heuss writes, "could not view the Bismarck Reich critically. . . . The feeling of gratitude prevailed, not only because the successful creation of the Reich appeared a great miracle but also because the Germans had acquired through it a political order vastly superior to all other European states." Most of his colleagues regarded Mommsen's critical attitude toward the development of the Reich with hostility or with condescending indulgence. "The demand for a parliamentary regime in Germany was simply ridiculous in the eyes of a satiated generation, grown-up in the admiration of Bismarck." The middle class, led by the universities, willingly and proudly accepted the ruling junkerism and militarism.

The old man stood almost alone and knew it. Few shared his critical insights. As the nineteenth century closed, the century culminating in Bismarck's glorious victories, Mommsen demanded the abolition of the celebration of the "day of Sedan," the anniversary of the surrender of the French army in 1870. In his last year he wrote an article, "A German to the English": "I am looking back upon a long life. Only a little of what I had hoped for my nation and for the world has been realized. But the Holy Alliance of Peoples was the aim of my youth and is the guiding star of the old man. And I maintain that the Germans and the English are destined to walk hand in hand." Looking back from the vantage point of an octogenarian, Mommsen projected an old man's insight into his younger years when concern for German power by far overshadowed with him all regard for other peoples. Yet even the old man could not have shared the attitude which Gladstone expressed in his last speech: "The ground on which we stand is not British, not European, but it is human."

Most German historians upheld the glory of Bismarck and the Reich even after 1918. One of them, Georg von Below, in 1923 wrote of Mommsen. "In his youth he had known better days as a political thinker, when with Droysen, Sybel, Treitschke he fought as a good German (*im guten deutschen Sinn*). But after 1880 we see him among those liberals who fight Bismarck's policy. The aggressive way in which without any real understanding he opposed Bismarck does not add to Mommsen's glory. He believed that some decades after his death the world would be convinced that he and not Bismarck was right. Today [1923] we can see that his faith was childish."

Old Mommsen's measured judgment differed: "The injury done by the Bismarck era is infinitely greater than its benefits. The gains in power were values which the next world-historical storm might destroy, but the subjugation [*Knechtung*] of the German personality, of the German mind [*Geist*] was a misfortune [*Verhängnis*] which can not be undone." An optimistic observer, while fully subscribing to Mommsen's judgment of Bismarck, could not share the pessism of the concluding five words. Mommsen's own development—and that of men like Gervinus and so many others—bears witness to the resilience and the infinite potentialities of the German —as of any human—personality and mind.

Chapter Nine

WAGNER AND HIS TIME

Richard Wagner in 1848

In the age of Bismarck only two other Germans loomed as large as he in the European scene—Wagner and Marx. The three had certain traits in common: they were great haters, supreme egotists who brooked no interference with their mission. Yet they differed widely in their background and in their aims. Bismarck belonged to the rural nobility of Prussia. Wagner, whose magic power of musical evocation was unrivaled in those times, was born two years before the statesman into a theatrical family settled in the Saxon city of Leipzig. Marx, whose name is better known today than that of any other German, was three years younger than Bismarck, and the son of a Jewish lawyer from the Rhineland.

Wagner and Marx were revolutionaries who had nothing but contempt for the nobility of which Bismarck was so unusual a representative. Rebels against the society of their day, they could scarcely approve the statesman's use of revolutionary methods to bolster the old order. Even in the Germany of the 1860's, Bismarck was an anachronism, and of his work nothing remains: the *Obrigkeitstaat* (authoritarian state) that he labored to reinforce lost its validity even before his death. But Wagner and Marx, both of whom died in 1883, fifteen years before the Chancellor, have had a powerful influence on Germany since their time.

Wagner and Marx scorned the bourgeois nineteenth century and yet were attached to that era of noisy bigness, stirred masses, and rapid technological advance. Marx's faith in the power and precedence of economics and worldly progress was even more intense than that of the great capitalists of his time, and his economic-social world was even more international than theirs Wagner was addicted to the theatrical splendor of the newly rich. His orchestra and singers resounded with the power of the triumphant industrial and imperial age. His ambition was limitless as that of Marx and while Bismarck was satisfied to be a Prussian statesman Marx and Wagner wished for nothing less than the remodeling of the modern world. The former was a systematic social thinker, rooted in the German classical tradition; the latter was a romantic artist who expected his total artwork—a never before consciously attempted unity of sound, word, image, and movement—to bring about the cultural and spiritual rebirth of the German people and, through its leadership, a new civilization.

Wagner left the world a magificent record of music. To the Germans he left even more: the almost untranslatable libretti of his music dramas, numerous essays and articles, and the circle of the Friends of Bayreuth. All this bore a message of specific and unique Germanic values, an interpretation of history and society, based upon the incomparable pre-eminence of Wagner's art and of German folkdom. Wagner saw himself not only as a musician of genius but as a prophet and savior. All his creative work was infused with, and served, this avocation. His music dramas thundered this message. His characters on the stage embodied his innermost desires protesting against the nineteenth century bourgeois world, against men without myth, passion and greatness.*

The German revolution of 1848 was a decisive event in the eyes of both Wagner and Marx. Defeat in May, 1849, drove both into exile. Marx ended his life in London, poor and relatively obscure. Wagner who made his peace, though a tenuous peace, with the conservative powers returned after eleven years to such a position of splendor, luxury and royal favor as no musician has ever achieved. But in 1848 Wagner was only second conductor at the Royal Opera House in Dresden, Saxony. He was not happy; he felt that his real value was not recognized by the aristocratic court society. A still unknown musician, he demanded royal rank for the artists, and wished to impose his ideas for a national stage upon the theater management. Living in great luxury and therefore always burdered by debts, he deeply resented his poverty and his humiliations. He had just fin-

---

* Wagner's biographer and not always uncritical admirer, the famous English music critic Ernest Newman, wrote rightly that for Wagner "Wotan, Siegfried, Titurel, Amfortas, Kundry (and all other main characters) were not stage fictions . . . but cosmic entities interwrought with each other in all sorts of strange ways."

ished the composition of *Lohengrin.* The Knight of the Grail and Elsa, his bride, anticipated most of Wagner's later work: Elsa in her purity embodied the Germanic folk-spirit, devotedly loving and, as long as she was not seduced by the cunning perfidy of dark and hostile forces, blindly trusting the Godsent savior and leader; at the same time she represented "that most fatal expression of sensual fatality which made of me a total revolutionary." Throughout his life Wagner was unable to solve the conflict between the artist's right to be a law unto himself and the laws of society, between worldly illusion and heavenly peace, between his addiction to the flesh and his longing for salvation. This unresolved conflict haunted him from *The Flying Dutchman* to *Parsifal.*

Wagner had hardly finished *Lohengrin,* when he turned in 1848 to his tetralogy *The Ring of the Nibelungen* which forms the center of his creative achievement and thought. In 1848 he wrote the poem "Siegfried's Death" and two significant essays closely connected with the tetralogy—"The Wibelungen: World-History from the Saga" and "The Nibelungen Myth as a Sketch of a Drama " From that moment on he dedicated twenty years of his life to this stupendous work. In 1852 he finished writing the text. The next year he began working at the music. By 1857 he had finished the *Rheingold,* the *Valkyrie* and the first part of *Siegfried.* Then followed a long interruption during which Wagner wrote *Tristan* and *Die Meistersinger.* Only in 1874, when he settled in his house "Wahnfried" in Bayreuth, did he finish the scoring of the last parts of the "stage-festival-drama," performed in August, 1876, as the first Bayreuth festival. The Kaiser himself was present on the first two evenings; he could not stay longer because he had to attend military maneuvers. But the *Ring of the Nibelungen* expressed the revolutionary spirit of 1848 rather than the conservative realism of 1876.

A French music critic, Henry Malherbe, wrote in his essay "Richard Wagner, *révolutionnaire total"* that "without doubt the Tetralogy is the most striking work of the 1848 revolution and the most outstanding artistic event of that period of European history. ... A savage gospel of anarchy, it is so deeply steeped in poetry and dreams that its dangerous significance may not be noticed. Thus its subterranean message, full of imagery, can permeate the souls with greater ease. Wagner wishes to attach himself to an ideal of guilelessness. To that end he sets out to cut all his ties with the human family and to ruin utterly the civilization of his time. The Germanic corner of his character can be detected in this frenzy as well as in the lack of precision, the naïveté and the nebulous

mysticism, with which he envisages the future, should the downfall he desires and foresees come to pass."

The theme of the *Nibelungenlied* was not unfamiliar to educated
Germans in the nineteenth century. The famous epic poem written
probably around 1200 by an Austrian poet has provided the subject
of several modern adaptations, of which the one by Friedrich
Hebbel is outstanding. Hebbel, born in the same year as Wagner,
was a conservative; in 1848 he did not call for revolution, but
headed a delegation which assured the Austrian Emperor—Hebbel,
born in Holstein, lived after 1845 in Vienna—of unswerving loyalty.
His Nibelungen Trilogy, written between 1855 and 1862, consists
of a short introduction *The Horny Siegfried* and two tragedies, of
five acts each, *Siegfried's Death* and *Kriemhild's Vengeance*. In the
epic poem and in Hebbel's drama, the characters are human figures
acting out of human motivations and in human freedom. The
ethos is that of the Merovingian period, but there shines through
it even in the old epic, and much more in Hebbel's adaptation, a
Christian message. In the epic poem mythical and historical
elements (the struggle of the Burgundians and the Huns) are
interwoven; Brunhilde, the fiery queen from Iceland, and Siegfried, the dragon-killer, represent the older stage of legendary giants
but they find themselves throughout among recognizable human
beings. Wagner reversed the trend. The human beings, the
Burgundians, appear only in the last part of the Tetralogy. Until
then mythical gods and demons alone hold the stage.

Wagner found his inspiration not in the *Nibelungenlied* but
in the older sagas of the *Edda*, the realm of primitive, pre-Christian
myth Wagner's interpretation turns them into a denial of civilized
life as such, into primordial forces hostile to good faith, to treaties,
and to law. These Nordic-Wagnerian myths, rediscovered and
adapted in the age of nationalism for nationalistic purposes, had
nothing in common with the Greek myths which moved Goethe
and Schiller, Hölderlin and Heine. In Greece the Olympians
triumphed over the primeval chaos and built over the frightening
abyss a world of beautiful appearance and luminous form. In
Wagner's art shapeless chaos triumphed over the Gods. Few
passages in world literature reveal as profound a nihilism as Wotan's
resignation (in *Die Walküre*, Act II, Scene 2): "In whatever I
do, I find always only myself, and I loathe it. . . I must leave
what I love; I must murder what I woo; deceitfully I must betray
whoever trusts me. . . . What I built must break down! I abandon
my work. One thing alone I demand, the end, the end! . . ."

What I deeply loathe I give it to thee as my heir, the futile splendour of the Divine: let thine envy greedily gnaw it up!" * Rightly Wotan can say of himself that he harbors in his heart the fury which throws a whole world into horror and chaos (*in Grauen und Wust*).

In the time of Aeschylus, with whom Wagner liked to be compared as the creator of a national drama, the Greek myths were still accepted by the Athenian audiences as part of their own emotional and spiritual life. The case was entirely different with nineteenth century Germans. Who among them believed in Wotan or Siegfried? Achilles and Odysseus were to them, as to all Europeans, infinitely more real than old tribal gods and heroes. A national drama must appeal to a past which is still alive, to clearly recognizable human characters with whom the spectator can identify himself and whose problems he understands. Wagner created only one truly national opera, *Die Meistersinger.* Its Hans Sachs, a poet and middle-class artisan, preserves, by his wise sense of restraint as a politician and mediator, the order of society and matrimony—the very order which Wagner's Wotan abhorred.

Primitive Nordic mythology, like the later Christian mysticism of *Parsifal,* remained isolated brilliant moments in the history of German art: outside the sphere of art, however, the Nibelungen, in Wagner's barbaric and weird interpretation, had their influence on the vagaries of German nationalism. The gods of fury, vengeance, and lust, the resurrection of which Heine had foreseen and dreaded, would have established their Reich if Hitler had won his war.

---

* *Zum Ekel find' ich*
ewig nur mich
in allem, was ich erwirke' . .
Was ich liebe, muss ich verlassen,
morden, was je ich minne,
trügend verraten, wer mir vertraut' . . .
Zusammenbreche,
Was ich gebaut'
Auf geb ich mein Werk,
eines nur will ich noch,
das Ende—
das Ende! . .
Was tief mich ekelt
dir geb' ich's zum Erbe,
der Gottheit nichtigen Glanz
zernage sie gierig dein Neid!

Hohenstaufen and Nibelungen

IN THE 1840'S WAGNER'S THOUGHT was under the influence of Ludwig Feuerbach and of Young Germany. In May, 1848, in a letter to Professor Franz Wigard, the Saxon representative in the Frankfurt Assembly, he demanded the sovereignty of the German Parliament, the arming of the folk, and a military alliance with France. In the same month he sent a poetical greeting to the revolutionaries in Vienna praising them for having drawn their swords and calling upon the Saxons to follow their heroic example. All this was in the general mood of the period. But a deeper, more personal, and perhaps more German enthusiasm took hold of Wagner the following year. In April, 1849, the *Volksblätter*, a paper published by his colleague and friend, the radical leader August Rockel, printed—anonymously—a long and dithyrambic article by Wagner. "The old world is in ruins," the article read, "from which a new world will arise, for the sublime goddess Revolution comes rushing and roaring on the wings of the storm, her august head rayed round with lightnings, . . . her eyes so . . . punitive, so cold; and yet what warmth of purest love, what fullness of happiness radiates from it. . . ." Revolution will destroy princes and courts but will bless the folk: "I come to you to break all the fetters that oppress you. . . . I will break down the power of the mighty, of law, of property. . . . I will destroy this order of things . . . for it makes unhappy men of us all."

In 1848 Wagner's thoughts were not only directed toward the future. He turned against the present and the recent past, but found comfort and promise for his revolutionary faith in the far-off realm of saga and myth. In the 1840's, like others of his generation, he was fascinated by the medieval splendour of the Hohenstaufen Reich. As early as 1832 he wrote an overture to Raupach's cycle *Die Hohenstaufen* and expressed his interest in Immermann's tragedy *Kaiser Friedrich II*. In the 1840's he sketched the text for two operas, one, *Die Sarazenin* dealing with Manfred, the son of Frederick II, the other glorifying Frederic I Barbarossa. When the *Nibelungenlied* began to prey on his mind, he felt the need of joining the two myths, that of the medieval world-empire of the Hohenstaufen and that of the Germanic *Edda*, in a way remarkable for its obscurity and extravagant fancy. Even among German metapolitical and metahistorical writings, with their profundity and lack of common sense, Wagner's long and confused essay on "The Wibelungen: World-History Out of the Saga" occupies a very high rank. In the German epic poem the Nibelungen were a noble race living on the Rhine, the Burgundian royal house, and Wagner used in "The Wibelungen" the name in this widely accepted sense. In the *Edda,* however, the Nibelungs are a demoniac dwarf race living in Nibelheim, the subterranean realm of mist and cold. Generally speaking, particularly in his Tetralogy, Wagner employed the word in its older meaning: "From the womb of night and death," he wrote, "a race was spawned that dwells in Nibelheim (the realm of mist)—Nibelungen they are called."

In 1848 Wagner did more than confuse the Nibelungen and a German royal house. At the time he was studying the life of Christ, for he was engaged in writing a sketch (in the printed edition its length exceeds fifty pages) for a drama *Jesus of Nazareth.* In the essay on *The Nibelungen* Wagner identified Siegfried as the mythical sun-god—victorious in death, first Light slaying Darkness (the dragon) and then Day slain by Night—who was mysteriously akin to the German folk and Christ. Siegfried, like Jesus, was God become man, "and as a mortal man he fills our souls with fresh and fierce sympathy· for as a sacrifice for his deed of blessing us, he arouses the moral motive of revenge—we long to avenge his death upon his murderer and thus to renew his deed." Wagner found in Siegfried a "striking likeness to Christ himself, the Son of God, who died, was mourned, and was avenged . . . as we still take revenge for Christ on the Jews of today."

But the confusion is not limited to Siegfried and Christ. For the Nibelungen Hoard won by Siegfried was mysteriously identified in the medieval German mind, according to Wagner, with the Reich, with the universal German monarchy of the Hohenstaufen. The Hoard was also spiritualized into the Holy Grail which Barbarossa was supposedly seeking when he set out on the Crusade in which he died. The Hohenstaufen became Siegfried's heirs, a truly unique royal house, the oldest and most divine of dynasties. "In the German folk," Wagner wrote, "the oldest lawful race of kings in the whole world survives: it springs from a Son of God, whom his nearest kinsmen called Siegfried and the other nations Christ. The closest heir (of Siegfried's deed) and of the power thereby gained are the Nibelungen, to whom the earth belongs in name, and this for the happiness of every nation. The Germans are the oldest nation, their blue-blooded king is a 'Nibelung,' and at their head he claims world leadersh.p."

The Frederic Barbarossa who claimed this world leadership was, to Wagner, a Nibelung and a new Siegfried. For this identification he used a strange etymology. The Hohenstaufen and then their followers were called Ghibellines, a name frequently though probably wrongly derived from Waiblingen, a Hohenstaufen estate in Suabia. Were not the Nibelungen really called Wibelungen, Wagner asked, and was it not clear therefore that the Hohenstaufen were Nibelungen, the rightful owners of the Hoard, of Siegfried's Sword, and of world power? Wagner concluded his essay with the picture of Barbarossa sitting in the Kyffhäuser guarding the Hoard and "by his side the sharp sword that had once slain the fierce dragon. . . . When comest thou again, Frederic, thou glorious Siegfried, and slayest the evil gnawing dragon of humanity?"

Might there not appear another true King of this kind, a folk-King who would promote Wagner's art and thereby the rebirth of Germany? In 1848 the Saxon court conductor put his hope in the Saxon King. In a famous speech in the Patriotic Club (*Vaterlandsverein*) on June 14 he called for the abolition of nobility and selfish privileges, for the creation of a republic, headed by the King, who would be the first of all republicans. Who but the prince could stand for the whole folk united in a classless society? Then the republican people would face the problem which lies at the root of the present social misery—modern capitalism, plutocracy. "Like a hideous nightmare this demonic idea of money will vanish with all its loathsome retinue of open and secret usury, paper-juggling, percentages, and bankers' speculations. This will mean the complete emancipation of the human race; this will be the fulfillment of Christ's pure teaching."

Wagner shared the political and social dreams of the radicals of 1848. The German folk, liberated from caste and class, no longer enslaved to money and property, would win the strength to march toward the highest tasks of civilization and to achieve the universal Reich. "Then we shall sail across the seas, plant here and there a young Germany . . . bring up the noblest of children, children like unto gods. Better we shall manage than the Spaniards, to whom the new world became a papal slaughterhouse, otherwise than the English who have made it into a peddler's tray. We shall do things Germanly and grandly; from its rising to its setting the sun will look upon a beautiful and free Germany, and on the borders of the daughter-lands as on those of their mother, no downtrodden unfree folk shall live: the rays of German freedom and gentleness (*Milde*) shall light and warm the French and Cossacks, the Bushmen, and Chinese."

In 1848 Wagner fused nationalistic and socialistic Germanic ideals —both equally vague and equally generous. One thing was certain to him then: the old order stultifying Wagner artistically and financially was doomed. A new world, a Wagnerian world, would magically take its place. Wagner looked forward to German world leadership, and to the freeing of man from the evil gnawing dragon, from the ring of gold which strangles mankind. Property—Wagner then owned none—was the root of evil. Wagner was more deeply addicted to gold than the average nineteenth-century bourgeois; he longed to enjoy the most extravagent refinements and pleasures which money could buy: at the same time he cursed and despised gold and blamed it as the great corrupter. But now nobility and capitalism, entrenched privilege and the power of the moneybag based upon laws and contracts, were, he gleefully anticipated in 1848, doomed by the miraculous folk-rising of that year. In March, 1849 Wagner wrote a poem *"Die Noth"* (Want or Misery), in which he rapturously welcomed the frenzy of the revolution. "Thy torch shall sever our bonds," the second part of the poem reads in John N. Burk's synopsis, "it shall consume the robbery wrought by paper and parchment! Brightly the firebrand burns, cities become skeletons, and the power which enslaved us is gone! Those who lived on the toils of others are now penniless—they must learn to earn their daily bread, and Want shall be their teacher! . . . Though all be ruin, life will spring anew; humanity is freed from chains; nature and man are restored—as one! What separated them is destroyed! The dawn of liberty has been kindled by Want!"

In the beginning of May, 1849, Wagner, together with his friend the Russian anarchist-aristocrat Mikhail Bakunin, took an active part in the short-lived Dresden uprising. Bakunin, one year younger than Wagner, at that time shared some of his generous hopes in a glorified folkdom (in Bakunin's case, of course, Slav folkdom), in a true folk-prince, and in the abolition of parchments and property. When Prussian troops crushed the revolution, Wagner was the only leader who succeeded in escaping trial and life imprisonment. But the incredible strength of conviction which animated his whole being and his determination to achieve his goal were not broken by the failure of the revolution. He abandoned the attempt to transform the world by political revolution; he set out to conquer it by his art which he consciously put at the service of a compre-

hensive revolution. Nietzsche, who knew only the later Wagner, said
of him that he "believed, half his life, as fervently in revolution as
ever a Frenchman did." Ernest Newman, a leading music critic
but no historian, limits Wagner's role in the German revolution.
"A man was needed," he writes, "to focus in himself all the elements of revolt, artistic, political and social, that had been slowly
forming in German music [in reality: not only in music but in the
German intellectual life as a whole, during the last half century
(since 1806–1813)], and in Wagner Nature threw up the man."
Wagner embodied, in his will and his work, the German revolution,
which had little in common with the revolutions in the West.

In 1849 Wagner wrote an essay "Art and Revolution," sending it
to a Paris journal, "but its Teutonic philosophizing and generaliz-
ing" to quote Ernest Newman, "being beyond the Gallic understanding, his manuscript was politely returned." A radical Leipzig
publisher accepted it and its success in Germany was so great that
soon there was a second printing. Revolution, Wagner proclaimed,
is necessary to found a true community of life (*Lebensgemein-
schaft*), which cannot be achieved by political means, but only
through art. At present the artist must also be a political man:
nobody can write creatively without writing about politics; pure
poetry will be only possible after the triumph of the revolution
which will render politics superfluous. The artist of today must be
a revolutionary.

An Athenian tragic poet, Wagner thought, was in a happier
position. In Greece the *polis* and the people were one; Greek
tragedy expressed the totality of the Greek people in unity with the
state and thus could be conservative. With the disintegration of the
polis, the total artwork of tragedy disintegrated into its various
elements and art decayed. This decay reached its lowest point in
the era of capitalism and industrialism. The State exists, but not
the folk—an organic and loving community of free individuals.
All great art originates only in the true folk-community, therefore
no great art can exist today. Under these conditions, the artist can
no longer be conservative. He must be a revolutionary, bent upon
the destruction of the State. His artwork will restore the loving
union of all arts and thus set the example of a true folk-community.
The theater must become a folk-theater, where all sit together
without distinction of rank; where everything belongs to everybody;
and none works for private gains. In the State, power and property
rule protected by law and custom. The revolution will transform
man and establish the reign of disinterested and sacrificial love.

Wagner's life and his theater in Bayreuth sharply contrasted with his teachings He was unable to write, as Schubert, Schumann, and Brahms did, under the inspiration of the German folk-song. Heine could bring the *Volkslied* alive and, as no other nineteenth century German could, enrich folk-poetry. From Wagner's work no road leads to the folk and their song. His music moved Baudelaire more than it did the German people. Internationally Wagner survives today as the great and self-centered artist who transformed and immeasurably enriched music. Nationally his revolutionary folk-message was of great potency. It did its part in bringing on the ruin of Germany. For his art grew out of his deep faith in his revolutionary message.

To his wife Wagner wrote in April, 1850: "With all my suffering, with all my self-consuming, I have within myself a great transcending faith, the faith in the truth and splendor of the cause for which I suffer and fight. . . . You cling to the peacefulness and permanence of existing conditions—I must break with them to satisfy my inner being; you are capable of sacrificing everything in order to have a respected position in the community, which I despise and with which I don't want to have anything to do; you cling with all your heart to property, to home, household, hearth— I leave all that so that I can be a human being. . . . All your wishes are directed toward conformity with the old, . . . I have broken with everything old and fight it with all my strength." Though Wagner wrote the long and pathetic letter in order to break up his marriage and join one of his many mistresses, he nevertheless gave a truthful picture of himself as a total revolutionary. With all due regard to the circumstances, the letter to his wife expressed the same fundamental attitude as did the article on the goddess Revolution published one year before in Rockel's radical paper.

The Doom of the Gods

FOR MORE THAN A DECADE Wagner lived in exile. During those years he did not long desperately for Germany as did Heine. He longed for the performance of his operas, for financial security, for home and love, sacrificial love (meaning that others would sacrifice for him). The year 1854 was decisive in Wagner's development. His philosophical brooding was crystallized by his reading of Arthur Schopenhauer's *The World as Will and Idea*. He presented a copy of the *Ring* to the philosopher. The old sage registered his displeasure at Wagner's use or abuse of German in the margins of his copy, a displeasure which would have grown had Schopenhauer ever read Wagner's prose essays.

Schopenhauer's philosophy confirmed Wagner's ever-growing romantic conviction—after his failure in 1849—that "night and death redeem man from the turmoil and burden of daylight and life," a conviction dominating *Tristan und Isolde*, which Wagner first conceived in 1854. "Since I have never enjoyed in life the real happiness of love," the forty-one-year-old husband and insatiable romantic artist wrote, at the end of 1854, to his friend Franz Liszt, in a statement which Schopenhauer would have strongly disapproved, "I will erect to this most beautiful of all dreams a memorial in which, from beginning to end, this love shall for once drink its fill."

Thanks to Schopenhauer's philosophy Wagner conceived of Wotan's "rising to the tragic height of willing his own destruction." In the original conception of the Tetralogy Siegfried was its central figure. He was *"Leben der Erde! Lachender Held!"* (Life of the Earth! Laughing Hero). The second part of the Tetralogy called *Siegfried* (originally *The Young Siegfried*) begins with Siegfried's wild laughter (*"er lacht unbändig"*), the naive and brutal laughter of the childish prank of a "noble savage"; it ends with laughter too, but a different laughter, which knows of its end and the end of all things and yet laughingly accepts doom. In the rapture of her love for Siegfried, Brunhilde herself becomes infected by Siegfried's laughter—*"lachend lass uns verderben, lachend zugrunde gehn,"* (laughingly we will perish, amidst laughter face our ruin). For the sake of this love, Brunhilde sacrifices the gods and the world. *Leuchtende Liebe* (luminous love) and *lachender Tod* (laughing death) are Brunhilde's and Siegfried's last words.

In Wagner's original concept Siegfried was the "Man of the Future," the herald of joyous victorious life. But soon he was replaced as central figure by a Wotan who longs for his doom, for the peace of nonbeing, the final nothingness. Out of the frenzied impulses and the lawless lusts of the Tetralogy grows a Schopenhauerian state of mind free of all desires and all illusions. At the conclusion of *Rheingold*, Loge, while watching the triumphant gods laughingly march over the rainbow bridge into resplendent Valhalla observed that "They who deem their power to be enduring hasten towards their end." He sneered at the blindness of these "most divine gods." Wotan lusting for power and women ignored Loge's warning, but in the course of the drama he came to accept his fate, rising to the tragic height of willing his own downfall. In almost Spenglerian words Wagner wrote that all history is governed by an immutable law of rise and fall. "This is the lesson we have to learn from the history of mankind: to will what is necessary, and bring it about ourselves."

At the conclusion of *The Twilight of the Gods* Brunhilde is the one who sets free the gods. She throws the brand into resplendent Valhalla. The ravens of Wotan can now return home with tidings (*bang ersehnte Botschaft*) of rest, of Wahnfried, peace from illusion and folly: "Ruhe! Ruhe, du Gott!" The world is left without a ruler or law.

What Wagner longed for was not redemption through love but the freeing of life, frenzied life and lust, from the fetters of law, contract, and custom, trust and good faith. In the last minutes of *Rheingold* the Rhine maidens proclaim that true faithfulness exists only in the dark depths of the river; falsehood and cowardice reign in the world of gods and men, in the world of Valhalla's light and joy. And at the close of *The Twilight of the Gods* Brunhilde sums up the meaning of the tetralogy in famous lines which Wagner did not set to music, because as he wrote their sense was fully expressed in the whole music drama as such. These words read: "Not goods nor gold nor divine splendor; not house nor estate nor lordly pomp; not the treacherous covenant of gloomy treaties nor the hard law of hypocritical custom: blissful in lust and woe, love alone sets you free." * Neither divine nor human law, neither treaty nor contract can limit the total freedom of passion as it accepts the risk of voluptuous self-annihilation. At the end even love is a deception: Brunhilde is left with nothing but hatred and vengeance. The nihilism of the tetralogy has little in common with that of Schopen-

---

* *Nicht Gut, nicht Gold,*
  noch gottliche Pracht,
  nicht Haus, nicht Hof,
  noch herrischer Prunk:
  nicht trüber Vertrage
  trügender Bund,
  nicht heuchelnder Sitte
  hartes Gesetz:
  selig in Lust und Leid
  lässt—die Liebe nur sein.

hauer, who for all his pessimism was fond of Mozart and Goethe. Nor can Wagner be considered merely a nihilist. No better antidote for *The Ring* can be discovered than Wagner's own *Die Meistersinger*. His hero, Walter von Stolzing, is a youth like Siegfried who has grown up in nature but is human and humanized, a Tristan reconciled to reality; Hans Sachs is a Wotan who does not lust for Eva but leads her toward a happy marriage. His serene upholding of the lawful order and the customs of society, proof of his worldly wisdom, would have been approved by Goethe; in modern music it is matched only by that of the Marschallin created by Hofmannsthal for Strauss' *Der Rosenkavalier*. But Strauss set his opera in the cosmopolitan world of eighteenth century aristocratic Vienna, Wagner's music in *Die Meistersinger* as in the tetralogy is steeped in nineteenth century German nationalism.

On September 11, 1865, Wagner confided to his diary: "I am the most German person (*der deutscheste Mensch*), I am the German spirit (*Geist*). Ask the incomparable magic of my works, confront them with everything else: you cannot say anything else but—this is German. But what is this German? It must be something wonderful, because it is humanly more beautiful than anything else! Why, my God! Should this 'German' take root? Shall I be able to find my folk? What a magnificent folk that must be! But I could only belong to such a people." Such words would have been unthinkable in the diaries of Goethe, Schopenhauer, or Nietzsche. Wagner wrote them at a time when, after long years of despondency and misery, Fortune had suddenly revealed itself to him as a kind and good fairy in a marvelous fairytale.

Wagner's Political Ideas

WHEN WAGNER WAS ALLOWED to return to Germany in 1860, he was not overjoyed. He believed that there "a new world of suffering was opening out for [him] as an artist, . . . new struggles, vain compromises, heartbreaking disappointments." He was right. Four years later, the fifty-one-year-old master found himself in Germany penniless, dreading arrest as a debtor, deserted by his friends, without love or home, and without hopes of seeing his great works performed. Suddenly this year of greatest despondency and despair turned into the annus mirabilis of his life. King Louis

II, a youth of eighteen, inherited the throne of Bavaria in 1864
An impressionable, romantic dreamer, who felt an unbounded
admiration for Wagner, he invited him to settle in Munich and
put the royal power and purse at his disposal. "My mission is to
live for him," the King wrote in November, 1865, "to suffer
for him, if that be necessary for his full salvation." Wagner used
and abused Louis in an often atrocious manner as he did all
his benefactors and friends. But whatever he thought of his
character the King never withheld his protecting hand from the
artist whom he continued to venerate. In 1876, after hearing
The Twilight of the Gods in Bayreuth, he called Wagner, in a
letter overflowing with gratitude, "the artist by the grace of God,"
who had come "to purify, bless, and redeem" this earth, "the
God-man who in truth cannot err or fail."

The annus mirabilis brought Wagner not only a royal patron.
In the twenty-six-year-old, tall and golden-haired Cosima, the
illegitimate daughter of Franz Liszt and a gifted aristocratic
French-woman, the aging master found his greatest love and his
closest collaborator. In 1864, when she was still the wife of the
conductor Hans von Bulow, Wagner's friend and admirer, and
mother of two children, she became Wagner's mistress. In 1870
she became his second wife. "She saw," Newman writes of her,
"the whole contemporary world, as Wagner did, under one sole
aspect, as something to be conquered for Wagnerian art, and that
not so much because it was Wagner's art but because it was the
only means to the salvation of European culture." Full of indomitable energy and will to power, she served for sixty-six
years the propagation of the new gospel of the Master's art and
of his political ideas. She survived him for forty-seven years and
died in 1930 at ninety-three, the uncrowned queen of Bayreuth.

Cosima shared Wagner's political ideas but she did her best (as
did Nietzsche's sister in the case of her brother) to interpret him
in a conservative sense appropriate to the Wilhelminian era. The
triumphal success which Wagner achieved in his later years, the
princely standard of living in which he freely indulged, the
royalty and plutocracy which flocked to Bayreuth, all this was
delightful to Cosima whenever she recalled her illegitimate birth.
She also shared Wagner's extremism—in his instinctive hatred of
the Jews.

"Emancipation from the yoke of Judaism appears to us the
foremost necessity," Wagner wrote. "Above all we must prove our
strength in this war of liberation. Now we shall never gain this

strength from abstract concepts, but only . . . from our feeling an instinctive repugnance of the Jewish character. Thus . . . it will become plain to us what we hate . . . ; through this exposure we may hope to rout the demon from the field where he can exist only in the shelter of a twilight darkness—a darkness we good-natured humanitarians have cast upon him ourselves, to make his look less loathsome." As early as 1851 Wagner wrote Liszt. "I have cherished a long repressed resentment about this Jew business, and this grudge is as necessary to my nature as gall is to the blood." Jews—directly or through their influence tolerated by un-suspecting gentiles—were responsible for Germany's decay, for the degradation of art, above all for opposition to Wagner. Cosima almost surpassed her husband in interpreting all contemporary history as a plot of Jews (and sometimes of Catholics) to destroy Germanic civilization, Wagner, and world salvation. Both agreed with the position taken by some Jewish nationalists, that a Jew was not a German or a European and could not think and create as a German. Jews remained forever aliens in their European homelands; by unbreakable mystical ties they belonged to their race and their distant ancestral soil.

In 1850 Wagner published an anonymous article "Judaism in Music," which he reprinted in an expanded form under his own name in 1869. Wagner's anti-Jewish racialism antedated the work of Count Arthur de Gobineau, whose *Essai sur l'inégalité des races humaines* began to appear in 1853, and whom Wagner met in 1876. Gobineau's racialist polemic against democracy made little impression in his native France; it was through the Bayreuth circle that Gobineau's influence began to spread. Tocqueville had fore-seen it. When Gobineau complained to him that his book received no hearing in France, the liberal nobleman answered: "I think that your book is fated to return to France from abroad, especially from Germany. Alone in Europe, the Germans possess the particular talent of becoming impassioned with what they take as abstract truth, without considering its practical consequences; they may furnish you with a truly favorable audience whose opinions will sooner or later re-echo in France, for nowadays the whole civilized world has become one."

Houston Stewart Chamberlain, an Englishman who turned vehemently against his native land, settled in Bayreuth, and married Wagner's daughter Eva, devoted himself to extolling German racialism. In his book *The Foundations of the Nineteenth Century* (1899) he fused the racial mysticism of both Wagner and Gobineau. This book, which went through many editions, stimulated the rising nationalistic megalomania in Germany before 1914, and influenced Hitler and his admirer Arthur Rosenberg. When, in 1924, for the first time since the war, the theater in Bayreuth was reopened, the swastika flew over the building: General Erich Ludendorff who had led the first Nazi putsch in Munich in November, 1923. was on hand, though Hitler was prevented from being there in person. He was writing the first volume of *Mein Kampf* in the fortress of Landsberg

In one respect Wagner and Hitler differed in their attitude toward Jews. Wagner was willing to accept Jewish admirers. Some Jews were among his most dedicated personal followers. Among them, three may be mentioned. first, Joseph Rubinstein, a Russian pianist, who lived from 1872 to Wagner's death in his house, and committed suicide in 1884, unable to envisage life without the Master. Second, Angelo Neumann, an Austrian musician and theater director, who worked with unsurpassed dedication to introduce Wagner's work on the European stage, and considerably increased Wagner's income. "If anything on this earth could astonish me," Wagner wrote him on June 13, 1882, "it would be you! Heavens, what restless energy, what faith, what courage!" and all this in the selfless service of Wagner's art and purse. Third, Hermann Levi, the son of a Hessian rabbi, principal conductor at the Munich Royal Opera House. Because Wagner had full confidence in his "extraordinary zeal and almost passionate devotion," he was entrusted with conducting the first performance of *Parsifal* at Bayreuth.

King Louis fully approved of Levi conducting *Parsifal*. "I am glad, dear Friend," he wrote to Wagner on October 11, 1882, "that in connection with the production of your great and holy work you make no distinction between Christian and Jew. There is nothing so nauseating, so unedifying as disputes of this sort: at bottom all men are brothers, whatever their religious differences." Wagner could not agree. In his own interest he had to accept Levi as a conductor, but he reproached the King with his ignorance of the true character of the Jewish race, "the born enemy of pure humanity and of everything that is noble in it. It is certain that we Germans will go under before them. Perhaps I am the last German who knows how to stand up . . . against the Judaism that is already getting control of everything." Here Wagner erred; he was not the last one.

Neither was he the first or last German in his insistence on the unequalled qualifications of the Germans. "I prefer the worst German book to the best of the French," the great Master declared in all seriousness; "the former always evokes something sympathetic of which the latter has no inkling." To Cosima who was of French descent and upbringing, the French were repugnant. No model of matrimonial faithfulness herself, she could not read love scenes in a French novel because in France "an honorable feeling between man and woman is impossible." "Richard said," Cosima wrote in her diary in 1870, "that the French capital, the *femme entretenue* of the world, would be destroyed. The burning of Paris would be the symbol of the freeing of the world from the pressure of everything that was evil. Richard wanted to write to Bismarck and beg him to bombard Paris." Instead, Wagner wrote a poem "To the German Army before Paris." In spite of its triteness he did not hesitate to publish it in 1873, together with his play *Eine Kapitulation.* This Ernest Newman calls a "tasteless farce, the loutish humors of which are ungraced by a single touch of literary finesse Only a man of a rather coarse fibre could have gone about in Wagner's deliberate way to make merry over the terrible sufferings of the starving Parisians."

In 1895 Max Koch, professor of German literature at Breslau University, wrote that Wagner's ideas and wishes were similar to those of Bismarck. Koch was wrong. There was little love lost between the Prussian Junker and the romantic artist. Wagner was proud of Prussia's military victories and the German warrior spirit, but he turned against Bismarck when the chancellor, who had little or no interest in art, refused to subsidize Bayreuth. Wagner eventually felt ill at ease in Bismarck's Reich, he found it dominated by Jews and capitalists. "Germany's princess," he wrote in 1878, "should have been as German as the great German master artists." The German princes, Wagner complained, mounted every spectacular Paris opera forthwith at their court theaters and Jewish agitators applied French maxims to government. Democracy was alien to Germany; it existed merely in the newspapers; "and what this German press is, one must find out for oneself." This "Franco-Judaic-German democracy," to secure a following among the people, aped a German mien; its catchwords like *Deutschtum* or German spirit or German loyalty (used so often by Wagner himself) now were declared to disgust "no one more than the man who possessed true German culture, who had to gaze in sorrow at the strange comedy of agitators from a non-German people pleading for his work, while he was not allowed to get a word in edgewise."

In 1880 Wagner, in the midst of his work on *Parsifal,* wrote an essay on "Religion and Art" in which he developed a new religion, based upon the message of his music, a de-Judaized Christianity and Schopenhauer's philosophy. Mankind, European art, and Germany were doomed, if the Germans did not purify their bloodstream by ridding themselves of the Jews. Wagner was appalled by the frivolity of so-called statesmen (Bismarck was one of them) who acknowledged Jews as Germans. Bismarck hoped to solve the Jewish problem in Germany by intermarriage. Moritz Busch, who served Bismarck as a publicist for a few years, wrote in a series of articles in the *Grenzboten,* which he edited, *"Israel und die Gojim,"* in which he differed from Bismarck and agreed with Wagner by declaring that Jews could never become Germans and that the best solution was to conquer their promised land for them and to send them there. But Wagner in 1880 went a step further. No longer were the Jews, democracy, and capitalism alone responsible for the degeneration of the human race; meat eating was apparently as great a sin as intermarriage.

In 1865 Wagner expressed the hope (in a *Journal* destined for the Bavarian King) that Germany's salvation would come from Louis II, who, inspired by Wagner, would restore the true German spirit. At the time Wagner was disappointed by Prussia and her militarism; but when the *Journal* was published in 1878 under the title "What is German?" Wagner omitted all passages critical of Prussia or of militarism; they were published only in 1936. In 1865, Wagner was convinced that "what the Folk lacked, it has now found—the German prince to lead it. . . . I believe it to be invincible when led by a truly German prince." Louis II, who would have loved to be such a prince, faded into relative obscurity when William of Prussia and Bismarck imposed Prussian leadership on Bavaria. Neither of the two men shared Wagner's ideas. Half a century had to pass and the Prussian monarchy had to disappear before a new kind of German folk-prince appeared who resembled Wagner rather than Bismarck, and who blended folkish racialism and authoritarian militarism.

Wagner and Nietzsche

FRIEDRICH NIETZSCHE who was thirty-one years younger than Wagner shared his contempt for Bismarck's Reich. But nothing was farther from his mind than racial mysticism or admiration for the German folk. Nietzsche had no part in Wagner's ideas. What he admired in Wagner was the incomparable artist, the great man, his vitality, and his insatiable will to power. Years after his break with Wagner, during the last autumn of his life, in his autobiographical *Ecce Homo*—a book in which Walter A. Kaufmann, Nietzsche's outstanding interpreter, sees the culmination of his philosophy and which he aptly compares to Socrates' *Apology*—he expressed his unique gratitude to Wagner: "All my other human relations I am willing to give away cheaply, but for no price would I eliminate from my life the days in Triebschen,* days of trust, of serene cheer, of sublime coincidences—of *deep* moments. . . . I do not know what others experienced with Wagner: over *our* sky never a cloud passed."

Nietzsche was too different from Wagner to remain his disciple. Wagner's background was the theater: to the end he remained essentially an actor and a magician of the stage. Nietzsche's background was a Protestant parsonage: his lasting concern was the re-formation of man. Wagner was the romantic artist and a German prophet. Nietzsche was a European moralist who was too much of an artist not to delight in the free play of thought. Wagner needed adulation, luxury, and the glare of publicity. Nietzsche retired after only ten years as university professor to lead a solitary life in the Swiss Alps and in Italy When, in January, 1889, madness closed in on him in Turin, his work was hardly known to the public. But at the time of his death, in 1900, it exercised a strong fascination on the European mind. What attracted young men at the time even more than his writings was Nietzsche's personality, the living example of protest against the halfheartedness, mediocrity, and vulgarity of the time, his uncompromising and unsparing quest for self-realization.

In his growing loneliness, Nietzsche, freed from all social ties and suffering deeply from the human, all-too-human, failings of historic Christianity and modern civilization, became their sharpest critic. He felt the approach of a century of world-wide moral and political crises. In order to meet their challenge he demanded the creation of a stronger and higher type of man. Nietzsche diagnosed the deep malady of civilization, for which he made western democracy and Christian sentimentalism primarily responsible, as a devitalization of all moral values and the ensuing feeling of

---

* Triebschen near Lucerne where Wagner lived from 1866 to 1872, and where Nietzsche, then as a young man of twenty-four, newly appointed professor of Greek at the University of Basle, visited for the first time on Whit-Monday 1869.

the meaninglessness of life. He accused philosophy from Plato to Hegel, and traditional Christianity as well, of having falsified reality and degraded life by proclaiming unchanging Ideas and an eternal God the only true reality; Nietzsche, on the other hand, saw reality in the ever-changing world of experience, in the growing and passing manifestations of life. Christian and Platonic values, based on unreality, had brought about a progressive weakening of vital forces until, in the nineteenth century, decadence and weakening of the will had become general and all the traditional values were fast loosing their validity ("God is dead"), leaving man in a void to face nothingness ("nihilism"). Nietzsche strongly felt the urgent need to overcome this crisis; to this end in aphorisms of deep psychological insight and in poetry of great dithyrambic beauty, he called for the emphatic affirmation of life and for the enhancement of man's will to spiritual, moral, and physical power.

In Wagner Nietzsche ultimately saw a representative of the decadence against which Wagner had claimed to fight but to which he had succumbed. "I am no less the child of this age than Wagner," Nietzsche wrote in 1888, "and that means a decadent: only I understood it, only I fought against it. The philosopher in me struggled against it." Nietzsche's life was a struggle for overcoming—overcoming himself and the dangers in himself. He recognized Wagner as the great temptation in his life. But man grows only in overcoming his temptations. "I regard it as my great good fortune to have lived at the right time and among Germans, to have been ripe" for Wagner's music, especially his *Tristan*, Nietzsche wrote in *Ecce Homo*. "So great in my case is the curiosity of the psychologist. The world is poor for those who have never been sick enough for this 'voluptuousness of hell': it is permissible, it is almost imperative to borrow in this instance the vocabulary of the mystics. I think I know better than anyone else the tremendous height that Wagner has scaled, the fifty worlds of strange enchantments which none besides him had wings to reach: and such as I am, strong enough to turn to my advantage even the most questionable and the most dangerous and thereby to grow stronger, I call Wagner the great benefactor of my life."

The meeting with Wagner gave Nietzsche the first opportunity to breathe freely in the Germany of his youth: Wagner as an artist, Nietzsche recognized, belonged to French romanticism, to Delacroix and Baudelaire. "What have I never forgiven Wagner?" Nietzsche asked in *Ecce Homo*. "That he *condescended* to the Germans—that he became *reichsdeutsch* [an adherent of the

German Reich]. As far as Germany reaches it *corrupts* culture."
What separated Nietzsche from Wagner, was not only the master's
Germanophilism and racialism but also Wagner's character, his
lusting for honors, women, and gold. Of himself Nietzsche could
truthfully write in his forty-fifth year, the last year of his creative
life, that he never strove for such ends.

Wagner confronted Nietzsche with the belief in the Germans
as the chosen people through whom salvation would come and
with anti-Semitism. On these issues Nietzsche stood at the opposite
pole from Wagner. Wagner denied that Jews could be Germans.
Nietzsche wished them "to grow into the German character," to
assimilate and intermarry. He welcomed the Slav and Jewish ad-
mixture in Germany as most beneficial. "Where races are mixed,
there is the source of great cultures." Among modern German
writers Nietzsche was most outspoken in his rejection of anti-
Semitism and of German nationalism. When the approach of
madness broke down his inhibitions he exposed his innermost self
in the last letters to his friends in Basel, the historian Jacob
Burckhardt and the theologian Franz Overbeck. "Wilhelm (the
Kaiser) and Bismarck must be done away with and all anti-
Semites. . . . Just now I am having all anti-Semites shot."

Though Wagner was neither Prussia's nor Bismarck's friend,
he longed for, and prided himself on, a powerful German Reich.
"One thing is now clear to me," he wrote to Constantin Frantz,
in 1868, "with Germany's well-being stands or falls my art-ideal:
without Germany's greatness my art was only a dream: if this
dream is to become reality, then as a matter of course Germany
also must achieve its predestined greatness." This was far from the
philosopher's point of view. As early as 1873, at the beginning of
Thoughts Out of Season, he pointed out the disastrous consequences
which the victorious war had had for Germany. Public opinion
praised the war and attributed victory to the superiority of German
culture. "This illusion is most dangerous: not because it is an
illusion—for there are most salutary and blissful errors—but because it can transform our victory into total defeat: into the defeat,
and even the extirpation of the German Mind (*Geist*) in favor of
the German Reich." German culture had not won the victory;
German military virtues did, which had nothing to do with culture.
"French culture continues to exist as before and we depend on it
as before."

Nietzsche never equated, as did most German scholars and
writers, *Geist* and *Macht,* cultural creativity and military power.

He distrusted the state and was convinced of its indifference or hostility to the creative mind. "One pays dearly for coming to power: power stupefies . . . *Deutschland, Deutschland über alles,* I feel, that was the end of German philosophy." For Nietzsche, as for the Swiss historian Burckhardt, civilization mattered—the artist, the philosopher, the saint were the highest type of man, not the statesman or the warrior. Hegel and Ranke had regarded the state as the essence of history. "But the state is always only the means for the preservation of individuals," Nietzsche objected in a note written in 1873, "how could it be the aim?"

Turning to the example of Greece, Nietzsche in 1875 took a position which Goethe would have fully shared. "The political defeat of Greece was the greatest failure of culture, for it has brought with it the revolting theory that one can promote culture only when one is armed to the teeth and wears boxing gloves . . . Being a Hellenophile means: being an enemy of raw power and dull intellects." And by 1878 Nietzsche drawing the conclusion from his reading of history was maintaining that a politically weakened people may rediscover its spiritual creativity after having lost it in the quest for power. "Culture owes its peak to politically weak ages." Two years later Nietzsche protested the armament race based on mutual distrust. "Disarming after one has been the best-armed, out of a true nobility—that is the way to achieve real peace. . . . Rather perish than hate and fear, and rather perish twice than make oneself hated and feared—this must someday become the highest maxim for every state." Nothing was farther away from Nietzsche's mind than the Roman *oderint dum metuant* (let them hate us, as long as they fear us), which, according to Seneca, was Emperor Caligula's favorite phrase.

In his contempt for force and for the arrogance which it confers, Nietzsche proved his independence from an age in which the cult of violence was rapidly spreading. He was, to quote Jacques Barzun, "against all manifestations of mob and snob, against militarism, against nationalism. . . . His superman is strong in that he can stand alone, that he thinks by cerebration and not imitation, that he acts by refined instinct and not by rote or rule." Nietzsche was the great nineteenth century Protestant, not in his religion but in his moral attitude. He has been recently compared to Kierkegaard—and there is some affinity in the purity and unsparing self-search of these two men, who lived similarly lonely lives and rejected the state and nationalism, conventional morality and normal virtues with equal vehemence. But Kierkegaard was a witness to an eternal and absolute truth which no longer was valid for Nietzsche. In his "Human, All-too-Human, A Book for Free Minds" Nietzsche included an aphorism on "To die for 'Truth,'" which in its use of the word opinion is infinitely removed from Kierkegaard's Christian martyrdom. "We shall not let ourselves be burnt to death for our opinions," Nietzsche wrote. "We are not too certain of them. But perhaps for the right to have opinions and to be allowed to change them." He was a Protestant in the sense of Henrik Ibsen and Ralph Waldo Emerson, who were the free minds to whom, among Germans, Nietzsche was most closely akin.

Nietzsche the Protestant

NIETZSCHE WAS SIXTEEN YEARS YOUNGER than Henrik Ibsen: madness closed his creative life sixteen years before Ibsen died. They lived in the same transitional period of the European mind: early forerunners conscious of the impending devaluation of all conventional values; deeply probing into the hidden recesses of the human heart; unsparingly searching for truth and for values by which men could live. Ernest Renan had already asked the two fundamental questions of the age of crises: *"Qui sait si la verité n'est pas triste?"* and *"De quoi vivra-t-on après nous?"* The same questions were asked by Ibsen and Nietzsche: both were infinitely more radical and daring than Renan, both were much more lonely men in revolt against their age. Ibsen went into a long voluntary exile to protest Norwegian nationalism, the Nordiphilism in language, literature, and politics which made many of his fellow citizens dedicate themselves to the creation of Norwegian independence in every field. Ibsen rejected the state and the church, all party lines, and all conformism. For both Ibsen and Nietzsche the individual alone, the single one, mattered, his faithfulness to himself, his self-realization, his growth by overcoming and disciplining himself. Ibsen with the wide range of his poetic imagination asked all the questions but did not attempt any answers. Nietzsche concerned with man's ethos, did not accept this wise limitation: his message in its inevitable ambiguity has led many of his readers—and even more those who read little of him—astray.

Yet his and Ibsen's tasks were not too different. The Norwegian's famous four lines could have been written by Nietzsche
too:

> To live—means to fight the [sprites]
> that infest heart and brain;
> to write—means to sit
> in judgment over oneself.

Ibsen and Nietzsche challenge the reader, to quote Walter
Kaufmann, "not so much to agree or disagree as to grow." Therein
they were at one with Emerson,* in the rejection of any conformism,
of the quest for group security, which they regarded as the false
idol of their time. "The surest way to corrupt a youth," Nietzsche
wrote in *The Dawn* (1881), "is to teach him to esteem more highly
those who think as he does than those who think differently."
The following two notes, written in 1875, could have been found
either among Emerson's or among Ibsen's papers: "The stronger the
state is established, the weaker is humanity," and, "To make the individual *uncomfortable*, that is my task."

Nietzsche, very different therein from all political, ideological,
or religious leaders, was passionately concerned with personal independence, his own and that of others. At the end of the first
part of *Thus Spake Zarathustra*—this book, affected and romantic
in its style, more Wagnerian than Ibsenian, was the one most

---

* While Ibsen did not influence Nietzsche, Emerson's direct influence was
great. It has been thoroughly studied by one German scholar, Edward
Baumgarten. To quote a few passages of Emerson, whom Nietzsche read
only in poor translations. "People wish to be settled; only as far as they are
unsettled is there any hope for them." "Experimental writing . . . Twice
today it has seemed to us that truth is our only armor in all passages of
life and death . . . I will speak the truth also in my secret heart or think
the truth against what is called God—Truth against the Universe " "With
consistency a great soul has simply nothing to do. . . . Speak what you think
now in hard words and tomorrow speak what tomorrow thinks in hard words
again, though it contradict everything you said today. . . . Is it so bad then
to be understood? . . . To be great is to be misunderstood." Nietzsche (in
Twilight of the Idols) praised Emerson's "benign and sparkling cheerfulness
(*gütige und geistreiche Heiterkeit*), which discourages all seriousness: he
simply does not know how old he is and how young he is still going to be."
The title of one of Nietzsche's greatest books *The Gay Science* perhaps de-
rives from Emerson who called himself "a professor of joyous science—an
affirmer of the one Law, yet as one should affirm it, in music and dancing "
But Nietzsche radicalized and overdid Emerson. Nietzsche lived in a social

widely read by German youth—Nietzsche in strongest terms rejected all believers and followers. "Now I go alone, my disciples,"
he wrote in the semibiblical style of his Zarathustra with its so
unbiblical calling. 'You too go now alone . . . go away from me
and resist—Zarathustra. Even better: be ashamed of him! Perhaps
he deceived you. . . . You say you believe in Zarathustra? But
what matters Zarathustra? You are my believers—but what matter
all believers? You had not yet sought yourselves: and you found me.
Thus do all believers; therefore all faith amounts to so little."
Nietzsche repeated these words in his final work *Ecce Homo*.
But years before he had written· "Convictions are more dangerous
enemies of truth than lies," clearly a youthful overstatement
dictated by the fear that men might succumb to the temptation of
the security of faith—religious, nationalist, or socialist—instead of
facing the danger of free questioning.

As the late-coming heir of the individualism of the Protestant
Enlightenment Nietzsche insisted that "nothing has been bought
more dearly than that little bit of human reason and sense of
freedom which is now the basis of our pride." As a young man of
twenty-one he wrote to his sister: "Here the ways of men part: if
you wish to strive for peace of soul and pleasure, then believe!
If you wish to be a devotee of truth, then inquire! Do we after
all seek rest, peace, and pleasure in our inquiries? No, only truth,
even if it be most abhorrent and ugly. Every true faith is infallible
inasmuch as it accomplishes what the person who has the faith
hopes to find in it. But faith does not offer the least support for
a proof of objective truth." And in his last year of sanity he wrote:
"One must be honest in intellectual matters to the point of hardness. A preference of strength for questions for which nobody today
has the courage, the courage for the forbidden." What he wished
to found was not a new metaphysical system or a new faith, but
an unfinished system with unlimited views, a world of free and
courageous inquiry in which man would not have only the courage
of his own convictions, but the courage for an attack on his convictions.

Ibsen, too, had the strength for questions for which very few
had the courage—the courage of the forbidden. From play to play
Ibsen, sitting in judgment over himself, questioned his own convictions. Some of his plays anticipated Nietzsche's later quest.

vacuum and felt himself forced to respond to nothingness while Emerson
was at home in Concord and remained within responsible human bounds

The overreaching will is prefigured in Ibsen's *Brand*. But Ibsen, deeply human, had his doubts about the unconditional extremism of *Brand*. "God is *Deus caritatis*" are the words with which the drama ends. For Nietzsche, however, there was no God of charity. Brand, like Kierkegaard, accepted the Christian God. Nietzsche like Ibsen's Rosmer, searched for a new joyful morality and a new joyful nobility. "For it is joy," Rosmer told Rebecca West, the young emancipated woman, "which ennobles the minds." "And don't you think," she answered, "suffering too? the great sorrow?" "Yes, if one can overcome it." Rosmer was unable to overcome it—his feeling of guilt, the burden of the past, was too strong. For Nietzsche the abandonment of the old values ("God is dead") meant as little moral license ("everything is permissible") as for Rosmer. Both were sons of Protestant parsons' homes. "There is no judge above us," Rosmer insisted, "therefore we must judge ourselves with greatest severity." And Nietzsche, after having met his emancipated young woman, Lou Andreas-Salomé, complained in the draft of a letter to Lou that she mistook the new morality for its very opposite, for egotism, lust, and love of pleasure —desires which one has in order to overcome them, to overcome oneself, and which were to Nietzsche *"das ganz Widerwärtige am Menschen* (the totally repulsive in a person)." In the draft of a letter to Lou's friend Dr. Paul Rée, Nietzsche complained that "she told me herself that she had no morality—and I thought she had, like myself, a more severe one than anybody else." Again Emerson, in his essay "Self-Reliance," had anticipated the strict antinomist morality of Rosmer and Nietzsche: "The populace think that your rejection of popular standards is a rejection of all standard. . . . And the bold sensualist will use the name of philosophy to gild his crimes. But the law of consciousness abides. . . . I have my own stern claims. If I can discharge its debts it enables me to dispense with the popular code. If anyone imagines that this law is lax, let him keep its commandments one day."

Emerson spoke for Ibsen and for Nietzsche when he wrote: "All men plume themselves on the improvement of society, and no man improves. . . . It may be a question of whether we have not lost by refinement some energy, by a Christianity, entrenched in establishments and forms, some vigor of wild virtue. For every Stoic was a Stoic; but in Christendom where is the Christian? Let a Stoic open the resources of man and tell men they are not leaning willows, but can and must detach themselves; . . . that a man is the word made flesh, born to shed healing to the nations;

that he should be ashamed of our compassion, and that the moment
he acts from himself, tossing the laws, the books, idolatries and
customs out of the window, we pity him no more but thank and
revere him; and that teacher shall restore the life of man to splendor
and make his name dear to all history."

"To restore the life of man to splendor"—that was Nietzsche's
deepest concern too. He knew, as Schopenhauer did, the tragic
character of life and history. But unlike Schopenhauer he refused
to bow to their meaninglessness. He wished to accept all their
perplexities, difficulties, and pain and regard them as a pledge
for the future. For that end greatness of mind, strong passions,
and their mastery and control were needed, qualities possessed by
the superman, whom Walter Kaufmann rightly prefers to call
overman—for *Übermensch* is closely related with *Überwindung*,
overcoming, self-overcoming, self-mastery. "The most spiritual men,
as the strongest, find their happiness where others would find their
destruction," Nietzsche wrote in *The Antichrist:* "in the labyrinth,
in hardness against themselves and others, in experiments: their
joy is self-conquest; asceticism becomes in them nature, need and
instinct. . . . They are the most venerable kind of man; that does
not preclude their being the most cheerful and kindliest."

In his conversations with Eckermann, Goethe insisted on October
11, 1828—and Eckermann agreed—that his writings could not
become popular and that whoever thought of it or worked for it
was in error. "They are not written for the mass but only for
single human beings who strive and seek for something similar
and who develop in similar directions." The same could be said
of Nietzsche. But he had not the wisdom of the old Goethe. He had
no patience with his time, with man, with himself. He demanded
too much of them and thus distorted all his perspective. His works
influenced men who did not wish others to think for themselves
but to follow the leader, who stressed mastery over others and not
self-mastery, who sought national fellowship and greatness instead of
the loneliness of the solitary thinker. Nowhere did Nietzsche, against
his intentions, exercise such a perverted and perverting influence
as in the Germany of the early twentieth century. In the preface
to his *The Will to Power* he had warned against it: *"The Will to
Power,* a book for *thinking,* nothing else: it belongs to those to
whom *thinking* is a *delight,* nothing else. That it is written in
German is at least untimely. I wished I had written it in French
in order that it might not appear as a confirmation of any aspirations of the German Reich."

Nietzsche the Portent

THOUGH NIETZSCHE WAS NO FORERUNNER of National Socialism, it would be futile to deny the dangerous implications of his influence. True, he was fundamentally a son of the Enlightenment, of its individualism and its fight against all "superstitions": he was as violently opposed to nationalism as to socialism in every form, to the glorification of workers or peasants, of the German folk and spirit as of any other folk-community and folk-tradition.

The Nazi philosopher, Alfred Baeumler, wrote before 1933 that "the German state of the future will not be a continuation of the work of Bismarck; it will be built out of the spirit of Nietzsche and that of the Great War" (1914–18). Baeumler was right in saying that Hitler's state was different from Bismarck's; but Nietzsche would have dismissed everything Hitler's Reich stood for just as he did in the case of Bismarck's Reich. Nevertheless, Nietzsche bears his share of responsibility for the fact that many educated Germans turned away from modern western civilization, and ultimately against all civilization.

In his last years, in the exuberance of his search for uninhibited truth, Nietzsche was ready to welcome any, even the wildest, changes of present day society and its morality. His critical warnings rose to a shrill denial of all accepted values of modern civilization and to the proclamation of himself as a new law-giver and as the leader of a coming harsh and heroic age. It was in this latter capacity that Nietzsche influenced, directly and, even more, indirectly, many central and eastern European writers and students who found in his heroic ecstasy a justification for their rejection of humanitarian liberalism and of the West. Nietzsche's notes at the time of his approaching madness, which had he remained alive might not have been published in their present form, are full of contradictions and complexities. While he frequently demanded the radical pursuit of truth for its own sake, he could write, "It is nothing more than moral prejudice that truth is worth more than semblance; it is in fact the worst proved supposition in the world." Of the philosophers of the future he said they would be "tempters, but assuredly they will not be dogmatists. It must be contrary to their pride and also to their taste that their truth should be truth for everybody." He called his free inquiring mind "ready for adventure." This lure of the forbidden did exercise a dangerous fascination, compatible with Nietzsche's belief that man grows by facing dangers, especially those of the mind.

In an unheroic and outwardly materialistic period, many young Germans were attracted by Nietzsche's call for dangerous living and the "fullness of life." In the famous chapter of *The Gay Science* "Men who prepare the Future" (*Vorbereitende Menschen*) Nietzsche welcomed the advent of a more manly, warlike age which would honor courage above all, an age in which a type of man who could not come "out of the sand and slime of our present civilization and the culture of its great cities (*Grossstadt-Bildung*)" would seek above all what is to be *overcome* in all things. They will *wage wars* for the sake of thoughts and their consequences. True, these men will be characterized by cheerfulness, patience, and magnanimity in victory; they will judge freely and sharply all victors and the share of chance in every victory and every fame. Yet Nietzsche tells them that to *live dangerously* is the secret of the greatest fruitfulness and the greatest enjoyment of life. "Build your cities under Vesuvius! Send your ships into uncharted seas! Live at war with your peers and yourselves! Be robbers and conquerors, as long as you cannot be rulers and owners, you who think and understand (*ihr Erkennenden*)! . . . At last, thoughtful understanding will reach out for its due: it will want to *rule* and to *own*, and you with it!" The words italicized were underlined by Nietzsche: to wage wars, to live dangerously, to overcome, to rule (*herrschen*), and to own. The wars were to be fought for the sake of ideas—and their consequences!—but wars for a faith can be, as the warlike twentieth century has shown again, the most dangerous and degrading of all wars.

In the section "On Old and New Commandments" in *Thus Spake Zarathustra*, Nietzsche asked, "O my brothers, am I cruel?" The answer is horrifying in its nihilism and its daring expectation of a miraculous rebirth out of total ruin: "But I say: what is toppling should be destroyed. Everything today is toppling and decaying: why should we interfere with the natural course of events? But I—*I* was born to destroy." The *hubris* of the absolute will proudly proclaimed: "For creators are hard. And it is blessed to inscribe your will to power on thousands of years as if they were wax. This new commandment, O my brothers, I give unto you: *become hard!*"

Nietzsche's language in his last writings expressed an extreme combative spirit, couched in violent language and extolling a pitiless struggle. Men are apparently divided by an unbridgeable gulf into two castes with entirely different roles and an entirely different morality. This division of mankind into elite and herd was foreshadowed by Dostoevsky, in the famous tale of the Great Inquisitor in *The Brothers Karamazov*. There the Great Inquisitor blames Christ for not having succumbed to the temptation of power offered by the devil in the desert. As a result, Christ has burdened the common man with the responsibility of freedom which is too heavy for the common man to bear and which makes him unhappy. The Great Inquisitor points out that the human happiness of the herd can be assured only when a few superior individuals, the really free and courageous men, renounce happiness, ease of life, and peace of mind, assume the burden for all the others, and become their unquestioned authority. Such men who understand the tragic character of life and history were announced by Nietzsche: "The masters of the globe shall replace God and shall acquire the deep and unconditional confidence of those over whom they will rule. They themselves renounce happiness and comfort. They give the expectation of happiness to the humblest not to themselves. They offer religions and systems, according to the rank (*Rangordnung*) of the people."

These words of Nietzsche were quoted by Richard Oehler at the end of his book *Friedrich Nietzsche und die Deutsche Zukunft*, published in 1935. Oehler, a nephew of Nietzsche's sister, Mrs. Elisabeth Foerster, was for many years secretary of the Nietzsche Archives and one of the few convinced Nazis among Nietzsche scholars. Oehler also quoted the passage from the first part of the *Genealogy of Morals* in which Nietzsche wrote: "Favor me with one glance only, one glance of something perfect, completely succeeding, happy, powerful and triumphant, . . . of man who justifies man, of a saving fortunate chance (*erlösende Glücksfall*) for man, for the sake of whom one can retain faith in man." Oehler was convinced that this one man who justified man had appeared in Germany: that the prophecy of Nietzsche, the Old Testament, was now being fulfilled in the fullness of time in the new Gospel which had come not as a system of thought but as a vital experience of a whole people which cannot be expressed in words. "The salvation has come, the fulfillment is growing."

The new superman replaces God, as Nietzsche said, at least in the beliefs of his followers, and to him everything will be permissible. Again it may be appropriate to quote another word by Dostoevsky, of the nightmare devil telling Ivan Karamazov: "Since there is in any event no God or immortality, the new man may well become Man-God . . . and promoted to his position he may easily do away with every former moral inhibition of the former Servant-Man." The image of the overman (or superman) may lead an Ivan Karamazov to lonely daring thoughts and a sincere search for truth, but Smerdyakov, his deformed half-brother, will misinterpret the overman into the leader to be followed, into the superman who makes everything permissible. Nietzsche himself distinguished the "strong spirit who has become free" whose instinct gives the highest honor to a morality of self-abnegation from the fanatics who impress the masses—"mankind would rather follow gestures than listen to reasons"—but unfortunately both the strong spirits and the fanatics are moved by the will to power and are its supreme embodiment.

Like Schopenhauer, Nietzsche reduced life and man to the one principle of the will superior to reason and ethos. Such a will cannot be a principle of morality or of rational living. Schopenhauer well understood that. His ethics negated the will. Nietzsche denied Schopenhauer's negation. He affirmed the will to live and turned it into a will to power. He believed it capable of creating the values of a new and higher morality. But the attempt to make will the fountainhead of morality led him by necessity into contradictions. Reality may be chaos, eternally creating itself, eternally destroying itself, subject neither to logos nor ethos, but it is life—it needs no justification from without, from any transcendent norm, it is for those who are strong an eternal experiment. In the last year of his creative existence he saw himself as a fatality. *Ecce Homo* ends with the chapter "Why I am a Portent." In the future, Nietzsche was convinced, the recollection of something monstrous (*Ungeheures*) will be attached to his name. "I am not a human being, I am dynamite." He called his discovery of the true nature of Christian morality—"an event that has no equal, a real catastrophe." Indirectly and unwittingly Nietzsche the portent helped bring about the catastrophe which Heine had foreseen for Germany—the triumph of nature over civilization.

Nietzsche proclaimed that our time was a turning point, in which the history of Christianity and of post-Socratic antiquity were coming to an end. Karl Jaspers has shown how Nietzsche, rejecting all Christian content, was still motivated by Christian premises: a vision of world history as an inclusive totality and the concept of man as a fundamentally vitiated being But Nietzsche de-Christian-ized these premises. He believed in man as potentially the creator and planner of history; true, man was less finished and less per-fected than an animal but for that very reason he could grow beyond himself. Nietzsche always wished to overcome, his time and himself, history and man. "But to overcome for what end?" Jaspers asks. "This remains obscure forever."

A year before he became insane, on January 3, 1888, Nietzsche wrote to Paul Deussen, a friend of his student days, that he expected from the years ahead "the subsequent (*nachträgliche*) sanction and justification of my whole being, a being which other-wise would remain for a hundred reasons eternally problematical." Fate did not allow him the years to find this justification, to explain himself, to make his life and work less problematical But in the one year granted to him, in the last book which he published, in *The Twilight of the Idols* he reached his own defini-tion of Goethe who, like Socrates and perhaps more than Socrates, appeared to him to be a superman. In these words Nietzsche revealed what he himself hoped in vain to become and what he expected that man might become: "He did not desert life, but placed himself at its center. He was not fainthearted but took as much as possible upon himself, into himself. What he aimed at was totality; he fought against separating reason from sensuality, feeling, will. He disciplined himself into wholeness, he created himself. He envisaged man as strong, highly civilized, graceful in every gesture, self-controlled, having respect for himself as a creature who might dare to afford the whole range and wealth of being natural, of being strong enough for such freedom, the man of tolerance, not from weakness but from strength, because he knows how to use to his advantage what would destroy an average character Such a mind, having attained real freedom, lives in the very center of all things with a joyful and confident acceptance of fate, lives in the faith that only the particular in its separateness is objectionable, and that in the wholeness of life everything is affirmed and redeemed. He no longer negates." But Goethe had an innate and spontaneous sense of measure and balance. Nietzsche succumbed to what he called "the magic power of extremes."

Chapter Ten

EUROPEAN HORIZONS

Nietzsche and Rilke

BY INCLINATION AND BY SYMPATHY, Nietzsche was a European. He prided himself upon his alleged descent from Polish nobility and he preferred the aesthetic and intellectual climate of France and Italy to that of Germany. After Bismarck had created the German Reich Nietzsche reacted sharply against the self-centered and self-satisfied provincialism of its thought and scholarship. He was still alive though slowly dying in madness when, before the turn of the century, and partly due to his liberating influence, German poetry and letters began to outgrow the narrow and confined horizons of the preceding generations. The German literary renaissance, which in many aspects followed the lead of France, was not an isolated phenomenon. It formed part of a general movement which made itself felt, at the beginning of the twentieth century, throughout the western world from the United States to Russia.

Among the new German poets three became of European importance: Stefan George, Hugo von Hofmannsthal, and Rainer Maria Rilke. In their work they owed a deep debt to the renewed close intercourse with foreign letters and civilization. They eagerly learned from developments abroad and revived the awareness of the unity of the western tradition. None of them was in the least touched by *Deutschtümelei* or by a Wagnerian preference for Germanic myths. In the field of letters, at least, Germany at the beginning of the twentieth century resumed the ways of Goethe's age, moving away from a confining nationalism to a fruitful cosmopolitan receptivity.

The three great poets were as different from each other as possible. They did not form a school or group. Two of them, George and Rilke, were deeply influenced by Nietzsche. Like Nietzsche, they were lonely and homeless men without ties to family, profession, or residence.* Whereas Nietzsche was of Protestant background and lived as deeply in the Protestant tradition as did Emerson or Ibsen, the three poets were born Catholics. George and Rilke turned against Christianity; their work and their minds were fundamentally pagan. Hofmannsthal, the only one of the three who lived the normal life of a man attached to family, home, and fatherland, remained a Catholic and was according to his wish buried in the garb of a member of the Tertiary order of the Franciscans.

The three poets came from borderlands outside of, or hostile to, the Prussian center. George was born in the Catholic Rhineland of a family of French Lorraine descent. Hofmannsthal was born and educated in Vienna, the imperial capital which was in antiquity, like the Rhineland, a Roman outpost and which later became the meeting ground of all the traditions of a cosmopolitan Europe to a degree found in no other city. The third poet, Rilke, was born in Prague, then an Austrian city, the centuries-old battleground of German and Slavic civilization. Hofmannsthal, part Jewish, part Italian, was deeply rooted in Vienna where he lived and died. Rilke left Prague—for which he felt no affinity—when he was still a youth and never returned. George remained a Rhinelander though he wandered, as did Rilke, through many cities and countries. Rilke and George died in voluntary exile in the Romance-speaking parts of Switzerland. According to their wishes they were buried there. Rilke left Germany for ever immediately after the First World War while George went to Switzerland, in 1933, in Germany's darkest hour.

Whatever their geographical wanderings, the three poets were even less confined in the breadth of their cultural contacts. The impact of Greece on George's thought and life was even greater than on that of Goethe and Hölderlin, Heine and Nietzsche. With him what Professor Butler has called "the tyranny of Greece over Germany" reached a degree of incarnation unknown in other German poets. But it was not only with Greek beauty, it was with the whole Latin western tradition of the priestly poet, from Dante to Mallarmé, and its dedication to form that George felt a

* Rilke, it is true, was married and had a daughter, but during most of his life he lived in every respect as a man without a family.

deep affinity. Hofmannsthal had an unusual familiarity with all western European literature of the past and of his own day; he was at home in the world of the baroque which had formed the bridge between the lands of the Austrian and those of the Spanish branch of the Habsburgs, and in the cosmopolitan atmosphere of the eighteenth century. Rilke, less well-read and less the heir of the past than the other two poets, embraced the whole of continental Europe as his own, from the Slavic east to France, from Scandinavia to Spain. In his younger years he was deeply impressed by his travels in Russia and by the Russian "soul." A quarter of a century later, in a letter of February 15, 1924, he thanked his Polish translator Witold von Hulewicz for proving a close relationship between his poetry and the "rich and deeply animated" (*innerlich bewegte*) Polish literature. "It corresponds more than I can say to my innermost feeling to suppose that the Slavic current may not be the least in the multiplicity (*Vielfältigkeit*) of my blood. . . . What you say—to my glory—of the fact that I could claim descent from Juljusz Słowacki,* has occupied my mind very often as a general proposition: the possibility that one could trace one's own descent in other languages and periods if all the hindrances which separate national minds would suddenly crumble." Nietzsche would have entirely agreed with these sentiments.

Of these poets, Rilke has become the most famous. His writings and letters have been frequently translated into English and other European languages. Perhaps more has been written about him in Germany and abroad than about any other modern poet. His affinity with Nietzsche was recently discussed by Erich Heller and Walter Kaufmann. Professor Frank H. Wood rightly called Rilke one "who seems in many ways to be Nietzsche's heir. . . . Like Nietzsche before him, Rilke came more and more in the end to identify himself with the warm pagan South, the Latin Mediterrané. Over much of the final poetry weaves the spell of Zarathustra's noon day hour and the *trop de clarté* of Valéry's poem *Cimetière marin*, which casts a magic light over the ribbon roads and sloping vineyards basking in the midday heat." In a poem written in his last year Rilke celebrated with almost Nietzschean words the Dionysian affirmation of life:

> *Uber dem Nirgendsein   spannt sich das Uberall!*
>
> (Over the nowhere   arches the everywhere!)

---

* Juljusz Słowacki (1809-49), one of the three great Polish Romantic poets.

Rilke like Nietzsche rejected the backward-looking traditionalism and the pessimism about life, men, and values which has characterized so much of modern German and European thought They did not seek to build their home in the security of tradition. They were courageous seekers for new experiences and they faced honestly the fullness and temptations of the life of their time, which they interpreted anew. In 1923, one year after T. S. Eliot's *The Waste Land*, Rilke published his most mature and in many ways final books of poems, *Duinese Elegies* and *Sonnets to Orpheus*. He explained their meaning in the same year in a letter to Countess Sizzo, in which Professor Kaufmann rightly finds a fundamental motive common to Rilke and Nietzsche· "Whoever does not affirm at some time or other with a definite resolve—yes, jubilate at—the terribleness of life, never takes possession of the unutterable powers of our existence (*die unsäglichen Vollmachte unseres Daseins*); he merely walks on the edge; and when the decision is eventually made, he will have been neither one of the living nor one of the dead. To show the *identity* of terribleness and bliss (*Furchtbarkeit und Seligkeit*), these two faces of the same divine head,—indeed, of this *single* face that merely looks this way or that, depending on the distance from which, or the mood in which, we perceive it—that is the essential meaning and concept of my two books."

To Rilke life was no wasteland nor was there any hope of an escape into the alleged security of dogma or tradition. His very last poems, written during his painful illness, continued to praise the rejuvenating forces of the earth *hic et nunc*. He was as lonely a man as any in modern or ancient times—it is a strange self-indulgence on the part of twentieth century intellectuals to imagine that they discovered human loneliness or the tragic character of life—but he did not advocate a "spurious retreat into other-worldliness." Life was tragic, but men had the power to face it and thus to grow. There was, of course, the imminence of death. He knew it as men have always known it. The thought of death was with Rilke from his youth to his long and painful dying. In his early poems he wrote in the affected manner which was then still characteristic of his poetry: -

Der Tod ist gross.
Wir sind die Seinen
lachenden Munds.
Wenn wir uns mitten im Leben meinen,

wagt er zu weinen
mitten in uns.

(Death is great. Laughingly we are His. When we think ourselves in the midst of life, he dares to weep in the midst of us) For him life and death belonged together, but he believed that life was stronger than death. In later years his *Sonnets to Orpheus* proclaimed, to quote William Rose, "that only he who has eaten of the poppy with the dead, only he who is aware of the jeweled realm of the dead and the living, may in full understanding sing in praise of life."

Rilke was not a prodigy like Mozart or Hofmannsthal. His beginnings were not only second-hand and second-rate, they were often outright embarrassing. Only slowly by hard work and discipline, by total dedication to his art, did Rilke become the greatest poet of his age. He grew not only in his art but also in his acceptance of life with all its anxieties, cares, and frights. That is the ever-recurring *motif* of his letters. In the fall of 1906 he wrote—and Goethe would have approved—that the man who has a courageous, resolute, and serious attitude toward life cannot be angered or disillusioned by it. The following year, thanks to the influence of life in Paris and of Rodin's example, brought a new stage in the development of Rilke's poetry, a dedication to close and disciplined observation and a new sobriety of form. But at the same time he started the *Notebook of Malte Laurids Brigge,* a prose narrative which is perhaps the most devastating document of human loneliness written by a great poet in the misery of a great city. Yet in 1912 Rilke commented, "I am just now more one-sided than ever; the lament (*Klage*) has prevailed, but I know that one should use the chords of lament so much only if one is determined to play on them later . . . also the whole jubilation (*Jubel*), which grows behind everything that is heavy, painful, and endured, and without which the voices are not complete."

For Rilke, the European and the human being, the war years were a time of forbidding misery. He had to leave Paris and his friends. He had to serve in the army. The war was to him a stark and unbearable tragedy. Yet on October 9, 1918, he confessed that he regarded life as a thing of unassailable delight and that the many disasters and horrors, "all that has grown these last years to a still increasing horror," could not disconcert him from acknowledging the fullness, goodness, and gentleness (*Zugeneigtheit*) of existence.

Immediately after the war Rilke was able to escape to Switzerland. There, thanks to Swiss patrons, he found in the lonely tower
of Muzot in the mountain canton of Valais, a home where he
spent most of the last years of his life. Writing from Muzot,
in March, 1922, to Rudolf Bodländer who found himself at the
bewildering threshold of life and art, he insisted that his work
did not call on anyone to revolt or seek revenge against life. "That
taking life seriously (*Jenes 'Schwer-nehmen' des Lebens*) with
which my books are replete, has nothing to do with melancholy
. . . it does not wish to be anything else but taking life as it truly
is, . . . no rejection; on the contrary, how much infinite assent,
an ever renewed assent to existence (*wieviel unendliche Zu-
stimmung zum Da-Sein*)!"

One year before his death Rilke explained to his Polish translator
the meaning of the *Elegies:* they proclaim that final assent to life
which the young Malte could not yet reach. Assent to life *and*
death are one in the *Elegies.* At the end of 1921, even before the
Elegies and the *Sonnets* appeared, Rilke prefaced a copy of his
Malte Laurids Brigge with a poem which begins:

> Oh sage, Dichter, was du tust?
> > —*Ich ruhme.*
> Aber das Todliche und Ungetüme,
> wie hältst du's aus, wie nimmst du's hin?
> > —*Ich rühme.*

(Tell us, Poet, what are you doing?—I praise. But how can you
endure, how can you accept, the deadly and dreadful?—I praise.)

There is the same winged lightness, the same "intellectual rational
ecstasy" in the *Sonnets to Orpheus* as there is in Nietzsche. There
is the same emphasis on *"über"* (*over*) as in Nietzsche, from *"O
reine Übersteigung!"* in the first sonnet to *"die herrlichen Über-
flüsse unseres Daseins"* in one of the last. The *Elegies* still show
despair and jubilation, "the terrible aspect of life passing into bliss."
The *Sonnets* only praise. Even the moments of life's pain are part
of the whole praiseworthy texture of life. Nietzsche's and Rilke's
world was one without transcendence. Both rejected Christianity
with its mediator. "Whenever the poet [Rilke] chose Christian
themes for his work," the German critic Hans Egon Holthusen
wrote, "he stripped them of their sacred meaning, substituting for
it psychological speculations, sometimes with a devastating effect."
Like Nietzsche, Rilke wished to remain faithful to this world.

Like Nietzsche, Rilke preferred the Old to the New Testament.
In a letter to Ilse Blumenthal-Weiss, in December, 1921, he spoke

of his "indescribable confidence" in tribal gods, those of the Hebrews, the Arabs, or the Mexicans, and his distrust of a religion of faith to which men can be spiritually converted. Though this stress upon the tribal and the archaic carries Nietzschean overtones Rilke went much farther than Nietzsche. With all his violent attack upon Christianity, Nietzsche was rooted in the Christian ethos. In him survived a puritan asceticism which was lacking in Rilke. Both assumed sometimes the irritating pose of a prophet, though neither went as far in that direction as did Richard Wagner or Stefan George. Rilke lacked the penetrating sharpness of Nietzsche's thought and the hardness of his will. There was a yielding and almost feminine softness in Rilke which Nietzsche would have scornfully dismissed. Rilke's *Requiem* for Wolf Graf von Kalck- reuth ends

> *Die grossen Worte aus den Zeiten, da*
> *Geschehn noch sichtbar war, sind nicht für uns.*
> *Wer spricht von Siegen? Überstehn ist alles.**

In an earlier poem Rilke defined growth as being deeply defeated by ever greater obstacles. Neither in life or in thought did Rilke reach Nietzsche's seminal greatness. Like Baudelaire, Rilke was a very great poet and fulfilled his life in his poetry. *"Gesang ist Dasein"* (*Song is Being*) proclaims the third sonnet to Orpheus. In a copy of *Les Fleurs du Mal* Rilke wrote in 1921

> *Der Dichter einzig hat die Welt geeinigt,*
> *die weit in jedem auseinanderfallt.*
> *Das Schöne hat er unerhört bescheinigt,*
> *doch da er selbst noch feiert, was ihn peinigt,*
> *hat er unendlich den Ruin gereinigt:*
> *und auch noch das Vernichtende wird Welt.*

Rilke proclaimed the god-artist through whom the world is being unified and recreated out of ruin and destruction into wholeness. It was a message of ultimate comfort, but one in which the warrior and the nationalist had no place. It is remarkable that in the twentieth century no other poet caught the imagination of German youth as much as this unpatriotic singer whose heart from the beginning turned away from Germany to the Slav and to the Latin, who ultimately preferred writing French to writing German, and in whose poetry the hardness of war and the glory of victory found no voice.

---

* The great words of the times, when things still visibly happened, are not for us Who speaks of victory? To survive is all.

An Unknown Rilke

THIRTY YEARS AFTER RILKE'S DEATH Renée Lang edited the letters which the poet wrote between 1921 and 1926 to the Duchess Gallarati Scotti of Milan. In the flood of frequently embarrassing letters which Rilke exchanged with his women friends and which were published after his death, this correspondence holds a unique place. It was carried on during the years when Fascism occupied the stage in Italy and the minds of so many intellectual spectators abroad. To understand Rilke's attitude, one should not forget how completely unfamiliar with political problems Rilke (and also Stefan George) was and how much more sophisticated observers misjudged Mussolini for many years. Even Ricarda Huch, the outstanding woman writer in modern German literature who strongly opposed National Socialism, wrote from Padua on December 11, 1923 to her friend Marie Baum: "I imagine that Mussolini is Italy's Bismarck and that if he remains alive he will lead Italy to great maternal flowering." She praised the Italian people for being able to produce out of their midst such an important man. Later her judgment of Mussolini changed. Rilke however remained fascinated by Fascism in spite of the objections of his correspondent, the Duchess, who like her husband was from the very beginning a staunch opponent of Mussolini, perhaps because she knew better what was going on, and in any case had much more political sense than the poet.

Rilke, who never regarded Germany as his spiritual home, was inclined to accept Fascism because it was a Latin movement, hostile to Anglo-American bourgeois civilization. It is true that, compared with Russia and France, Italy played only a secondary role in Rilke's spiritual evolution. What Italy was for so many Germans of an older generation France was for Rilke. The two great artists whom he acknowledged as masters and friends, Rodin and Valéry, were incapable of reading a line of his poetry. But in spite of this lack of comprehension he never longed like Heine for Germany. He felt Germany was alien to him and that France was his true home.

Rilke's feelings of attachment and homelessness were personal and spiritual, they had nothing to do with political issues. Only

in respect to one such issue did he take a decided stand—in the
rejection of Prussia. "In politics," he wrote the Duchess in January, 1923, "I have no voice, none—and I deny myself any sentimental involvement in it . . . But I confess that I have never
been able to love Germany except its hidden root; politically I
have disapproved of everything I saw happen there. . . . The year
1866 seems to me the beginning of many errors from which we
today suffer. For that year marks the birth of the terrible Prussian
hegemony which by brutally unifying Germany suppressed all
the simple and likeable Germanies of the past. Prussia, the least
civilized and least German state, this incorrigibile *parvenu*, has
succeeded in imposing upon hardly formed faces the coldly fixed
mask of a greedy demon who attracts and provokes doom (*ce
masque figé d'un démon profiteur qui attire et provoque le
mauvais sort*)."

Rilke's correspondence with the Duchess exhausts itself generally in brief letters dealing with literature and his memories of
former visits to Italy rather than with the events of the day. Only
in the last year of his life, when he was a very sick man, did
Rilke turn explicitly to the events which shook Italy after the
brutal murder of Giacomo Matteotti in June, 1924. Rilke several
times hinted of his admiration for Mussolini, until finally the
Duchess found it necessary to explain to him why she thought
any adherence to Fascism impossible. "I detest violence," she wrote,
"and I can accept it even less when this violence is exercised in my
favor or in favor of my social class than when it is exercised by
my enemies. And I believe that the tranquility of the country
can only be assured when liberty allows us to gain an exact idea
of what the country thinks and wants."

Rilke answered in the beginning of 1926 in two lengthy letters.
They reveal not only a little-known aspect of the poet's thought
but also a then widespread mood among many intellectuals on
the European continent. This mood combined dangerous aspects of
Nietzsche's thought, his glorification of aristocratic virtue and
steely heroism, which were then overemphasized by D'Annunzio and Mussolini and by Spengler and Ernst Jünger, with the
fashionable deprecation of the soulless machine, of industrial
democracy, and of middle-class society. Rilke referred the Duchess
to a Swiss Catholic author, Gonzague de Reynold, whose article
"The European Balance Sheet" in the Paris *Figaro* of January 14,
1926, praised Italy's order and progress, growing self-confidence
and recovery. The authoritarian regime of the great man had put

an end, it was claimed, to the disorders of parliamentary democracy and was restoring to Italy her rightful greatness which history had destined for her. Similar words and claims were applied to France thirty-three years later. "Everywhere, the economic situation is worse than two years ago," Reynold wrote in 1926, "except in Italy, where one works as never before. Why? Because security reigns. And why does it reign? Because a government governs. . . . The Continent passes through a crisis of regime. . . . Certainly Fascist Italy offers a refreshing spectacle, a solution which arouses envy, an example which one is tempted to follow: hence the conspiracy of silence or this campaign of vilification through which the enemies of Fascism try to hide or defame it. Certainly Spain too, more than ever vilified by a whole sect, is also being revived through dictatorship."

In her letter the Duchess had written of her friendship with Rabindranath Tagore. In his reply Rilke rejected the humanitarianism of a Rabindranath Tagore or a Romain Rolland. Rilke was of course right when he maintained that good intentions do not make good poets, but he was on dangerous ground when he continued: "*La liberté! Mais n'est-ce point d'elle que le monde est malade?* . . . *Il me semble que les meilleurs d'entre la jeunesse* . . . *ont besoin non tant de liberté, mais d'une fière et volontaire obéissance qui les unit, en développant en chacun la conscience de leur force et de leurs capacités.*" * There is little of the true Nietzsche in this late and fatigued Rilke, little of Nietzsche's daring quest, even less of the luminous heritage of the Enlightenment to which Nietzsche remained faithful in all his aberrations.

Rilke turned back to the "security" of the Middle Ages, to the alleged superiority of the peasant and artisan of the pre-industrial age over the modern worker, to order as if it were a desirable supreme goal in itself. True, he excused himself for writing about political questions: "As for politics, I am so removed from it, so incapable of following and of explaining to myself its movements and repercussions that it would be ridiculous to wish to express myself on any event in its domain." True, he took into account his personal condition: "Is it because I myself am a sick man that I recommend the use of a regimen, of a remedy that always requires authority, a certain temporary violence and the deprivation

---

* "Liberty! But isn't it all because of her that the world is sick? . . . It seems to me that the best among our youth need not so much liberty, . . but a strong and freely given obedience that unites them in developing in each the consciousness of their power and their capacities."

of liberty?" Despite all these reservations he did not hesitate to declare that "the Italy of 1926 shows admirable vitality and good will while the disorder in surrounding countries continues to undermine them and to work toward their destruction. It is a fact to which, meanwhile, I do not hesitate to sacrifice some ideas and some sentiments, so great and impatient is my desire for order."

In her answer the Duchess insisted that the poet's vision of Italy's grandeur was far from the truth. She foresaw the catastrophe to which Fascism led Italy. With deep apprehension she asked, "Where will that spirit of nationalism which this government promotes spend itself?" To these arguments Rilke reacted strongly. He saw in Mussolini "the architect of the Italian national will, the man who forges a new national consciousness." Rilke proceeded even to a general defense of nationalism, though he was careful to exclude from his approbation German nationalism in which he found too much vanity and bad taste, as if these two were lacking in Mussolini's or in any other strong nationalism.*

His love of the Latin world betrayed him into writing lines which in their crude oversimplification are embarrassing to read today: "I think that all peoples must have those bluntly nationalistic moments in order to become conscious of themselves or simply to know themselves. . . . People need that fury of nationalism in order to touch their own mysterious heart, in order to feel themselves *one* and united to each other individually and at the same time collectively to their country and their past. For nations that have a true tradition to recapture, such a recollection can become a means of rejuvenation and inner rebirth. . . . What would have been difficult for me elsewhere, I could have done in Italy or France, if I had been born there, to serve with conviction and enthusiasm as an Italian or French soldier, in a fraternal spirit, even to the extreme sacrifice. So much nationalism in these two countries seems to me allied with the gesture, with action, with a visible example. In your country, even more than in France, the blood is truly *one* and in certain moments the idea carried by that blood can be *one*. The Roman idea is one of those rare ideas which at certain turning points of history could acquire a universal

---

* To Marie von Mutius Rilke wrote in 1918, in the war's last year, that one should be able to write in all languages: "This lack of a fatherland (*Vaterlandslosigkeit*) should be confessed jubilantly in a positive form as an allegiance to the whole [of mankind]. My heart and my mind have been directed from childhood on toward this cosmopolitanism (*Welt-Ebenbürtigkeit*); I cannot retreat one step, and thus you will understand how I suffer."

value, not because it strove to be international but because its pure national force is so intensely true that it radiated all over the world." *Heureuse Italie!* Rilke exclaimed, forgetting that Italy has been unhappily haunted in modern times by the ghost of the Roman idea. Therein she shared the fate of Germany which, haunted by the idea of the Reich, its German-centered adaptation of the Roman idea, also courted spiritual and political catastrophe. Was there still an affinity, in these late letters, between Rilke and Nietzsche? D'Annunzio would have thought so. In reality, when Rilke, as a Latin and not as a German, paid tribute to nationalism and to order in the state he expressed sentiments which Nietzsche throughout his mature life treated with scorn and indignation.

Another great German poet of Rilke's generation took up these sentiments and applied them, no longer as a Latin but as a German. Stefan George started as Rilke did, a disciple of Nietzsche and an admirer of the Latin sense of form. But as the authoritarian high priest of his own art he later turned away from Nietzsche's loneliness and Mallarmé's modesty to become the venerated lord and master of a devoted circle of disciples. They thought of themselves as preparing the coming of the Reich, a Reich conceived in the spirit but identified with Germany. In the eyes of George's disciples Nietzsche became the poet's forerunner. George was what Nietzsche allegedly wished to be: founder of the new Reich embodied in a new nobility of men.

George, Rome, and Hellas

TODAY GEORGE IS LITTLE READ. Abroad and in Germany he has been overshadowed by Rilke. But at least in Germany the situation was different thirty years ago. In 1927 Fritz Strich, a well-known literary historian, wrote that Rilke's star paled in Germany in the 1920's so that he was then almost forgotten and his last works—the *Elegies* and *Sonnets*—remained unknown and without an echo. George's star was then at its zenith. His prophetic gesture, his prediction of the new *Reich*, his call for leadership aroused a fervent echo in the feverish intellectual climate of the time.

It should not be overlooked, however, that George's and Rilke's influence, like that of great art everywhere, was confined to relatively small circles. At the turn of the century, when George and Rilke looked to the West, the popular writers appealed to an over-sentimentalized Germanophile nationalism which glorified the un-equaled depth of the German soul and the unsurpassed might of German power. Walter Bloem and Rudolf Herzog may have no place in the history of literature but their novels captivated the hearts and minds of millions of readers. More important were three North Germans, Gustav Frenssen, Hermann Löns, and Hans Friedrich Blunck, whose work combined masculine nat-uralism and racial religiosity, poor taste and pretentious verbosity. Löns was idolized after he fell in battle in the early stages of the War of 1914. "We Germans," he wrote, "pretend that we are Christians, but we are nothing of the sort and never can be. For Christianity and race consciousness are incompatible as are socialism and culture."

The other two writers lived long enough to support enthusi-astically the National Socialist movement. Frenssen, whose best-selling novels created a sensation at the beginning of the century, started as a pastor and a liberal. But he soon discarded Christianity and liberalism for the sake of the folkish religion of nature whose sway over Germany Heine had dreaded. Like Blunck who was his junior by twenty-five years Frenssen predicted the coming of the savior who would save the Germans from Christian morality and western civilization. In 1923 Blunck published a novel in a trilogy which he called *Werdendes Volk* (*The Birth of a People*). Its hero, the leader of the Saxons in their struggle against Charlemagne and Christianization, was a god-seeker bearing traits of Christ and Baldur. He preached a pseudo-Nietzschean gospel of hardness and of sacrifice in war. He was later hailed as the herald of the Third Reich. Interestingly enough, the longing for a strong and evil leader—the word evil was meant in a laudatory sense on the part of Frenssen and Blunck—was frequently ac-compained by the assurance that the Germans as a people were much kinder and more humane than the western nations. The oversentimentalized approach to their own virtue contributed to that self-pity which many Germans exhibited after the unexpected defeat of 1918.

There was nothing narrowly nationalistic or sentimentally pro-vincial about Stefan George. His beginnings were consciously European and Latin. Yet Hofmannsthal and Rilke were European events; George could only happen in Germany. It was an older and more spiritual Germany than that with which the world became familiar through Bismarck and the Bismarckian scholars. Like Goethe, George believed that the smaller German states could promote cultural life better than Prussia, which he defined in 1901 as "a very efficient system which was, however. hostile to all art and culture" (*ein allerdings sehr wirksames aber aller Kunst und Kultur feindliches System*). For Bismarck he felt not only the antipathy found so frequently among the inhabitants of the territories which were annexed by Prussia in 1814 and in 1866, but he also resented the lack of spirituality and the preponderance of militarism in Bismarck's creation.* George even wrote a poem *"Der Preusse,"* which he read in 1902 to friends in the house of his publisher Georg Bondi and which he later destroyed. In it he called Berlin *"die kalte Stadt von Heer-und Handelsknechten"* (the cold city of military and commercial serfs) and Bismarck the "herald of soulless decades."

Like Heine, George was born a Rhinelander and felt himself as such. During his childhood French was spoken in the home and his family called him Étienne. He visited Paris for the first time in 1889, when he was twenty-one, and was deeply impressed by the Symbolist poets and above all by Mallarmé. In a poem *"Franken,"* which he included in his *Der Siebente Ring* (1907), he expressed his disgust with everything which was praised in Germany, where he found no poets and where his gods were mocked. His gratitude went out to France for all she gave him when he, a Frank, returned to France

Returnent Franc en France Dulce Terre.

George as a young man invented his own Lingua Romana. "I can not write to you in this short space the reasons why I do not like writing in German," he informed his friend Arthur Stahl in January, 1890. "This is also the reason why I have not written anything for months, because I simply don't know in which language to write."

In May, 1892, George wrote to Hofmannsthal: "Who knows, whether if I had not met you . . . as a poet, I would have con-

---

* *"Gegen Bismarck hatte George nicht nur die Antipathie des Muss-Preussen, die ich selbst aus der Heimatstadt Frankfurt kannte und in der ich aufgewachsen bin, sondern hier empoerte sich sein eigener Taeter-Willen gegen die folgenschwere Unzulaenglichkeit, die den preussisch-deutschen Kanzler die ungewoehnliche Gunst einer grossen Stunde verpassen und ihn statt einer geistigen Neugestaltung des Staates ein romantisch-pietistisch-militaristisches Reich zusammenzimmern liess."* Edgar Salin.

tinued to write poetry in my mother tongue," and in 1911 he told Ernst Robert Curtius that he wrote five of six poems in French and later translated them into German. "There was a time when I had to face the decision of becoming either a German or a French poet."* He was then convinced, as he wrote to Arthur Stahl, that he could prove that the short French domination had been an important element in the formation of the German national spirit, and that close contact with other peoples and their wisdom was the best way of eradicating all that was bad in each nation. George's love went out not only to French, but to all western languages. German literature owes much to George for rendering into German besides contemporary poets, Shakespeare's *Sonnets* (1909), Baudelaire's *Les Fleurs du Mal* (1901) and, above all, a model translation of Dante (1912).

As a Rhinelander, as a *Rheinfranke,* he felt close not only to France but to Rome and the whole Latin world. He found in his blood a *"römischer Hauch,"* a breath of Rome. Porta Nigra, a city gate of Trier (formerly Augusta Trevirorum), is the most important Roman ruin in Germany. In a poem named after the gate, George celebrated the German city on the Moselle river as Rome's sister. Standing in the eleventh century cathedral in Speyer on the Rhine, where eight German emperors are buried, he was attracted above all by the tomb of the Southern princess who was the ancestor of the later Hohenstaufen, among whom Frederick the Second was declared to be the greatest because he, whose home was Sicily and the Mediterranean, had broadened his German heritage by

> *Des Morgenlandes ungeheuren traum,*
> *Weisheit der Kabbala und Romerwürde*
> *Feste von Agrigent und Selinunt.***

In 1892 under Mallarmé's influence George started the publication of his *Blätter für die Kunst,* an esoteric periodical dedicated

---

* André Gide saw Stefan George when the latter visited Paris for the last time in 1907, and wrote in his *Journal* of April 7: *"Il s'exprime dans notre langue sans faute aucune . . . et fait preuve d'une connaissance et compréhension surprenantes de nos auteurs, poètes en particulier; tout ceci sans fatuité mais avec une conscience évidente de son évidente supériorité."* George himself wrote that the Germans have nothing to learn from the Nordic spirit, but from the Latin spirit they can learn what they do not possess, clarity, breadth and sunniness.
** "The Orient's prodigious dream, the wisdom of the cabala and the dignity of the Romans, feasts of Agrigent and Selinunt."—two ancient cities in Sicily (the second named Selinus) famous for early Greek ruins.

to a new austere purity of German language and poetry. A few years later the *Blatter* described the type of young men whom George gathered around him: "A ray from Hellas lighted upon our lives. No longer does our youth look down on reality. It begins to look upon it with fervor. It strives for perfection of proportions in body and mind. It has freed itself from enthusiasm for shallow general education and from obsolete military barbarism. It shrinks away from both stiff rigidity and humble cringing, which it sees all around it. It wishes to walk through life in beauty and as its own free master. It understands its nationality grandly, not in the narrow tribal sense." These words define the attitude of the early George circle; the rejection of Bismarckian Germany, the aristocratic contempt for democracy, the Hellenic deification of form and beauty. Goethe was influenced by Greek poetry and wisdom, George by Greek plastic art. The Hellenic example alone could assure perfection of form, the highest goal for which the young George strove. E. K. Bennett aptly quotes a statement from the *Blätter* (1910) which elucidates George's Hellenistic concept of the divine: "Of all the utterances of thousands of years which are known to us, the Greek idea that the body is god—the body which is the symbol of transitoriness—was by far the most creative, . . . by far the boldest and the most worthy of mankind, and surpasses in sublimity every other, including the Christian one."

Nietzsche had proclaimed that God was dead; the age which Europe was entering was an age without God, but also an age of incessant god-seeking. To George it was given to proclaim the apparition of the divine in his own time, the embodiment of the deity and the deification of the body, in a youth whom he called Maximin and who died in 1904, one day after his sixteenth birthday. George's beautiful poems to Maximin recall Shakespeare's sonnets, but George's poems are of a certainty and radiance unknown to the Elizabethan poet. Perhaps Maximin finds a parallel in Dante's Beatrice, but Dante, with whom George loved to compare himself, was a Christian and Beatrice was therefore never for him a divinity. For George, Maximin was the new god whom Nietzsche had sought in vain. But like Beatrice's beauty Maximin's was asexual, he represented Eros not as violent physical desire but as the embodiment of the longing for the beautiful and the good.*

---

* Little is known of Maximin, Maximilian Kürnberger (1888–1904), a native of Munich, a city which George praised for having given birth to a god,
"*Preist eure Stadt die einen Gott gebar,*
Preist eure Zeit in der ein Gott gelebt"

The Maximin experience forms the center of George's most famous book of poems *Der Siebente Ring* (1907). Eight years had passed since the appearance of his preceding book, which contained two significant and often quoted poems One of them described the circle of young men around George. It was then a small group advancing quietly and proudly, equally removed from the noisy utilitarianism of the marketplace and the grave enthusiasm of Christianity. The banner under which the group marched carried the inscription "Hellas eternally our love." * The other poem announced a turning point in George's life and work. In it the poet bade farewell to Rome and the Mediterranean and abandoned them for Germany and the Rhine.

> *Schon lockt nicht mehr das wunder der lagunen*
> *Das allumworbene trummergrosse Rom*
> *Wie herber eichen duft und rebenbluten*
> *Wie sie die Deines volkes hort behuten—*
> *Wie Deine wogen—lebengruner Strom!*

(No longer is the miracle of Venice alluring, nor Rome, courted by all and great in her ruins, as much as is the fragrance of austere oaks and vine blossoms, as are those which guard the hoard of thy people—as are your waves, oh river green with life.)

George and Germany

THE YOUNG GEORGE who began to publish the *Blätter für die Kunst* wished, like Rilke, to serve art and not the state or society. "The worth of a poem is determined not by its meaning, otherwise it would be wisdom or instruction, but by its form." Art was as important a value to George as it was to his French masters. By an unremitting effort he wished to reach perfection of form and word. Even in the presentation of his work he

George was throughout his life a lonely man He was intimate with none, unapproachable in art and life alike He was surrounded by young men, generally of exalted minds and physical beauty, who venerated him. The only woman whom it is known that he loved as a young man was Ida Coblenz, a fellow Rhinelander who later married the German poet Richard Dehmel.
* *"Hellas ewig unsre liebe"* It is noteworthy that none of the great German Hellenists—Winckelmann, Goethe, Hölderlin, Nietzsche, or George —ever visited the country of their longing.

insisted on perfect typographical form, on a spelling and printing of his own distinctive choice. All this stressed the aloofness of the artist's work which can be approached only by a few and through a conscious effort. A similar self-stylization regulated George's severe and exemplary life. His very remarkable head and face resembled more and more that of Dante. A young Englishman, Cyril M. Scott, who met George while studying music in Germany and later was the first to translate some of George's poems into English, wrote of him in his autobiographical *My Years of Indiscretion* (1924): "Both in appearance and manner George was the most striking and unusual personality I have ever encountered. . . . He was not only a great poet but looked one." And at another time a striking comparison came to Scott: "I felt as I had so often done before that he represented among persons what a place like Siena represents among towns."

After the turn of the century George turned not only to Germany but to contemporary events. Feeling the bitter need of the time, he believed himself, like Hölderlin, the bearer of a message to his people, calling for the building of a new community based upon the poet's ideals. Not by accident was Hölderlin, after many decades of oblivion, discovered by George's circle. George, too, became now a prophet to his contemporaries. His *Der Siebente Ring* started with a cycle of poems, called *"Zeitgedichte,"* ("Poems about my Time"), a title already used by Heine. The poet's voice sounded like a 'zealous trumpet" (*eifernde posaune*), but he did not forget that "tomorrow all beauty, strength and greatness may arise from a boy's calm flute song." He wished now to speak as his people's conscience and judge, to fight the degeneracy which he saw all around him, and to call for a new heroism. From then on, and in the two remaining books of poems which he published, *Der Stern des Bundes* (1914) and *Das Neue Reich* (1928), he alternated between the knowledge of approaching doom and the hope of regeneration. Even before the outbreak of the war, the poet foresaw the inescapable calamity.

During the war George did not share the bellicose patriotism of his followers. Many of them enthusiastically joined the armed forces; some died in battle. Some of them dreamed, while they were fighting in the trenches, of the destruction of the hated Prussian Reich and of a new Confederation of the Rhine with the poet-king at its head. But George remained reserved: *"Am streit wie ihr ihn fühlt nehm ich nicht teil"* (I do not participate in the struggle as you feel it). He did not identify the victory of

German arms with the victory of the spirit. He was afraid that an easy German victory might cause a German spiritual debacle. One of his disciples Walter Wenghöfer wrote in 1916 to Hanna Wolfskehl, *"la première nation que les boches aboliront est l'allemande."*

From the early spring of 1916 on George emphasized in his conversations with friends—he of course never wrote or spoke publicly—the necessity of concluding an early peace. "The Germans have already been told what they need at the beginning of the century. . . . It is naturally easier for weaklings to send armies into battle than to govern a people in peace." During the latter part of the war he surprised his young admirers by insisting that "if Germany had the strength to renounce Alsace-Lorraine, it might not be too late—there would be peace and Germany would be greater than ever before." They replied almost spontaneously, as Edgar Salin reports, "but that is impossible *(aber das geht doch nicht)."*

In 1917 George published his poem "The War." In it he opposed the widespread illusion that war and victory might bring peace. He stressed the fact that he had foreseen the catastrophe and had lived through years of great anxiety long before the war, when people played with fire; he had shed so many tears that he no longer had any left for the present struggle. "Much had happened and nobody saw it. The darkest hour is yet to come and nobody sees it." He assured his readers that he could not grow enthusiastic about German virtue or alien knavery. "There is no reason for jubilation· there will be no triumph but only many downfalls without dignity. . . . The old god of battle is no longer. Sick worlds feverishly end in the turmoil."

George's contempt for democracy convinced him that in the war "the idea of an enlightened humanity has definitely failed, and so has Anglo-American Christianity." There was more hope in Germany, especially in German youth, than in the West. George even went so far as to tell Ernst Robert Curtius in Heidelberg in 1917 that "the French have only literature, not poetry." Heine had said the same. But Heine had never turned to the French as masters in the art of poetry. George's antidemocratic and antiwestern stand in the war completely alienated one of his oldest friends and companions, the great Dutch poet and scholar Albert Verwey, "a personality of exceptional stature and integrity."

How far George could go in expressing publicly his disdain of liberalism can be seen in a short poem to a Jesuit.

Return clever and deft Fathers!
Your poison and dagger are a better custom
Than are equality-praising traitors
No worse enemy of the people than the middle!

Here poor poetry goes hand in hand with poor judgment. Poison
and dagger are not "the custom of the Jesuits" except in the popular
legends of anti-Catholic thought, nor are poison and dagger a
better way than liberal humanitarianism, except in the distorted
world of national or social extremism. George's disciples went even
further than he did in the rejection of western liberalism and of
middle class civilization.

The companions of George's earlier years, creative poets and
scholars in their own right and close to him in age, were later
replaced by much younger men. George became now the master
and the law-giver. For his disciples his poems became sacred books.
They expected the rise of a new hidden Germany and saw in
George the hidden leader and savior. Edgar Salin described the
circle around George as "youth hungry for and open to the wide
world, united in a passionate rejection of the old world and in
an intoxicated feeling of being the bearers of a new world."
They still looked to Hellas and Rome, but they felt more and more
Nordic and German. Catholicism appeared to them originally as
a bulwark against the liberal bourgeois world which Protestantism
had helped to bring into being. But now, they feared, Catholicism
too was fast traveling on the road to becoming protestant. It
no longer fulfilled the great task of preserving pagan vitality in
western civilization. Very different from Goethe, the circle of
young men around George saw in America the world of satanic
perversity.

After the collapse of Imperial Germany in 1918, George became convinced that the Germans were now ahead of the West;
the defeat had made them more inclined to receive the new word
and to change their lives. Therefore they were nearer to the possibility of a true rebirth than the West. George overlooked the
continuous strength of the Bismarckian-Wilhelminian tradition
after 1918. He idealized the spiritual potentialities of Germany.
Yet his very attitude helped to accelerate the growth of a German
nationalism which repeated all the old mistakes while at the same
time it regarded itself confidently as a new and higher form of
life. The German youth movement which had started at the
beginning of the twentieth century as an antiauthoritarian revolt
of a generation longing for self-responsibility in freedom, changed

under George's influence after 1918. No longer was freedom the central concept; it was replaced by *Bund*, a close fellowship of young men, trusting in the guidance of their leader, to whose authority they felt deep emotional ties. The underlying concepts of *Gefolgschaft, Herrschaft,* and *Dienst,* the devoted allegiance of followers, the authority of the master, the sense of dedicated service, were popularized by the influence of Stefan George.

In this acceptance of George as a forerunner of National Socialism, of George as a John the Baptist of Hitler, there was certainly a strong element of misunderstanding. George did not regard himself as anybody's John the Baptist. One of his disciples, Hans Brasch, reported a conversation of 1919 in which George accepted the new position of a defeated Germany in Europe, and saw in it the possibility of a new freedom in which men could again talk to men without the fetters of Prussian serfdom. George always rejected militarism, state-power and conquest. He always cautioned against political hopes (*Hoffnungen staatlicher Art*). Yet, despite the warnings of Friedrich Gundolf, one of his most prominent older followers, George changed the signet for the *Blatter für die Kunst* from the Amphora which Melchior Lechter, another friend of his early years, had drawn, to the Swastika. The contemporary use of the Swastika originated with an early follower of George, Alfred Schuler, who found this symbol in Bachofen, an early student of ancient myths and rituals. He promoted it, to quote Ludwig Curtius, "to its fateful role in recent German history. His hatred of Jewish Christianity belonged to the sources which fed German anti-Semitism."

Worse still was the fact that in the 1920's George collaborated closely with the most nationalist wing of his followers, much to the dismay of his older friends, and never disavowed Friedrich Wolters' nationalist interpretation of George as Germany's savior. Wolters died in 1930, before the National Socialists came to power. Many of George's disciples joined them. Professor Hans Naumann dedicated the sixth edition (1933) of his very popular and influential *Deutsche Dichtung der Gegenwart (Contemporary German Literature;* the first edition appeared in 1923) to "Our Leaders" (*Unsere Führer*), meaning Hitler and George, saying that both cherished the same ideals of race and leadership. As Hitler's war seemed to bring Germany's ruin, some former disciples of George, now bitterly disappointed, turned against National Socialism. Among them was Count Claus von Stauffenberg, who set a bomb on July 20, 1944, with the intention of killing Hitler.

But it should not be forgotten that after 1918 George was a
prematurely old and ailing man. The sufferings of the war of
1914 had aged him visibly. His great poetical powers quickly ebbed.
His last book (1928) contains a beautiful poem "Hyperion" in which
he voices the hope for a new age of love which he knows he shall
not live to see. "My suffering life inclines toward slumber. . . . I
shall become the clod of earth which holy scions will approach
for their fulfillment. With this the new age will come. Love
gave birth to the world; love will give birth to it anew. . . .
Before darkness overtakes me, a high vision carries me away; soon
on light soles the god will wander through the beloved fields,
visible in his glory." It was of Maximin that George thought. The
lofty and lovely poem with which this last volume closes once
more paid tribute to the pure, calm, and noble beauty of the
youth. George did not think of Hitler. In August, 1933, when
George left Germany for the last time and when the ship which
brought him to Switzerland was crossing the lake of Constance,
the old poet remarked half jokingly that now he could breathe
more freely. The National Socialists invited George to become
President of the German Academy of the Third Reich. George
communicated his refusal through one of his Jewish disciples,
Ernst Morwitz. At the end of 1933 George died in the Italian-
speaking Swiss canton of Ticino. His silence carried the secret
of this great and lonely poet into the grave. Southern laurel
trees surrounded the coffin and surround the tomb.

Perhaps nothing showed George's hold over the minds of some
great Germans of his time as clearly as Karl Wolfskehl's loyalty
toward the master, a loyalty unshaken for more than half a
century in spite of fundamental differences in their temperaments
and ways of life. Wolfskehl, one year younger than George, was
himself a great and original poet. While George lost his creative
power during his fifties, Wolfskehl reached a new height of
creative splendor in his sixties and seventies. Like others of
George's most prominent followers Wolfskehl was Jewish. For
many centuries his family had been settled in western Germany,
in Hessen. Deeply rooted in German tradition and culture,
Wolfskehl knew throughout his life the mystery of Jewish existence and history. As early as 1913 he published a brief essay,
a confession and self-analysis *"Das jüdische Geheimnis"* in a
symposium *Vom Judentum*. Wolfskehl was always aware of the
two aspects of Jewish destiny: its potential greatness and its tragic
calamity. Twenty years later when a perhaps unprecedented calamity

seemed to threaten Jewish and German destiny, Wolfskehl became, in the most beautiful German poems of that deeply stirred but artistically sterile time, the exemplary singer of Jewish destiny, of the ever renewed tragedy and temptation of Job.

After a few years in Italy, Wolfskehl, so profoundly rooted in the German and Latin tradition, emigrated to distant New Zealand, an outpost of the English-speaking world with which he had felt all during his life the least affinity. Yet there in dismal exile the poet expressed the meaning and triumph of his life in two of his greatest poems, "The Song Out of Exile" and "To the Germans." The first of them celebrated his "Mediterranean homeland," Hellas, the beauty of which no death can extinguish. The second poem expressed his eternal gratitude and allegiance to Germany and to Stefan George, the master, an allegiance based upon the indestructible power of the spirit. The poem was written over a period of ten years—started in Rome in March, 1934, completed in New Zealand in the beginning of April, 1944— a decade which belongs to the darkest in German and Jewish history alike At the end of the poem the master, by then dead for more than a decade, appears and calls his ever faithful companion to endure and remain at the helm, even in the despair of exile. For where Wolfskehl is, 'the freest of all the free, the one who preserves and dares and prays, there the German spirit is." For many years before 1933 Wolfskehl had been haunted by visions of the damnation of European society and of approaching apocalyptic terrors. When the terror came it did not break Wolfskehl's spirit. In the midst of Job's vexations and trials he rose to the triumphant reaffirmation of his life and of the power of the spirit. He found a voice, where the master was silent; he showed exuberant strength, when the master withdrew in fatigue. This spiritual victory of the disciple, ending his life miserably yet gratefully in a hated distant exile may compensate for the strange and embarrassing ambiguities of his master.

Hofmannsthal and Austria

IN DECEMBER, 1891, STEFAN GEORGE, then twenty-three years old, met the eighteen-year-old Hofmannsthal, who had by then published some of the most beautiful poems in the German language.

George recognized Hofmannsthal's genius. In his terrible loneliness he hoped to find in Hofmannsthal a companion in the struggle for the realization of a new art and a new man. He wooed him passionately but the younger poet politely resisted George's entreaty. There could be no true understanding between the two. George was intolerant and dictatorial, he was certain of the narrow path on which he intended to travel. Hofmannsthal's humane nature was attracted, but at the same time frightened and repelled by George's demonic power. His gentle sensibility which was open to all influences, his knowledge of the secret interrelationship of all things and beings, made him George's antipode in temper and endowment. But for the youth of eighteen the meeting with the so much more self-assured George was, as Hofmannsthal wrote many years later, "of decisive importance. It confirmed me in the feeling that I was not an entirely lonely eccentric, when I thought it possible to produce in German something which moved on the same poetical plane as did great English poetry from Keats on, and was at the same time endowed with a firm Latin sense of form."

George was not the only one to testify to the impression which the young Hofmannsthal made upon his older contemporaries. Hermann Bahr, who became a successful playwright and critic and was active in every literary movement between 1890 and 1920, was, though an Austrian subject, a Pan-German who deprecated Austria. This attitude changed completely when he met the young Hofmannsthal in 1891. "The strange boy, so terribly sad in his precocious art of living, became for me a vision of Austria," Bahr wrote in his *Selbstbildnis* (1923). "For the first time he made appear before me my forgotten fatherland." Hofmannsthal rendered Austria, then in her last glow, so rapturously beautiful, "that I mistook her smiling agony for a sacred spring." Bahr's last novel, published in 1929, the year of Hofmannsthal's death, was entitled *Österreich in Ewigkeit* (*Austria in Eternity*). The following year Max Kommerell, a former disciple of George, in his inaugural lecture as professor of German literautre at Frankfurt University greeted in Hofmannsthal that part of Germany whose melancholy profundity is music, and whose light-hearted levity has something of the spirit of Hellas.*

Many great Germans—Goethe and Hölderlin, Rilke and George

---

* "*Wir grüssen in ihm den deutschen Stamm, dessen Tiefsinn Musik ist und dessen Leichtsinn noch etwas Hellenisches hat*"

—sought non-Germanic lands: Rome and Hellas, the Mediterranean and the West. Hofmannsthal did not seek them: they were part of his heritage. Rilke and George had to decide between the Germanic and the Latin worlds; Hofmannsthal never felt the conflict for he was equally and naturally at home in both. Austria had never grown into a circumscribed nation; it could never be defined ethnically or territorially. With continuously changing boundaries it was a complex historical phenomenon, long predating the age of nationalism. Vienna lies at the crossroads of Europe, geographically and culturally. At the time of the Roman Empire and again under Charlemagne, it was Europe's eastern frontier post, and later for centuries it was the point from which western civilization radiated out to the east and southeast. But through Vienna the West did not only give to the East, it also received from the East.

In "The Austrian Idea" (1917) Hofmannsthal called Austria the conciliator and mediator between the old European Latin-Germanic world and the Byzantine and Slavic worlds. In this conciliation and mediation he saw Austria's *raison d'être*, which was obscured after 1848 by the growth of nationalism, which saw Austria as a German outpost for the control and ordering of central Europe, not as a European factor. The decades between 1848 and 1867 were as decisive for Austria as they were for the whole of central Europe. The American historian John Lothrop Motley, who was his country's minister to Vienna in the 1860's, remarked then that "the problem, how to create a nation out of nationalities . . . an Empire out of provinces and states is as old as history, and one of the most difficult and most important for human sagacity to solve." Unfortunately Austria was unable to solve the problem. The most promising attempt in this direction, the constitution of 1849, which was regarded in America as "a liberal and efficient constitution, resembling that of the United States," was still-born.

Austria was not only a mediator between East and West, but also between North and South, between Germanic and Latin civilizations. The Habsburgs ruled not only over Germans but over Spaniards and Italians as well. For centuries they were a European dynasty. Archduke Frederick the Younger, who died in 1493 as the Emperor Frederick III, a man of little energy who seemed "asleep on his throne," laid the foundations of these European connections through the marriage of his son with the heiress of Burgundy. This mediocre prince must have had a strong premonition of the coming greatness of his house. He expressed it in the strange combination of the five vowels A E I O U which he used to inscribe on buildings and belongings. In his own interpretation they meant *"Austriae est imperare orbi universo"* (Austria must rule the universe). This naive confidence was, in the stress and storm of later periods, reinterpreted into the still confident but rather obscure apocalyptic *"Austria erit in orbe ultima"* (Austria will be the last on earth).

Frederick's descendants ruled Spain and the New World, Italy and the Low Countries, Bohemia and Hungary, and bore the German Imperial crown. But even prior to Frederick III the small Austria of the Middle Ages was not simply a German state. Already his predecessors kept only one foot within the German orbit and stepped out of it with the other. They constantly intermarried with the royal houses of Bohemia and Hungary and for centuries prepared for the union of the three crowns which came at the beginning of the sixteenth century. The political mysticism of the baroque era saw in the union of Austria, Bohemia, and Hungary—in the *Monarchia Austriaca*—a parallel to the Holy Trinity, or to the three wise kings as represented through their patron saints, St. Leopold, St. Stephen, and St. Wenceslaus. Austria's mission has appeared for centuries not primarily as German but as supranational and European; the formation of the monarchy, with its deep roots in the Middle Ages, as well as its growth were not conditioned or made possible as part of Germany but by its orientation toward the other peoples and kingdoms of Europe. Austria was not a German march, it was a bridge on which Germany and Europe met, where all European civilizations mingled for mutual stimulation. Under these circumstances, it became characteristic of Austria to show tolerance and moderation, to avoid extremes, to be even-tempered, to permeate its life with a broad-minded catholicity and a strong tendency to ease the living together of different types and races. A mellow and easygoing charm, a richness of color and music, and a balanced reasonableness made life different from any stiff or drab uniformity, from any cutting and steely hardness that might be exhibited in other nations. But this even temper was threatened in the nineteenth century by the aggressiveness of German (and Hungarian) nationalism just as it had been in the seventeenth century by the burning intolerance of the Spanish Counter Reformation.

Spain played a minor role in Rilke's and George's formation, but a very large one for the Viennese Hofmannsthal. The baroque style became representative of Viennese architecture; Calderón influenced Hofmannsthal's theater more than did the Greeks or Shakespeare. The Viennese—and that too may be an inheritance of the baroque era—are passionately addicted to the theater in all its forms, to the serious drama and to the popular comedy, to the mystery play and to the opera. Rilke and George were pure poets; Hofmannsthal was equally interested in the novella and in the literary essay, in the theater and in music; he was the only one among the three who was trained in and had a high respect for scholarship. Above all, no aspect and no form of the theater remained alien to Hofmannsthal. He tried to renew all of them. He successfully revived mystery plays from *Everyman*, an English morality play, to Calderón's allegorical *Gran Teatro del Mundo*. With Richard Strauss he created new musical possibilities for the modern theater and gave it in *Elektra* its greatest tragedy and in *Rosenkavalier* its most gracious comedy. Hofmannsthal did not write, as did George, for a small exclusive minority. Rather, in his refined art he tried to appeal, as did Calderón and Shakespeare, to Everyman. His influence was hindered not by the esoteric character or the difficulty of his work but by its timelessness—Hofmannsthal was more at home in the past than in the present. He never assumed the posture of an intellectual or of a period, neither of a rebel nor of a bohemian. He shared his fate and the unostentatious quiet and retiring dignity of his life with his native Austria.

There was nothing exclusive in Hofmannsthal. He was "the hidden friend (*Genosse*), the silent (*lautlose*) brother of all things. ... I would not wish to strengthen anything in me which would separate me from the human beings." He embraced peoples and civilizations with an equal receptivity and recognition. "The Germans especially," he warned in 1901, "should always remember that they are not the prominent representatives of the spirit of classical antiquity or of humanity; they are a nation like any other."

Spanish influences were in no way preponderant in Hofmannsthal's work. Venice exercised similar fascination. It was another meeting ground of East and West with its blending of Italian statecraft and folk life with Byzantium and the Levant, and with Habsburg and Spanish reminiscences. Hofmannsthal was as much at home in the West as he was in the South of Europe. He knew the English poets and loved the French language. He wrote some of the best essays on the great French writers and he even thought of becoming professor of Romance Literature at Vienna University.

With this in mind he wrote a study of the development of the poet Victor Hugo. Like Goethe he was not confined in his interests to Europe. Throughout his life he was attracted by the tales of the Arabian Nights and during the war he turned to China in his *Die Frau ohne Schatten,* as Goethe had turned in similar times of trouble to Hafiz. "Hofmannsthal's attitude," wrote Ernst Robert Curtius, "was universal as before him only Goethe's had been. He could well have said of himself as the great Leibniz said· *je ne méprise presque rien.'*

Hofmannsthal's *humanitas Austriaca* was rooted in Austria's past rather than in the Austria of his day. Yet at the beginning of the century Austria, though decaying politically, lived through a period of great intellectual and artistic creativity. Sigmund Freud, Karl Kraus, Otto Weininger, and Ludwig Wittgenstein presented an astonishing variety of original approaches to the problems of man and civilization. The two greatest German composers after Wagner, Anton Bruckner and Johannes Brahms, had died in Vienna within a year of each other; the new school of Gustav Mahler, Arnold Schonberg, Anton von Webern, and Alban Berg continued to make Vienna a musical center. In literature Arthur Schnitzler's name may represent here the older generation; among those who were twenty or thirty years his juniors, Robert Musil, Franz Kafka, Hermann Broch, Georg Trakl, Franz Werfel, and Joseph Roth, each in his own way, opened new avenues for German poetry and prose. Most of these Austrians were revolutionary in their outlook and techniques. Hofmannsthal, on the other hand, was in every respect a conservative. He was not only the heir of the Austrian tradition but of the ages. There have been few poets or scholars with a similar power of feeling their way into many civilizations and modes of artistic expression. Hofmannsthal's conservatism, in its humane, cosmopolitan and deeply civilized form found no following in the period after 1918, when the search for a valid tradition led German "conservatives" into so many feverish nationalist or restorative aberrations. Hofmannsthal feared "the eruption of chaos into a world from whose order the spirit has departed." He spoke of the need for a conservative revolution. But this phrase was widely abused: the movement which took up this name helped to lower or destroy the defences which protected civilization from chaos and barbarism.

After the collapse of the Austrian monarchy, which destroyed the intellectual and social climate which had nourished his life, Hofmannsthal saw himself as the preserver of the old Europe and its civilization, of which the Austrian monarchy had formed part Though Rilke loved the aristocratic society of the old Europe he felt no social responsibilities. George wished to oppose his own esoteric aristocracy to society. Only Hofmannsthal cared, in a time of disintegration, for the preservation of society and its institutions. To his young Swiss friend Carl J. Burckhardt he wrote in 1923: "To me matrimony is something lofty, truly a sacrament —I would not like to imagine a life without it," and two years later he repeated· "Matrimony is an exalted institution and stands in our restless and uneasy lives like a castle built of one solid rock." In those years he also returned to the Catholic religious tradition. In the Europe after 1918 he no longer felt at home. The democratization of the world which set in after the First World War was beyond Hofmannsthal's perceptive powers.

A contemporary Austrian historian wrongly compared Austrian conservatism to that of England and Spain. It was his error and Austria's misfortune that they did not apparently perceive the sharp and unbridgeable gulf between the two kinds of conservatism. England was conservative in the liberal sense of the word. She understood how to accommodate herself to the spirit of the times, to the industrial revolution, to the broadest democracy, to the emancipation of dependent territories, and yet to maintain a respect for living traditions. Spanish conservatism on the other hand proudly refused to adapt itself to the *Zeitgeist*. It preserved intolerance and fanaticism, stagnation and backwardness. In Spain the *"verengte, intolerante, aberglaubische und herrschsüchtige Katholizismus der Gegenreformation"* (the narrow, intolerant, superstitious, domineering Catholicism of the Counter Reformation) as it was characterized by Friedrich Heer, one of Austria's leading Catholic historians, has prevailed intact almost until today. Austria, however, was not Spain. The spirit of the Enlightenment of the eighteenth century and of the liberalism of the nineteenth century influenced the Austrian church as much as did the spirit of the baroque. Austria (though not the Hungarian part of the monarchy where a backward feudalism still held sway until recently) solved her agrarian problem long ago and was stimulated by a powerful and disciplined socialist movement. Nevertheless, there was perhaps too much of the Spanish influence in Austrian society to allow Austria to follow the example of England or, to mention a country which like Austria had formed part of Germany and in which the German language predominated, of Switzerland. Switzerland showed a spirit of creative tolerance and of courageous innovation coupled with respect for tradition similar to that of England.

Of the three great German poets Rilke represented only himself; George a small, though in the 1920's growing, circle of aristocratic youths; while Hofmannsthal alone represented a country and its traditions, which were representative of a Europe which ended in 1918 and which had been in decline long before then No return to this old Europe or to the Habsburg monarchy is feasible or desirable. Vienna no longer is a cosmopolitan metropolis. The expulsion of the Jews from Vienna has had a devastating effect upon its cultural life. Hitler made Vienna a provincial city in the greater German Reich. After his fall the former *"Kaiserstadt"* has not regained its stature. From there the Reich cannot be re-established, nor can Occidental or Christian culture be saved. Wishful thinking is as dangerous to peoples and civilizations as are utopian expectations.

A century ago, the great German Catholic poet Joseph Freiherr von Eichendorff recognized this clearly. At that time, under the leadership of Joseph de Maistre, an attempt was made to undo the intellectual revolution which had transformed Europe from the Renaissance to the Enlightenment. Eichendorff opposed all attempts to restore the old Reich or to establish a new Reich. To him the Reich was an ostentatious baroque castle (*spatbarocker Prunkbau*) which the storms of history had proven to be ram-shackle; in its collapse he saw the sign of an unappealable judg-ment. The fairy palace of the baroque appeared to Eichendorff as a dangerous temptation in modern times. Something of this temptation survived in Hofmannsthal's nostalgia. The heritage of the past lives on in the present; it is good for great poets to recall the values of the past, especially the humane and the universal aspects. But an emphasis on the past may hinder the difficult task of learning to adapt oneself, without sentimentality and without a sense of tragic loss, to the realities of the present time, and to the task of permeating them with the spirit of humane consideration and broad tolerance which one can find in some, but only a few, past traditions.

Germany, the West, and the War

GERMAN LITERATURE SINCE GOETHE reached its highest point of achieve-ment in poetry. Goethe created the concept of *Weltliteratur*. "It must not be assumed that all nations should think alike," Goethe

wrote, "but they should become aware of one another and understand one another; and if they cannot love one another, they
should at least learn mutual toleration." George, Rilke, and
Hofmannsthal, each one in his own way, carried on Goethe's
tradition of *Weltliteratur*. They kept the roads between Germany
and the outside world wide open. Their horizon was truly
European.

Of lesser European importance than German poetry was the
German novel. Its typical form, the *Bildungsroman* was the story
of the formation of an individual from youth to maturity through
his contact with society. It frequently contained an autobiographical
element, and this element is present in the works of the two great
German novelists of the twentieth century, Thomas Mann and
Hermann Hesse. Both wrote first novels—*The Buddenbrooks*
(1900) and *Peter Camenzind* (1904)—which became immediate
successes. Both were later awarded the Nobel Prize for Literature.

George, Hofmannsthal, and Rilke never doubted the rank of art
and the value of the life of the mind On the other hand, Mann
inclined in his work to regard culture as a symptom of degeneracy
and the poet or artist as a somehow indecent misfit. With a
masterly technique, with a high artistry of style, and with a playful
irony Mann questioned in his early work cultural and intellectual
values. In a different way Hesse's early novels showed the impact
of extreme and almost demonic sensuality upon the ever-threatened
existence of man.

Mann and Hesse did not confine themselves to works of
creative imagination. In a number of essays both expressed their
attitude toward Germany and the times. Both grew in their work,
in artistic power and in wisdom, from *The Buddenbrooks* to
Doctor Faustus, from *Peter Camenzind* to *Magister Ludi*. The
following remarks are not concerned with their art but with their
judgment of Germany and the West during and after the war of
1914. Their attitudes were representative, although they expressed
opposite points of view. It would be mistaken to consider one without the other.

In considering Mann, one should remember what he wrote
about Goethe· "There was a kind of imperial faithlessness in him,
so that it would amuse him to abandon his followers, to confound
the partisans of every principle by carrying it to the ultimate—
and its opposite as well. He exercised a kind of universal dominion
in the form of irony and serene betrayal of mutually exclusive
points of view, one to the other. There was in this a profound
nihilism; there was also art's—and nature's—objectivistic refusal to

analyze and evaluate. There was an ambiguous impishness, an element of equivocation, negation, and all-embracing doubt which led him to make self-contradictory pronouncements." These words had no application to the real Goethe who throughout his life was deeply faithful in all essential matters. Mann's words apply rather to Mann himself. They present an ironical apology for his own views. Yet the words do not truly apply even to Mann. For he showed a greater loyalty and consistency than he acknowledged.

During the first half of his life, Thomas Mann was uninterested in political issues. The problem of the artist in a bourgeois society preoccupied him, and the phenomena of human morbidity and disintegration fascinated him. He shared with Dostoevsky and Nietzsche the interest in the perplexity of the human predicament, which heightened his artistic power and deepened his human appeal. It did not help, however, to form the basis of sound political judgments. It took the First World War to awaken Thomas Mann, who was then forty years old, to the importance of the political issues then at stake. He dedicated the war years to political writings, in which he revealed himself as a German nationalist, proudly supporting Prussian militarism and its claim to moral superiority over the West. Throughout the war Mann continued to misinterpret Germany and the West in a way which seemed to justify the most extreme anti-German suspicions and oversimplifications voiced in the West during the two world wars. "In Kant and Nietzsche we have the moralists of German militarism," Mann wrote in November, 1914.

In the usual way Mann opposed German *Kultur* to western civilization. The latter was to him technological, superficial, rational, and bourgeois; the former a sublimation of profound and instinctive forces, the matrix of all true art and ethics which expressed itself in German militarism. To these nationalistic platitudes he lent the supple splendor of his language. His essay *Frederick the Great and the Grand Coalition* excused and glorified Friedrich II's aggression against Saxony in 1740 in the typical fashion of Prussian historical hagiography. He welcomed the war of 1914 as the best safeguard against the democratization of Germany, as "purification, liberation, an enormous hope. . . . The victory of Germany will be a paradox, nay a wonder: a victory of the soul over numbers. The German soul is opposed to the pacifist ideal of civilization, for is not peace an element of civil corruption?"

More important are his highly personal *Betrachtungen eines*

Unpolitischen (Reflections of a Nonpolitical Man), a work of great weight and substance which he wrote in 1917 and which presents the most brilliant and penetrating summation of anti-western and antiliberal German nationalist sentiment written in the twentieth century. It is not a political book in the usual sense of the word; in fact, it shares the widespread German contempt for politics; it is, to use Peter Viereck's expression, a metapolitical philosophy of history, civilization, and the German mind. Mann categorically denied that western democracy could ever take root in Germany. He insisted that Germany was, in 1914, unanimously and enthusiastically for the war, "which is being called with every possible justification the German war." Mann saw the war essentially as a new and perhaps the most splendid eruption of the ancient *(uralten)* German struggle against the spirit of the West, and as a new attempt of the Roman world to repress unyielding Germany. He never doubted that in spite of the great physical danger which threatened Germany from the East, the real enemy was in the West, where Germany was confronted with a unified western world, which included the United States. The West was determined to force upon Germany a western bourgeois democracy, which would make Germany stupid and un-German. Mann was convinced that the war of 1914 was more than a war for power and for economic gain, it was a war of ideas. He found then (and not without some justification) opposite ideas facing each other, ideas which officially were acknowledged only later, in the war of 1939.

The peace of Europe, Mann maintained, could be only a German peace; the Germans were the most highly educated people and loved justice and peace most truthfully *(das gebildetste, gerechteste und den Frieden am wahrsten liebende Volk)*, therefore they had to be the most powerful and dominant people. In this truly seminal book Mann anticipated the later identification of German nationalism with a true socialism, a position asserted by Spengler a few years later. "It remains," Mann wrote in 1917, "the specific character of German individualism that it goes well hand in hand with ethical socialism, which one calls state socialism, and which is different from Marxist socialism with its doctrine of human rights."

With great contempt Mann turned against the West which believed that the Germans had been driven by their masters against their own will into the war and that they longed to be liberated from their masters. With even greater indignation he ridiculed those who believed that the Germans did not approve of the atrocities, the invasion of Belgium, the sinking of the Lusitania, or the unlimited submarine warfare.* Looking toward the future, Mann hoped for a German form of government which would unite monarchy and caesarism with Marshall Hindenburg as the Reichs-chancellor. Only under such leadership seemed the democratization of Germany, which was then discussed by German liberals and socialists, bearable to Mann.

To the familiar denunciations of the West, Mann added a new note. Like his remarks about socialism and Hindenburg, it also showed foresight into the nature of German antiwesternism. While Germany was at war with Russia, he proclaimed the solidarity of Germany and Russia against the West. "Has anybody ever understood the human meaning of nationalism in a more German way than the greatest Russian moralist?", he wrote of Dostoevsky. "Are the Russian and German attitudes toward Europe, the West, civilization, politics and democracy, not closely akin? . . . If spiritual affinity can form the foundation and justification of political alliances, then Russia and Germany belong together: their agreement now, their union for the future, has been since the beginning of this war (the war of 1914) the desire and dream of my heart. It is more than desirable: it is politically and spiritually necessary should the Anglo-American alliance endure." Understandably in 1927 a German high school teacher (*Studienrat*) Martin Havenstein recommended in a book on Thomas Mann his *Reflections* as a means of strengthening patriotic defiance and faith. "We are now outwardly defeated and probably condemned to be powerless for a long time," Haverstein wrote, "therefore we must do everything possible to resist and assert ourselves spiritually and morally against the superior power of our enemies, for fundamentally they continue to be such. For

---

* *Das Weltvolk des Geistes, zu überschwanglicher Leibeskraft erstarkt, hatte einen langen Trunk am Quell des Ehrgeizes getan; es wollte ein Weltvolk, so Gott es dazu berief, das Weltvolk der Wirklichkeit werden,—wenn es sein musste (und offenbar musste es sein) vermittelst gewaltsamen Durchbruchs. . . . Das deutsche Volk als Volk durchaus heroisch gestimmt, bereit, Schuld auf sich zu nehmen und ungeneigt zu moralischer Duckmäuserei . . . hat die Vernichtung jenes frechen Symbols der englischen Seeherrschaft und einer immer noch komfortablen Zivilisation, des Riesenlustschiffes "Lusitania" gebilligt, und dem welterfüllenden Zetermordio humanitärer Hypokrisie die Stirn geboten. Den uneingeschränkten Unterseebootskrieg aber hat es nicht nur gebilligt, es hat danach geschrieen und bis zur Auflehnung mit den Führern gehadert, die zögerten, ihn walten zu lassen.*

this struggle the valiant author of the *Reflections* provides us with a better arsenal of weapons than anyone else."

After the First World War and the unexpected collapse of military monarchy, Thomas Mann slowly rallied to the Weimar Republic, but he never really became a democrat in the western sense of the word. In 1920 he upheld in a letter to Count Hermann Keyserling his *Reflections* against the democracy, which a new Freemasonry was now offering as a remedy to an astonished Germany. The book, he wrote, dealt with "a religious and not a political problem; it was a question of what is more beneficial for us, virtue or sin—and I equated virtue with rationalism, with humanitarian enlightenment, while sin was another word for Romanticism." In an esssay on Freud (1928) Mann called the Great War "a gigantic explosion of unreason, in which the positive cosmopolitan forces of the time, the Church and Socialism, were defeated by the negative cosmopolitan power, imperialistic capital and international capitalism." Mann hoped that Germany would keep "a beautiful and dignified, a German balance" between western democracy and its own romantic-aristocratic tradition. "What is necessary," he wrote in 1929, in an essay on "Culture and Socialism," "and what could be definitely German, would be an alliance between the conservative culture idea and the revolutionary social thought."

Mann's penchant for the ambiguous and the romantic was reflected in his novel *The Magic Mountain* (1924) in which he introduced three leading types: the representative of liberalism was an Italian who spiritually was a descendant of Mazzinian thought and thereby not a convincing spokesman for the modern West, a pleasant and ineffectual doctrinaire, and an easy object for irony. More incisive was the second type, the spokesman of authoritarianism, ironically enough a Jew converted to Catholicism. They both tried to win over a naive and decent young German, Hans Castorp, whose education forms the central theme of the novel and who grows to maturity in his contacts with the two opposite political philosophies. It is a criterion of the artistic value of the novel that it is impossible to say where Mann's sympathies lie. Perhaps, even when he wrote *The Magic Mountain,* they lay with neither of the ideological protagonists, both of whom he treats with superior irony, but with Castorp's cousin, a young Prussian officer, without any intellectual or artistic interests, a nonpolitical man, who in the face of death shows what the Germans call *"Haltung,"* a stoic and disciplined attitude. The political-ideological issues remain unresolved. The German hero himself goes off at the end of the novel, to fight in the world war and dies in a battle on the western front.

The Magic Mountain, a great novel which may well rank in sweep and importance with *The Brothers Karamazov*, shows hardly any understanding of, nor any true interest in. the problems of modern liberty. The one woman who attracts Hans Castorp and contributes to his growing awareness of the world is, characteristically, a Russian who embodies the somewhat disorderly strangeness which the Germans liked to associate with the mysterious East. and also the intimate fascination which the Russian East has exercised upon so many German intellectuals in the twentieth century.

When National Socialism came to power in Germany—partly as the result of the existence of the many nonpolitical men in whose name Mann had spoken in 1917—Mann turned, after some initial hesitation, against Hitler, in whom he rightly saw the demonic seducer who would lead Germany to the abyss. Even after 1945 Mann was never aware of any affinity between Hitlerian and Stalinistic totalitarianism, though Communism was equally convinced of the inevitable doom and moral inferiority of the liberal West and of the inescapably approaching victory of totalitarianism on a global scale. But to Mann resistance to Communism appeared as "the fundamental foolishness" (*Grundtorheit*) of the era. He disapproved of many things in Stalinism, but there were many things in the United States of which he equally disapproved, and he apparently never saw any fundamental difference between the liberal West and totalitarian Russia, whatever their momentary shortcomings or their professed aims might be. "Because I am not a capitalist, I do not [much] fear the Russian threat to the capitalist-bourgeois way of life," Mann declared on November 7, 1948, to a German language communist periodical in New York. "But as far as I can see, Russia doesn't threaten the thing that matters most, peace."

The wishful and confused thinking which characterized many circles in the twentieth century found exemplary expression in Mann's political utterances after 1945 as well as in 1917. In his creative work Mann treated with serene irony the tension between the security of the bourgeois world, to which he, rich in success and honors, belonged, and the dangerous temptations of the world of the artist with its lure of the illicit. But in his political views he revealed a naïveté similar to that of many German historians who had to their credit solid and enduring achievements of scholarship.

Yet Mann's antiwesternism was not shared by the great German writers at the beginning of the twentieth century. His older brother Heinrich, against whom the bitterness of Thomas Mann's *Reflections* was aimed, championed the cause of French Enlightenment and directed the biting sarcasm of many of his novels against the ideology and the ruling class of the Reich. Gerhart Hauptmann, who started as Germany's leading playwright of the naturalist school, later fell under the spell of classical antiquity. A journey to Greece in 1907 had a similar significance in Hauptmann's life as had the Italian journey in Goethe's. But Hauptmann did not, as Goethe did, view antiquity in the light of classical humanism. In the sun-drenched Greek landscape Hauptmann felt the sensuous presence of archaic gods Dionysus moved him more than Apollo did, Nietzsche rather than Goethe guided him. "Tragedy," Hauptmann wrote in Delphi, "means enmity, persecution, hatred, and love of life s frenzy." But like Goethe, he opposed in the name of the timeless beauty of antiquity the national passions of the day.

In 1913 Hauptmann, as the representative German writer, was commissioned to write a play for the official celebration of the centenary of the battle of Leipzig, where the Allies defeated Napoleon, a victory in which the Prussian army claimed a major share. The *Festspiel* which Hauptmann wrote expressed more Goethe's spirit than enthusiasm for the War of Liberation. It did not glorify resistance to the West, but international harmony. Athene-Germany turned from the bloodsoaked battlefields of Germany longingly to the purifying air of ancient Greece.

> Still shuddering from the bath of a night heavy with dreams,
> I enter now the pure peak of Olympus,
> The serene home of blessed gods. I grow
> high and far into the different bath of radiant ether.

In her final words Athene-Germany proclaimed the deeds of peace and not those of war as the meaning of her existence. She called war naked murder, and she protested the fratricidal division of Europe. "Neither languages nor rivers nor seas separate us, neither gods nor the unknown god separate those who care deeply for the well-being of all men. Error alone separates, error alone lets loose hatred. . . ." *

---

* *Uns trennen Sprachen, trennen Strom und Meere nicht.*
  Nicht trennen Gotter, noch der unbekannte Gott

On May 31, 1913. Hauptmann's *Festspiel* was staged by Max Reinhardt in Breslau, the city in which, a century before, the Prussian king had proclaimed the War of Liberation. Understandably it was bitterly attacked by the nationalists Upon the intervention of the German Crown prince it closed after the eleventh performance Yet it was an event of no slight significance that the greatest German playwright of the period celebrated a victory against the national enemy in a spirit of humanitarian internationalism. It was a courageous protest against the preparations for another war against the same enemy, which were then going on. Thirty years later. Hauptmann, living then in retirement in his native Silesian village, turned again to Greek tragedy to express his despair over the possible triumph of the forces of darkness, the forces of Germany. His *Iphigenia in Aulis* was conscious of what was at stake in the war.

> Well-being is no longer at stake, Oh Queen,
> A little less or more of it. No:
> Everything is at stake! Civilized manners, beautiful appearance,
> The high nobility of priceless custom
> Have fallen prey to unleashed demons *

The most uncompromising stand against German nationalism was taken by the Swabian novelist Hermann Hesse. In his opposition to the German atmosphere in the years preceding the outbreak of the war in 1914, he left his fatherland in 1912 and settled in the Italian-speaking part of Switzerland, where he has lived ever since. He never lamented his exile as Heine had in Paris, and never longed to return to Germany. He acquired Swiss citizenship in 1923. In December, 1918 he was one of the few Germans who dared to answer the challenge presented by the defeat in war which, according to Thomas Mann, most Germans had fervently desired. Hesse called upon the German people to abandon the "most sacred ideals" (*die heiligsten Güter*) of the past and to continue on the new road. "Ahead of us lies the task of the

---

die, denen aller Menschen Heil am Herzen liegt.
Was trennt, ist Irrtum, Irrtum, der allein den Hass entfesselt. . .

* *Es geht nicht mehr um Wohlsein, Königin*
Ein weniger, ein mehr davon, o nein
Es geht um alles!—Sitte, schoner Schein,
Der hohe Adel kostlicher Gewohnung
Ward losgebundener Dämonen Raub

vanquished," he wrote. "It is the ancient and sacred task of all those who are unhappy on earth, not only to bear their fate but to make it their own and to understand it, until the misfortune is no longer felt as something alien which has suddenly come down upon us out of distant clouds but as something which belongs to us and which guides our thought. . . . Then this long war and this painful defeat will turn out to have become our good and well-deserved fate, no longer a sickness and wound from which we suffer, but a valuable promise for our future."

In 1919 Hesse appealed to the German youth in his *"Zarathustras Wiederkehr: Ein Wort an die deutsche Jugend"*: "Have you never considered how it has come about that the German is so little loved, that he is so much hated and feared? Did you not find it strange to see how in this war, which you started with so many soldiers and with such good prospects, slowly and ir-resistibly, one people after the other joined your enemies and decided against you? You did see it, with deep indignation, and you were proud to be so alone and so misunderstood. But you were not misunderstood! It was you yourselves who misunderstood.

"You young Germans have always boasted of the virtues you did not have, and blamed your enemies for vices which they learned from you You spoke always of 'German virtues' and you regarded faithfulness (*Treue*) and other virtues almost as your inventions. But you were not faithful. You were unfaithful to yourselves, and this brought the world's hatred upon you. You say: no, it was our wealth and our successes! Perhaps the enemy thought so too. But the causes always lie more deeply than we think, especially if we think in a shallow, economic way. Perhaps your enemies envied your money. But there are other successes which arouse no envy and which the world approves (*denen die Welt zujubelt*). Why did you never know such successes? Why only the others? Be-cause you were unfaithful to yourselves. You played a role that was not yours. You made out of the 'German virtues' with the help of your Emperor and of Richard Wagner, an operatic display which no one in the world took seriously but yourselves. And behind this pretty humbug of operatic splendor you allowed all your dark instincts, your servility and your swagger to proliferate. . . . And you gave yourselves away by pretending that your enemies always cheated in the same way! Listen, you always said, how they talk of virtue and justice, and look what they mean in reality! Where did you get this knowledge of their hypocrisy if not from your own heart?"

Hesse's appeal was in vain. No soul searching of the kind he asked for was forthcoming. In fact, the talk of "German virtues," of faithfulness and justice, swelled to unprecedented dimensions after 1919, until it almost drowned the never completely muted protest of reason. The operatic display of National Socialism surpassed by far that of Wilhelm II and Richard Wagner. The Germans after 1919 misunderstood and misjudged the outside world even more than they had done before 1914.

One year before Hitler came to power, Hesse wrote in a letter: "Germany has completely neglected to appreciate her appalling share of responsibility for the World War (*ungeheure Mitschuld am Weltkrieg*) and the present situation of Europe. She should have acknowledged it (without thereby denying that her enemies too bore a heavy share of responsibility), and undertaken a moral purification (as for instance France did during the Dreyfus Affair). Instead Germany has used the harsh and unjust peace treaty as a pretext to lie to the world and to herself about her own guilt. Instead of understanding her own errors and sins and correcting them, Germany talks big again, as she did in 1914, of her undeserved pariah position and reproaches others, sometimes the French, sometimes the Communists, and sometimes the Jews, with the responsibility for every evil." The mood of 1932 dangerously resembled that of 1914. The European horizon was rapidly shrinking. Many Germans, convinced of their superiority over their neighbors in the West and in the East, tried to build a Germany cut off politically and culturally from its neighbors. The German-centered view of scholars and educators, before and after the First World War, played an important part in the growth and in the hardening of the attitude against which Hesse had warned.

Chapter Eleven

GERMANOPHILISM

The Nature of the State

I~ his *Reflections of a Nonpolitical Man,* Thomas Mann, stressing the similarities between Russia and Germany, asked, "Don't we also have our Slavophiles and our Westernizers (*zapadniki*)?" He alluded to the fact that during the nineteenth century two trends of thought vied in influencing Russia's development. One trend wished to integrate Russia as closely as possible with the West and make it part and parcel of the European development. The other trend insisted, for the sake of Russia and of world civilization, if not of world salvation, on the need of preserving Russia's distinctiveness from Europe, her original Slav character and traditions which were regarded as superior to those of the West. These Slavophiles felt that capitalism and rationalism doomed the West and they opposed to the rotting West the alleged social justice and love of peace characteristic of Russia. The West was torn by party conflict and social struggle whereas Russia formed a true community. The Slavophiles were convinced that the approaching struggle between Russia and the West would, for reasons of her moral and social superiority, end with Russia's victory. Though this Slavophile thought was strongly influenced by German Romanticism, the Slavophiles regarded Germany as forming part of the hostile and doomed West.

A similar struggle between Germanophiles and westernizers went on in late nineteenth century Germany and was intensified after 1914. As in Russia, the dividing line between the two camps was not clearly drawn. Many westernizers harbored Germanophile sentiments, many Germanophiles adopted and helped to develop

262

western techniques. There were, of course, fundamental differences between Russia and Germany, based upon their different stage of technological and economic development and upon their different spiritual traditions. Russian Slavophilism was on the whole deeply Christian, identifying Russia and her mission with the national Russian Orthodox Church. No such identification was possible in Germany. Even Lutheranism was not specifically German though of German origin: for instance in Scandinavia, Lutheranism had developed differently from the German model. Some Germanophiles—before 1933 only a tiny minority—dreamt of a specific form of Christianity or turned to the pre-Christian German gods. Many Germanophiles were found in the Protestant camp. They all shared with the Slavophiles the conviction of their moral and social superiority over the West, of which they knew very little. Their one-sided perspective made them overestimate Germany's strength and treat the West with contempt.

Like Slavophilism in Russia, Germanophilism expressed itself in the emphasis on a state concept different from the western one and on its superior value. Ernst Troeltsch and others have pointed out how German political and social thought after 1806 developed in a direction opposite to that of the general trend of western thought which until then had been shared by Germany. In the eighteenth century politics was considered the art of assuring a good life for man, of creating the conditions which would enable men to live, as they should live, a worthy human life. The doctrine of man's individual rights, including the right of the pursuit of happiness, was a logical outcome of this concept of politics. This concept has continued as the dominant one in the political thought of the English-speaking countries.

German political thought after 1806 came under the one-sided influence of Machiavelli's realism and of the *raison d'état, die Idee der Staatsräson*, a concept for which, characteristically, there is no English equivalent. Politics now became a technique of acquiring, preserving, and expanding power. The state was no longer a society established by men for securing as far as possible the good life for its members and of reconciling conflicts of group interests. Instead it was regarded as an instrument of power which had no higher purpose than itself, a system of domination of men over men based upon force; that was the characteristic definition given by a leading German social scientist, Max Weber (*ein auf Gewaltsamkeit gestütztes Herrschaftsverhältnis von Menschen über Menschen*). At the same time the state as embodiment of the nation or the folk was raised to the highest dignity. The human individual, basic to the western state concept, was replaced by the higher organic individuality of the state or nation.

One of the early expressions of this Germanophile view of the state was presented by Ranke in his *Dialogue on Politics*. He opposed the western liberal view that power was merely an instrument to further the general welfare. The state for him was not a member of an international community, not a "subdivision of something more general, but a living thing, an individual, a unique self. . . . The position of the state in the world depends on the degree of independence it has attained. It is obliged therefore to organize all its internal resources for the purpose of self-preservation. This is the supreme law of the state." Such a theory, as Ranke himself acknowledged, "relegates politics to the field of power and of foreign affairs where it belongs." Each state has the tendency to grow incessantly according to its own unique and specific nature.

In commenting on Ranke's view, Professor Theodore H. von Laue pointed out its momentous consequences for German political thinking. Ranke's view implied a break with western developments; it expressed Prussia's refusal to follow the more pacifist western evaluation of international relations. Ranke's philosophy "was one of the landmarks in the revolt against the West, upholding against the advocates of western liberalism a new Prussophilism which in time grew into a Germanophilism. . . . His theory . . . was carried forward . . . in a destructive but inevitable chain reaction into Slavophilism, Sinophilism, Indophilism, etc. Wherever the standards of the most advanced western nations clashed with local traditions, a similar ideological revolt was the logical consequence of local nationalism. The Prussian and German revolt was the first one. It supplied the essential guides of thought for all subsequent ones. And up to the present it is the most odious rebellion only because it occurred so near the heart of Western Europe, in a situation in which the competition between western universal liberalism and local nationalism was very close."

Germanophilism insisted, to a degree unknown to Christian Slavophilism, on the power character of state and politics and on the precedence of foreign over domestic policy. It shared with Slavophilism the conviction of its country's unique spiritual character, of its moral superiority over the West, and of the legitimacy of its claim to leadership. Adolph Lasson, who was born the year after Hegel's death and died the year before the First World War ended, was a Hegelian who taught philosophy at Berlin University. The *Kantstudien* in 1918 called Lasson "the torch bearer of universal idealism." This strange universal idealist wrote in 1871, in his *Principles and Future of International Law*. "The more powerful state is the better state, its people are the better people, its culture is a superior culture. Whoever suffers defeat must acknowledge that he deserved it. The victor can be sure not that he is good but that he is the better one of the two." Strangely enough, this philosophy of 1871 was not accepted by the Germans in 1918. But in 1882 Lasson was so convinced of the strength of Germany that his *System of the Philosophy of Law* asserted that "the decision of war is just. The victorious people will become the leading, the model people."

In a similar spirit Otto von Gierke, the greatest exponent of the Germanic point of view in the interpretation of legal history, wrote in his *The German Folk Spirit in the War* (1915): "If we achieve our war aims the triumph of our arms will bring about the triumph of the truth. For in world history success utters the decisive word. Even those formerly incapable of being taught this, will now realize that success in war is not an accident, but rather the outcome of eternal laws, in which God's rule reveals itself." Gierke upheld this point two years later in "Our Peace Aims" in which he not only demanded wide annexations but also proclaimed the victor's right to determine the existence of the defeated. At the same time the historian Erich Brandenburg contrasted in "Wilson and World History" (*Tägliche Rundschau*, January 31, 1917), Anglo-American and German concepts of state. To the Germans the state "does not exist to protect the interests of its citizens, it is rather the power organization of a people and has primarily the task of securing the latter's independence, individuality and rank in the world. . . . Consequently the relationship between the state and the individual is here entirely different from what it is on the other side of the Ocean." Nations as conceived by Wilson—or, as Brandenburg forgot to add, by Kant—could organize themselves into a league of nations. That was not the case with states as understood by most modern Germans. The nature of such states lies in their growth as power organizations in sharp competition with other states.

Many people everywhere and at all times have succumbed to the demonic temptations of power, but German intellectuals sanctified this acceptance with the halo of a philosophy which they extolled for its deep or realistic understanding of the alleged forces of history. Modern German thought turned away from rational natural law and the universal ideas of the eighteenth century and conceived universal history as the progressive differentiation of nations according to each one's peculiar character. German historians, while increasing the perfection of their methods, became more and more provincial in their horizons. They knew little of foreign countries and conditions. This was not due to the fact that they did not travel.* Goethe and Kant traveled less, and yet while living in small provincial towns their horizons were world-wide, and they were sympathetically concerned with events and movements everywhere. They never regarded Germany's situation as peculiar or unique. The leading German scholars at the turn of the century made little effort to understand western thought. They knew that the West emphasized individual liberty and that it regarded war as a misfortune. They saw therein proof of the superficial optimism and humanitarian sentimentalism of the West. In their enthusiastic affirmation of the German state the German historians educated their people to accept wars as a contest of moral energies. They saw their nineteenth century history, from Goethe to their own age, not as a decline, not as a loss of value-substance, but as a steep ascent to a higher and more permanent reality. This feeling was expressed by Friedrich Meinecke in his first major work, *Cosmopolitanism and the Nation-State*

---

* When, in 1904, Friedrich Paulsen, professor of philosophy and education at Berlin University, traveled in England, a country to which he had always felt drawn in so many ways, the reactions of this truly liberal scholar were typically German "In Germany, far into the middle classes, people have the idea that the policeman's business is to order them about, in England, everyone regards him as a man who is there for everyone's safety and protection. In England, everybody is a citizen, in Germany, everybody is a subject At least another century will have to go by before we can attain this self-assured attitude toward the State. Perhaps we shall never attain it. The relation of a German to the State is based principally on the place he holds in the army, whereas that of an Englishman is based on the part assigned to him in the political and judiciary organization of the State. So long as that holds good in Germany—and I do not see how it could be altered, our external political situation being what it is—the great majority of Germans will continue to identify the State with the person of the supreme war lord on the one hand and with that of the noncommissioned officer on the other. And after all it cannot be denied that our military discipline has its good side, too; it has been remarkably successful in instilling into our population a taste for good deportment, orderliness, and cleanliness. In England I have heard my wife exclaim more than once· 'One would have to go a long way in Germany to see such slovenliness among both sexes of the lower classes!' "

(1907), which he dedicated, in recollection of the "great times" through which they had lived together, to his nationalistic fellow-historian, Erich Marcks, Bismarck's biographer

This power-proud smugness was as superficial and optimistic as were the most shallow expressions of western liberalism but it contained less consideration for humanity and carried more dangerous implications In 1870, Rudolf Haym, professor of the history of literature at the University of Halle and biographer of Herder, wrote in the preface to his *Die Romantische Schule* of the "confident and joyous work of progress on the foundations, won as by a miracle, of power-proud national independence." Thirty years later when the last New Year's Eve of the nineteenth century was celebrated in the home of the famous liberal theologian Adolf von Harnack, a neighbor, Max Delbrück, brother of the historian Hans Delbruck, in a spirit of buoyant confidence proposed the toast to "the greater Germany, the greater navy" of the new century.

This spirit of power-proud self-confidence spread from the universities to the secondary and elementary schools, where it became oversimplified. At that time German schools devoted much time to recent history and its glorious fulfillment. William II, opening a conference of Prussian school principals in December, 1890 called upon teachers to bring up nationalistic young Germans, and not young Greeks or Romans. "More than ever, the instruction in history must provide an understanding of the present, and especially an understanding of our country's position in the present. For this purpose, German history, particularly that of modern and contemporary times, must be stressed." As the result of a study of textbooks of that time, Walter Consuelo Langsam found that "the material presented in books and in the school rooms appeared to have been much more militaristic in spirit than either the government regulations or the courses of study seemed to demand."

This nation-centered self-glorification made the period around the turn of the century a time in which people lived with a feeling of unshakable security and great expectations. This smugness was felt throughout the western world in general; it was nowhere more pronounced than in Germany. The people, from the Emperor to the farm hand, from the university professor to the village schoolmaster, were convinced that history demanded them to enter *Weltpolitik* and that they were the *Weltvolk* of the immediate future. In the preface to the third printing of

Cosmopolitanism and the Nation-State Meinecke regarded the war of 1914 as "the event which will definitely raise us to the rank of the leading world nation" (*der uns endgültig zum Weltvolke erheben soll*). Yet neither German leaders nor intellectuals were able to think in a world-political framework. The Germans entered the war of 1914 unprepared for the trial of strength which they were to face. They had no understanding of the real and moral forces of the outside world. They overestimated the advantages of sheer military preparedness and of organizational discipline. In all decisions military and technical points of view took precedence over political and moral ones. Under these conditions the defeat in the war came as an unexpected shock. It ran counter, the Germans were deeply convinced, to the laws of history and of divine justice.

Of the innumerable expressions of this Germanophilism, it will suffice to quote one chosen on account of the importance and influence of the correspondents involved: the letter which Houston Stewart Chamberlain, whose book was then the leading best seller,* as twenty years later Spengler's was to be, wrote to William II on November 15, 1901. Chamberlain, who was born an Englishman, a well-read and well-traveled author of serious books on Kant, Goethe, and Wagner, thanked God that he had become a German. "It is my deep conviction, which I have gained as a result of my long years of study, of those solemn hours when the soul wrestles with the divine for understanding as Jacob wrestled with the Angel, that the moral and spiritual salvation of mankind depends upon what we call the German (*das Deutsche*). In that moral world order of which Your Majesty has sometimes spoken, the German element now forms the pivot. The language itself irrefutably proves it, for scholarship, philosophy and religion cannot advance one step today, except in German. . . . Because the German soul is indissolubly tied up with the German language, the higher development of mankind is tied up with a powerful Germany, a Germany which is spread far over the earth and everywhere maintains, and imposes upon others, the sacred heritage of its language. The *Realpolitik* of the German Reich which cannot be sufficiently sober and matter-of-fact, nevertheless signifies, at least in my eyes, something different from the policy of other nations. . . . Only a planned organization em-

---

* Even the English translation, *Foundations of the Nineteenth Century*, went through five large printings between November, 1910 and June, 1914.

bracing the minutest detail, not the free civilization of emancipated individuals as it exists with the English speaking peoples, can assure German victory. Political liberty for the masses is an obsolete idea (*hat abgewirtschaftet*); but through organization Germany can achieve everything, everything! In that respect no one can equal her."

As a man of non-German origin Chamberlain was perhaps more enthusiastic about Germany than most Germans. But the sentiments he expressed were typical. He did not understand that Germanophilism could not provide the foundation of a sober and matter-of-fact *Realpolitik*. Intoxicated by the knowledge that the German was different from, and better than, other nations, the Germans discarded Bismarck's sober foreign policy. Adalbert Wahl, professor of history at the University of Tübingen, saw the task of the state in its will to make the unique and specific character of its own people triumph in all political and cultural fields, a philosophy which Bismarck would neither have approved nor understood. Such a philosophy ran counter to the conduct of a realistic foreign policy in Bismarck's style as well as to the building of a peaceful international society as envisaged by Gladstone or Woodrow Wilson.

Conservative Germanophilism

GERMAN POLITICAL DEVELOPMENT suffered from the absence of conservatives and of liberals in the western sense of the word. Germany had neither a Disraeli nor a Gladstone, neither a Theodore Roosevelt nor a Woodrow Wilson. Its liberals—to name only two of the most famous, Max Weber and Friedrich Naumann—were not primarily concerned with individual rights but with national power. They opposed autocracy and aristocracy not for the sake of liberty but on account of their insufficiency when it came to safeguarding and enhancing Germany's position as a world power. To that end they wished to modernize, and to a degree westernize, Germany's political and social structure.

Before 1918 the liberals had no practical influence. This was equally true of the leading representatives of conservative thought. Whereas the liberals based their program on power politics the conservatives took their stand on cultural and ethical grounds.

But they were so reactionary in their political and economic outlook that they lost themselves in romantic dreams far removed from the reality of the modern age. Their influence did not even reach the conservative parties, which in smugness and philistinism out-did the less conservative parties and had become merely the champions of economic interests and social privileges.

One of the remarkable representatives of conservative thought under Bismarck was Paul de Lagarde, professor of oriental lan-guages at the University of Göttingen. In his *Deutsche Schriften* he proposed the return to true Germanism—which meant the end of interdependence with other civilizations. The adoption of Roman law, the influence of the Enlightenment, modern urbanization and parliamentarism, all of these threatened the very foundations of Germany. Lagarde opposed Bismarck and the new Germany on two grounds· they conformed too closely to the modern pattern and they spurned ethical principles. According to Lagarde the develop-ment of personality was a German principle. But Bismarckian Germany was too centralized and bureaucratic, tending to suppress individuality. Only a self-sufficient Germany, whose own individ-uality, eternal and divine, was developing according to its own laws, could develop German personalities.

In Lagarde's eyes the Bismarckian Reich lacked ethos; it adored success and power. This was not surprising because it had been established by irresponsible followers of Machiavelli. "It will be difficult," he wrote, "to find anything bleaker (*trostlos*) than the fatherland's history between 1871 and 1890." Where were the ideas which could guide national life? Glorification of the state was not one of them, Lagarde insisted, nor was the accumulation of wealth. Rather, both tended to corrupt the true life of the nation, which as a divine creation embodied a high moral principle. What the Germans needed was not so much external as inner unity. To that end Lagarde wished to replace Protestantism and Ca-tholicism, which divided Germany, with a German national church. Such a church would be able to arouse the German sense of nationality, "the invisible force which lives in everything that grows and thrives in Germany, and to bring out in every single German that divine image which is in him from birth." Thus Lagarde's national church would transform the whole nation into a religious body outside of which there would be no salvation for the members of the nation.

Sceptical of the whole Christian tradition, Lagarde clung to the true teachings of Christ without being able to define them.

Like many others, Lagarde made a sharp distinction between
Jesus on the one hand and Paul and Augustine on the other,
regarding the latter two as destroyers of the true Christian spirit.
Lagarde never went so far as to wish to revive the old German
gods, though he stressed the value of old Germanic traditions.
He never took part in the Wotan-cult, which had then become
acceptable to a few writers, thanks partly to Wagner's resurrection of the Germanic myths. Among others, the novelist Felix
Dahn and the playwright Ernst von Wildenbruch made use of
this new cult. In a poem "Allvaters Anrufung" (1884) the latter
called upon Wotan to stand always and everywhere on Germany's
side and to give her strength in her struggles. "We, of thy blood,
God of the Germans, approach Thee; we, lost among alien folk,
call upon Thee, Father of All!"

> *Wir, von deinem Blut geboren,*
> *Gott der Deutschen, nahen dir,*
> *Wir, in fremdem Volk verloren,*
> *Dich, Allvater, rufen wir!*

The conclusions which Lagarde drew from his idealistic ethics
ran counter to the whole modern development. For that reason
Thomas Mann approved of Lagarde in his *Reflections of a Nonpolitical Man.* "One must clearly understand," Lagarde wrote,
"that voters constitute a people as little as a canvas and color
molecules constitute a painting by Raphael. . . . Individuals as
such, that means as egoisms, are in opposition to the people. The
people's voice is not heard at all when single individuals speak,
of whom the people consist. The people speaks only when the
soul of the people (*Volkheit*) speaks through the individuals, that
is to say when the consciousness of the fundamentally common
roots, common to all individuals, is awakened and finds a common
response to the great events of history" (e.g. great wars). . . .
"As regards individual laws, the people really has nothing to say,
even if everyone votes. Where universal suffrage is regarded as
a blessing one does not weigh the votes, one counts them. My
students should recognize that this immoral method of arriving
at a political decision is immoral."

Needless to say Lagarde was not an admirer of democracy. "The
principles of 1789 can find even less application in Germany than
in France. They originated out of pure theory, not out of any
real necessity or truth. Under Louis Philippe the French lost the
merciless honesty of their fathers, who at least had strong con-

victions and were ready to murder and die for them. Thus these principles have no claims to being universal principles. The specific Celtic taste which they imported from Paris made them for Germans neither more palatable nor more justifiable. Celtic egalitarianism could make Germany, which is by nature aristocratic, only more un-German and thereby unhappy." Lagarde was convinced that in his time liberty and self-government were impossible in Germany. Before Germany could become ripe for self-government a small elite would have to be created through an entirely new system of education. This elite would be selected not by birth but by ethical and intellectual endowment, and working on behalf and for the people, it would be able at some future time to realize self-government for Germany. But of course, Germany could never be governed by the people themselves.

It is important to note that Lagarde's ethical idealism was confined to the Germans. In international relations he indulged in an aggressive imperialism going far beyond anything known in the age of bourgeois imperialism. He was an opponent not only of the domestic spirit of Bismarck's Prussian German Empire, but also of its moderate foreign policy. He demanded the creation of a greater Germany which would include the lands and peoples of the Habsburg monarchy and expand beyond into southern and southeastern Europe. He disagreed with Bismarck's pro-Russian policy. He saw in Russia a force in which all that he disliked, "Catholicism, Judaism and North America," were symbolically represented. He was convinced of the inevitability of a Russo-German war. Such a war would open the possibility of the settlement of German farmers throughout eastern Europe. "By pushing the Muscovites back we could find room next door to us for those Germans who are now lost to us by emigrating to America, and at the same time we could create conditions for an independent, non-Russian development of the southern Slavs which would thereby no longer be dangerous to us. . . . May Russia be kind enough to move voluntarily some five hundred miles into Asia where there is room enough. May she give us sufficient access to the Black Sea so that we can settle our beggars and peasants in Asia Minor. If Russia does not accede to our wishes, she will force us to exercise the right of eminent domain, and that means war. . . . This policy is somewhat Assyrian, but there is no other alternative for us."

Lagarde's fundamentally unpolitical ideas about Germany were shared by the author of a book which appeared anonymously in 1890. Entitled *Rembrandt As Educator. By a German,* it aroused

immediate and widespread attention. In the year of its publication it went through thirteen printings. The following year the
thirty-seventh much enlarged and revised edition was published.
Though the book was widely discussed in the 1890's and enthusiastically supported by Rudolf Eucken, a popular professor of
philosophy at the University of Jena, it really came into its own
only after 1918, a decade after the death of its author, Julius
Langbehn. What made him popular after 1918 and prevented his
full success in the 1890's was his insistence upon race as a decisive
factor in human life. Langbehn rejected the division of nations
according to political frontiers, history or language. "Blood is
mightier than political nationality and mightier even than language; blood affinity inescapably produces spiritual affinity." Langbehn concluded from his assumption that blood determined men
and that inborn qualities were more important than acquired ones.
Upon this hereditary element rested, according to him, the natural
superiority of aristocracy as a social-political system over democracy.

In his emphasis on race Langbehn went far beyond Lagarde.
He also had no part in Lagarde's Greater Germany program with
its eastward expansion. Langbehn was a Low German, born in
the then Danish Schleswig-Holstein. The Low Germans were
for him the true born aristocrats. His racialism was distinctly Low
German, not German, and the Low German race included the
Dutch and a large part of the English, and even New Englanders.
"Bismarck, Cromwell, William of Orange, Shakespeare, Rembrandt,
Beethoven—two Germans, two Dutchmen, two Englishmen—these
are the most beautiful flowers and leaves in this [Low German]
wreath . . . and this glorious wreath circles the North Sea, the
Low German Sea." * He contrasted the Low German spirit with
that of Berlin-Borussia which, through Bismarck, had triumphed
in Germany. In Prussia, Slavic, French, and Jewish influences corrupted the Low German character. Prussian discipline was good but

---

* Langbehn loved Venice and found there a people akin to the Low
Germans. "It is a truly aristocratic city. If Rembrandt had not been a
Dutchman he would have deserved to have been a Venetian That is equally
true of his person as of his art. At the mouths of the Po and of the Rhine
the inhabitants combine the strong sense for home which is characteristic
of inhabitants of marshlands with the wide horizons which characterize
seafaring people. . . . Venice the single aristocratic city of former days, faces
North America, a whole democratic continent of today. Yet it should not
be difficult for the present Germans to choose between these two models.
Venetianization is superior to Americanization "

it had brought with it arrogance, brutality, a lack of moral seriousness and the irresponsibility of the rulers. Langbehn regarded
William II as a man who dissipated the inheritance of his ancestors. "Do you know of a German intellectual," Langbehn asked,
in November, 1900, "who strongly and seriously opposes this personality which now radically dominates Germany? I do not know
of one. And can you understand the consequences of this? I can.
The people is becoming demoralized and brutalized if they are
not so already." Langbehn found the atmosphere in Bismarckian
Germany soul-destroying. "Present day Germany succumbs more
and more to an increasing moral rottenness. I feel neither the
inclination nor the calling to counteract this. Certain historical
processes cannot be arrested. May the well-deserved curse be fulfilled."

Langbehn put his hope in the German youth. "At the time of
the old *Burschenschaft,* German youth rose for the ideal interests
of the fatherland," he wrote. "It fought hostile forces in Germany's
inner life and thereby prepared a later national resurgence. Today the situation in Germany is such that a similar impulse is
required; some signs even point to this possibility." Langbehn
appealed to the German youth—and to that end helped dis-
seminate Lagarde's writings—to form a new nobility, an elite
of social aristocrats who would put upon their banner two words:
German honor. German honor meant above all a struggle against
materialism, against the capitalistic mentality, against the mechani-
zation of intellectual life, and against the typically German educated
barbarian. Art seemed to Langbehn superior to scholarship, which
was mechanical, abstract and international "Everything now
depends," wrote Langbehn, "on the preservation of the continuity
of folk life. It is a principal task of our day to dig ancient folk
rights out of the soil, and one of the most important fundamental
rights of the German folk is its right to a thoroughly native art,
a thoroughly native intellectual life. Therein the German heart
must be the determining factor." But Langbehn insisted also on
measure and moderation as a criterion of all true art and opposed
romantic ecstacy. For that reason he dismissed Wagner. "Wagner
wishes to dominate and he dominates, but for how long? . . .
Wagner does not offer simplicity and quiet greatness and yet these
are the core of all true art and of all folkdom. That stunning and
intoxicating element which is so characteristic of Wagnerian art
is entirely un-German. He out-Meyerbeers Meyerbeer."

In the later editions Langbehn altered two of his original positions. On the one hand he denounced Jewish influence more

strongly; on the other hand his attitude toward Christianity became more positive. Born of a Protestant family—his mother was a pastor's daughter—Langbehn left the church at the age of twenty-four and turned against Christianity. After the publication of his book he came under the influence of his fellow Holsteinian Momme Nissen, who in 1900 became a convert to Catholicism. Living as a hermit and shunning all political activity, Langbehn abandoned his emphasis on race before his death in 1907. Yet his book had a greater influence on German youth after 1918 than Lagarde. Before Nissen—Langbehn's literary executor —died, in 1943, the book had reached its ninetieth large printing.

A third conservative thinker was Konstantin Frantz, the son of a Protestant pastor. For many years in Prussian governmental service, he left the service and Berlin in 1873 and withdrew to Saxony where he died in 1891. Frantz became Germany's foremost advocate of federalism and thus gained in influence after 1945. Though he was a declared enemy of Bismarck's Reich, he was neither a democrat nor even a friend of a moderate constitutional monarchy. Bismarck's Germany was not a true Reich, he complained, but imitated France's political and social immorality, becoming an eastern replica of France, *ein östliches Frankreich*. In a mad power-drive Bismarck's empire had abandoned German morality and the German principle of federation. Yet a true federation of all central European peoples, not their annexation by Prussia, was demanded by the world situation.

Frantz regarded the United States and Russia as the two real great powers of the future; he felt that only a federated central Europe under German leadership could check their imperialism. He wished to recreate the German Confederation which would include Germany and the Habsburg lands as the nucleus of a wider central European federation. There were undoubtedly sound elements in Frantz's political vision. He believed in the federal principle on all levels of political life. He demanded a friendly relationship between the Germans and the western and southern Slavs, especially the Poles, and respect for every nationality He wished to found politics on a moral basis which in his case was not purely Germanic as it was with Lagarde, but Christian and universal. "Where will it lead us if we replace the Gospel by a so-called *Realpolitik* which divests itself in principle of all ideal demands and strives only for national power and greatness and wishes to confine our mind within the narrow sphere of alleged national interest? It will certainly not lead us to a system of peace. . . . Good God, what is not being done in the name of progress, even if it leads to catastrophe! But what are your Germanias, your Borussias, your Berolinas, and similar images which you call up before the eyes of the nation, so that it will pay homage to it? What else but the most tasteless inventions of artificial refurbished paganism. And the sacrifices which these new idols will demand will be human sacrifices!"

Frantz not only rejected modern nationalism; he also rejected democratic constitutionalism and demanded the return to a true or premodern national economy based upon transformed medieval institutions. The Prussian state, even before Bismarck, appeared to him, as it did to many German liberals, to be an embodiment of modern principles in economy and administration. Whereas the liberals praised Prussia for it, Frantz blamed Prussia for undermining "the Christian-Germanic principles." In his pamphlet "National Liberalism and Jewish Domination" (*Der National-liberalismus und die Judenherrschaft*, 1874), he saw Berlin as the center from which the Jews and the stock exchange dominated Germany. The year 1866 meant in his eyes the final triumph of the pro-capitalist, pro-Jewish policy. "This most desirable situation for the Children of Israel we owe to Herr von Bismarck who has done more for them than has ever been done before." Frantz maintained that by descent and tradition a Jew always remained a Jew and that the Jewish religion was inseparably tied up with Jewish nationality. Therefore he saw only one solution, to exclude the Jews, who were by nature aliens, from German life and to have them lead their own segregated life. The violent anti-Semitism of Frantz was not religiously or racially motivated: it had its roots in his rejection of modern ideas of liberalism and emancipation. In the same way his concept of Europe was not that of Nietzsche or of the good Europeans. it was antiwestern and excluded not only Russia, but also France and above all England. It was a Germano-centered Europeanism based upon antiliberal foundations, a romantic longing for a renewal of the medieval nonnationalist Holy Roman Empire, pacifist and Christian. In his utopian way Frantz longed for the rebirth in Germany of a deep and authentic Christianity, freed from divisive church ties, a Christianity based at the same time on exact science. Through federation and true religion Germany would point the way for mankind. Frantz concluded his *Federalism as Guiding Principle for the Social, Political and International Organization* (1879) by quoting Friedrich Gentz: "Europe which fell through Germany's fault, shall rise up again through Germany."

Though some of the ideas of the Germanophile conservatives bear a resemblance to some National Socialist ideas—and how could it be otherwise?—it would be a profound mistake to see in these romantics forerunners of National Socialism. Their ethos and their concern with cultural and spiritual values were entirely alien to National Socialism. The conservatives were profoundly opposed to the vulgar adoration of the masses, of technology and organization which characterized the National Socialists, in spite of their authoritarianism, as it characterizes Communism. But by their hostility to western liberalism, by their disregard of the fundamental importance of the modern rights of man, these conservatives contributed to that mental and moral confusion, out of which later, when war and chaos had brutalized the masses, a mass movement could grow from which they would have shrunk in horror.

Yet even without the National Socialist last act of the tragedy Germanophilism had a dangerous implication. It emphasized, as Slavophilism did, uniqueness (though not always on racial grounds) and separate destiny. Germany had the task of regenerating Europe, so Frantz believed. George's disciple Friedrich Gundolf, himself a scholar of high rank, spoke for many highly cultured and prominent Germans at the turn of the century when he wrote, comparing Germany with the West: "Only Germany is not yet 'completed'—how often did this incompletion torment and intimidate us, when we faced the form, the sureness, the perfection of the Latins and the Celts! Around all German figures there seemed to hover a chaos of yet indeterminate forces. But our people, the only people in possession of a wealth that is still intact and formless and, at the same time, of a creative force to mould that wealth, the only people, in short, which is still young, is thereby entitled and in duty bound to regenerate Europe." A Russian Slavophile could have written in the same terms about Russia.

Liberals and the Power State

MORE DISTURBING THAN THE FAILURE of the conservatives to understand western thought, was the similar failure on the part of the German liberals. The depth of the misunderstanding is indicated by the fact that even in the German Federal Republic of the 1950's Ernst Moritz Arndt is apparently regarded as a liberal It was Arndt who wrote in his *Germany and Europe* that "Germany needs a military tyrant who is capable of exterminating whole nations."

When we think of influential and representative liberals at the beginning of the twentieth century, the names of Friedrich Naumann and Max Weber come to mind first. Both were men of high personal integrity, both, with a perspicacity rare among the members of their class, were interested in social reforms which they regarded, however, as a means to strengthen the power-state. There was no philistine smugness in their views. They were critical of the government and the people and fully understood the need for modernizing Germany's political and social structure. But the idea of the German power-state was central to all their thought. They explained the emphasis upon the need of growing national power—realistically, not ethically—by pointing to Germany's uniqueness. They believed that Germany, as a stepchild of history, had come very late into her own and that as a stepchild of geography she found herself in a most vulnerable location.

Of the two men Weber was the younger and more influential. The son of a National Liberal member of the Reichstag, Weber studied jurisprudence and became one of Germany's leading scholars in the social sciences. He never questioned, as Frantz did, the German power-state as constituted by Bismarck Throughout his life he differed from Bismarck by being, like Lagarde and Frantz, anti-Russian. From 1892 on he was critical of the Kaiser and also became critical of Bismarck's legacy, not because he saw any flaw in its fundamental conception, but because he became convinced that Germany as constituted in the 1890's was not strong enough to succeed in carrying out her mission as a great power.

As a student in Berlin Weber listened to Treitschke In 1887, in a letter to his uncle Hermann Baumgarten, who was highly critical of Treitschke's influence upon the students, Weber defended Treitschke by putting part of the blame upon his fellow students. His characterization of the young generation in the late Bismarck period agreed with Nietzsche's and Lagarde's strictures: "If among my contemporaries there did not exist the adoration of militaristic and other ruthlessness, the cult of so-called realism and philistine contempt for all those aspirations which hope to reach their goal without appealing to the worst side of men's character,—then the innumerable and often harsh cases of one-sidedness, the passionate struggle against other opinions, and the predilection, under the powerful influence of success, for what one calls today *Realpolitik,* would not be the only impression which the students take away with them from Treitschke's lectures. Under these conditions, however, Treitschke succeeds in degrading serious and conscientious work, which is interested in truth alone. He calls forth a boorish self-conceit (*flegelhafte suffisance*), which becomes insupportable here even in conversation, and an unusual coarseness (*ungemeine Roheit*) in judging everything which is not purely opportunistic."

In the atmosphere of uncritical adoration of the German regime which prevailed in academic circles, Weber was one of the very few to foresee the catastrophe to which the Kaiser's regime was leading Germany. On December 14, 1906, he warned Naumann against supporting the Emperor. "The degree of contempt with which we are met as a nation abroad (in Italy, the United States—everywhere), and justified contempt—that is decisive—because we tolerate *this* regime of *this* man, has become a factor of greatest importance in world politics. We are becoming isolated, because this man rules us in this way, and *because we tolerate and excuse it."* Weber knew where the responsibility lay: not only with the Kaiser "who was dealing with politics from the point of view of a young lieutenant," but with the whole system of sham-constitutionalism and with the Conservative Party, which prevented its change. "The dynasty of the Hohenzollern," he wrote again to Naumann on November 18, 1908, "knows only the corporal's form of power: to command, to obey, to stand to attention, to boast." But the fault was not the Kaiser's alone. "Don't overestimate the quality of the person; it is the institutions and your lack of temperament, which are responsible. Both are the result of Bismarckism and of the political immaturity which it promoted. . . . Bismarck's terrible annihilation of all independent convictions among us, is the reason, or one of the main reasons, of all the defects of our situation. But do we not bear at least the same responsibility for it as Bismarck does?"

Yet Weber never doubted the principles on which Bismarck and the Hohenzollern had established the Reich of 1871. The *Machtstaat* idea was, as J. P. Mayer, the great student of Toqueville, writes, the *Leitmotif* of Weber's thought, it never changed throughout his life and it survived the downfall of the Hohenzollern monarchy. "Bismarck's example made Weber understand the lesson of Machiavelh's *Principe."* In reality, Weber, like most German scholars, never understood the implications and limitations of Machiavellianism. He was "unable to see the moral element inherent in any political power."

As a young man Weber joined the Pan-German League and the Association for Social Policy (*Verein für Sozialpolitik*). The latter was founded by the "socialists of the cathedra," professors who advocated an active interest in the betterment of the workers. These men regarded the struggle against English and French economic and political liberalism as the mission of Germany, whose ethically superior national social community confronted the individualistic or atomistic democracy of the West. The Association sought, as its program stated, the union of state, people, and economy for the advancement of national greatness. One of its moving spirits was Adolph Wagner, whose nationalism, according to Professor Evalyn A. Clark, fused irrational romanticism, ruthless *Realpolitik*, Pan-Germanism, and racialism. He taught economics in the 1860's at the University of Dorpat (today Tartu in Estonia) then a town in Russia's Baltic provinces inhabited mostly by Germans. From his association with the aggressive nationalism of the borderland, Wagner took over its insistence on the supreme importance of maintaining and spreading one's own national language and destroying that of the enemy nation by means of schools and economic pressure. From Treitschke and the whole climate of opinion of *Machtpolitik* and social Darwinism, Wagner appropriated the belief in the forcible assertion of national superiority. "The nation must assert its right over all individuals within it and prove its right to existence among other nations by a war of all against all in which only the stronger survive."

In 1870, when Wagner was called from Dorpat to the University of Berlin, he published *Alsace-Lorraine and Its Recovery for Germany,* a pamphlet whose point of view was too extremist even for Treitschke. It claimed Germany's right to bring all people of Germanic descent—the Dutch, the Flemish, the Swiss, and others—home into the new German Reich. The same spirit of Pan-Germanism animated Wagner's *Vom Territorialstaat zur Weltmacht* ("From Territorial State to World Power," 1900) and *Gegen England* ("Against England," 1912). But his outlook was broader than that of most Pan-Germans. He was sincerely interested in improving the lot of workers and peasants: the workers to wean them away from Marxism to patriotism, and the peasants because he saw in them "the fountain of youth of our military power."

In 1878 he helped Pastor Adolph Stocker, court chaplain in Berlin, found the Christian Social Workers Party. Stocker combined a thoroughly conservative point of view with modern mass agitation methods. He wished to prevent the Marxist social revolution by sound social reforms, based on a Christian foundation. He saw, as did Frantz, Marxism, liberalism, capitalism, and the Jews as the enemy, finding a common root in all four of them. He became, as Professor Koppel S. Pinson called him, "the most volatile, stormy, and controversial political agitator and demagogue of the Second Reich. In this agitation anti-Semitism was his most formidable weapon." Stöcker was largely responsible for the Conservative Party adopting anti-Semitism as part of its platform. "Previously anti-Semitism had been represented," a German writer quoted by Pinson remarked, "only in various small splinter parties; now it became the legitimate property of one of the biggest parties, of the party nearest to the throne and holding the most important positions in the state. Anti-Semitism had become close to being accepted at the highest level of social respectability." The alliance between the Conservatives and Stocker did not last. In 1887 a political party basing its program entirely on anti-Semitism competed for the first time in the Reichstag elections.

In 1881 Friedrich Naumann, a Lutheran pastor's son who himself became a pastor, helped Stöcker to found the nationalist and anti-Semitic German Student Association. Later on Naumann abandoned Stocker's ostensibly Christian outlook. Under Max Weber's influence, he no longer regarded politics as applied ethics, but as a method to assure Germany's power position. He developed into "a nationalist, whose lifetime of public service sought its object in strengthening the German nation." One of the ways to strengthen it was to win the adherence of the workers, whose importance in modern industrial society he fully understood, to a sense of civic responsibility and awareness of the importance of the power-state.

Weber's inaugural lecture at the University of Freiburg (1895) changed Naumann's outlook. In this lecture the brilliant young economist discussed the relationship between the nation-state and political economy. Characteristically he started from the nationality conflicts in Prussia's eastern provinces, the economic and social struggle between the Germans and the Poles. He proclaimed Germany's right to strengthen and broaden the German character of the Polish provinces. The economic and social policy of the nation-state must be governed by national egotism, the famous *sacro egoismo*, as the Italian nationalists called it. "It is not our task to pass on to our descendants peace and human happiness," Weber said, "but the eternal struggle for the maintenance and enhancement of our national way. . . . The power and interests of the nation . . . are the last and decisive interests which economic policy has to serve. . . . The national state is for us the secular power organization of the nation and in this national state the *raison d'état* is for us the ultimate yardstick for economic considerations." Therefore the economic policy of the German state and the value standards of the German economic theorists could only be German, making international economic co-operation and scholarship impossible and undesirable.

In her biography of Weber, his widow wrote that he demanded "from economy, technology and governmental machinery first of all, that they be the proper pillars for Germany's great-power-position. . . . His passion for the national power state sprang clearly from an innate instinct which no reasoning could call in question. The powerful nation is the expanded body of a powerfully endowed man; its affirmation is his self-affirmation." Germany was Weber's ultimate norm. Economic and political leaders were only justified in Weber's eyes if they recalled this fundamental truth to the people. Germany's domestic situation caused Weber to be deeply concerned about the future. The Junker class, which had done so much to raise Germany's power, was decaying and the bourgeoisie and the workers were in Weber's opinion, politically too immature to assume the responsibility for Germany's power-position. "An immense task of political education lies before us," he told his fellow scholars, "and there is no more serious duty for each one of us than to collaborate in the political education of our nation which must remain our ultimate aim." Unfortunately the German scholars were hardly qualified for this task, and Weber's infatuation with the power-state did not make them better qualified.

Looking back upon the road traveled by Germany between 1871 and 1895, Weber in his inaugural address asserted that the unification of Germany was meaningless if it meant the end and not the beginning of German world-power-politics (*wenn sie der Abschluss und nicht der Ausgangspunkt einer deutschen Weltmachtpolitik sein sollte*). At that time Weber was still a member of the Pan-German League. He left it soon afterwards, not because he disagreed with its imperialism but because he objected to its rigid antilabor policy. Twenty years later, during the First World War, Weber fully adhered to his position of 1895. "If we did not wish to risk this war, we might just as well have dispensed with the creation of the German Reich." Like so many others, he saw—and not without justification—that the spirit in which the Bismarckian state was founded conditioned its future dynamic drive for greater power and expansion, an urge for constant growth without concrete, limited political or economic aims. This sheer power drive belonged to the realm of metapolitics, which raised it above the level of reasonable discussion. Naumann well expressed it when he wrote, "You must have the will to conquer something, anything in the world, to be something."

Weber's inaugural address made Naumann change from his emphasis on a Christianity winning and helping the proletariat, to a social policy supporting imperialist expansion. In his weekly *Die Hilfe* (*The Help*), with its significant sub-title "God's Help, Self-Help, Brotherly Help," he asked in July, 1895: "Is not Weber right? Of what use is the best social policy if the Cossacks are coming? Whoever wishes to concern himself with domestic policy must first secure the people, fatherland and frontiers. We must consolidate national power." To Naumann, socialism made sense only when it was linked with German nationalism. It must recognize the precedence of foreign policy.

In 1896 Naumann founded the National Social Party. In discussing its program Weber protested against the humanitarian and Christian elements which then still existed in Naumann's draft. "We must face without illusion the one fundamental fact," Weber insisted, "the inevitable eternal struggle of men against men on this earth." Social Darwinism, then fashionable throughout the western world, made a deep impression on Naumann and Weber. They did not apply it so much to economic life as to international power-politics. When Hellmuth von Gerlach attacked Prussia's policy against her Poles, which reduced the Poles to second class citizens, Weber countered that the opposite was true: "We alone made out of the Poles human beings" (*Wir haben die Polen erst zu Menschen gemacht*). Such views expressed by leading German liberals who today are regarded as representative of German liberalism help one to understand the German catastrophe.

The membership of the Pan-German League did not consist, as is often assumed, mainly of Prussian Junkers, but of the academic intelligentsia and the upper middle class. Naumann himself, though he had nothing in common with the Pan-Germans' reactionary anti-labor views, agreed largely with their foreign policy. His sincere domestic liberalism supported an illiberal imperialism. "Before 1914," Professor William O. Shanahan writes, "no one propagated the German liberal view more effectively than Friedrich Naumann. To this task he applied his warm and sympathetic personality backed by the resources of his quick intelligence. He charmed his generation with a wit and style previously unknown in German politics or political journalism. To eloquence he added the magic of a lucid prose. His pen could ease Germanic sentences of their pedantic burdens. He could simplify erudition and he could dignify the commonplace. His literary gifts compensated for lack of originality to give his political writing a luster which reflected the hopes and aspirations, as well as the doubts and fears of Wilhelmian liberalism."

Naumann's and Weber's chauvinism was enhanced by their knowledge of Germany's political immaturity. They felt that no real national unity existed in Germany and that no common ideals, no agreed-upon social compact bound the various warring classes, parties, and religions together. They doubted the continuity and vitality of the Reich. They dreaded its enemies without and its inept leadership within. They forgot that their own imperialism created and united their enemies and that despite their grumbling, their half-hearted toleration gave Wilhelm II a free hand as a later generation was to give to Hitler. This longing for true national unity became intensified in the Weimar Republic with its sharper conflict of classes and *Weltanschauungen* and formed the most important single idealistic appeal of National Socialism. It was the weakness of Weber's and Naumann's nationalism—as it was later that of National Socialism—that it had no human or universal ideas to offer to inspire the Germans, but only a *sacro egoismo* and a cult of power for its own sake, adorned by some vague metaphysical ideas about German destiny.

Weber's attitude in the First World War and in 1918 bore out his Pan-Germanism. "It is open to doubt," J. P. Mayer writes, "whether Weber's war aims were *de facto* much different as compared with the war aims of the *Alldeutsche* (Pan-Germans). More subtle they certainly were. Weber still firmly believed in the conception of the State as power-State, a conviction to which he adhered to his death. Germany, the German people was *his* supreme law." When Weber addressed a Munich meeting called by the Progressive Liberals in October, 1916—his first public address in nineteen years—he explained the historical meaning of the war. He saw its cause in Germany's development as a great power which the Germans had to go through, not out of vanity but out of their responsibility before history. Otherwise, Weber feared, the world would have been divided between—and its civilization determined by—the regulations of Russian officials on the one hand and the conventions of Anglo-Saxon society on the other, perhaps with an infusion of Latin *raison*. Against this dreadful prospect the small Germanic peoples, the Scandinavians, the Dutch, and the Swiss, could do nothing, but Germany could and therefore had to fight "because we can throw our weight on the scales of history, therefore we have the duty before history, before posterity to throw ourselves against those two powers which threaten to engulf the whole world. Our national *honor* ordered us to do it . . . and this war concerns *honor,* and not territorial changes or economic gain."

As the war revealed more and more the weakness of the Reich's social and political structure, Weber ascribed the responsibility for the poor quality of Germany's leadership no longer to the Kaiser, but to Bismarck. "Bismarck left behind as a political heritage a nation without any political education, far below the level which, in this respect, it had reached twenty years earlier. Above all he left behind a nation without any political will, accustomed to allow the great statesman at its head to look after its policy for it. Moreover, as a consequence of his misuse of the monarchy as a cover for his own interests in the struggle of political parties, he left a nation accustomed to submit, under the label of constitutional monarchy, to anything which was decided for it, without criticizing the political qualifications of those who now occupied Bismarck's empty place and who with incredible ingenousness took the reins of power into their own hands." Bismarck's legacy survived the catastrophe of 1918 and so led to that of 1933.

A man of Weber's views could hardly be helpful when the time came to establish democracy and to adapt the new Germany to peaceful co-existence of nations. Weber, who even after the armistice continued to admire Ludendorff, went to see him shortly before the armistice in an effort to persuade him to surrender as a true heroic soldier to the enemy. The hearts of the two men, Weber's widow wrote, "were beating with the same feeling of heroic patriotism" (*schlugen gleich in heldischem Patriotismus*). In his conversation with the General, Weber explained his concept of democracy: "In democracy the people elect their leader, in whom they have confidence. Then the chosen leader says: Now shut up and obey! People and parties are no longer allowed to interfere with him." Ludendorff of course replied that Weber's democracy might be acceptable to him. Weber went on: "Afterwards the people can judge—if the leader made mistakes, let them hang him!" On the strength of this interpretation of democracy Weber insisted on Article 41 of the Weimar constitution, which stipulated the election by the people of the Reichspresident. Article 48 of the constitution gave the president extraordinary powers in times of emergency and these powers became in the hands of Hindenburg the main constitutional instrument for ending the constitution. Yet Weber was regarded by many as the hope of liberalism for the Weimar Republic.

Weber had as little understanding of an international order based on peace as he had of domestic democracy. After the acceptance of the Versailles treaty, he declared that he would from then on concentrate on the one problem: how to get once more a great General Staff for Germany. Before and after the armistice, he repeatedly demanded that should Polish troops invade Danzig or Thorn (Toruń), a German irredenta must be bred (*gezüchtet*) and a nationalist revolutionary terrorism must be set in motion. In talking with students he insisted that the first Polish official who dared to set foot in Danzig must be shot. In his eyes it was inevitable (*unvermeidlich*) to follow such a method. Weber's incitement to terrorism (which as the events after 1945 proved was in no way inevitable) was followed, and naturally broadened beyond the limits which Weber might have set.

In a letter to Friedrich Crusius, professor of classical philology at Munich, Weber wrote on November 24, 1918, that Germany had to start anew as she did after 1806, but this time with greater speed and energy. He expressed this with strong Germanophile overtones. "We have shown to the world, 110 years ago, that we—and *we alone*—were able to be one of the great cultural peoples under foreign domination. *This* we shall demonstrate again! Then history, which has already given us—and *us alone*—a second youth—will give us also a third one. I have no doubt about it. . . ." Weber took his reference to a second youth from Treitschke. His insistence that the Germans *alone* were able to be one of the great cultural peoples under foreign domination was mistaken: he could have easily remembered, for instance, that the Italians of the Renaissance were a very great cultural people under foreign domination In fact, Italians and Germans have never regained as an independent nation the level of cultural creativity obtained under foreign domination. This is of course no plea for foreign domination but a warning against the belief that national independence is necessarily favorable to culture.

The essence of Weber's political thought and the unfortunate influence of his "liberalism" on Germany can best be summed up in the words of a recent American interpreter of Weber and Spengler, Professor H. Stuart Hughes: "In a less extreme and apocalyptic form Weber's vision of the future has disconcerting resemblances to Spengler's." Both were Germanophiles in their attitude toward democracy and the West. "Weber's hankering after personal leadership—along with his ineradicable nationalism—is enough to make us question the whole basis of his political thinking."

Naumann's political thought was far less scholarly but due to his religious roots, more complex than Weber's. "I am a Christian, a Darwinist and an Imperialist," he gladly proclaimed. But of this trinity, Christianity was the weakest member. It abdicated before the supposed necessities of history. Illustrative of his attitude was Naumann's reaction to the famous speech with which Wilhelm II in the summer of 1900 sent German troops off to China to crush the Boxer uprising. He admonished them to take no prisoners and to spare no lives. The soldiers were to leave a record in history similar to that of Attila's Huns, "so that the name German will be confirmed by you in China for one thousand years in such a way that at no time again will a Chinese dare to look askance at a German." These words which were characteristic of many of Wilhelm's utterances, aroused sharp criticism in some German liberal and socialist papers. Naumann, against the protest of Friedrich Paulsen and others, defended the Kaiser. A nation which wished to rise in the world would have to be hard. Politics, he wrote, had nothing to do with applied ethics but were only a technique to use in the power struggle. There was only one part of the Emperor's speech to which Naumann objected. Wilhelm called the war against China a vehicle for the propagation of Christianity, an interpretation of religion by a Christian monarch which Attila certainly missed. The Emperor wished to fuse inhuman power politics with the Gospel. Naumann went to the other extreme. He recognized no connection between ethics and politics. "We fight," he wrote, "because we are a nation, not because we believe in the Gospel. For the sake of the Gospel we send missionaries, for the sake of politics we send naval captains. Crusades are undertaken for the sake of the Holy Cross; our soldiers go to Peking for the sake of our power." That both attitudes, that of the Emperor and that of

the liberal spokesman, would degrade Christianity as well as
European power politics in the eyes of the Chinese, and ultimately
work against both, was beyond the understanding of the two men.
Naumann took a similar position on colonial questions. Public
opinion in Germany as in other European countries at the time,
was deeply divided on some of the horrors connected with colonial
expansion in Africa. But perhaps it was only in Germany that a
leading liberal came forward in defense of heinous inhumanity in
backward areas. Against the prevailing liberal opinion in Germany,
Naumann joined the Pan-Germans in defending Karl Peters, who,
after being an instructor in philosophy at Berlin University,
opened up and governed East Africa for Germany. In 1896 a
murder charge forced his dismissal. In Naumann's eyes Peters'
inhumanity was more than outweighed by his service to German
expansion. Naumann regarded Peters as a symbol of Germany's
world-power aspirations, which should not be tarnished by public
criticism based on moral grounds. The arguments which he advanced—the precedence of respect for the realities of national
existence over moral law—were fundamentally the same as those
advanced about the same time by the French anti-Dreyfusards. But
the anti-Dreyfusards were not regarded as liberals and did not
regard themselves as such. Naumann of course had a moral justification for his attitude; he proudly contrasted German candor about
colonial brutality with British liberal hypocrisy in condemning
colonialism while continuing to practise it. That the British liberals
from Gladstone on tried to humanize colonialism escaped Naumann's attention.

Needless to say, Naumann supported to the hilt German naval
armaments with their accompanying risk of war with Britain.
Nietzsche's admonition to "live dangerously" fascinated Naumann
and many of his contemporaries. "Expansion means great danger,"
Naumann wrote. "But without such risks there is generally no
political greatness. Without daring no individual and no people
has ever become strong." Naumann was convinced that world
civilization depended upon Germany's growing strength; no sentimental considerations could be allowed to interfere with it.

The heady wine of imperialism even went to the head of the
contributors to Germany's leading liberal intellectual monthly *Neue
Rundschau*. It published in 1907 an article which demanded
German expansion into the barbaric lands east of the Vistula.
Germany's enlightened national interest required, the Russians were
told in a periodical deservedly famous for its intellectual and

aesthetic standards, the dissolution of the Russian empire and the subordination of eastern and southeastern Europe to German administration and settlement. It was not the German government nor the Prussian army which harbored such plans; they were discussed openly by German intellectuals. That they frightened Russia—as Germany was frightened not by any concrete plans of the Russian government but by the vague aspirations of Pan-Slav intellectuals—is understandable. They helped to bring about the unexpected Anglo-Russian Entente of 1907 as they had engineered, at least unwittingly, the equally surprising Anglo-French Entente Cordiale of 1904. Professor Sell rightly insists that when after 1918 liberal apologists for Germany claimed that only a small reactionary Pan-German minority before the war had advocated expansionism, the facts were otherwise.

Theodor Heuss warned in his biography of Friedrich Naumann (1937) that one ought to beware of the misunderstanding that democracy was for Naumann a kind of ethical demand (*eine Art von sittlicher Forderung*). Democracy was to him a means of strengthening the nation. Only a democratic Germany, in Naumann's sense of the word, would in the age of industrialism which Naumann fullheartedly accepted, find enough healthy soldiers and skilled workmen to realize Germany's historical task. Only a democratic state would be able to channel the great potential strength latent in the people for the good of the nation. To that end the workers must receive full political rights and their wellbeing must be assured. These rights, however, could not be based upon the natural rights of man. Naumann despised such theories which he regarded as obsolete (*ein überwundener Standpunkt*). For him rights could only be based on power. A nation struggling for more power could not indulge in the sentimentality of natural law. "In our political activity we do not wish to imagine that we shall thereby enhance the happiness of individuals, . . . our concern is not happiness but the duty we have to fulfill towards the nation in which we were born." Naumann was convinced that he was thinking historically, and that historical thought in the realm of politics was infinitely superior to ethical thought. He never asked himself whether his interpretation of history, which was supported by most German historians of his day, corresponded to the real forces moving the world in modern times.

Under these circumstances it is not surprising that Naumann was among the most determined opponents of the ratification of the Treaty of Versailles. After the ratification he became an advocate of a purified Pan-Germanism. The Germans outside the frontiers of the Reich had to be included into the German nation The folkish German faith—*"der volksdeutsche Glaube,"* as Theodor Heuss calls it—became Naumann's guiding principle: "The spirit which now unites all Germans from Riga to Strasbourg, from [northern] Schleswig to Bozen [in south Tyrol], is rising up now more mightily than ever before *(der steht jetzt erst recht auf)*!" Thus, a few days before his death, Naumann set the tone for the nationalism of the Weimar Republic.

The German Reich, defeated after an unprecedented effort, was to rise again mightier than ever before. The previously scorned principle of national self-determination, of the natural rights of men and peoples, was to become the instrument of Germany's revenge. Most liberals and socialists in the Weimar Reich refused to accept the eastern borders of the new Germany and the principle of self-determination for the Poles. (The Germans were, however, not the only people to interpret self-determination one-sidedly in their own favor and to deny it to their neighbors). All of the liberals and socialists demanded the expansion of the Reich to include Austria and thus to enlarge Germany after defeat by much more land and population than she had lost in her Polish, French, and Danish borderlands. None asked themselves whether France, her territory devastated and her population dwindling, could agree to face after her hard-won victory a Germany superior in population and potential power to the one which had been so formidable in 1914. In 1919 German liberal thought was as German-centered as it had been before 1914. The experience of the First World War taught the German liberals nothing. Though in the event of Germany's victory they would have demanded vast territorial gains and huge indemnities, they regarded with sincere horror the loss to Germany of her non-German borderlands, which Germany had acquired by the partitions of Poland and her annexations of 1864 and 1871.

The Drift to War

THE WAR OF 1914 and the events of 1917 marked the great divide in modern history. The Second World War only brought into relief what had happened in the previous war, which marked the end of

the four-century-old phase of European world leadership. During
that period this leadership asserted itself all over the globe and
thereby prepared an unprecedented intercourse and interdependence
among all continents and civilizations. The Germans and the other
great European powers, however, regarded the First World War as
another struggle for hegemony in Europe; none realized its true
implications. This incomprehension of the character of the war
made its resumption twenty years later possible and perhaps inevitable. All the participants in the first war, with the exception of
Leninist Russia, continued their pre-First World War policies
fundamentally unchanged after 1918.

Before 1914 the democratic forces in Germany were growing in
numbers but not in influence. They were the opposition, but the
opposition in Bismarckian Germany played a different role from
that in western countries. The opposition was not an alternative
government but was regarded by the government as a force hostile
to the State, even if it represented a majority of the voters. In the
last prewar Reichstag elections of 1912 the Social Democrats
emerged as the strongest single party. More than 85% of the
electorate went to the polls, and of them more than one-third
voted for the Social Democrats, who received more than 4,200,000
votes and had 110 representatives in the Reichstag. The second
strongest party in votes and deputies was the Catholic Center
Party. In 1912 the Progressive Liberals, a democratic group to the
left of the National Liberals, received more votes than in any
previous Reichstag election. In addition four smaller parties in the
Reichstag were in opposition to the Bismarckian Reich—the Poles,
with eighteen deputies; the Alsatians, who in the course of more
than forty years had not become reconciled to their separation from
the French fatherland, with nine; the Guelphs who continued to
protest the annexation of Hanover by Prussia in 1866, with five;
and the Danes of northern Schleswig with one. Together the
opposition parties counted 276 out of a total of 397 deputies.

Twice in 1913 the Reichstag voted a motion of nonconfidence in
the Government, in January because of the expropriation of Polish-
owned estates for the purpose of settling German colonizers and in
December because of the famous Saverne affair. In that little
Alsatian town the long smoldering tension between Alsatians and
Germans came to a head as the result of the highhanded and
illegal behavior of German officers. The military and civilian
authorities backed and rewarded the officers, against the protests
not only of the Alsatians but of many Germans. The Chancellor

who defended the government point of view was Theobald von Bethmann Hollweg, a man of generally moderate and civilian views. Thus once more, to quote Professor Pinson, the camouflage character of German parliamentary institutions became manifest, and the source of real power was still there where Bismarck had placed it, in the Emperor and the high command. Throne and Altar as the seat of all power in the period of Metternich had been replaced by Throne and Army. It was hardly an improvement. "In Prussia," wrote Wickham Steed in *The Times* (London) of January 12, 1914, "the army is supreme, and through Prussia, the army rules Germany. This is the first lesson of the [Saverne affair] for those who lightly imagine the German Empire to be even as other states."

The Saverne affair demonstrated to Europe the military character of the German government and the semicolonial attitude which it assumed toward its Polish, Alsatian, and Danish citizens. Even a conservative professor like Hans Delbrück protested, out of deep concern for Germany's future, against this attitude. He was Treitschke's successor as professor of history at Berlin and as editor of the *Preussische Jahrbucher*. "If there really existed a way to transform the two and a half million Poles into Germans," Delbruck wrote in 1894, "one could then seriously discuss the government's policy. But . . . too many of our German politicians are like this: If only the word national is mentioned, they begin to roll their eyes, pound on the desk, and breathing hard they shout 'energy'! One would think that we are on the verge of declaring war on Russia, of conquering Holland, and of being obliged to transport all our Poles and also our Jews and Social Democrats to Africa." But instead, only some small scale measures were being taken. "In reality we would like to exterminate all the Poles, but actually we limit ourselves to expropriating several hundred Polish estates and paying the highest compensation; we annoy them with some language regulations, we do not appoint Poles to the better civil service posts, and we teach Polish children the German language in an unintelligent rather than an intelligent way. Away with such a policy of pinpricks, which is as unworthy of a great nation as it is useless."

To Delbrück it was inconceivable that less than half a century later the Germans would carry through some of the radical policies which were implied in the big words used at the turn of the century. But he realized that these extreme statements, though they were followed by no real action, did irreparable moral harm to

Germany. They proved, as a young German historian Annelise Thimme remarks in her brilliant biography of Delbrück, the existence of a spirit which if unloosed one day would have devastating consequences. The Prussian government, Delbrück wrote, received its proper coloring from the bureaucracy "which always saw only the immediate object, the authority which has to assert itself, the adversary who has to be crushed, but disregards the moral and other consequences which are out of its immediate province (*Ressort*)."

Delbrück was one of the most likeable among the German historians. Like practically all of them he started as an arch-conservative. As editor of the *Preussische Jahrbücher* he defined its position in 1884: "For the Emperor, against the Pope, against federalism, against parliamentarism and against capitalism."* In this programmatic declaration Delbrück did not even mention the socialists. Opposition to them was at that time tacitly understood. Like some other German historians, Delbrück slowly developed toward a more liberal conception, though his heart remained even in the 1920's faithful to the *ancien régime*. But more than other German historians he was sensitive to ethical questions. He condemned the persecution of minority groups not only because of the repercussions such a policy was bound to have on Germany's relationship with her neighbors but because of the deterioration of the German national character which he saw as a consequence of such a policy. "I regard the effect," he wrote in 1907, "of our policy against the minorities on the German national character as equally important and equally calamitous. We are facing the task of developing among us a more refined respect for law and a higher regard for the individual, in which respect we are manifestly lagging behind the English-speaking nations. But the acceptance of the principles which we employ in our policy against the minorities, even if one should regard them as politically necessary, blunt the respect for law among our officials, and in view of the fact that public opinion did not only not oppose but even approved our policy, this border war against the minorities depresses our whole ethical-political life and thus revenges itself upon us." Delbrück took a similar stand against the persecution of the Danish minority. He protested the expulsion of some Danes from northern Schleswig. "Even worse than the brutality which arouses the horror of the civilized world," he wrote in 1898, "is the delusion that we can

* *"Für die kaiserliche Partei, gegen den Papst, gegen den Partikularismus, gegen den Parlamentarismus und gegen den Kapitalismus."*

achieve by such means lasting successes in the struggle among nationalities." Turning against his fellow historian Erich Marcks, who supported extreme measures against the Danes, Delbruck sadly remarked in 1911: "This has been the essence of religious or political fanaticism· that it silences criticism and that it blurs, even on the part of men who are otherwise intelligent and reasonable, the insight into the simplest and most manifest facts."

But Delbruck never doubted that the Prussian German state was the best of its time. Like the other German historians he pressed forward for a German *Weltpolitik*. The continental hegemony achieved by Bismarck was no longer enough. In the interest of mankind, of civilization, of the freedom of the small nations Germany had to break British hegemony on the seas. Delbrück's demand for the construction of a powerful German navy took precedence over concerns for domestic policy and liberty. Later on he was not as incautious as many of his colleagues or Naumann were. Writing in the *Preussische Jahrbucher*, in 1905, he understood very well that it was the building of the German navy and not economic competition which provoked British fears. A defeat in a naval war with Germany would mean for Britain, Delbruck recognized, the end of her great power position. But he was determined that Germany should take a leading role in the future "War of the English Succession," which Max Lenz predicted at the time of the Boer War. Delbrück was convinced that out of England's defeat a new world balance of power would emerge in which Germany would be recognized as an equal by Britain on the seas.

Ludwig Dehio in his *Germany and World Politics in the Twentieth Century,* the most original reinterpretation of the international situation at the beginning of the century, has shown the influence on German *Weltpolitik* exercised by Ranke's theory of continental power-politics. It made the German historians, and through them public opinion, underestimate the strategic and moral role of maritime power. Therefore they could seriously believe that Germany in her war against England would find allies among all the smaller nations "We hope," one of them wrote, "that sooner or later, other nations who are oppressed by the yoke of English supremacy at sea will also pluck up courage and decide to shake off their yoke. It is our aim to complement the balance of power on land with the balance of power at sea. . . . The effects of German naval armament are clearly making themselves felt in the peripheral territories of the Pacific. Japan is developing into a position of power, and we may soon hear the cry, Asia for the Asians. The rise of Islam points in the same direction. The dream of a world governed by the white race is beginning to dissolve."* It was Germany's duty to help create this future by fighting England and her obsolete hegemony.

No one put it more strongly than Friedrich Meinecke who in republishing Ranke's "The Great Powers" interpreted the First World War as a German struggle against universal monarchy which he accused the British of wishing to establish. "Universal maritime supremacy is only another form of universal monarchy, which cannot be tolerated and must, sooner or later, fail. England is fighting against the spirit of modern development. . . . Her significance as a world nation and a world civilization, which we recognize, will not suffer if the balance of power, which she has tried in the past to restrict artificially within the limits of Europe, is extended to include the oceans and the world beyond. Only then will every nation have the free breathing space it requires."

German public opinion before 1914 was systematically prepared by historians and publicists for the War of the English Succession, for the moral need of a new division of the world, in which Germany had to play the leading role.** For her historical mission,

---

* In this passage, written in 1916, Otto Hintze meant by the white race primarily the English. Other German historians, like Erich Marcks, tried to frighten the British with the claim that the United States was more dangerous to England's future than was Germany. Marcks thought that the First World War might be followed by a struggle between the two Anglo-Saxon empires for Canada and Australia.

** The desire to replace England went back to the middle of the nineteenth century, though it was then expressed, not by scholars and certainly not by responsible politicians, but by men of letters. A prominent Viennese literary critic, Ferdinand Kurnberger, published in 1855 a novel *Der Amerikamude*, in which he portrayed a German immigrant disenchanted with America. Kurnberger himself was never in the United States His portrayal of the country, so different from that of Goethe, was influenced by the unhappy German poet Nikolaus Lenau, who had gone as a pioneer to the wilderness on the banks of the Missouri river and became understandably disillusioned. America seemed to him a vast continent where men and culture were doomed to decay. He anticipated Spengler's judgment when he characterized American life and institutions as typical examples of *Bodenlosigkeit*, lack of rootedness in the soil or nomadism

Kurnberger's hero shared Lenau's disgust with the United States. Living a quarter of a century later and having shared in the nationalist exuberance of 1848, he was also an enthusiast for Germany's unity and power. Envisioning the future of America and his share in it, he wrote: "What the German farmers in Pennsylvania were able to do unconsciously, to preserve German

296 THE MIND OF GERMANY

and not for the defence of her commerce, Germany needed naval
equality with the British. "Although foreign observers often over-
estimated the power of the Pan-German League in specific cases,"
Professor Dehio writes, "their suspicions later proved to have been,
on the whole, too modest. Though they may have exaggerated the
influence of the Pan-Germans in the Foreign Ministry, this influence was indisputably at work in the Admiralty, whose chief, and
not the Imperial Chancellor, was the man of destiny in the years
before the war." The common desire of those Germans who thought
about foreign policy—obviously a minority, though their ideas
trickled down to the masses through popular journalism—was to
eliminate English maritime supremacy.

Germany's hopes of mobilizing the lesser powers in a war
against Britain was in vain. Napoleon had harbored similar hopes.
He was convinced of the mastery of the world if he could conquer
Britain. In this struggle he claimed to represent the interests of
mankind and to defend the liberties of all peoples against British
universal monarchy. These peoples however did not agree: they
feared Napoleon and the French more than the English. The
English employed the advantages of commerce and inspired jealousy; Napoleon used the means of war and imposed tyranny. In
the chapter *"Du caractère des nations modernes relativement à la
guerre"* of his *De l'esprit de conquête et de l'usurpation dans leurs
rapports avec la civilisation européene* (1813), Benjamin Constant
saw in war the instrument of the past, in commerce that of enlightened civilization: "War and commerce are only two different
means of arriving at the same goal—the possession of what one
desires. Commerce is an attempt to receive by agreement what one
no longer hopes to conquer by force. A man who would always be
the strongest, would never think of commerce. It is experience
which, in demonstrating to him that war—this is to say, the
employment of his force against that of another—is exposed to
various resistances and checks, leads him to have recourse to commerce—that is to say, to a more pleasant and certain way of

life through a whole century so strongly that even today whole communities
of theirs do not understand one English word, should I be less able to do,
with my enthusiastic consciousness of German kind and culture? I am not
afraid of it. No, I shall last, a German in Yankeedom, and the fall which I
foresee for this racial mixture can worry me . . little." What seemed a
writer's phantasy around the middle of the nineteenth century, Germany's
rise in place of England, became at the end of the century the concern and
desire of influential German public opinion. *Der Amerikamüde* is interesting
today in the light of developments just prior to and following the First
World War

compelling the interests of others to consent to what accommodates his own interest. . . . Carthage, fighting with Rome in ancient times, had to succumb; it had the force of circumstances against it. But if the fight between Rome and Carthage were taking place today, Carthage would have the universe on its side (*Elle aurait pour alliés les moeurs actuelles et le génie du monde*)." Constant warned the French, unfortunately with as little effect as a similar warning to the Germans would have had later, against the spirit of military glory, an ancient and hallowed spirit but one opposed to modern civilization which was animated by the commercial instinct prevailing over "the narrow and hostile emotion which people masked with the name of patriotism." Constant called war a savage and passionate impulse, commerce on the other hand, a civilized and rational calculation. He called upon the French to draw closer to England, "that noble country, the generous asylum of free thought, the illustrious refuge for the dignity of the human race." Though Constant was not a man of lofty character he had a clearer insight into the forces of modern times and the aspirations of civilized people than most German historians who personally were men of much greater integrity.

The German philosopher Max Scheler added a pseudo-Marxian interpretation to the anti-English agitation which later became fashionable. Germany's struggle against Britain, transferred to the international stage, represented the rise of the proletariat whose revolutionary ethos was expelling the bourgeois *beati possidentes* from their paradise. In such a struggle Germany was to be supported, in their supposed self-interest, by all other have-not nations. But this was not to be. The German attitude before 1914 forced Britain into agreements with France and Russia. Before 1914, as before 1939, Britain made repeated efforts to arrive at an understanding with Germany. At both times she was rebuked. When she finally declared war on Germany, the majority of mankind was on her side. Germany's faith that the wind of history was swelling her sails as she set forth against England proved to be a miscalculation.

The War

DURING THE WAR Germany shifted her main targets. At the beginning there was an upsurge of anti-British feeling. The Germans had expected, and because of their feeling of superiority accepted, war against Russia and France. Twenty-five years later the same attitude prevailed with regard to Poland. However, Britain's declarations of war both in 1914 and in 1939 came as a surprise and—in spite of all the anti-British agitation in Germany which preceded the conflict—were regarded as treachery motivated by envy. *"Gott strafe England* (God punish England)" was the most popular German slogan in 1914. When victory against Britain was slow in coming and when the mighty German fleet proved of no avail and turned out to be a poor investment, the Germans shifted their arguments about their mission and purpose in the war. In his *Der Genius des Krieges* Max Scheler proclaimed that it was Germany's task to unite the whole continent against Russia. The other European nations would certainly realize that only a mighty Germany stretching from the Baltic to the Mediterranean could defend them against Russia's towering threat. In their claim that they were leading and protecting the West against the threat from the East, Napoleon's France and the Germany of Wilhelm and Hitler acted, to quote Professor Dehio, "like the man who sets a house on fire and then invites the other occupants to help him put it out." After 1918 Germany regarded France as her main enemy and German historians like Erich Marcks and Erich Brandenburg hoped to find in Britain an ally against France, while other Germans preached cooperation with Russia against the West.

At the beginning of the war Werner Sombart, one of the leading economists of his generation—once a Marxian socialist—gave classical expression to anti-British feeling. In his *Händler und Helden* he contrasted the nation of shopkeepers with the nation of heroes. The term itself was not of German invention. In his novel *The Young Duke* (1831) Disraeli had referred to the English as "indeed a nation of shopkeepers." As early as the eighteenth century a British economist Josiah Tucker in his *Four Tracts on Political and Commercial Subjects* (1766) wrote: "A shopkeeper will never get the more custom by beating his customers, and what is true of a shopkeeper is true of a shopkeeping nation." Heroes, of course, had interests and habits different from those of shopkeepers. Sombart stressed the ancient and dominant German tradition of love for war, condemned Kant's pacifist writings as senile, and regarded Nietzsche as "merely the last singer and seer who decending from heaven announced to us the tidings that from us would be born the son of God whom he called superman."

Sombart was wrong about Kant and Nietzsche; in his case an economist spurred on by war became himself a kind of dithyrambic

singer and seer. "German thought and German feeling," he proclaimed in 1915 in a typically Germanophilic fashion, "express
themselves in the unanimous rejection of everything that even
distantly approximates English or western European thought and
feeling. With deepest disgust, with exasperation and resentment the
German spirit has risen against the ideas of the eighteenth century
which were of English origin. Every German thinker, even every
German who thought in a German way, has always resolutely
rejected all utilitarianism and eudaemonism. . . . We must recognize everything which resembles western European ideas or which
is even distantly related to commercialism as something much
inferior to us."

Sombart dedicated his book to the young heroes fighting the
enemy and reminded them that the struggle must go on even
after they returned from the battlefield. "I pray that the ideas
contained in this book," Sombart wrote at the end of his dedication, "might become the seed which falls on fertile soil and will
bear fruit a thousandfold times." Sombart's wish was fulfilled. He
praised war as the greatest ethical force and Treitschke as the man
who had best described its moralizing influence. "Militarism is a
supreme manifestation of the heroic spirit. It is the highest form of
union of Potsdam and Weimar. It is Faust and Zarathustra and the
Beethoven scores in the trenches. . . . Above all, militarism means
the primacy of military interests in national life. Everything that
refers to military matters takes precedence with us. We are a
nation of warriors. The highest honors in the state are paid to the
warriors. . . . All other branches of the life of the people, especially
the economic one, serve military interests." *

Sombart welcomed the war as Germany's great opportunity
to heal the wounds western civilization had inflicted on her before
1914. Before the happy event of the outbreak of the war Sombart
confessed that, like so many others, he had been deeply pessimistic
about the future of culture. Now everything was changed. Great
times were here. "The miracle happened, the war came. A new

---

* *"Militarismus ist der zum kriegerischen Geist hinaufgesteigerte heldische
Geist. Er ist Potsdam und Weimar in höchster Vereinigung. Er ist Faust und
Zarathustra und Beethoven-Partitur in den Schützengräben. Vor allem wird
man unter Militarismus verstehen müssen das, was man den Primat der
militärischen Interessen im Lande nennen kann. Alles, was sich auf mili-
tärische Dinge bezieht, hat bei uns den Vorrang. Wir sind ein Volk von
Kriegern. Den Kriegern gebühren die höchsten Ehren im Staate. . . . Alle
anderen Zweige des Volkslebens dienen dem Militärinteresse, insbesondere
auch ist das Wirtschaftsleben ihm untergeordnet."*

spirit surged forth out of a thousand sources." It was the old German heroic spirit that had smoldered under the ashes. "We Germans [are culturally independent]. No people on earth can give us anything that we really need, in the field of scholarship, technology, art, or literature. From no people on earth can we learn anything about domestic policy, the constitution or administration. Let us think of the inexhaustible wealth of Germanism which includes every real value that human culture can produce." Sombart had no use for the idea of the good European. He did not wish the Germans to develop into Europeans, but into ever better Germans. "How," he asked, "could a European emerge from a mixture of a heroic German and a calculating Englishman? If a European would emerge who would think half as a shopkeeper and half as a hero, that would mean the elevation of the Englishman but the degradation of the German." That, of course, would not be desirable.

Sombart found it natural for England with her imperialist greed to expand. Germany, he asserted, had no similar desire. She was not driven by greed. "If it is necessary that we expand so that our growing people have space to develop, then we shall take as much land as we regard as necessary. We shall also put our foot where we think it essential for strategic reasons to maintain our unassailable strength. Therefore, if it is useful for our power position on earth, we shall establish naval bases in perhaps Dover, Malta, and Suez. Nothing more. We do not wish to expand at all. For we have more important things to do, we have to develop our own spirit, we have to keep the German soul pure, we have to take precautions against the enemy, the commercial spirit, invading our mentality. This task is tremendous and full of responsibility. For we know what is at stake: Germany is the last dike against the muddy flood of commercialism which threatens to cover all other people because none of them is armed against this threat by the heroic spirit (*Weltanschauung*) which alone provides protection and salvation."

A Slavophile like Dostoevsky might have written in much the same style, only he would have appealed to the truly religious and not to the heroic spirit. Again like the Slavophiles, Sombart proclaimed his people the chosen people of modern times. He showed a certain modesty by declaring that the Germans were "the chosen people of this century." He saw the Germans surrounded by hatred and incomprehension because they were the chosen people. "Now we understand," Sombart wrote, "why other peoples hate us. They do not understand us but they fear our tremendous spiritual superiority." Like the Slavophiles, Sombart was convinced that foreigners could not understand Germany. But he made exceptions for a very few prominent personalities,—perhaps he thought of Houston Stewart Chamberlain—"whom a kind fate has lifted up to the towering heights of the German spirit" (*die ein gütiges Schicksal in die Flughöhe des deutschen Geistes emporgetragen hat*).

A similar Germanophilism inspired many other German scholarly writings of the period. Max Scheler proved that the openly acknowledged war ethic of the Germans was superior to the cunning business ethic of the English. For spiritual, not for political, reasons Scheler praised the war against England. The war, he wrote, arouses the Christian ideal of love much more than peace does, which is only a nonwar of people who exchange goods and rely on the principle, Do nothing to me and I shall do nothing to you.* Scheler was even ready to accept England as a partner in a coalition led by Germany against Russia and the rest of the world— as soon as England was cured of her English malady, a malady which Scheler defined as an overvaluation of commerce and money making, of favoring the natural sciences above the humanities, of misunderstanding civil liberty.

It was quite clear that the views of Sombart and other leading German intellectuals did not make it easy for Germany to win moral support during the war. When Matthias Erzberger, a member of the Center Party, undertook such a task early in the war, he ran into almost insurmountable difficulties. One of them, as Klaus Epstein, Erzberger's biographer, writes, was "the utter indifference shown to what influential people in the neutral countries thought about Germany. To serve as propagandist for a nationalist, militarist, and semiautocratic country, whose war effort was challenging the liberties and equilibrium of Europe, was to assume a task where great successes could not be expected." **

---

* "*In diesem grossen Erlebnis aber liegt eine metaphysische Erkenntnisbedeutung des Krieges, . . Auf höchster Stufe geht uns in jener Gottinnigkeit heiliger Liebe, in der wir uns schon als Menschen, ja darüber hinaus als Inbegriff aller personlichen Geister, alle als Brüder und als Kinder eines gottlichen Vaters fuhlen und sehen, die ganze Ausdehnung des geistigen Reiches auf*"

** Even Erzberger started in 1914 with an extremist program which demanded the annexation of all of Belgium and the French channel coast; the acquisition of the iron ore of Briey-Longwy; the separation of Poland, the Baltic provinces and the Ukraine from Russia and their constitution as

On July 8, 1916, 1,314 intellectuals, among them 352 university professors, submitted a memorandum supporting the most extreme Pan-German war aims. The initiator of the petition was Reinhold Seeberg, professor of theology at Berlin University. Many thousands more sent in their signatures later. A memorandum drafted by Delbrück and opposing extreme annexationism received no more than 141 signatures. Only after the failure of unrestricted submarine warfare in July, 1917, could Erzberger have a very vague peace resolution adopted by the Reichstag and to this Ludendorff was bitterly opposed. But even the moderates who desired a negotiated peace hoped that it would open the door for further advances once Germany had recovered and, above all, disintegrate the western coalition. The struggle of the more moderate elements in the Reichstag to assert themselves did not help; it increased the "hopeless confusion that prevented Germany from developing any coherent foreign or domestic policy." The real power in Germany, though without any constitutional authority, remained in the hands of Ludendorff.

This whole spectacle increased the distrust of German war aims abroad. Returning from a trip into neutral countries, Delbruck recognized that "the fear of German despotism . . . was one of the most effective facts and strongest factors in favor of the enemy," which Germany had to take into account. He asked publicly whether the peace resolution of the Reichstag was ever meant sincerely. Two months before the German collapse Delbrück in vain implored the German government to repudiate the Pan-German demands. Even outside the Pan-German camp, German public opinion insisted at a time when defeat clearly loomed on the horizon upon Germany emerging from the war in so strong a position that no one and no coalition would ever again dare to attack her. Delbrück was one of the very few who dared to point out that a power which was so strong as to be superior to any coalition would represent a permanent and unacceptable threat to the outside world. "The world demands, and has a right to

satellites of Germany and Austria, the creation of a German African empire, including the Belgian and French Congo; and finally huge reparations of at least 10 billion marks and the payment of Germany's entire national debt, in addition to establishing funds to provide for German veterans and for their housing needs. Only gradually did Erzberger abandon these war goals. He remained a nationalist though with greater moderation until 1917. He had the wisdom, Professor Epstein writes, "unlike most of his annexationist colleagues, to abandon such foolish aims in the further course of the war."

demand," he wrote, "that the German people give it a guarantee, that the Pan-German spirit, the spirit of arrogance, of the cult of power, of paganism is no longer the German spirit." In quoting this passage Dr. Thimme added: "Today we shall hardly be able to say that this was an exaggeration. Rather, Delbrück underestimated the general acceptance of Pan-German thought." The events after 1918 proved how strong a hold Pan-Germanism and Germanophilism retained on the German mind.

Their disastrous effects were deepened by the acceptance of war as the supreme test of human worth and by the praise bestowed upon this attitude as a typically Prussian or German virtue. The defenders of this attitude acted from high idealistic motives. Characteristic in this respect was Walter Flex, a young officer who fell in battle at the age of thirty. Flex, who was born in Eisenach, a city in the Grand Duchy of Saxony-Weimar, embraced the ideals of Prussianism with great moral earnestness. Before the war he was tutor to Bismarck's grandchildren and played an active part in the German youth movement. Among his war poems, the "Oath to the Prussian Flag" achieved the greatest popularity. It idealizes the man who overcomes all love of self and every trace of self-will and devotes his whole life and soul to Prussia. The two lines

Wer auf die preussische Fahne schwört,
Hat nichts mehr, was ihm selber gehört.

(A man who swears an oath on the Prussian flag no longer has anything that belongs to him) were an inspiration to many young Germans before and after 1918.

Flex became even more popular through his war novel *The Wanderer Between Two Worlds* (1916).* It is the story of his friend Ernst Wurche, who was killed in battle and to whose memory Flex dedicated the book. When Flex visited the mother of his dead friend, she asked him softly after a long silence: "Did Ernst participate in an attack (*Sturmangriff*) before his death? I nodded yes. 'That was his great wish,' she said slowly, as if she rejoiced, despite her suffering, that something about which she had been long anxious had been fulfilled. A mother certainly must know what the deepest wish of her child is. And that must have been a

---

* The copy available to me shows that over 480,000 copies were sold. His collection of "poems and thoughts from the battlefield" called *Vom grossen Abendmahl* reached, in the edition available to me, a printing of 120,000 copies.

deep wish, about whose fulfillment she had been anxious even after his death. Oh you mothers, you German mothers!"

From the novel, which became a favored book with the youth of Germany, two sentences were widely quoted: "To serve as a lieutenant means living as a model for one's men; to show them how to die is of course only a part of this model life. Many men are capable of showing others how to die—but it will always be a much finer achievement to show them how to live. It is also more difficult. . . . How to remain pure and yet to grow to maturity—that is the finest and most difficult thing in the art of living." Wurche always carried in his knapsack a small volume of Goethe's poems, Nietzsche's *Zarathustra,* and the New Testament, all of them well-thumbed. He had intended to become a Protestant pastor and had just begun his theological studies when war broke out. His case, Professor S. D. Stirk points out, proves the close connection of the best kind of Prussianism with a definite and confident Protestant piety. Professor Pinson has shown the influence of pietism on the rise of German nationalism. There was in German Protestant nationalism a deeply ingrained religious enthusiasm and earnestness.

The elevation of nationalism to an almost religious personal pathos has rarely been so clearly experienced as by some idealistic German youth in 1914. Flex himself has referred to the religious character of his national devotion in a letter: "I am today as willing to volunteer for the war as on the day it broke out. I am willing not, as many think, out of national but out of ethical fanaticism. What I wrote of the eternity of the German people and of the world-saving mission of Germanism (*der welterlosenden Sendung des Deutschtums*) had nothing to do with national egoism but is an ethical faith which can realize itself in the defeat or as Wurche would have said, in the death in battle of a people. . . . I have always maintained that human development reaches its most perfect form for the individual and his inner development in his love for his nation. I believe that the German spirit reached in August, 1914 a height no other people had previously seen. Happy the man who stood on this peak and does not need to descend again. This is my faith, my pride, and my happiness, which lifts me above all personal worries."

As religion has done in the past, nationalism too can misuse and pervert some of man's noble sentiments. A cosmopolitan tolerance alone can prevent these misuses and perversions. But Germans were little inclined to such a tolerance, for which pragmatic people—

or shopkeepers as Sombart called them—are perhaps better predisposed. Defeat in the First World War did not disillusion the Germans in their ideals. On the contrary, it confirmed them in their belief in their distinctness and in the moral superiority over their victors. Again this one-sided perspective led them to overestimate their strength and to despise and challenge the West.

Chapter Twelve

OUT OF CATASTROPHE

The Weimar Illusion

THE GERMAN NATIONAL ASSEMBLY, meeting at Weimar in the summer of 1919, adopted the new German constitution. The democrats, brought into power by the disastrous imperial policy, indulged in optimistic illusions. The Socialist Minister of the Interior, Eduard David, was convinced that "not only political but economic democracy as well is anchored in it [the constitution]. . . . Nowhere in the world is democracy more consistently achieved than in the new German constitution. . . . The German Republic is henceforth the most democratic democracy of the world." Konstantin Fehrenbach, a member of the Center Party and president of the National Assembly, added: "We now lay the constitution in the hands of the German people, whom we have made thereby the freest people on earth." But a democracy is not made by a constitution; traditions of liberty under law, which become part of the moral and social climate, are its premise. Such traditions existed in Germany, but they had not become part of the national mores and were without vitality. They were unable to assert themselves against nationalist pride and passion. Nationalism, the drive for national power and unity, undermined democracy after 1918 as it had done in 1848.

The antidemocratic forces asserted themselves immediately in the National Assembly by insisting that the republic was simply the continuation of the Reich. The Kaiser had gone, but his Reich remained. The liberal author of the constitution, Hugo Preuss, defended this view with the characteristic words: "The word, the thought, the principle of the 'Reich' has for us Germans such deeply rooted emotional values that I believe we cannot assume the responsibility of giving up this name. Traditions of centuries, all the yearning of a divided German people for national unity are bound up with the name 'Reich,' and we would wound the feelings of wide circles without reason and to no purpose if we gave up this designation."

The lack of strong democratic traditions was made more calamitous by two unexpected factors to which Professor Pinson has drawn attention. During the years of the Weimar Republic, a period of political weakness, cultural life was superior to that of the Bismarckian age: it was more dynamic and advanced on a broader front "Germany recovered its position of intellectual eminence even more rapidly than it achieved economic recovery. During the first years following the end of the war Germany seethed with new and experimental movements. Berlin and Munich soon came to rival Paris as the cultural meccas for artists, literati and scholars." But this sudden effervesence tended to confuse and irritate rather than to exhilarate the German mind, accustomed as it was to discipline and order. Practically all the new movements and trends were radical, whether to the left or the right. They depised and rejected the middle road, reasonableness, and common sense, the live and let live, the practical art of politics, the foundation of democracy.

One of the most interesting of these literary movements was Expressionism, so named in 1914 by Hermann Bahr. Its style was explosive and often ecstatic, its contents a mixture of reality and superreality. It corresponded to a certain extent to *futurismo* in Italy and Russia and to the beginnings of *surréalisme* in France. But nowhere was the movement so numerous and influential as in Germany. It was full of apocalyptical expectations of a coming great transformation of man and mankind. Its two most prominent periodicals, *Sturm* and *Aktion,* founded around 1910, set its tone. In the first period which covered the four years from 1910 to 1914, Expressionism was full of prophecies of war or revolution or both. In the next four years the expressionist writers interpreted the war as a world conflagration, a divine judgment of the world, a cosmic *dies irae,* out of the chaos of which a new cosmos would be born in terrifying labor pains. Among the early representative works of the movement were Georg Heym's poem "Der Krieg" (1911), Ernst Stadler's "Der Aufbruch" (1914), and Kasimir Edschmid's *Rasendes Leben* (1916). The most talented members of the movement were the poet Franz Werfel and the dramatist Georg Kaiser.

Expressionism entered its last stage after the war and came to a close by 1924, when a wave of prosperity ended, for the time being, the feverish radicalism of the preceding fifteen years. Some of the expressionist writers like Johannes R. Becher became Communists, others like Hanns Johst and Kurt Heynicke became National Socialists, while still others accepted their disappointment over the nonrealization of their utopian hopes for a transformation of mankind.

The second astonishing postwar factor was the sudden brutalization of German political life. "Where did such brutality come from," Professor Pinson asks, "to a people who had a reputation for discipline and order and whose history lacked any such manifestations since the time of the Peasants' War? How were such cruel and unrestrained outbursts of political passion possible in a country described by Heine as a *fromme Kinderstube und keine romische Mördergrube?*" The war of course did its share as did the example set by Lenin's revolution. But German traditions of extolling power played their role too. What had held them in check before was the equally traditional awe before throne and church. The throne was now gone and the church had been losing influence for many decades. A similar collapse of traditional authorities unchained elemental brutality in Russia in 1918. Neither Germans nor Russians had been accustomed to self-restraint by democratic checks and balances. They had relied on authority to maintain order, on the *Obrigkeit*. After 1918 no recognized authority developed in Germany capable of making the people feel that there was a state to be venerated and obeyed, as they had been accustomed to. The government of the Weimar Republic lacked the brutality and the messianic appeal to mass instincts which characterized Lenin's government. The Weimar government inspired neither awe nor utopian hopes. There were no heroes and no heroics. The German people missed them. Actual power and intellectual authority in the Weimar Republic remained in the hands of the unregenerated bureaucracy, the university professors, the judiciary and the army officers, who in their overwhelming majority looked longingly to the past. They rejected the parliamentary regime on principle. It was not only alien; it seemed to fail in what was to them the decisive factor,—to provide an "efficient" government to restore German power and to unify the German people for the inevitable resumption of the power struggle. Treitschke,

Meinecke wrote, "had influenced as hardly anyone else had, the attitude and ideas of the leading strata of German society before the November [1918] Revolution," and the same attitude and ideas continued to determine the policy and mentality of the influential circles in the Weimar Republic.

The universities were centers of nationalism. In 1919 Reinhold See-berg, a leading theologian of Berlin University, began the official memorial service for students who had died in the war with the words: *Invictis victi victuri,* To the undefeated, the defeated ones who will be the future victors. Later the School of Medicine of the University of Königsberg, where Kant had taught, bestowed on Ludendorff the honorary degree of Doctor of Medicine. The citation read: "To the master of strategy whose art has saved the health and life of innumerable German warriors from hostile guns; . . . to the leader whose strong arm carried the immaculate glory of the German arms and the splendor of German culture from the shores of the Atlantic to the Arabian desert; to the hero who protected the German people who were surrounded by a world of greedy enemies, with the sharp blows of his undefeated sword, until the people, trusting false words, abandoned its unbroken arms and the strong leader; to that German, whose image, shining forth from the darkness of the present, gives us faith in a future savior and avenger of our people." No school of medicine anywhere has ever succeeded in packing so many dangerous legends and false-hoods into one citation. Unfortunately, these legends and false-hoods were accepted throughout Germany. They were based on the dominant *Weltanschauung* of the Bismarck period: they made it possible for the Germans to welcome Hitler.

When theologians and physicians made up their minds to in-terpret history, historians had to have their say. After 1918 the great majority of German historians, instead of re-examining the founda-tions of the Bismarckian Reich and of the Ranke tradition, set their hearts on the vindication of the past and on the fight against the war-guilt lie. In a surge of self-pity and self-justification, many German intellectuals viewed the world situation as if it had begun with the Allied crime of Versailles. Even leading national liberals like Hermann Oncken, the biographer of Ferdinand Lassalle, put all their talents at the service of the nationalist attack upon the consequences of the defeat. The powerful autosuggestion of having been wronged in history—in comparison with the western nations —created a sense of living in a unique situation which justified unique measures.

Max Lenz, who after many years as professor of history in Berlin taught history at the relatively liberal University of Hamburg, published in 1922 a collection of addresses under the characteristic title *Wille, Macht und Schicksal* (Will, Power, and Fate). He regarded Germany's situation as *Knechtschaft* (serfdom). In an address, "Bismarck as a Prophet," he praised what was the weakest point in Bismarck's foreign policy after 1871, his attitude toward the Poles. "Who among our enemies," Lenz asked, "who three years ago tore parts of Germany's soil out of the body of our Reich and people, inflicted the worst on us? . . . We had to suffer the greatest humiliation, the greatest and most unbearable ignominy at the hands of the Poles . . . these Sarmatians who never were able to create anything out of their own strength. . . . That we shall never forgive or forget."

The whole essay was a paean to Bismarck's immaculate creation of the Reich. "Iron and blood has created our Reich. Iron and blood had to decide [in 1918], whether we could breathe freely in the world or would have to live henceforth in servitude and misery." Bismarck might have been a good prophet; Lenz was as poor an educator of his people as Treitschke. It was the reliance on iron and blood which made Germany lose her two great wars. Nor was Germany henceforth to lead, as Lenz asserted in 1922 that she would, a life of servitude and misery. Within three years, with the help of her former enemies, she was on the high road to economic recovery and fifteen years later she was rich and strong enough to challenge Europe again. What led Germany, then, into another period of servitude and misery was that reliance on iron and blood which Lenz and so many others preached as salvation. Where did Lenz find the root of Germany's misfortune after the First World War? In democracy. In an hour of weakness, he insisted, the German Emperor promised his people to introduce parliamentary democracy. Thereby he himself broke the scepter which Bismarck had forged and extinguished the will to power and the faith in the right of might. The political parties could now rise to influence in Germany, and with Germany's enslavement their rule began. "Because our Will languished, our Power was broken, and Fate decreed what only our Will could have averted." Rarely has the faith in will and power as the foundations of political and moral life been so clearly proclaimed as by Professor Lenz. In this spirit the official organ of the National Socialist youth movement was ten years later called *Wille und Macht.*

Professor Lenz set the general tone for most German scholars "Delusion kept us from any sober recognition of the true causes of our failure," Professor Dehio writes about the German historians after 1918. "No critical analysis was made of our limited possibilities in the realm of power politics. The defeat was ascribed to the deceit of our enemies, and to errors and treason at home We brooded over our defeat, but in order to prove to ourselves that it was undeserved, not to understand why it was deserved."

The collapse of November, 1918 was entirely unexpected In the spring of 1918, after they had imposed the annexationist peace of Brest-Litovsk on defeated Russia, the Germans were certain of the coming victory. Until the very end the official bulletins did not reveal the true situation. Ludendorff and Tirpitz continued to be venerated as heroes. Yet in November, 1918 Germany signed the armistice of defeat. Dynasties vanished What had seemed so secure collapsed. The Germans did not ask, What was our share in bringing about this war, which we expected to win and which we welcomed and praised as long as it promised victory? Instead they asked: How could it end in defeat? Throughout the war, the Germans had demanded vast annexations and indemnities. Professor Hans W. Gatzke's recent book, *Germany's Drive to the West,* recalls what even Germany's victims so easily forgot Now, after their own extreme demands, which were not officially disavowed, and after the peace of Brest-Litovsk, the Germans showed themselves sincerely disturbed by the peace treaty of Versailles. How could the enemies do that to them, to the Germans? Did it not prove the immorality of the West, the hollow pretensions of all its talk about justice and civilization? The better people had lost the war: if there was justice in the world, their hour had to come. German interpretation of history became even more one-sided than it had been, more German-centered, less world-open. German military valor was overevaluated, that of the enemy nations was ignored. Germans asked themselves. How could so many sacrifices go unrewarded? That the other nations had made sacrifices too, was overlooked. Even chivalry among soldiers—which had existed in Germany too—seemed dead.

Germany and Russia

INSPITE OF ALL THIS SELF-PITY, Germany emerged fundamentally un-
weakened from the war and the peace treaties. Mutual jealousies
and recriminations among the western allies, the creation of so
many new small nation-states on Germany's eastern and southeastern border, the bolshevization of Russia—all these factors made
Germany's position stronger than it had been in 1914 and seemed
to make it easy for her to reassert her hegemony, this time not by
naval competition but by eastward expansion. Communism and
Fascism added a new passionate element to political life, an element
which by its nature encouraged the dynamism of wronged or
frustrated nations. Communism, Fascism, and German national
aspirations were one in their desire to destroy the order established
in 1919 and to undermine the unjust position of the senile western
democracies. "The great gamble on the disintegration of the
western bourgeois world" was facilitated by western disunity and
disarmament, by widespread intellectual cynicism and indifference,
and, a few years later, by the economic depression.

Practically all the liberals and socialists in the Weimar Republic
supported the program of eastward expansion. They all desired
Anschluss with Austria and the annexation of former German or
German-inhabited territories in Poland and Czechoslvakia Thus
Germany after the loss of her first world war would be much stronger
than before its start. By the occupation of Vienna she would gain a
position from which she could economically and strategically
control the Danubian basin and the Balkans. She would thereby
gain the firm continental basis which would enable her to resume
the world war with much better prospects for enduring victory.

Under the circumstances the future relationship with Russia
occupied after 1918 a much larger place in German thinking than
it did in the West. Two roads seemed open to Germany: was she
to achieve her future greatness in co-operation with or in a life-
and-death struggle against Communist Russia? The final answer
to this question was given only on June 22, 1941.

As early as December 21, 1914, after the defeat of the Russian
invasion of Eastern Prussia, General Hans von Seeckt, later the
Commander-in-Chief of the Reichswehr and the foremost ad-

vocate of Russian-German military co-operation against the West, wrote: "The decisive question is What nation could be our best springboard against England? The answer, in my judgment, is and must be for a long time to come the determining factor in our policy. There is no other choice because I think a real end of the struggle with England now is out of the question. [A decision] will probably be postponed and then be reached in a second and third explosion. . . . France would be a welcome ally, and geographically speaking, the choice would be easy. But France is a weak ally even if we can have her. Therefore Russia. She has what we don't have. All forces can be concentrated on the final struggle with England. *On ne se marie pas avec un cadavre?* Let's wait and see. Certain powers have an inexhaustible vitality. Our thirst for revenge in East Prussia might be quenched by blood in Poland." Two years later, in a letter to Seeckt, Walter Rathenau advocated a similar eastward policy. "The German-Russian combination," says Professor Erich C. Kollman in summing up Rathenau's letter, "would make all Balkan countries, including Turkey, dependent on these great powers, give them an outlet to the Mediterranean, and lay the foundations of a future policy toward Asia. Without the Russian alliance, German political activity and expansion in the Near East and the Balkans would be only a poor and most unsatisfactory substitute."

Their common opposition to the West, and their common hatred of the new Poland brought Germany and Russia together after 1918. In a memorandum addressed in July, 1922, to the then German Chancellor Joseph Wirth, Seeckt declared that Poland's very existence was "incompatible with the vital needs of Germany." Three months before, on Easter Sunday, Rathenau, as German Foreign Minister, had signed the Treaty of Rapallo with Soviet Russia. Though the text of the treaty was innocuous enough, it marked a decisive success for Soviet policy. It ended Russia's isolation and it bore out Lenin's prediction that Soviet Russia would grow by exploiting the fundamental differences among the imperialist nations. In Germany the Rapallo treaty was welcomed as a sign of a new independent power-policy which represented a break through the circle of enslavement imposed by Versailles. But the pacifist and left-wing weekly *Die Weltbühne* warned: "At a moment when after four years of war and three of postwar confusion, the European powers have assembled in order to take counsel as to their future, Germany—apart from Russia the one country utterly dependent on the help of others—commits this escapade and isolates herself voluntarily, excludes herself from the conference table, rises in opposition to all other powers . . . and falls again under the suspicion that she is the disturber of peace in Europe."

Much still remains unknown about the co-operation between the armed forces of Germany and Soviet Russia which began as far back as 1923. From that time on the Reichswehr produced weapons forbidden to Germany under the Treaty of Versailles—military aircraft, poison gas, tanks and heavy artillery—in Russia. Both powers profited from this co-operation. It facilitated the secret German rearmament which in violation of the peace treaty went on under all the Weimar governments from 1919 on; it brought to Russia the benefit of the most modern technology in armaments. When Gustav Stresemann a few years later sought a rapprochement with the West to facilitate Germany's plans in the East, he followed the Locarno treaty with the West by a treaty of friendship with Russia concluded in April, 1926.

Germany's Russian policy after 1918 was motivated not only by political and strategic considerations. Many German intellectuals felt a stronger sympathy for Russia than for the West. Such a sympathy was expressed by others than Thomas Mann. Ricarda Huch wrote from Munich in February, 1919: "Do you know what always strikes me here? How much sympathy there is among intellectuals for Bolshevism, for the ideas which are its foundation, and not for the Russian methods. And I too believe that the changes here will have to be more radical than it seems now. . . . The opinion that the Germans are called to carry through what Russian Bolshevism would like to do but cannot do, appears to me correct. Germany will again have the task of being the mediator between East and West." Russia's hostility to the West, the supposed youth of the Russian nation, the Bolshevik method of violence, of ruthless determination and of self-confident élan, appealed to many young Germans. In the 1920's Germany—and not France or Italy—had the strongest Communist party outside Russia. In the elections of September, 1930, the party received over 4,500,000 votes, and two years later, in November, 1932, it reached almost 6,000,000 votes.

An interesting German development was National Bolshevism. It never achieved any numerical strength. It was a movement of intellectuals, not of the masses. Its most prominent spokesman was Ernst Niekisch, who resembled in many ways the radical-revolutionary conservatives. His confused thought represented many sentiments and resentments prevailing in Germany after 1918; the hatred against the West and Versailles, the loathing of capitalism and the bourgeoisie, a pride in German barbarism compared with the sated civilizations of Rome and the Occident, and finally the impatient demand for something fundamentally new. Originally a Marxist, Niekisch tried to fuse Marxism with an extreme German nationalism. His weekly *Resistance* propagated a socialist-nationalist-revolutionary policy of emancipation from all western and bourgeois influences, from Romanism and Americanism, and an alliance with Russia or any other force which wished to destroy western civilization.

In many ways Niekisch, like Spengler or Jünger, shared the fundamental attitudes of National Socialism and influenced them. But more courageously and radically than the two others—animated by a stronger ethos than they—he turned against Hitler, publicly and openly, and suffered many years in concentration camps. In 1932 he published a pamphlet *Hitler—ein deutsches Verhängnis* (*Hitler—a German Fatality*) in which he sharply attacked him as the culmination of Wilhelminian Germany and not a new beginning, and as a demagogue without true Prussian discipline. In his anti-Russian policy Hitler seemed willing to repeat the old mistake of playing the East against the West. Niekisch was convinced that such a policy would fail. Only with Moscow could Potsdam triumph. "The Russian-Asian bloc is so full of energy that the future probably belongs to it," Niekisch wrote. Only Prussianism with its ascetic ideal of duty could by co-operation with the Russian-Asian bloc hope to preserve some of the European cultural values for the future.

"It is difficult to remain sober when so many are intoxicated," Niekisch wrote in the introduction to his pamphlet against Hitler. "It pains one not to be able to hope and believe with others at a time when hardly anyone doubts any longer. But the force of numbers cannot relieve a man from responsibility when he must account to his own conscience. No one is allowed to keep silent when he sees an abyss while others are still blind. Many will be hurt; they may comfort themselves by being allowed to live on in a state of intoxication. They do not worry about the future of our nation. The man who can't help worrying has to speak up." Niekisch had called upon the young Germans who had returned from the front to have "courage to face the abyss" (*Mut zum Abgrund*). Too late he saw that the forces which he had helped to unleash were driving Germany into a spiritual and moral abyss.

Like Nietzsche and Lagarde, Niekisch was a man of integrity. Yet he prepared the way for an entirely unethical demagogue bent upon achieving personal political power, whom the people welcomed because he realized in a debased form the revolution of nihilism, which better men had prepared. Germany had talked herself, through her intellectuals and historians, into an intoxication of despair, feeling unjustly wronged and compensating for it by great expectations.

During the First World War the historian Otto Hintze threatened: "If worse comes to worse, we shall let ourselves be buried beneath the ruins of European civilization." After the war the conviction became general that man—at least in central and eastern Europe—lived in a time of transition, which would usher in an unprecedented new age, provided man freed himself from the fetters of the past, from the restraints of civilization, and surrendered to the idea of his destiny. To achieve the break-through to the new age, everything appeared permissible. In his play *Die Massnahme* (*The Measures Taken*, 1930) Bertolt Brecht wrote:

> With whom should the just not join
> To forward the cause of justice?
> What kind of medicine tastes bad to the dying?
> What kind of depravity would you not bring about
> In order to root out depravity forever?—
> Yes, submerge us in filth,
> And embrace the executioner,
> But transform the world!
> It needs it!

A Democracy with Few Democrats

THE WEIMAR REPUBLIC CONTINUED—and outdid—the characteristic traits of the Reich. With an understandable distrust the outside world watched the developments in Germany. That the Germans resented defeat and the peace treaty was understandable. France had equally resented the defeat and peace treaty of 1871. The Third Republic was born under auspices as unfortunate as those of the Weimar Republic: collapse of an empire; loss of national territory; imposition of a huge war indemnity; civil war. But less than a decade after 1871 the republic was firmly established, republicans were in power, and French intellectuals defeated, in the Dreyfus affair, the attempt to reintroduce militarism, authoritarianism, and a self-centered nationalism. In France, too, such trends emerged repeatedly to impose themselves, in spite of their anachronism, upon France, for the sake of imperialism and *gloire*. But the French republic, born out of defeat and the deeply resented peace treaty, lasted seventy years.

The Weimar Republic lasted hardly a decade. In France the Imperial Marshal Maurice de MacMahon, a courageous soldier, an esteemed conservative patriot who led a simple and unostentatious life, and a man devoid of any capacity for statecraft, was forced out of the presidency in January, 1879, to make room for a convinced republican. In Germany in April, 1925 in the first popular election, the Imperial Marshal Paul von Hindenburg, another honorable conservative without any political capacity, was elected Reichspresident. He was not forced out by the German republicans and democrats but confirmed as their representative in 1932. In that role he helped Hitler to power. In the elections of 1930 and even more so in those of 1932 the parties of the right and left, opposed to the republic, received the majority of seats. In 1925 and again in 1930 the majority of the people rejected the democratic republic.

Many Germans blamed the Allies for the weakness of democratic Germany. The truth, however, was that the essential framework of the Treaty of Versailles was not upheld by the Allies. One concession after another was made to the Weimar Republic: the sympathy of the world turned toward Germany; German complaints and the German interpretation of the war were accepted at their face value, especially in Britain and the United States; economic assistance permitted Germany to modernize her industrial structure to a point beyond that of her former enemies. By the end of the twenties Germany impressed every visitor as being much better off than Britain, France, or Belgium. Splendid new housing projects, schools, hospitals, parks, monuments, official buildings, and post offices adorned every German city. Amidst all this ostentatious wealth the Germans regarded the payment of reparations for the wanton destruction which their armies had done in the war as an unjust imposition. They continued to complain about the disastrous consequences of the peace treaty. This failure on the part of the educated German classes, even more than their unfamiliarity, with, or dislike for democracy, wrote the death warrant of the Weimar Republic.

The lament of so many decent, conservative, liberal, or socialist

Germans about the burdens and cruelties inflicted by the Allies upon an innocent Germany, which even in defeat proved its moral superiority, undermined democracy in Germany and facilitated the rise of Hitler. When the world economic crisis, which wrought greater havoc in the United States and Britain than in Germany, reached the latter country, it too was ascribed to the Versailles Treaty. The Germans refused to see that unemployment was as high and bankruptcies as numerous in America as in Germany. This self-centered view prevented a democratic or evolutionary solution of their economic problems. The catastrophe which in German opinion had fallen upon their country in 1918 had assumed in their imagination such a unique and radical character, that it could be solved only by something more radical than they imagined possible in 1914.

From the beginning the Weimar Republic was undermined by the bureaucracy, the judiciary, and the universities on which a government has to rely. It could perhaps have consolidated itself if it had not been subject to irresponsible criticism. The Weimar Republic—like the Giolitti cabinet in post-First World War Italy and the Fourth Republic in post-Second World War France—was accused of inefficiency and corruption at home and above all of lack of militant vigor abroad. Critics on the right and left incessantly attacked the republic with great impatience and sharp wit for its alleged or real shortcomings. The corruption in the Weimar Republic and in Italy under Giolitti was, however, very minor compared with the corruption in the Fascist regimes which came to power after having held up to ridicule the slowness, moderation, and venality of the preceding systems which they did not deign to honor by the title of government. Their nationalist policy of empire and glory proved to be, in the long run and in spite of initial successes, disastrous for their nations. The constant carping at parliamentarianism rendered the republic contemptible in the eyes of the people and weakened its will to defend the people's liberties. The masses grew weary of all politicians, except those who proclaimed themselves to be something better than politicians and promised to lead the nation to a wonderland of national glory. This devaluation of political life and of democracy was intensified among the Germans by the leading publicists of the post-First World War period. They did not look for a restoration of the ancien régime as most older Germans did; they were conscious of a revolutionary change which they interpreted in a peculiar Germanophile fashion. They were often highly gifted men and scholars who all did their share in leading the Germans from the defeat of 1918 to the infinitely greater disaster of 1933. By all kinds of arguments they proclaimed the inevitably approaching doom of western democracy and the coming age of authoritarian-. ism and military glory, until the Germans, easily seduced by metaphysical phrases, believed them and tried to live accordingly.

Amidst the general trend away from democracy, there were, however, individuals and groups in Germany who opposed the race to the abyss, who rejected Germanophilism and who upheld the validity of universal values. Some drew from the experience of the war conclusions different from those of the majority of their countrymen and turned away from a narrow nationalism. Forty years before, Karl Christian Planck, a philosopher in Württemberg, had hoped for such an outcome in his *Testament eines Deutschen,* published in 1881, one year after his death. He predicted the coming of a great war which he saw as an inevitable result of Bismarck's foundation of the Reich; at the end of the war he expected Germany's rejection of the power-state and her return to her older traditions. "If such a universalist people, situated in the heart of Europe," he wrote, "forms in sharpest contrast to all its preceding history a centralized unified nation-state and thereby establishes for all other nations the example of increased armaments, what, in an age of acute nationalism, can the consequence be but a total conflict? Yet this conflict may lead to the understanding that an order based upon nation-states is insufficient. Such an order can certainly not apply to the universal position of the German nation which lives intermingled with many non-German elements. From this understanding this bloodiest of all wars will draw its lasting significance. It will open the mind of the nation, which today is concentrated on external interests and power, for its true vocation. Amid blood and tears the insight will grow, that the mere nation-state and its acquisitive national society can never bring peace and reconciliation."

The war of 1914 did not bring about the change of heart which Planck had hoped for. Most German historians continued proudly to affirm the separation of German from western political thought. They regarded liberalism and pacifism as forms of hypocritical utopianism in which the demon of power "hides its true face behind the mask of justice." The German Machiavellian *Machtstaat,* on the other hand, based its right frankly upon its "immanent power drive and vitality." But there were some who like Planck warned that German thought had, for the last one hundred years, taken the wrong path, and so sought to direct it back to the older traditions which it had held in common with the West. Among them was Ernst Troeltsch, a Protestant theologian who drew out of the experiences of the First World War the lesson that western utopianism was less utopian than the Machiavellian power-state, and that moral forces, though they never appear in history in anything approaching perfection, help to shape history more enduringly than military successes.

Even during the war Troeltsch insisted that Machiavellianism was heathenish. He opposed the dominant conviction that sacrifices for national greatness and heroic courage were moral values in themselves. Writing to the liberal Protestant theologian Martin Rade, editor of the excellent weekly *Die Christliche Welt,* Troeltsch asked him to join an organization to combat Ludendorff's emphasis on "victory and the full enjoyment of victory." He complained that his fellow Protestants did not wish to join the organization because its stress on moral principles and on reasonableness seemed to them sentimental. Instead they preached a theology of war and extreme annexationist demands, referring to Luther as their authority (*Hier herrscht die Kriegstheologie und die schneidige Annexionspolitik mit der Berufung auf Luther als den nationalen Mann*). With Delbrück and a few others, Troeltsch tried to moderate the German demands for war gains.

After the war Troeltsch went farther. In a lecture on "The Ideas of Natural Law and Humanity" (1922) he insisted that behind the present practical controversies between Germany and the West arose the more permanent problem of the contrast between German thought—in politics, history, and ethics—and that of western Europe and America. Western thought was rooted in a long tradition from Stoicism and Christianity to the Enlightenment. German thought had fully shared in this development until the beginning of the nineteenth century when "the typically German romantic counter-revolution" rejected the premises of western thought. In this German thought, Troeltsch wrote, "the State becomes the embodiment of a particular spiritual world as it exists at a given time, and the justice and law it enforces also become particular and positive. . . . The result of this view is a total and fundamental dissolution of the idea of a universal Natural Law; and henceforth Natural Law disappears almost completely in Germany. . . . Morality . . . becomes altogether a matter of the inner self, in its own particular spiritual substance. The moral code is distinguished not only from the rules of Law, but also from the demands and requirements of social well-being. This concept . . . made Law something which lay outside the bounds of morality. . . . This demoralized Law was associated . . . with the idea of a spiritual and divine essence inherent in the community. This meant a deification of the actual particular State. . . . The whole of this line of argument assumed the inequality of individuals. . . . It placed leadership in the hands of great men, from whom the spirit of the Whole essentially radiated, and by whom it was organised. . . ."

Troeltsch did not underrate the great contribution which German romantic thought had rendered to our understanding of history. But this positive achievement had led to dangerous consequences because it was not balanced by an awareness of supranational values. As a consequence "the conception of a wealth of unique National Minds turns into a feeling of contempt for the idea of Universal Humanity: the old pantheistic deification of the State becomes a blind worship of success and power; the Romantic Revolution sinks into a complacent contentment with things as they are. . . . The political thought of Germany is marked by a curious dualism, which cannot but impress every foreign observer. Look at one of its sides, and you will see an abundance of remnants of Romanticism and lofty idealism: look at the other, and you will see a realism which goes to the verge of cynicism and of utter indifference to all ideals and all morality; but what you will see above all is an inclination to make an astonishing combination of the two elements—in a word, to brutalize romance, and to romanticise cynicism."

Troeltsch demanded a more universal outlook on the part of German historians, a greater regard for the political and ethical forces which dominated the nineteenth century western development, and which had been treated by German scholars "with an ill-advised antipathy, which astonishingly combines an exaggerated romanticism with a habit of reliance on Prussian militarism for the support of law and order." Troeltsch warned that the Germans must no longer neglect the theory of the Rights of Man, rights which are not the gift of the state but the ideal postulates of the state, and indeed of society itself, in all its forms, and that they must accept the indestructible and moral core at the heart of the League of Nations. "We may clearly see its difficulties and its abuses: we may seek with all our strength to overcome them, but what we cannot do, and must not do, is to deny the idea itself, its ethical significance, its connection with the philosophy of history." By accepting western universalism and humanitarianism, the Germans, Troeltsch maintained, would only recover ideas which they had allowed themselves to lose and adapt their thought to the vastly altered conditions of the modern world.

In the final part of his lecture Troeltsch regarded the enthusiastic reception of Spengler's book as proof of how little the Germans were yet prepared to do this, and how much the current was flowing in the opposite direction from that which he advocated. Spengler, Troeltsch wrote, "is encouraging men to formulate, in their extremist form, all the deductions which can be drawn from Romantic aestheticism and Romantic ideas of individuality, to foster the cause of scepticism, of amoralism, of pessimism, of belief in the policy of force, of simple cynicism. 'Decay' (*Untergang*) is indeed a consequence which follows logically on such a basis; for with such ideas in their minds men simply cannot exist, or fight the battle of the future. Spengler's book is an absolute confirmation of the reproaches which western Europe brings against us· it is nothing less than a hauling down of the flag of life in the course of man's perpetual struggle to keep it flying. He who desires to survive—and our nation *does* desire to survive—can never go in that direction."

In his postwar political writings Troeltsch drew the consequences of his broader vision: he warned that the time of world power politics for Germany was past. "Even the splendid French power position of today appears to me hollow and deceptive," Troeltsch wrote in February, 1921. "All European states will have to renounce world policy backed by military power (*grosse Welt- und Militärpolitik*) and will have to establish themselves on the basis of an international treaty system, which will allow them to promote their spiritual and economic forces within a framework set by the non-European world powers. For France, too, the hour of resignation will come. Europe's salvation depends on its not coming too late for all concerned. Our own hour is now. . . . I write this down at the risk of being attacked as un-heroic and of lacking the true Prussian spirit." Unfortunately Germany did not heed Troeltsch's warning after the First World War, and France did not heed it after the Second World War.

One year later, Troeltsch protested against the German policy of playing communist Russia against the West or vice-versa. He warned that co-operation with Bolshevism against the West would lead to cultural catastrophe (*Untergang unserer Kultur*). The only reasonable policy, he wrote, was Germany's close co-operation with the West, in spite of the harsh peace treaty. "I do not wish to make a secret of the fact that I can see salvation only in the Anglo-Saxon system." Germany needed not a new Yorck but a new Talleyrand.* Germany must not set any hope in her militarism. As a viable system it was clearly finished because the war had revealed its insufficiencies: its political and military strategy had failed and the obsolete relationship between officers and soldiers had undermined its morale.

Troeltsch's premature death at the beginning of 1923 was a loss to Germany and to the western world. A lecture on "Politics, Patriotism and Religion," which he had prepared for delivery in England, ended with a warning against German radicalism and with a tribute to the spirit of English politics: "Many of us in Germany regard 'compromise' as the lowest and most despicable means to which a thinker can have resort. We are asked to recognize a radical disjunction here, and to choose either *for* or *against*. . . . Among you in England, the principle of compromise is given its due. Political experience and the influence of empirical systems of thought have given you a different outlook, though you have not lacked your uncompromising thinkers, from the Puritan fathers to the disciples of Rousseau, Tom Paine, and Bentham. In spite of a natural distaste for purely empirical philosophy, I have found this a particularly attractive and instructive feature of your literature.

"It is thus easier for me to confess my adhesion to the principle of compromise here than in my own country. I know of no other principle and I am unaware of any practical thinker who does. It is true, however, that in the use of compromise we have to guard against all precipitate capitulation to the course which presents itself as momentarily expedient, or as the easiest way out of a difficulty, but which may be thus expedient and easy only for the moment, and, once more, we have to guard against any fundamental abandonment of the ideal. Indeed, it is only by keep-

---

* Count Yorck von Wartenburg was a Prussian Field Marshall who commanded the Prussian corps in Napoleon's Grande Armée and after Napoleon's retreat, deserted the French and concluded an agreement with the Russians which put the Prussian army on their side against Napoleon It was the beginning of Prussia's War of Liberation. Talleyrand, on the other hand, reintegrated France, after her revolutionary struggle for hegemony and defeat, into the European system.

324 THE MIND OF GERMANY

ing this ideal ever before our eyes that we can continue to hope and
to strive for a better future in the midst of a cold and sinister
world."

Troeltsch was not the only representative of the German educated
classes who, independent of all party politics, understood the need
for the integration of Germany into the general stream of western
civilization and policy. Men as different in their points of view as
the Catholic Kierkegaard scholar Theodor Haecker, the radical
publicist Carl von Ossietzky, and the Eastern Prussian regional
novelist Ernst Wiechert agreed on this one point.

While most German historians after 1918 supported an extreme
nationalism, Max Lehmann, a Prussian through descent and upbringing, took the opposite stand. He was the well-known biographer of the Prussian general Scharnhorst and the Prussian reformer
Freiherr vom Stein and the editor of the political testaments of the
Hohenzollern princes. He was also Prussian state archivist and
instructor at the Prussian War Academy before becoming Professor
at Göttingen. At the end of a long life of scholarship devoted
to the study of Prussian history, he interpreted Bismarck to his
students in a way which contrasted sharply with that of Treitschke
and Marcks. His lectures were not published until 1948, almost
twenty years after his death. They are not primarily an original
contribution to scholarship; their significance as a human and
German document can hardly be overstressed. This septuagenarian,
who had lived through the events from 1866 to 1918, wrote his
lectures with astonishing forcefulness, ethical warmth, and psychological penetration. His western point of view proves, if proof
be needed, that the human spirit is not determined by origin or upbringing. The old man freed himself from the fascination with
success, from the belief in the supposed Machiavellian necessities of
political life and in the moral autonomy of the *raison d'état.* "The
historian should not only try to understand success and victory," he
wrote, "he fulfills his high task completely only if he makes an
effort to do justice to the vanquished, too." Though Lehmann wrote
several years before Hitler's name became known, the reader of his
book will be impressed by the similarities in the German reaction
to the achievements and appeal of Bismarck and Hitler, despite the
unbridgeable differences in origin and personality between the two
men.

It may suffice to mention three other representatives—by the way,
all of them Prussians—of the western and antimilitarist spirit in
the Weimar Republic. They belonged to three very different realms

of life—an aristocratic diplomat; a scholar and teacher; and a professional officer who turned poet The first of them, Prince Karl Lichnowsky, formerly German ambassador to Britain, warned toward the end of the First World War: "Is it not understandable for our enemies to declare that they will not rest until a system is destroyed which represents a permanent menace to its neighbors? Must they not otherwise fear that they will be obliged after a few years to take up arms again and to see their provinces invaded and their cities and villages destroyed? Were not those men right who predicted that the spirit of Treitschke and Bernhardi dominates the German people, a spirit which glorifies war as an end in itself and does not abhor it as an evil, that in Germany the warrior caste rules and that it, and not the civilian gentleman, determines ideas and values?" Thus Prince Lichnowsky restated out of his own experience what the German historian Gervinus had predicted in 1870 as the most likely outcome of Bismarck's policy.

None attacked more radically the thesis that the *raison d'état* requires and excuses actions and attitudes which do not conform to general ethical standards than Friedrich Wilhelm Förster, the son of a professor at Berlin University who himself became an educator and teacher of ethics. He saw in the glorification of the *raison d'état* the original sin of German thought. Around 1910 he pointed out that the sabotage of the Hague Peace Conference by German diplomacy would only strengthen the general distrust of Germany. During World War I he denounced before his students at Munich University the spirit of power politics. "We must," he said publicly, "abandon national egoism and join a new European cultural order." At that same time the faculty of philosophy of the University protested against Forster's opinions which should "make every German blush." With great courage Förster insisted that the reports about the German atrocities committed at the time of the invasion of Belgium in 1914 were true, and that more than 4,000 innocent hostages had been executed. After the Second World War German historians of the younger generation confirmed from documentary evidence not only that the atrocities— widely believed in the United States to have been fabrications of British war propaganda—were actually committed, but that they were not provoked by Belgian *franctireurs*.

Early in 1919 Förster was in Switzerland as minister of the shortlived Bavarian Republic. From there he wrote his father that the continuation of the blockade was not due to devilish wickedness but to the scarcity of food in France and Switzerland and to the paucity and disorganization of transportation facilities, caused by the devastations of war. "In France the people sit weeping amid their ruins and do not know how to rebuild it all. If the Germans knew what has happened in France, they would think differently of what happens to them now." Prophetically he concluded the letter: "I have not lost faith in Germany. But I must think of the words which Hilty * wrote in 1906: 'The German people will have to pass through much suffering before they will turn away from their idols.' Now everything will depend upon whether the Germans recognize in the peace treaty the natural consequence (*Reflex*) of what we have done for the last fifty years or will see it only as the shameful vileness of the Allies. . . . I shall do my share that the correct interpretation of recent history not be forgotten." Förster did his share, despite the bitter hostility and derision with which he was met. After 1918 he proposed to the then Chancellor of the Reich that a few hundred thousand German volunteers be called up to help rebuild Belgium and northern France. During the Weimar Reich Forster called attention in his periodical *Die Menschheit* (*Humanity*) to German secret rearmament. Förster lived long enough—he passed his ninetieth birthday in 1959—to witness· his heretical interpretation of recent German history being shared by a growing number of Germans in the German Federal Republic.

The third of the critics of Prussian-Bismarckian traditions was Fritz von Unruh, a Prussian officer whose ancestors had served in a similar capacity. The war taught him to question the moral concepts on which he had been brought up. In his story *"Opfergang"* a soldier commented upon duty, the sacred word of the Prussian tradition: "It is certainly a fine word and overcomes all personal feelings. But what lies behind it has degenerated. Duty is the cancer in the heart of the [German] people." In his verse play *Ein Geschlecht* Unruh stressed the orgiastic and destructive passions let loose by war. Whereas Flex admired the mother who willingly sacrificed her son for the state, in Unruh's play the son curses the mother in whom he sees a tool of the state producing sacrifices for the state. There were many Germans in the Weimar Republic who turned against militarism and extreme nationalism; some of them were sincere democrats, others decent conservatives who upheld general moral standards, but they were too few and

---

* Carl Hilty (1833–1909), professor of law at the University of Berne, Switzerland

too poorly organized, devoid of any fighting spirit, and unsupported by any strong traditions to be able to stop the race to the abyss.

Into the Abyss

WITHIN LITTLE MORE THAN A DECADE German intellectuals succeeded in leading the German people into the abyss. They could not have done so except for the generations of preparation, in which Germanophilism and antiwesternism became more and more characteristic of German thought. In its last stage, German nationalism rejected not only western civilization, but the validity of civilized life. "The new nationalism," Ernst Robert Curtius warned in 1931, "wishes to throw off not only the presently so much maligned nineteenth century, but all historical traditions." Extreme nationalist thinkers in France—Charles Maurras or Maurice Barrès—never went so far as to turn against civilization. In Germany the anti-intellectuals were not the mob but leading intellectuals, men frequently of refined taste and great erudition.

Looking at everything purely from the German point of view, they became convinced that western civilization was everywhere as deeply undermined as it was in Germany. From partial observations they drew the most sweeping conclusions. They identified their situation as they interpreted it, with that of mankind, even with that of the universe. Gottfried Benn had no doubt that the Quarternary period of geological development was coming to an end, that homo sapiens was becoming obsolete. No expression was extreme enough to voice the hatred of western civilization, of liberalism, of humanitarianism. The philosophy of Martin Heidegger, the political theory of Carl Schmitt, the theology of Karl Barth—all these convinced the German intellectuals that mankind had reached a decisive turning point, an unprecedented crisis, into which liberalism had led man. These intellectuals looked down upon the West with the same contempt later displayed by the leaders of National Socialism. At the same time they were arrogantly certain that German thought, because of its awareness of the crisis, was the only thought worthy of the new historical epoch.

In the introduction to the fourth edition (1941) of his

Literaturgeschichte der deutschen Stamme und Landschaften
Josef Nadler wrote that the Germans had never before been so
passionately and so exclusively the people of thinkers and poets
as in the quarter of a century from 1914 to 1939, during which they
went through an experience which made them incomprehensible to
other people. His work, Nadler maintained, proved that the German people was called, on the very strength of its unique experience, to become the trustee (*Treuhander*) of the whole European
community of nations. "And thus it should be, as it is [1941] or it
should not be at all." (*Und also moge es sein, wie es ist, oder es
soll nicht sein*). No wonder that Nadler had no use for Goethe.
He regarded him as long outdated, addicted to form alone, which
meant for Nadler supreme sterility.

Nadler's judgment of Goethe revealed, as Walter Muschg
pointed out, that Nadler had hardly any feeling for poetry.
Nietzsche, who was a great artist himself, understood not only
Goethe but also the meaning of form in art. In his *Human, All Too
Human* (I, 221) he praised the French dramatists for the strict-
ness of form which they imposed upon themselves. "Thus one
learns step by step to walk graciously even on narrow planks
which bridge dizzying abysses, and acquires greatest suppleness of
movement. . . . Lessing held up to scorn in Germany this French
form, which is the only modern art form, and pointed to
Shakespeare." Thereby the Germans lost the possibility of a continuous development from the necessity of strict form to the
appearance of freedom. German poetry fell back into naturalism,
into the earliest stages of art.

"From this Goethe endeavored to save himself, by always trying
to limit himself anew in different ways; but even the most gifted
only succeeds by continuously experimenting, once the thread of
development has been broken. . . . After Voltaire, the French
themselves suddenly lacked the great talents which would have
led the development of tragedy out of the constraint of form
to the appearance of freedom. Later on they followed the German
example and lept into a sort of Rousseaulike state of nature in
art and experimented. It is only necessary to read from time to
time Voltaire's *Mahomet,* in order to perceive clearly what
European culture has lost forever through that break in tradition.
Voltaire was the last of the great dramatists who controlled with
Greek proportions (*Mass*) his manifold soul, which was equal
even to the greatest tragic storms He was able to do what no

German could, because the French nature is much more akin to the Greek than is the German. Voltaire was also the last great writer who in the wielding of prose possessed a Greek ear, a Greek artistic conscientiousness, simplicity and grace. He was also one of the last men able to combine in himself greatest freedom of mind and an absolutely unrevolutionary way of thinking, without being inconsistent and cowardly. Since then the modern spirit with its restlessness and its hatred of moderation and balance came to dominate all fields. . . .

"True the 'senseless' fetters of Franco-Greek art have been thrown off, but unconsciously we have grown accustomed to regard all fetters, all limitations as senseless, and thus art moves towards its disintegration and in so doing it reverts to all the phases of its beginnings, its imperfections, its former audacities and excesses. . . . Does not Goethe's mature artistic insight in the second half of his life say practically the same thing?—that insight by means of which he made such a bound in advance of whole generations, that it may be said that Goethe's influence has not yet begun and that his time has still to come. Just because his nature held him fast for a long time in the path of the poetic revolution, just because he drank to the dregs of whatever new source had been indirectly discovered through that breaking down of tradition, . . . his later transformation and conversion carried so much weight. It showed that he felt the deepest longing to recover the tradition of art and to restore, with the imagination of the eye at least, the ancient perfection and completeness to the ruined remnants and colonnades of the temple, when the strength of the arm should be found too weak to build, where such tremendous powers were needed even to destroy."

The classical understanding of tradition, so alive in Goethe, was lost in the 1930's in Germany as it was in Russia. "Art" became "popular," "new," and utilitarian; form did not count. Nadler could object to Goethe because "a man like him could not transform a people." Now the people were being "transformed"; at least their spokesmen were proud of it. A highly regarded German periodical, *Hochschule und Ausland,* which was devoted to contacts between German and foreign universities, changed its title in April, 1937 to *Geist der Zeit* (*The Spirit of the Times*) and stated with becoming modesty in its editorial: "There is no nation in Europe and there has never been one outside Greece, in which the spirit was so alive as it is today in Germany." But the German in-

tellectuals were wrong when they mistook their spirit of the times
for the actual spirit of the time. In their Germanophile dislike
of the West they misread history.

Outside the world of the universities, Moeller van den Bruck,
Spengler, Jünger, and the circle around *Die Tat* were the foremost
influences shaping and expressing German thought in the Weimar
Republic. For all their personal differences their fundamental
attitudes were much alike. Though they acknowledged Nietzsche's
influence they parted company with him by linking the future of
man with the German power-state and Prussian military virtues.
Nietzsche believed in, and overdid, the freedom of the individual.
His later self-styled followers found the fulfillment of the individual in his subservience to an irrational force. Spengler was
convinced, as he wrote in December, 1917 in the preface to the
first edition of his *magnum opus, The Decay of the West (Der
Untergang des Abendlandes;* the usual translation of *Untergang* by
decline is much too weak), that he was writing *"the* philosophy
of our times." In the preface to the revised edition (December, 1922)
he felt the urge to name once more those to whom he owed "practically everything," Goethe and Nietzsche. The claim to these two
great ancestors was typically German. In reality, Spengler had
no affinity with Goethe and distorted Nietzsche. But less proudly
than in 1917 when he regarded his work as "the philosophy of
our times," he now called it *"a German philosophy."* No critic can
take exception to this; no one could imagine Spengler's philosophy
as being other than *a* German philosophy.

Moeller, Spengler and Jünger believed that the lost war would
turn into a German victory, if the Germans would realize that
they represented the spirit of the times. Moeller began as a literary
critic and the foremost German translator of Dostoevsky. The
war turned him from a cultural into a political philosopher. In
The Right of Young Peoples which appeared early in 1919, he
asked recognition for the right of young nations to expand. They
had new ideas, while the aged West was a continuation of the
outdated eighteenth century. Among the young peoples Prussia
was to assume leadership. "The time will come once again in
which all peoples that are young, in which everyone who feels
young, will recognize in Prussian history the most beautiful, the
noblest, the most manly political history of all European peoples."
Moeller disagreed with Spengler on one point; for him history
was not subject to any deterministic law. History was the story
of the incalculable; there was always the possibility of a fresh

beginning. The young peoples were characterized by their will for what the German nationalists called *Aufbruch*, breaking camp, a passionate departure toward the new historic age. "Mankind has always been a new departure (*Aufbruch*) to which it made up its mind without being sure of the way, let alone the goal." In Moeller's writing, to quote Roy Pascal, "despair takes on the form of strength and confidence, insecurity turns into fanatical faith, emotive passion disguises itself as sceptical realism, arbitrary judgments are given the standing of metaphysical truths, revolt against past and present appears in the form of a philosophy of history, adventurism clothes itself in the robes of Destiny."

Neither the theory of young or proletarian peoples nor the voluntaristic interpretation of history, the glorification of movement in itself, was typically Prussian or German. Italian nationalists had proclaimed the Italian nation a proletarian nation in the international context. The nationalist movement led by Enrico Corradini demanded before 1914 subordination of employer and worker to the nation. The Fascist movement did not start from a doctrine nor had it a definite goal, as Mussolini himself admitted in his famous article on Fascism in the *Enciclopedia Italiana*. It was an *Aufbruch*, a march into the future, determined by irrational forces. "Life is not actually what it is, but what it ought to be," Giovanni Gentile, the philosopher of Fascism, wrote with words which could have been written by Moeller, "a life altogether full of duties and difficulty, which always demands efforts of will and abnegation and hearts disposed to suffer to render possible the good: the only life worthy of being lived. An antimaterialist conviction, essentially religious."

In 1923, two years before he committed suicide, Moeller published his most influential book *Das Dritte Reich*. The title cannot be translated as *The Third Empire*. It is the essence of the Reich to be much more than an empire. There are several empires, there can be only one Reich. "German nationalism," Moeller wrote, "is a champion of the final Reich: ever promising, never fulfilled. . . . There is only One Reich, as there is only One Church. Anything else that claims the title may be a state or a community or a sect. There exists only The Reich." In building the Reich, the Germans were not working for themselves but for Europe. Their Reich was urgently needed for western civilization had not elevated but debased humanity. "In the midst of the sinking world which is the victorious world of today, the German seeks his salvation. He seeks to preserve those imperishable values, which are imperishable

in their own right. He seeks to secure their permanence in the
world by recapturing the rank to which their defenders are
entitled At the same time he is fighting for the cause of Europe,
for every European influence that radiates from Germany as the
centre of Europe. . . . The shadow of Africa falls across Europe.
It is our task to be guardians on the threshold of values."
    Moeller called the Reich "a fine old German idea which goes
back to the Middle Ages, and is associated with the expectation of
a one-thousand-years-Reich." This Reich will be a truly socialist and
antiliberal Reich. The third chapter of Moeller's book carried as
its motto the significant words "Through Liberalism the People
Perish." German socialism had nothing in common with Marxian
historical materialism and international class war. It was the national solidarity of a people exploited by foreign plutocracy; it
was the idea of selfless service to the common good instead of the
pursuit of personal profit. "Where Marxism ends," Moeller wrote,
"there begins socialism: a German socialism, whose mission is to
supplant in the intellectual history of mankind all liberalism.
German socialism is not the task of a Third Reich. It is rather
its foundation." Moeller accepted Lenin's antiliberal and anti-
plutocratic revolution as a national socialism peculiarly suited to
Russia and was ready to co-operate with it provided that Russia
directed her expansion toward Asia and conceded Germany's
mission in the German-Russian borderlands.
    The idea of a German socialism was widely discussed after 1914.
In 1922 the economist Karl Pribram wrote on German nationalism
and German socialism in the *Archiv für Sozialwissenschaft und
Sozialpolitik*: "Perhaps one can say, reversing the materialist interpretation of history, that German socialism represents the revolt
of the masses against the economic system created by a commercial
middle class whose thinking has always remained alien to the
people in general, not only to the workers, but to the peasants, the
officials, and the armed forces. That makes it understandable that
from the beginning the planned war economy with its stringent
regulations was willingly accepted by the people [in Germany]
and why the ideas [of a planned national economy] were enthusiastically praised as the ideas of 1914. They were nothing fundamentally new. They had been dominating Germany for a long
time. They had been accepted by German nationalists as well as
by the working class. But it was only during the war when in
order to support the armed struggle, everything which intellectually
and morally separated the Germans from the enemy was em-

phasized, that the Germans became conscious of the fact that the individualistic nominalism which was characteristic of the ideas of 1789 had always remained alien to a large majority of the German people. . . . They began to discover the outline of a true socialism in the German mind (*Geist*), in the German economy, in the German constitution and administration, a socialism which demanded from the German people a definite ethos (*ethische Gesinnung und Haltung*)." German socialism meant the voluntary absorption of the individual will into the will of the whole, into the *volonté générale,* the renunciation of selfish profit for the good of the whole.

Oswald Spengler in his *Preussentum und Sozialismus* (1919) went a step further. "Only German socialism is real socialism!" he proclaimed. "The old Prussian spirit and socialism, although today they seem to be opposed to each other, are really one and the same." Spengler's early and relatively short book remained unknown to the English reading public but captivated many more German readers than the two stout volumes of his chief work. The ideas propagated in *Prussianism and Socialism* were as Spengler himself stated, the seed (*Kern*) out of which his whole philosophy developed. *Prussianism and Socialism* is a basic book not only for the understanding of Spengler but for the understanding of the Weimar period. Naturally, Spengler contrasted his socialistic Prussians with the individualistic, money-conscious Englishmen, where each was for himself, whereas in Prussia all were for all. When the English worked, they did it for the sake of success; the Prussians worked for the sake of the task to be performed. In England wealth counted, in Prussia the performance. Marx's socialism was deeply influenced by English ideas. Marx, like the English, did not think in terms of the state but of society. To him as to the English work was something to be bought and sold, a merchandise in the market economy, whereas to the Prussian all work, that of the highest official down to that of the lowliest laborer, was a duty, performed as a service to the community. For Spengler Frederick William I, the Prussian soldier-king of the eighteenth century, and not Marx was "the first conscious socialist." Only Prussia was a real state and therefore a socialist state. "Here, in the strict sense of the word, private individuals did not exist. Everyone who lived within the system, which worked with the precision of a good machine, was in some way part of the machine."

Spengler went far back into history to explain the difference between the English and the Prussians; the English character stemmed from plundering Vikings, the Prussian character from the dedicated Teutonic Knights. In spite of his often brilliant and often spurious historicism, Spengler's writings were not intended to be detached scholarship; they were *littérature engagée*. His *Prussianism and Socialism* was a fervent appeal to German youth, launched in the hour of defeat and despondency. "I count in our struggle," he wrote in the introduction, "on that part of our youth which feels deeply, behind all the idle talk of the day, . . . the unconquerable strength which marches on in spite of everything, a youth . . . Roman in the pride to serve, in the humility to command, demanding not rights from others but duties from oneself, all without exception, without distinction, to fulfill the destiny which they feel within themselves. In this youth there lives a silent consciousness which integrates the individual into a whole, into our most sacred and deepest, a heritage of hard centuries, which distinguishes us from amongst all other peoples, us, the youngest and last of our civilization. To this youth I turn. May it understand what thereby becomes its future task. May it be proud, that it is allowed to do it."

Spengler's appeal to youth became even more fervent at the end of the book: "I call upon all those who have marrow in their bones and blood in their veins. . . . Become men! We do not want any more talk about culture and world citizenship and Germany's spiritual mission. We need hardness, a bold skepticism, a class of socialist mastermen. Once more: socialism means power, power, and ever and again power. The road to power is clearly marked: the most valuable among the German workers must unite with the best representatives of the old Prussian political spirit, both determined to create a strictly socialist state, a democracy in the *Prussian* sense, both tied together by a common sense of duty, by the consciousness of a great task, by the will to obey in order to rule, to die in order to win, by the strength to make tremendous sacrifices in order to fulfill our destiny, to be *what we are* and what without us would not exist. *We* are socialists. We do not intend to have been socialists in vain."

Spengler's philosophy of history was concisely expressed in a passage in his *Prussianism and Socialism:* "War is eternally the higher form of human existence, and states exist for the sake of war; they express their readiness for war. Even were a weary and lifeless humanity desirous of renouncing war, it would become instead of the subject of war, the object of war for whom and with whom others would wage wars" The same theme was repeated in the second volume of Spengler's *The Decay of the West*, which appeared in 1922. There he wrote: "Life is harsh. It leaves only one choice, that between victory and defeat, not between war and peace." And in the last book that he published, eleven years later, *The Hour of Decision*, he repeated with almost Hitlerian repetitiveness: "Struggle is the fundamental fact of life, is life itself. The weary procession of reformers, leaving as their only monument mountains of printed paper, is now ended. . . . Human history in the period of highly developed civilization is a history of political powers. The form of this history is war. Peace is only . . . a continuation of the war by other means. . . . A state is the 'being-in-form' of a folk, which is formed and represented by it, for actual and possible wars." This oversimplified "philosophy" of history carried Ranke's precedence of foreign over domestic policy to an extreme which becomes manifestly absurd. Civilization and religion, institutions and constitutions, economy and domestic welfare no longer count in history, only foreign policy, which itself is reduced to war and preparation for war. Wars are no longer exceptions or incidents in history, they are now the central fact of life and history, their meaning and fulfillment. The first modern nation to understand this, in Spengler's opinion, was Prussia. On this understanding her claim to leadership in the new age was based. "Prussian," Spengler wrote, "is above all the unconditional precedence of foreign policy over domestic policy, whose sole function is to keep the nation in form for this task."

The first volume of *The Decay of the West* was conceived before the outbreak of the war of 1914 and was finished in 1917, at a time when the Germans still expected victory. It found a publisher only with difficulty. The second volume appeared in an entirely changed atmosphere in 1922. It brought comfort to the Germans. The victorious West was doomed. The future belonged to the martial races. Spengler predicted the coming of new caesars who with their warrior elites would break the dictatorship of money together with its political weapon, democracy. Before the breakthrough of elemental forces, the intellectual world built up by the conscious mind would vanish. History has always sacrificed truth and justice to might and vitality and doomed people to whom truth was more than deeds, and justice more than power, Spengler taught. Was he even empirically right? Did not the Jews survive after the days of their great prophets and the second destruction of their state because they preferred justice to power? But Spengler had the indomitable will to dominate history by anticipating it. Thus he set forth the future he desired as inescapable. "The essential therefore is to understand the time for which one is born." Only he who senses its most secret forces will be of the stature of accomplishing the task of historical necessity. To Spengler, as to Hegel and Marx, history was subject to inexorable laws; his laws however, did not belong to the realm of the idea or of society but to biology. Whoever understands and accepts them, will be the master of the future. He can face the world, which is full of uncertainty and confusion for the others, with the confidence of victory. *The Hour of Decision* carries as a motto Wotan's words from Wagner's *Siegfried:* "The Norns weave doom on the world's loom; they can change nothing." Like Marx, Spengler was bent on unmasking the real moving forces in history and in men. But Marx believed in men, while Spengler was a nihilist. "Contempt for humanity is the essential requirement for a profound knowledge of it," he wrote. But too great a profundity can blind us to the obvious.

Professor Hans Barth pointed out the fundamental contradiction in Spengler. He did not believe in reason, the mind, the spirit (*Geist*) which were to him an anachronism, and yet he presented a highly intellectualized philosophy himself. He hated "paper" and longed for deeds, he hated the "bookworm" and longed for life. "I have taken my stand in full consciousness on the other side, the side of life and not the side of thought." Yet he tried to overcome literature by more literature, thought by more thought. When the youth upon whom he called tried to translate his thought into life, Spengler shrank back from life and its stark aspects. His books fascinated many by the daring of their vision and the brilliancy of their style. The rise of Mussolini and Hitler seemed to bear out his prediction of the coming of an age of caesars. In reality democracy survived the assault. Spengler understood neither the strength of communist Russia nor of democratic America. He found both fundamentally alike. He expected, in all seriousness, that they would unite for a war against Britain. But the effect of his writings had little to do with their truth. They intensified the German contempt for liberalism, tolerance, and humanitarianism and justified it by a philosophy of world history which proved the inevitable decay of western liberal values. Spengler died in 1936, before he could witness where his call to the beast in man would lead.

The political theories which Spengler proclaimed as a seer were put forward on a more scholarly footing by Carl Schmitt, professor of international and constitutional law at the University of Bonn and the most influential German teacher of public law for two decades. His writings, related to those of Spengler, introduced a new concept of politics which received its meaning not from what has been considered the normal life of society but from extreme situations. No longer did the normal aim to control the abnormal. The abnormal, the exceptional, that which had previously been the *ultima ratio*, determined and directed the normal. "One can say that here as elsewhere," Schmitt wrote in his *Der Begriff des Politischen* (*The Concept of the Political*, 1933), that "the exceptional case has a particularly decisive meaning and reveals the heart of the matter. . . . From this most extreme possibility the life of men gains its specific political tension." In his theory about the origins and legitimacy of justice, which he called decisionism, Schmitt proclaimed that justice should be determined by the legislator who has the power to realize and enforce the decision. Ideal justice and positive law are discarded as norms of lawmaking Starting from the extraordinary situation, the *Staatsnotstand* ("*Not kennt kein Gebot*," Necessity recognizes no Law), which demands the disregard of abstract justice or of the existing positive law, Schmitt applies this abnormal case to the normal course of existence. Right is thus always dependent upon the concrete situation and has its source in the decision with which the supreme power-authority meets the situation. "*Jegliches Recht ist Situationsrecht*" (Each law corresponds to a concrete situation). As each situation is unique and concrete, there cannot be any general and abstract norm. Each decision is valid only for its own situation. Justice becomes the function of the power which makes the essentially political decision; political and judicial functions are no longer separated, although political decisions continue to be made to appear as judicial ones. But in practice, and frequently in theory, the judicial function is subordinated to the political. In 1936, in his address to the Deutsche Juristentag, the Convention of German Jurists, Rudolf Hess repeated Treitschke's words: "*Alle Rechtspflege ist eine politische Tätigkeit*" (All justice is political).

This exaltation of life over law, of the instinctive necessities over conscious control—in Spengler's terminology of *Dasein* over *Wachsein*—ends in a precarious existence on the rim of the abyss. Carl Schmitt based his concept of politics on the inescapable antagonism between friend and enemy, an antagonism as fundamental as that between good and bad, or between the beautiful and the ugly. Political conflicts are, therefore, for Schmitt not rationally or ethically determined or solvable; they are existential conflicts in which existence itself is at stake. "The enemy is in the existential sense another and alien, with whom in the extreme case conflicts are possible in which existence itself is at stake. Such conflicts cannot be decided by a general agreement previously concluded, nor by the judgment of a third party which is not involved and therefore impartial. . . . Enmity is existential negation of the existence of another."

For this political theory war is a high point of political life and of life in general; the inescapable friend-enemy relation dominates all life. "The culminating points of great politics," Schmitt writes, "are the moments in which the enemy is visualized in concrete clarity as the enemy." This political philosophy corresponds to the supposed primitive combative instinct of man who tends to regard anyone who stands in the way of the realization of his desires as a foe who has to be done away with. Traditional western statesmanship, on the other hand, consists in finding the ways and means to overcome the primitive instinct by patient negotiation, by compromise, by an effort at reciprocity, above all by the acknowledgment of universally binding laws.

The totalitarian philosophy of war was well summed up by Schmitt: "War is the essence of everything. The nature of the total war determines the natural form of the total state." Understandably, Carl Schmitt looked back upon the nineteenth century with utmost contempt as a "century full of illusion and fraud." In his ideal state of the twentieth century, which apparently was free of illusions and fraud, the totality of life is subordinated to armed conflict. In this spirit Professor Karl Alexander von Müller, the editor of the *Historische Zeitschrift*, the official organ of German historians, ended an editorial about the war in the issue of September, 1939, with the words: "In this battle of souls we find the section of the trenches which is entrusted to Germany's historical scholarship. It will mount the guard. The watch word has been given by Hegel: The spirit of the universe gave the command to advance; such a command will find itself blindly obeyed." Professor von Müller knew, as did Professor Schmitt, what the Spirit of the Universe, the *Weltgeist,* and naturally also the *Zeitgeist* and the *Volksgeist,* commanded. They blindly obeyed.

Like Spengler and Schmitt, Ernst Jünger, a writer who had no pretension to scholarship, saw in life and history not a meaning but a pattern, determined by violence. He was the only one of the

three who saw war service. As a youth in 1914 he volunteered and
joined an infantry regiment. During the four years he spent in
the trenches he was awarded high military decorations for exemplary courage. For the next twenty years Jünger published a
number of well-written books, all of them glorifying total war as
the most powerful expression of the totality of life. The titles of
his books—*In Storms of Steel, War as an Experience of the Soul
(Inneres Erlebnis), Fire and Blood, The Total Mobilization*—
show that he resorted again and again to his central theme. In
1925 he demanded a "faith in Folk and Fatherland that will flare
up like a demon from all classes of society. . . . Everybody who
feels differently must be branded with the mark of the heretic
and exterminated. We cannot possibly be nationalistic enough.
A revolution which inscribes this on its banners will always
find us in its ranks. . . . The integration of all Germans into the
great Reich of the future which will merge a hundred million,
that is a goal for which it is worthwhile to die and to beat down
all opposition."

Frequently, however, Jünger had not even a nationalist goal.
"For what purpose one exists, may never be learned," he wrote in
Das abenteuerliche Herz (The Adventurous Heart, 1929), "all so-
called goals can only be the pretexts of history. . . . It is essential
to find will and faith, quite apart from and irrespective of any
contents of this will and faith." War in itself was a fulfillment,
it was an adventure of magic beauty and the occasion for sharing
one's heroic attitude, irrespective of success or goal. "When the
last men of a ship sunk in battle go down with a hurrah and
flying flags, then a radiant transfiguration spreads over the waves,
as infinite and eternal as the sea itself. And even if they went
down for a cause which children ridicule (*über die längst die
Kinder spotten*), we must weep and be proud at the same time.
Blessed is the man who can feel this."

Two of Jünger's later books *Die totale Mobilmachung* (1931)
and *Der Arbeiter: Herrschaft und Gestalt* (1932) carried to a logical
conclusion what Spengler had in mind when he wrote *Prussianism
and Socialism,* a system of a military super-industrialism, in which
the borderlines between industrial society and army disappear, the
factories become barracks, and the same discipline and devotion
are demanded in both. Jünger's worker is the apotheosis of the
depersonalization of modern man. Worlds separate this mass-man,
this type-man from Nietzsche's individual. To Nietzsche the
thinker, the poet, and the saint represented the higher man and

the purpose of creation; they were men creating and daring in
solitude. For Spengler and Junger the soldier and the technician,
the *homo faber*, the disciplined cog in the machine, warrior or
worker or rather warrior and worker, represent the new type.
Jünger's mechanized soldiers and skilled factory hands, like so many
puppets were mere extensions of their technical function. "The
face which looks from under the steel helmet or the crash helmet
upon the observer has changed," Jünger writes. "It has lost in
variety and thereby in individuality, while it has gained in the
clearness and definiteness of its separate features (*Einzelaus-
prägung*). It has become more metallic, its surface has been, as
it were, galvanized, the bones stand out clearly, the features are
sparse and tense. The gaze is calm and fixed, trained to observe
things which can be perceived only in a state of fast movement.
It is the face of a race which begins to develop under the specific
demands of a new landscape, in which the single man represents
not a personality or an individual but a type. . . . We see here
develop a kind of elite-regiment (*eine Art von Garde*), a new
backbone of the organization of fighters,—an elite (*Auslese*)
which can also be described as an Order. It is the new type of the
twentieth century." These "workers" are living in a state of permanent and total mobilization, always on the alert, incessantly
armed, always ready to obey a summons, to follow a call.

Jünger was the leading representative of nihilism and propagandist of the beauty of total war in Germany. He accepted the
fact that the elemental forces of life which the bourgeois regarded
and dreaded as immoral and unreasonable had come into their
own with the war of 1914. But he never joined the National
Socialists or any other party. He was far removed from politics
and the masses. He was a proud and lonely man. His writings
were free from anti-Semitism to a degree rare even among
moderate German writers. During the Second World War, Jünger
found that he "had passed the zero line of nihilism," and discovered, after the warrior and the worker, the civilian who
cherishes the dignity of man more than life.

Moeller, Spengler, Schmitt, and Jünger were the most prominent representatives of the new revolutionary mood which seized
the conservative nationalists after 1918 and which was not so
different from the mood of the revolutionaries on the left. Both
expected the millennium, though the former first thought it would
be brought about by the German folk, and the latter by the
proletariat. The two movements were bitterly hostile, though from

time to time they co-operated against the common enemy, the West. One should not overlook the fact that in the West peace returned with the armistice of 1918. In Germany and in eastern Europe civil wars went on for the next five years. Germans continued to fight on Baltic and Polish territory and the domestic civil war, with uprisings, assassinations, and paramilitary storm-troopers, went on at least until the end of 1923.

This civil war, in Germany and elsewhere in eastern Europe, even more than the Great War, gave birth to an extreme radicalism. It was popularized by widely read novelists like Ernst von Salomon and Edwin Erich Dwinger. Salomon, who participated in the assassination of Rathenau, described the experiences of those years in his novel *Die Geächteten* (*The Outlaws*, 1930). "If there is a power," Salomon wrote, "whose destruction it is our task to accomplish by any means, it is the West and the German class that has allowed itself to be alienated by it." Like Moeller and Spengler, Salomon saw salvation in Prussian socialism which he called "a metaphysical socialism," which existed in Prussia before she became corrupted by European influences; it represented a third force between western capitalism and eastern Marxism and it gave to the nation that true unity, "of which the nineteenth century cheated us." Only the German idea, Salomon was convinced, can create a new order which will determine the next century and "perhaps the next thousand years." Like Jünger, Salomon never joined the National Socialists, and objected to their plebiscitary mass-democracy and their extreme anti-Semitism. His autobiographical novel, the best-seller *Der Fragebogen* (*The Questionnaire*) published in 1951, showed that he did not change his radical outlook. Outside Germany it is often not realized that men who were not National Socialists, who were hostile to them and often very courageous in their opposi-tion—this was the case with Niekisch and others, though not with Jünger or Salomon—were in many ways as antiwestern and anti-liberal as were the National Socialists.

In contrast to Salomon, Dwinger joined the party. As a boy of seventeen he volunteered for the cavalry in 1914 and became a prisoner of war in Russia. In his trilogy—*Die Armee hinter Stacheldraht* (*The Army Behind Barbed Wire*, 1929); *Zwischen Weiss und Rot. Die Russische Tragödie* (*Between White and Red. The Russian Tragedy*, 1930); *Wir rufen Deutschland. Heim-kehr und Vermächtnis* (*We Call Germany. Return and Legacy*, 1932)—he described life in the prison camps, the civil war, and finally the return to Germany. As he wrote in the last of these three novels, he hated collectivism as much as capitalism Discussing Dwinger's novels in *Dichtung und Volkstum* (1936) Professor Hermann Pongs wrote: "This is a sharp-shooting work (*in dem scharf geschossen wird*) against the Republic, which is no state but a mutual life insurance company, . . . ; against Bolshevism, in which the trash rules, who made a revolution to avenge themselves on their masters; against the false romanticism of those eternal adolescents who dream of political life on a moral basis. The heroism of the last desperate German battle is marvellously contrasted with, on the one hand, the bestial cruelty of the masses of eastern peoples, who emerge from the primeval slime, and on the other hand with the cold and calculating cruelty of England, who betrays her own race."

Dwinger's novels were published by Eugen Diederichs, one of the deservedly famous German publishing houses which reflected the personalities of their founders. Diederichs, a Low German of confused generous and semireligious aspirations, who fell under the influence of Lagarde, started publishing in Florence in 1896 and later moved his firm to Jena, a city in the middle of Germany and the seat of the early romantic circle. As a publisher Diederichs became the center of the neoromantic movement in Germany and revived the vague nationalist mysticism of the generation which lived through the War of Liberation. His interest in the myths, thought and literature of other peoples was as comprehensive as that of the romanticists. In that way he rendered a definite service; but in his wish to serve his times by seeking out the creative influences and forces shaping the future he concentrated more and more on reviving Germanic primitive and folkish traditions. In the volume which he published for the thirtieth anniversary of the founding of his publishing house, entitled *The German Face. A Road to the Future,* he stated: "The events of the war have united not only European lands but all countries, so that the coming civilization can be only a world civilization. It will then be of decisive importance, whether Germany will arrive in the next decade at a firm, intellectual position (*festen geistigen Haltung*) which will give her the inner right to leadership. . . . Mankind needs a Germany spiritually alive, for Germany is the heart of Europe and therefore of the world. But the consciousness of being chosen, which expresses itself in such a faith, is coupled with love." The same claim to cultural leadership was raised at the same time by mightier voices which coupled it not with love, but with hatred.

An arrogant dismissal of the West characterized Diederichs' monthly *Die Tat.* In 1928, two years before his death, he abandoned the editorship to younger men, who declared themselves ready to work for a "most radical solution." Among them were Giselher Wirsing, Hans Zehrer, and Friedrich Zimmerman, who wrote under the pseudonym of Ferdinand Fried. "The *Tat* men," Professor Klemperer writes, "turned on the Nazis for reasons of snobbism rather than principle. While the Nazis were the mob, they were the intellectuals. . . . Can we say which one of the two was worse? Surely the *Tat* had done a thorough job in undermining the Weimar Republic." In 1931 Zimmerman predicted in his *Das Ende des Kapitalismus* (*The End of Capitalism*) that "in the coming world political conflicts, the greatest role, perhaps the leadership, will fall to Germany." * The *Tat* editors did their full share in discrediting the forces that could have resisted National Socialism. Perhaps they hoped that Hitler, once in power, would fail and that leadership would then fall to them. They were mistaken. Zehrer, like Spengler and Junger, did not join the party; Wirsing and Zimmermann did. But whether they joined or not, all of them by their contempt for western liberalism and their overestimation of Germany's role in the world—an overestimation based partly on provincialism and misinterpretation—made many Germans in 1933 accept, even welcome, the confident leap into a spiritual and moral abyss.

Out of Catastrophe

HALF A CENTURY BEFORE, in the heyday of the success of Bismarckism, Planck knew that Bismarckian power policy would involve Germany and Europe in a war of unprecedented horror; he hoped that out of it a reformation of Germany would come. He was too optimistic: the defeat of 1918 brought no reformation but an intensification of the trends of the Bismarckian Reich. The gulf between Germany and the West grew wider during the years of the Weimar Reich. It led to the catastrophe of 1933 and this in turn to the war of 1939. This second war confirmed Planck's hope for a reformation.

* *"Deutschland ist in den kommenden weltpolitischen Auseinandersetzungen die grosste Aufgabe, vielleicht die Führung zugewiesen."*

Few men could have foreseen in 1920 or 1940 the Germany of
1960. The unexpected German reformation can teach us to view
the future in history as an open future containing potentially new
developments. Of course the present is always a product of the
past; retrospectively, the historian can show how the present grew
out of the past. But the present is always also something new and
itself pregnant with future developments. Though the past does
not determine the future it sets certain limits within which
future developments can take place. By means of their moral understanding, intelligence, and imagination men at any given moment can decide freely among several possibilities, thereby affirm-
ing their humanity. They have to decide within the limits of a
concrete situation which is the result of past developments. Only
by recognition of the conditions created by the past and thereby
of the true nature of the concrete problem can men find an
answer which is neither destructive nor utopian. Such a response
to the challenge of the situation demands both historical understanding and ethical standards which are above and beyond historical understanding but cannot be fruitfully applied without it.

German reaction to the defeat in 1945 was different from that
of 1918. As a leading foreign correspondent in the German Federal
Republic pointed out: "Bonn is not Weimar." Though doubts of
the sincerity of the change of heart persist, German democracy
in 1959 was more stable than it was at any time after 1918. Fourteen
years after the end of the First World War Hitler was in power.
Fourteen years after the end of the Second World War there has
been no sign in Germany of the rise to power of extreme nationalism. The German reaction to defeat differs in the 1950's
from what it was in the 1920's, and so does the European framework with which German policy has to deal. The 1920's offered
Germany a tempting chance for resuming her drive toward
European or world hegemony. Spengler and Hitler regarded
Russia and the United States as feeble and unstable countries,
the one disintegrating through Bolshevism, the other through
capitalism. The years since 1942 have revealed the error of this
assumption. Today a united, heavily armed Germany could not
hope to defeat the Soviet Union. The weakness and isolation of
Germany's eastern and southeastern neighbors which tempted even
German liberals and socialists to a campaign against Poland, no
longer exists. Today these nations are undergoing a process of
rapid industrialization and are protected by the power of the
Soviet Union. Even more important for a limitation of German

aspirations for a new power-policy is the close union of the western democracies, above all Britain and the United States. If such a unity had existed in the 1920's it could have prevented the rise of Hitler and the outbreak of the Second World War. The two main weapons of post-1918 Germany in preparing her new war—the successful agitation against western unity and democratic confidence and the independent power game between Russia and the West—have become blunted, perhaps irreparably so.

The effect of these world political changes is increased by domestic structural changes. Prussia, the center of German power-policy and militarism after 1862, when Bismarck defeated the Prussian parliament, no longer exists. Königsberg, where the Prussian kingdom was proclaimed in 1701, has been named Kaliningrad. The junker class has lost its economic hold on, and its political influence in, the lands east of the Elbe. There is no reason to expect that it can ever regain its former position. The whole way of life in Germany east of the Elbe has changed beyond recognition. Even after 1918 it preserved its feudal agrarian character. To protect the obsolete economy of their estates, the Junkers prevailed upon Hindenburg to dismiss Chancellor Brüning and a few months later, Chancellor General von Schleicher, and to appoint in their stead first Herr von Papen and then Hitler. Fighting for their most selfish class interests, these archconservatives opened the gates to a radical revolution which in its consequences extinguished them.

The outcome of the war of 1939 led Germany out of catastrophe. It put an end to tyranny in the larger part of Germany. The success of the combined Anglo-American forces in landing in Normandy, introduced a democracy ideologically and structurally stronger than that of Weimar. It was founded without pretensions and without the illusion of the Weimar constitution-makers of establishing the best democracy in the world. Its birth was not accompanied by the two unexpected factors which characterized the years after 1918, a rich but confused cultural and artistic flowering on the one hand and a wave of violence on the other. No great writers or musicians, no brilliant publicists, film or stage directors came to the fore to give Germany the leading vanguard position which she occupied in the 1920's. Paramilitary organizations, secret cells of violent resistance to the occupation forces, political assassinations did not again disturb the evolution of a democratic order. The Germany liberated by the West from German tyranny was not reconstituted as a Reich but as a German

Federal Republic. The center of gravity of German life shifted to the seat of its older traditions, away from the east to the Rhineland and to southwestern Germany, those German lands where liberalism was alive in the early nineteenth century. Berlin, which became Germany's capital only in 1871, as a result of Prussia's victories over the German Confederation and over France, was replaced by Bonn, a city on the western bank of the Rhine without any association with military triumphs or imperial grandeur. The geographic change was symbolic of the shift in general policy, from a self-centered nationalism to co-operation with the West. Whereas the Reichstag after 1918 soon became unworkable through the multiplicity of parties and the growth of parties which rejected democracy, the Bundestag after 1948 has developed toward a stable two party system and both major parties fully accept the democratic structure of the Republic. No party favoring an extreme nationalism has so far been able to attract any large number of voters.

German democracy was also strengthened when the Fascist claim to be the wave of the future was shown to be a fraud. Before 1945 Fascism attracted many continental Europeans, not only in Italy and Germany. Thirty years ago, in a speech delivered on October 27, 1930, from the balcony of the Palazzo Venezia in Rome, Mussolini boasted: "By the year 1950, Italy will be the only country of young people in Europe, while the rest of Europe will be wrinkled and decrepit. (That was, of course, before Hitler and Franco came to power.) From across all the frontiers people will come to see the phenomenon of the blooming Spring of the Italian people. . . . Today I affirm that the idea, doctrine, and spirit of Fascism are universal. It is Italian in its particular institutions, but it is universal in its spirit. It is therefore possible to foresee a Fascist Europe which will model its institutions on Fascist doctrine and practice. Today, even as yesterday, the prestige of nations is determined absolutely by their military glory and armed power."

History has not borne out Mussolini's confidence. Fascism held up to ridicule the weakness of parliamentary democracy and its assumed inability to sustain a great industrial and military effort. The experience of Britain and the United States in the Second World War disproved this assumption. Nor did the events bear out the Fascist thesis that the West had no other choice but that between Communism and Fascism. All these circumstances explain why Germany in the 1950's lived politically and intellectually in a context very different from that of the 1920's and 1930's. Germany's experience in the 1950's has shown that a nation is not weakened by the loss of her imperial ambitions, but on a limited and undisputed territory may grow in economic prosperity, political stability and world-wide influence.

The change in the political and intellectual climate of the late 1950's should warn us against taking the events of thirty years ago as the starting point to predict Germany's future in 1960. The impact of this new climate has produced a slow change in the German mind, a questioning of the foundations of German life from Bismarck to Hitler, and an attempt to find the way back to older traditions which Germany shared with the West. A reinterpretation of German history which was not undertaken after 1918 has been under way since 1945. Meinecke, who started his academic career as a Prussian archconservative and who, after 1914, slowly moderated his attitude, published *The German Catastrophe* in 1946. Here, as Professor Richard W. Sterling points out in his *Ethics in the World of Power,* he finally came, at the end of a long life, to divesting the nation-state of the aura of the absolute, which he had conferred upon it, and to proclaiming the ultimate primacy of individual conscience. Meinecke's strongly nationalistic *Das Zeitalter der deutschen Erhebung 1795-1815,* which glorified the birth of German nationalism in the struggle against France, was republished in 1940 twenty-four years after the original edition. In the introduction to this new edition he then wrote that this little book written for a popular audience had always remained dear to him and that in his old age he still agreed with its fundamental outlook. The book was brought out again in 1957 and this time Professor Siegfried A. Kaehler insisted that Meinecke's scholarly principles and political ideals were determined by the three concepts of individual, nation, and state. Professor Kaehler hoped that many readers would regard the national uprising between 1806 and 1813 as "the model-situation of Prussian German history."

The concept of a universal or European community and regard for other nations as a political ideal, did not play a role in Meinecke's thought. But in 1946 he stressed the need for regard of the welfare of other nations and drew the attention of the Germans to the cosmopolitan late eighteenth century as their guiding star, to a period, to quote Professor H. Stuart Hughes, "when Germany had not yet diverged from the western European norm, and when men like Goethe and Kant were still working within the assumptions of Anglo-French thought to raise the common intellectual heritage to a higher plane of intuitive grasp. In short, Meinecke had gone back to the last and greatest of the products of the Enlightenment."

In 1951, in his last public address, Meinecke answered in the affirmative the question whether the present could be called a great time. The issue, he announced, was the highest and most sacred good of mankind—the freedom, honor, right, and dignity of the individual. The old man would not have spoken such words before in his half century of academic teaching. Unfortunately most historians of the older generation hesitated to proceed with the revision of their historical values similar to that which Meinecke started under the immediate impact of the collapse of the Reich. Some excused themselves by saying that a change of their attitude could be taken for an opportunistic adaptation to the political powers of the hour. But German historians had shown no such hesitation to adapt themselves to the political powers of Bismarckism or nationalism. Now some of them tried to justify German history since 1806 as a tragic history the course of which was inevitable and therefore, guiltless. Meinecke felt that no one should criticize a tragic hero for having taken a wrong path if, filled with the proud sentiment *"in hoc signo vinces,"* he performed deeds which first carried him to the height of victory and finally plunged him into the abyss. In answering Meinecke's article, Professor Hajo Holborn found such an excuse for the course to the abyss wholly untenable. "For, in my opinion, the essential difference lies in whether [one] fights under the sign of the cross, the star symbol of the Prussian Guard, or the swastika. Moreover, the memory of what irreparable wounds were inflicted not only on one's own people, but on other peoples, in the course of such events, should indeed never be forgotten."

Other German scholars insisted with greater consistency than Meinecke, on the need for a revision of the values dominant in German thought. "When an edifice breaks down," the philosopher Theodor Litt wrote in his *Wege und Irrwege geschichtlichen Denkens* (1948), "which was thought to be built on rock, we must look into the mistakes the builders made when they laid the foundations. Similarly we must ask what has been able to survive the catastrophe and promises to endure for the future. The revision of our conception of [German] history must correspond to the size and force of the catastrophe which happened to us and through us. Only then our new understanding of [our] history will be in accord with the changed situation." A few years later Litt repeated:

"Unconditional honesty with oneself is the indispensable means to recovery. This requirement would in no way be less binding if it should be found that other peoples have not escaped, or not entirely escaped, the same self-undoing," which the Germans brought upon themselves.

Among older German historians the Catholics Franz Schnabel and Karl Buchheim had long been critical of Bismarck's Reich. Since the war others, among them two North Germans, Ludwig Dehio, who was born in Königsberg, and Johann Albrecht von Rantzau, have joined their ranks. They represent many others, among whom, fortunately, younger historians are associated. The *Institut für Zeitgeschichte* in Munich and the *Vierteljahrshefte für Zeitgeschichte* do excellent work in acquainting the Germans, in an objective and critical way, with the history of the last fifty years and Germany's role in it. The Federal government in Bonn, through its *Bundeszentrale für Heimatdienst* helps to spread and strengthen democratic and European thinking among the Germans. Its weekly *Das Parlament* reports the proceedings of the Federal legislative bodies and of the organs of the various European communities. Special attention is being paid to the democratic education and information of teachers. Similar training courses and manuals on democracy and on the new European spirit exist for the officers and men of the Federal army, in which a new western and civilian (*staatsbürgerlich*) spirit is being nurtured. Nothing of that kind was attempted in the Weimar Reich.

In 1952, in the *Historische Zeitschrift*, which he then edited, Dehio stressed that "the prerequisite for any really creative German response after the period of the two World Wars is the unconditional recognition of the terrible role that we have played in this period." Dehio insisted that a fundamental change occurred in the middle of the twentieth century, not only in Germany's position but in the whole world context. The function of historical writing about the present time "is no longer to demonstrate the continuity of history, but rather to show the break that has occurred—to knock down what must fall." What must fall, at least in western Europe, is the self-centered nationalism which has dominated for so long the writing of history. The old European system of conflicting nationalisms which emerged in the Renaissance has collapsed in the two World Wars. Within the new world context Europe can only take her place if her nations stop being fascinated by past glories and empires. As early as 1953 Dehio clearly saw that "it is extremely difficult for the remaining free nations of Europe in their changed surroundings to master anachronistic instincts that they have formed during the centuries of the European system, and the task is hardest of all for the two great neighbors, Germany and France, in whom the continental mentality has crystallized in its most typical form."

The new Germany, after 1945, was made possible by a new development of even wider scope and importance, the trend toward closer co-operation among the western European and north Atlantic nations. To have integrated Germany into this trend will remain the historical achievement of the first German Federal Chancellor Konrad Adenauer, who with unflagging determination has led Germany in that direction. He changed the trend of modern German history. In that respect his work can be well compared with that of Bismarck. The first German Reichs Chancellor led Germany into the opposite direction, a trend which culminated in, and was reduced to absurdity by, the work of the last German Reichs Chancellor. A new element in the present situation is the fact that the possibility of a Franco-German war, which for three hundred years belonged to the regular pattern of European history, has disappeared from the calculations of statesmen. But this auspicious development of a Franco-German entente can gain its real value only from its North Atlantic framework. German reintegration into the West for the sake of strengthening democracy and of weakening the appeal of military glory and imperial grandeur in Germany and elsewhere must proceed in closest co-operation with the English-speaking countries and with the neighboring small Germanic democracies; thus alone can Germany develop a secure free and civilian society.

The new German democracy must ask how far its policy will safeguard free society. This criterion applies also to the practical pursuit of the problem of German unity. Germany's return to the western community, German freedom, and German unity are three interdependent problems. In that respect, too, Professor Dehio has spoken out with courage. "Today liberty—that is the liberty of the individual, not of the state—can only be preserved as the common property of a consolidated group of nations, and any nation which draws aside to save its own unity will lose it. A hundred years ago the most pressing goal was national unity; for the preservation of freedom offered no problem in the sense in which it does today, whereas unity was the natural demand within that system of nation-states which is lying in ruins today. Now, however, after the Third Reich has abused and thrown away our unity by denying freedom, unity must be subordinated to the superior and wider aim of freedom, for today a demand for unity surely has an anachronistic flavour about it. No political watchword can be transplanted into a new situation without carrying with it traces of the soil in which it grew previously."

The present division of Germany is not the result of western mistakes but of German *hubris*. In 1939 Hitler, by extinguishing Poland and dividing her with Russia, as Frederick II did in the eighteenth century, helped the advance of the eastern empire westward. Hitler's invasion and wanton devastation of Russia two years later brought the Russian armies to the Elbe river. By imposing their system on part of Germany the Communists did not replace liberty by tyranny. Germany lived then under a heinous tyranny. But National Socialism had not been satisfied to impose tyranny on Germany. German aggression directly or indirectly implanted tyrannical regimes in several non-German lands east of Germany. All friends of liberty desire the end of tyranny in all these lands. In the general misery, brought about by National Socialism, the German territory still under tyranny can hardly expect to receive preferential treatment.

Fortunately the question of unity and eastern frontiers does not exercise today that obsessive fascination for the German mind that undermined democracy in the Weimar period. Outside of relatively small groups, the German Federal Republic has not succumbed to the lures of excessive nationalism. Yet some talk of reunification is dominated by obsolete ideas. Berlin is still longingly called *Reichshauptstadt,* the capital of the Reich. Many seem to regard the Federal Republic as something less desirable than a Reich. The memories which cling to the Berlin of the nineteenth and early twentieth century promote wishful thinking. To which frontiers should Germany return? To those of 1939, sanctioning Hitler's moves? To those of 1919? But public opinion in the Weimar Reich, even among socialists and democrats, then regarded these frontiers almost unanimously as unbearable. Or should Germany return to the frontiers of 1914, possibly enlarged by the addition of Austria and the Sudetenland? Karl Goerdeler, the leader of the German resistance movement in the Second World War, who was executed by the National Socialists in 1945, demanded as late as 1942 that Germany should retain Austria and the Sudetenland, Polish Poznań and western Prussia. Goerdeler and some of his fellow conspirators apparently never realized, to quote Professor Sell, "what a threat such an enlarged Germany with or without Hitler would represent for her neighbors. Fundamentally, they still revered Bismarck, which means they followed the policy which tried to gain the maximum of aggrandizement which a reasonable calculation of the risks allowed." Talk of the restoration of the Reich and of the Reichshauptstadt sometimes appears based on the assumption that the German Federal Republic is not the new Germany which emerged out of catastrophe, but only the continuation of that Reich which had led Germany into catastrophe. The Weimar Republic perished because many citizens thought of it and its frontiers as a temporary makeshift imposed by Allied victory.

Closely connected with this problem is that of Germany's adherence to the West. Many regard that adherence, too, as temporary; only a united Germany will later decide whether it will remain part of the western world or start again to play a solitary power game between East and West. Such restorative daydreams are easily understandable. In a nation with a recent past such as Germany has it is rather astonishing that these trends are not stronger or more violent than they are. Fifteen years after the defeat of 1945 the number of Germans is still great who know that under today's conditions a free society can only be preserved by close co-operation with other free societies, and that, different therein from the past century of German history, freedom must take precedence over unity, in the interests of the Germans and of the western community.

Seen in the perspective not of Bismarckism but of a common western civilization, the German Federal Republic is not a temporary makeshift; it is the first consolidated German democracy, the first German state for well over one hundred years to be part and partner of the western community, a community united in its desire for a free society, but rich in its diversity. In this diversity the German Federal Republic has its place. Its frontiers may change. Germans now living under a régime of no freedom will, we hope, one day share the freedom of the German Federal Republic. But whatever its frontiers, it is important that the present fundamental structure and outlook of the German Federal Republic be preserved.

The German Federal Republic is as little a model of perfection as it is a mere makeshift. Like all other states it is beset with many serious imperfections, perhaps it is in some respects more imperfect than older and more stable democracies. All peoples are carrying the burdens of their history, and the last one hundred years through which the German people have lived have naturally left their deep scars. Only if viewed in perspective will the Germany of today appear as a very great improvement and her achievements will be fully appreciated. As in other democracies, German public opinion must be wide awake to the ever present threats to democracy and to all imperfections and abuses and strive for the necessary reforms. It would be, however, less than helpful if the attitude of carping criticism, the revelation of minor incidents out of all proportion to their real importance, and the malevolent suspicions which undermined democracy in the Weimar Reich should again poison the atmosphere.

A national and personal past with which one cannot cope, which one has not mastered, the *"unbewältigte Vergangenheit,"* is a continuing source of danger. Such a past presents a problem for other people besides the Germans, it haunts them too like a *revenant,* a ghost which can turn into a demon because one does not dare to face it in the clear light of a responsible and reasonable realism. The Germans are, as a result of their modern history, perhaps more threatened by such demonic ghosts than some other peoples. In a warning published in the *Frankfurter Allgemeine Zeitung* of June 9, 1959, Professor Franz Böhm pointed to the fact that many parents and teachers who were fervent nationalists, who resent the triumph of the forces—western democracy and humanitarian liberalism—which they fought and despised, now face the questions of young people about the recent past. But there is not only the danger of willful misinformation of the younger generation. Large numbers of German young people—as apparently the majority of young people everywhere in the late 1950's—are indifferent to ideological issues which so strongly moved their elders in the 1930's. Indifference to Fascism or Communism does not transform the young into democrats. But again there is no reason to overstress the danger involved in such an attitude. German youth has tired of the extremism of Nietzsche and George, and even more, of that of their followers. Until recently many Germans inclined to accept intellectual myths and legends and to press impatiently for their realization. This inclination has been widely replaced by a desire for *le petit bonheur,* the good life of the average man, which Nietzsche, Spengler and George so much despised.

If, in the present time, the German Federal Republic is allowed to follow her democratic course, if the spirit of mutual tolerance grows and if passionate concentration on unity, frontiers and the efficient power-state does not again overwhelm the concern for building a stronger and better free society, then there is every reason to believe that out of catastrophe a new Germany will arise.

For the last one hundred years the question of Germany and Europe dominated much of German thought and political life. The similar question of Russia and Europe was and in a varied form still is today, foremost in the Russian mind. In Germany, however, this question, which was such a burning issue only thirty years ago, is no longer of the order of the day. The German Federal Republic is part of the western community. The Germans have thereby given new strength to that community to which only a short while ago they presented a deadly threat. Germany's two hegemonial wars in the twentieth century brought the peoples and the civilization of Europe to the brink of catastrophe. Out of this catastrophe one great gain has come, a democratic Germany which is finally taking its due place in modern western life.

Suggested Readings

THE FOLLOWING LIST is purposely confined to a very small number of recent books. It represents neither a bibliography nor a guide to the sources on which the present book is based. The list has a purely practical and very limited purpose, to draw the attention of the reader to a few books which he might find useful in following up some of the problems developed in the present study.

An excellent introduction to the background of the present study is provided by Koppel S. Pinson, *Modern Germany, Its History and Civilization* (New York: Macmillan, 1954). The book also contains a useful bibliography.

Other recent works in the English language, which readers may find valuable, are:

Edgar Alexander, *Adenauer and the New Germany* (NEW YORK · FARRAR, STRAUS AND CUDAHY, 1957).

Maurice Baumont et al., editors. *The Third Reich* (NEW YORK: FREDERICK A. PRAGER, 1955).

Ludwig Dehio, *Germany and World Politics in the Twentieth Century* (NEW YORK: ALFRED A. KNOPF, 1959).

Andreas Dorpalen, *Heinrich von Treitschke* (NEW HAVEN: YALE UNIVERSITY PRESS, 1957).

Walter Kaufmann, *From Shakespeare to Existentialism* (BOSTON: BEACON PRESS, 1959).

355

Klemens von Klemperer, *Germany's New Conservatism: Its History and Dilemma in the Twentieth Century* (PRINCETON: PRINCETON UNIVERSITY PRESS, 1957).

Louis L. Syyder, *Documents of German History* (NEW BRUNS-WICK: RUTGERS UNIVERSITY PRESS, 1958).

FOR THOSE who read German, the following additional books will be of interest:

Walther Hofer, *Geschichte zwischen Philosophie und Politik* (BASEL: VERLAG FÜR RECHT UND GESELLSCHAFT, 1956).

Golo Mann, *Deutsche Geschichte des 19. und 20. Jahrhunderts* (FRANKFURT: S. FISCHER, 1958).

Harry Pross, *Die Zerstorung der Deutschen Politik* (FISCHER BÜCHEREI, 1959).

Friedrich G. Sell, *Die Tragodie des Deutschen Liberalismus* (STUTTGART: DEUTSCHE VERLAGS-ANSTALT, 1953).

On the German Federal Republic the following two books will be found useful:

Fritz René Allemann, *Bonn ist nicht Weimar* (COLOGNE: KIE-PENHEUER & WITSCH, 1957).

Alfred Grosser, *La Démocratie de Bonn* (PARIS: ARMAND COLIN, 1958).

Index

Printed in the USA
CPSIA information can be obtained
at www.ICGtesting.com
LVHW020008310324
775953LV00001B/70